SAGE was founded in 1965 by Sara Miller McCune to support the dissemination of usable knowledge by publishing innovative and high-quality research and teaching content. Today, we publish over 900 journals, including those of more than 400 learned societies, more than 800 new books per year, and a growing range of library products including archives, data, case studies, reports, and video. SAGE remains majority-owned by our founder, and after Sara's lifetime will become owned by a charitrust that secures our continued independence.

Los Angeles | London | New Delhi | Singapore | Washington DC | Melbourne

India's 2019 Elections

India's 2019 Elections

The Hindutva Wave and Indian Nationalism

Edited by

Paul Wallace

SAGE

Los Angeles | London | New Delhi
Singapore | Washington DC | Melbourne

First published in 2020 by

SAGE Publications India Pvt Ltd
B1/I-1 Mohan Cooperative Industrial Area
Mathura Road, New Delhi 110 044, India
www.sagepub.in

SAGE Publications Inc
2455 Teller Road
Thousand Oaks, California 91320, USA

SAGE Publications Ltd
1 Oliver's Yard, 55 City Road
London EC1Y 1SP, United Kingdom

SAGE Publications Asia-Pacific Pte Ltd
18 Cross Street #10-10/11/12
China Square Central
Singapore 048423

Published by Vivek Mehra for SAGE Publications India Pvt Ltd. Typeset in 10.5/13pt Bembo by Zaza Eunice, Hosur, Tamil Nadu, India.

Library of Congress Cataloging-in-Publication Data Available

ISBN: 978-93-5388-244-0 (HB)

SAGE Team: Abhijit Baroi, Shruti Gupta, Mahira Chadha and Rajinder Kaur

Robin Alison Remington

Not only has she been my wife and best friend

As we collaborated across India and Europe

But as colleagues critiquing each other's work

Inspiring scholarship and moral values.

Contents

Part II: Analytical State Studies

List of Figures

List of Tables

Acknowledgements

This sixth consecutive volume on India's national elections with SAGE Publications has received superfast track publication that I did not think was possible. I have been the editor or co-editor of all the previous books in this series and so became jaded when comparing promises to performance.

First, special recognition must be accorded to our 29 contributors whose expertise and professionalism helped produce the 20 chapters. I did not believe that academics could adhere to such a rigorous timetable. 'Disciplining academics is like herding cats' is the accepted cliché that I have long accepted as absolute truth. I now happily stand corrected.

Second, I also have had lengthy experience with various bureaucracies both private and public, and I am generally familiar with the literature on large-scale organizations and their difficulty in changing long-established routines. Publishing houses are no exception. SAGE Publications demolished the stereotype at least for this superfast project.

Finally, leadership always is a consideration for any endeavor. I have worked closely with a large number of commissioning agents, editors, sub-editors and other personnel over the years. My virtual hat is off in recognition of the kind but relentless; intelligent but not overbearing; professional but not unbending leadership of Abhijit Baroi. His title is Commissioning Editor, Academic Books, but he exercised roles performed by many individuals in the past all done with grace, understanding, professionalism and effectiveness. In this endeavor, he was ably assisted by the meticulous editing of Shruti Gupta, Associate Production Editor—Editorial (Books).

Paul Wallace
Columbia, Missouri, US

Introduction
Hindu Nationalism and TINA Propel BJP Wave

Paul Wallace

The 2019 parliamentary elections culminated after three phrases with election results announced on 23 May 2019. S. Y. Quraishi, former Chief Election Commissioner (CEC), provides the incredible logistics for the world's largest democratic elections in Chapter 3 of this volume.[1] Politically, a Modi-led Bharatiya Janata Party (BJP) wave follows his sweep in 2014.

BJP alone won 303 of the 542 parliamentary seats, 354 when its National Democratic Alliance (NDA) totals are added. By contrast, the Congress party won only 52 seats with Rahul Gandhi forced to rely on a seat in Kerala while losing his 'family' Amethi seat in Uttar Pradesh. The broader United Progressive Alliance (UPA) added 40 seats for a total of 92, but for a second consecutive Lok Sabha, the total will be insufficient for a formal opposition. The bulk of the non-Congress contribution comes from the 23-seat sweep in Tamil Nadu by the Dravida Munnetra Kazhagam (DMK), and five each from its alliance in Kerala and the Nationalist Congress Party (NCP). See Table I.1 for comparative results with the past two elections to the Lok Sabha. Complete results by party are provided at the end of the Introduction. Voluminous amount of data are presented in the following 20 chapters.

A second five-year term for Prime Minister Narendra Modi had been anticipated, but its depth and extent are surprising, especially the enhanced majorities and penetration of areas seemingly controlled by the regional parties. Two factors arguably can be emphasized: muscular Hindu nationalism with its *parivar* (family) of devoted organizations and 'There

Table I.1 *Seats and Vote Per Cent Won by Coalitions, BJP and Congress 2009, 2014 and 2019*

	2019		2014		2009	
	Seats	Vote (%)	Seats	Vote (%)	Seats	Vote (%)
NDA	354	45.00	336	38.00	159	25.0
BJP	303	37.36	282	31.45	116	18.8
UPA	92	27.00	60	23.00	262	48.3
Congress	52	19.49	44	19.31	206	28.55

Source: Election Commission of India (ECI), 2017, 2018, 2019; Indian media.

Is No Alternative' (TINA) emphasizing the leadership gulf between the charismatic Modi who clearly dominates his party and a comparatively ineffectual set of opposition leaders. A complete list of parties and number of seats won is provided in Table I.2 at the end of this introduction.

MODI VERSUS RAHUL IN A PLEBISCITARIAN CAMPAIGN

NaMo (Modi) and his chief lieutenant Amit Shah adroitly executed a presidential–plebiscitarian campaign for 2019 as they did for 2014 that energetically and tirelessly covered India combining adroit use of the media, modern technology and unending mass rallies. They succeeded in a large measure invalidating a weak Rahul Gandhi and his Congress party as the national alternative to a strong Modi—'the *Chowkidar*' (watchman)—and his BJP. Election returns and the media followed this pattern by comparing the BJP-led NDA with the Congress-led UPA.[2] A second successive BJP sweep reduced Congress to a regional party leaving it in control of only two major states, Kerala and Punjab.[3]

There appeared to be a basis for equating India's grand old party with the BJP. The Indian NCP led India to Independence under Mahatma Gandhi, and Rahul Gandhi is the latest leader of the dynasty that included Jawaharlal Nehru, India's first prime minister, his daughter Indira Gandhi and her son Rajiv Gandhi, all popular prime ministers. Rajiv's wife, Italy-born Sonia Gandhi, successfully held the party together aided by veteran Congress functionaries until son Rahul appeared to be ready.

Economist Manmohan Singh served essentially as a non-political prime minister during the two Congress-led UPA governments prior to 2014 when Rahul failed in his initial efforts against the BJP. In the 5th volume in the SAGE series that I edited for the 2014 elections, I posed a question in a section of the introductory chapter in boldface: *Are the Congress and the Dynasty Finished?* A number of reputable sources severely criticized Rahul, Manmohan Singh and the Congress campaign.[4]

Even stronger criticism assailed Congress following its debacle in 2019. Guardedly, the Print commented that Congress leadership appears to be 'in disarray following Rahul's resignation' and recommended that a new leader should not be part of the family.[5] Reputable private sources that anticipated and favoured a Congress resurgence were bitterly unhappy:

- 'Congress is dead, there is no one who is opposing Modi.'
- 'It is Not a Party, but A Court bereft of ideology with grassroots leaders long since cast aside….'
- 'Rahul failed to energise…effectively use his grassroot leaders.'
- 'Rahul and his mother are culpable…. They wasted 15 years during which they should have had elections within the party…right up to the CWC (Congress Working Committee). NaMo prefers them to run the Congress, as they offer an easy target and No Opposition.'[6]

In comparing the two leaders and their parties, Rajesh Dev in his analysis of Northeast India in Chapter 20 concludes that the BJP under a charismatic leader like Modi 'has been able to incorporate new elites from a cross-section of the region's communities'. This change relates to the 'disillusion of regional elites with the Congress' unable to 'ensure upward mobility of existing elites within the party' and accommodate 'newly emerging elites'. Congress is beset with 'in-fighting, factional rebellion, resistance to dynastic incorporation and centralisation of decision-making in a "high-command" (thus) "reducing the authority of" powerful regional leaders'.[7]

At least Rahul Gandhi won his 'family' Amethi seat in Uttar Pradesh in 2014, allegedly due to the efforts of his sister Priyanka. That was not possible in 2019. Rahul lost in Amethi having to be content in securing a seat in Kerala. This attitude of despondency, an end of the world depression, also is a reaction to Congress optimism in December 2018 following state assembly elections five months before the May 2019 Lok Sabha elections. Congress defeated BJP in state assembly polls heading new governments in Rajasthan, Madhya Pradesh and Chhattisgarh in the northern Hindi belt. Alliances between the formerly antagonistic regional parties, especially in electorally rich Uttar Pradesh,[8] seemed to many reputable political pundits to predict significant BJP losses in northern India compared to 2014 and thus to miss the even larger tsunami in 2019.[9]

Economic issues reinforced opposition optimism. Poor agricultural production caused rural distress and a continuing high level of farmer suicides. Increasing unemployment and a significant decline in the GDP contrasted with BJP's promises. Poorer parts of the population suffered most from the failure of demonetization designed to eliminate 'black money' announced in November 2016. New large rupee currency notes replaced suddenly worthless former currency. Fake news (see Chapter 6 in this book) popularized the following misinformation:

- UNESCO declared the new ₹2,000 note the best currency in the world.
- BBC reported that 'thousands' of Indian WhatsApp users 'forwarded the message along with joyful emojis'.
- New notes have a GPS chip to detect black money and have a radioactive ink.
- The income tax department was using the isotope to trace large quantities of cash held at a particular spot.[10]

The introduction and implementation of the Goods and Services Tax (GST), a levy on consumption in 2017, was intended as a radical tax simplification benefitting the economy, but 'it has proved complex and cumbersome in practice'. Unemployment, a major problem prior to the parliamentary election, became even more acute as Indian household debt after unemployment rose to a 45-year high in August 2019.[11] GDP also has decreased significantly as *The Economist* reports.[12]

THE BRIEF OPPOSITION'S DREAM

What enabled Modi and the BJP to engineer a turnaround despite their apparent vulnerability in December 2018? A BJP landslide swept most of India by May 2019 despite Congress' election victories in December and BJP's arguably poor economic performance following parliamentary elections in 2014. It is truly surprising despite the old belief of the distinction between state and national elections. Even in Andhra Pradesh, political veteran Chandrababu Naidu apparently viewed himself as dashing off to Delhi to contest for leadership of the disparate, but possible victorious regional satraps only to being revealed as the equivalent of the emperor without clothes as he lost power in his own state![13] Chief Minister K. Chandrashekar Rao of Telangana apparently had similar aspirations and along with Naidu 'had to bite the dust in their own states'.[14] Karli Srinivasulu in Chapter 15 provides the context for their political problems as 'related to the nature of state division' following the bifurcation of Andhra in 2014, and issues involving centre–state relations.[15]

Chief Minister Mamata Banerjee in West Bengal, allegedly with comparable national aspirations, provides a very rough parallel situation as BJP absorbed most of her former Leftist and Congress opposition to become a formidable political threat in the supposedly secular state. One veteran commentator colourfully concluded: 'The smug view that "Jai Shri Ram" had no resonance beyond the Hindi-speakers of Burrabazar has been punctured'.[16] The BJP and Mamata Banerjee and her All India Trinamool Congress (AITC) are both seen as contributing to the problems of secularism in the state by Jawhar Sircar, currently Chairman of the Board of Governors of the Centre for Studies in Social Sciences, Kolkata, in a hard-hitting insightful article with the headline 'There Is Still Some Hope Left for Secularism in Bengal'.[17] Sriroop Chaudhuri provides detailed coverage on West Bengal in Chapter 13.

Rumours during the brief period of opposition optimism also revolved around Chief Minister of Bihar, Nitish Kumar. He left his 2014 Lok Sabha alliance with the BJP to win assembly elections in 2015 against the BJP, subsequently rejoining the NDA during a complex realignment of parties in Bihar. Would he leave the BJP-led alliance in a bid to secure leadership of a secular opposition? Would Rahul and the Congress plus other regional leaders accept him? These dreams came to naught.

MUSCULAR HINDU NATIONALISM

Muscular Hindu nationalism intervened in the five-month period between December 2018 and the parliamentary elections. India and Pakistan engaged in carefully limited military exchanges following a *jihadist* suicide bombing of an Indian paramilitary convey killing 40 soldiers in Pulwama, Jammu and Kashmir, on 14 February 2019. An Indian air attack then retaliated bombing the *jihadist* Jaish-e-Mohammed[18] base in Balakot, Pakistan, followed by a limited battle with Pakistan planes. Both sides claimed victory. Our contributing author on Madhya Pradesh insightfully phrases the consequences for BJP's much higher than expected electoral dividend in the parliamentary elections: The BJP 'saw it as an opportune moment to weave its ideology of Hindutva into the politics of muscular nationalism'.[19]

Indian nationalism resonated as Hindu nationalism through the aggressive 'muscular' campaign led by Prime Minister Modi and his long-time lieutenant Amit Shah. Shah has been by his side since Modi served as chief minister of Gujarat, and after the elections has been elevated to home minister in the central government. Elections reports from almost all states, including the chapters in this book, attest to the patriotic significance of what is often referred to in a shorthand manner as 'the Balakot issue' as overriding other issues and demonizing the opposition. A poll conducted by the Lokniti research unit at the Centre for the Study of Developing Societies dated 24 March to 31 March 2019 reported by Swansy Afonso has the headline, 'Modi's Popularity Back to Peak Levels on Air Strike, Survey Says'.[20]

BJP emphasizes the 'surgical strike' against the *jihadists* in Balakot, Pakistan, which it claims to have destroyed along with a large number of Jaish-e-Mohammed *jihadists*, perhaps as many as 300 or more. Pakistan denies the casualty claim with its version of the bombs destroying only trees. Independent observers have not been allowed access, so both sides claim victory. Balakot is an important issue, but not the decisive electoral one. BJP would have remained in power according to virtually all reputable sources, but possibly with a reduced majority and the necessity of reliance on its NDA alliance.

Hindu nationalism also appears to operate with a strong communal bias against Muslims, despite Modi's magnanimous reaction to the election results in his victory statement in party headquarters in New Delhi on 23 May. He dedicated the 'massive mandate' to all citizens stressing that the next five years will be dedicated to eliminating poverty and nation-building. In his remarks, Amit Shah, however, 'reflected an endorsement of nationalism'.[21]

An active parliamentary citizenship bill in regard to refugees enumerates the many religions that would be acceptable. Muslims conspicuously were not included. In India's north-east, in the state of Assam, another citizenship bill going back to 1971 focusing on refugees from Bangladesh, primarily Muslims, roiled the parliamentary elections, but not sufficiently so as to alter the BJP victory.[22] Following the elections, the controversy continued with *The Hindu* stating that over 1.9 million people faced statelessness, and alleged that 'the Union Government is preparing detention centres', pointing out 'that only a veritable "prison state" can house such numbers'. It is possible that the National Register of Citizens bill will be contested all the way to the Supreme Court.[23]

A negative reaction to Hindu nationalism by former 'liberal' defenders of Prime Minister Modi took place even before the 2019 elections at the *India Today* Conclave in March 2018. Pratap Bhanu Mehta combined disappointment in Modi's promise of economic development with fear of the focus on Hindu religious identity. Expectations of 'growth and inclusion and job creation...have been deeply disappointed', Mehta begins. 'Religion...is being reduced to the identity that marks you', and 'nationalism is being used to divide people'. 'He asserted that unless there is a massive repudiation of the public culture that we have created in the last five years...you will not be able to recover either the nation, or your freedom, or your truths, or your religion. That's what is going to be at stake in 2019'.[24]

Sadanand Dhume, Ashutosh Varshney and Gurcharan Das had also 'shielded Narendra Modi from detractors and doomsayers on his way to the prime minister's office. Today they have joined the ranks of those they once pilloried'. The very long *Caravan* article details each of the intellectual's journey from defenders of Modi and his many programmes and aspirations to the cultural and political conclusions most clearly expressed by Varshney in an e-mail to the author of the *Caravan* article:

> I have never supported Hindu nationalism, and I never will.... Modi's is 'not a right-of-center government, which the institutional framework of politics would have pushed him towards. Instead, he has pushed institutions to their limit, and produced India's first right-wing, not center-right, government'.[25]

Walter Andersen, author of two major books on the BJP as well as Chapter 1 on the BJP in this book, is much more reserved about the consequences of the elections. He disagrees with those 'who consider this mandate as a dramatic inflexion point for the country'. He concludes that 'while there will be Hindu-centric assertions...it is not the end of secularism in India as some people fear. India is too complex and diverse for such a dramatic change, and this complexity is also its strength'.[26]

All of these concerns reached a new level of concern on 5 August with the elimination of Jammu and Kashmir's autonomy under Article 370, the splitting of the state into union territories and a lockdown of communications and movement two months following the elections.[27] Sumit Ganguly explains the actions in Chapter 2 as well as in an article in *Foreign Affairs*[28] as does Reeta Tremblay in Chapter 10. Reaction, according to the normally conservative *South Asia intelligence Review*, is 'divided between triumphalism in the Hindutva Right, and extends along the spectrum from dismay to dire imaginings among those opposed'. An unexpectedly strong conclusion emphasizes the following:

> erosion of constitutional norms, the undermining of institutions, the rising communalism of the environment, the overwhelming and disturbing shift towards the religious right, and the emergence of a whole new paradigm, where the ruling party's ideological objectives and electoral commitments will be the principal movers of policy and strategy, with little concern for long term outcomes. Those who seek to bind the nation by force may well unravel the constitutional fabric that holds its infinite diversity together.[29]

Jyotirindra Dasgupta and Anshu Chatterjee also are concerned about the fabric that binds India's diversity together. In Chapter 5, they explore the rich diversity of organized public action in relation to political accountability. They conclude that BJP has been taking 'more interest in reducing the importance of rights than actually strengthening them' during the past five years despite the many government programmes for various sectors of society that they examine. They are apprehensive about ideas of 'majoritarian nationalism…as pursued to promote religious and patriotic themes in different spheres of public life'. They also examine how citizens can 'hold authorities to account'. India's institutional richness from the panchayat to the Supreme Court level as well as civil society organizations do provide the means for effective representation. How they fare in the future is to be seen.[30]

Women's developing roles unquestionably are critical to Indian society and are becoming a marginally more significant part of political life. Rainuka Dagar in Chapter 4 presents an impressive amount of data and analysis about women's political participation and concerns being registered over gender rights, BJP promises and programmes that are targeted for traditional women needs. The BJP, she points out, 'highlighted women entitlements and rights into their political campaign, but as a strategy of political gain rather than a promotion of democratic rights'. Gender equality in the political arena has not been achieved. Empowerment and 'the reframing of the power relations remains seemingly intangible though fundamental to democracy'. The majority of women elected to office are 'dynasts, a part of political families, rather than independently evolved voices for "women interests" or promoting deliberative democracy from different perspectives'.[31]

THE SOUTH AND REGIONAL POLITICS

BJP's national sweep doesn't include the south where it failed to win a single seat in the three southern states of Andhra Pradesh, Tamil Nadu and Kerala, and also losing the union territory of Puducherry (formerly Pondicherry). Nonetheless, it has made inroads into southern India, especially Karnataka and to a lesser extent in Odisha (formerly Orissa). Odisha traditionally is included in eastern India but its politics like that of neighbouring West Bengal in 2019 reflect a strong regional leader with BJP emerging as the major opposition. Overall, the region's states primarily reflect local politics marked by distinctive languages, rich state-wide cultures and being averse to perceived domination by the Hindi-speaking north.

BJP swept parliamentary elections in Karnataka winning 25 of the 28 seats polling over 50 per cent of the votes. The electoral shock upended the ruling Congress-JD(S) state coalition government resulting in defections, political turmoil and change to a BJP government as described by our co-authors in Chapter 16. Their analysis includes the tenuous Congress-JD(S) alliance, local factors such as the dynastic politics of the Deve Gowda family and BJP's success with Muslims. BJP proved that it is not 'untouchable' because of incidents such as attacks on Muslims elsewhere according to Patagundi and Desai. 'The longstanding myth that the BJP would not be able to divide the larger social coalition of MOD (Muslims, Other Backward Classes and Dalits) which has always favoured the Congress, has been broken', they conclude.[32]

In addition to what is presented about the leadership in Andhra Pradesh and Telangana in the earlier part of this introduction are the inroads BJP made in Telangana. Srinivasulu in Chapter 15 emphasizes the 'significant performance of the BJP' with four seats and a 19.45 per cent vote share 'thus registering a quantum jump' since 2014 as well as its increase since the 2018 assembly elections. BJP stressed that 'Telangana would be important for the BJP march into the south after Karnataka'. The regional parties continue to dominate in Andhra Pradesh as BJP lost two of the MP seats won in 2014.[33]

Odisha presents a mixed picture for the BJP. Long-time leader Naveen Patnaik won a fifth consecutive term and his Biju Janata Dal (BJD) maintained its dominance in the Legislative Assembly. But the BJP is now the major opposition party at the state level and has improved its parliamentary toll from 1 in 2014 to 8 in 2019. Pradeep Nayak's conclusion in Chapter 14 emphasizes common strengths for both the BJP and BJD that include personal leadership for both Modi and Patnaik, organizational strengths and 'populist schemes' that he describes in his chapter. Patnaik's image is 'as a strong, incorruptible and simple living leader'.[34]

Tamil Nadu and Kerala provide the NDA and Congress with the bulk of its 92 seats. Complexity is a feature of the politics of both states, but Tamil Nadu especially provides a kaleidoscope of parties, report Manikandan and Wyatt in Chapter 17. Each major party has a splinter party, 'caste parties add 3–4 extra; and then the BJP. It has been about 20 parties in both alliances the last few elections'.[35] Tamil Nadu provides MPs from 8–10 parties following the 2019 elections. Major election results appear to be much simpler.

The DMK and its allies in the NDA won 37 of the 38 seats it contested as against its long-term major rival, the All India Anna Dravida Munnetra Kazhagam (AIADMK), reduced to one seat as opposed to the opposite result in 2014. Leaders of both major parties died prior to the 2019 elections, but DMK lacked a leadership struggle. M. Karunanidhi's son M. K. Stalin along with strong middle-level leadership seamlessly replaced his father.

AIADMK had the opposite result as the party split following the charismatic, all-powerful J. Jayalalithaa's death. BJP lost its one MP seat from Tamil Nadu as its local relationship with the losing AIADMK and 'national developments combined with grassroots protests since 2017' such as education and other policies resulted in an anti-Modi climate. 'Whenever the Prime Minister visited Tamil Nadu, #GoBackModi would trend on Twitter'.[36]

Kerala's election results confirm the importance of the south in showing that a nationally dominant party 'has not been able to sweep all before it', according to James Chiriyankandath in Chapter 18. BJP despite the Sangh Parivar, the family of Hindu nationalist organizations, was unable 'to forge the kind of coalition with the significant regional parties as in other states outside the Hindi belt'. Kerala remains the 'only state of any size in the country not to have ever returned a BJP MP'.[37]

BJP focused on four constituencies each of which has a major temple complex. Sabarimala became a national as well as local issue with the Supreme Court ruling that women of menstruating age should be allowed to enter the Ayyappa shrine in Sabarimala. The shrine attracts millions of Hindus from across India and elsewhere. BJP sought to exploit the issue but failed as Chiriyankandath explains in detail. Congress with its United Democratic Front (UDC) alliance won 19 of 20 MP seats proving 'more resistant' than elsewhere to the appeal of the 'ideology of Hindu nationalism' and Modi's national leadership. Whether this continues to be true in the future as the supporters of that ideology 'mould a pervasive pan-Indian Hindutva culture is a moot point'.[38]

Punjab is in north-west India but shares two characteristics with southern Kerala. They have the least Hindu population among major states, and both supported the Congress party in the 2014 elections. Thus, demography and regionalism combined against the Modi wave. Captain Amarinder Singh of the Patiala princely house is a Sikh leading the Congress party in a Sikh majority state. His past includes opposition to Congress as well as semi-retirement during a colourful life. It can be argued that Congress won because of him rather than the reverse. M. J. Akbar without qualification asserts that 'In Punjab Congress has won only because of Captain Amarinder Singh'.[39]

Thus, it is not surprising that the Captain, as he is universally referred to in Punjab, focused on regional concerns rather than blindly following his national leaders. He supported Indian patriotism, rather than Hindu nationalism, in the Balakot limited conflict with bordering Pakistan in 2019. He also, according to Pramod Kumar in Chapter 8, 'entered into an understanding to defeat the AAP' (Aam Aadmi Party) in the 2017 assembly polls. The AAP continued its decline losing three of its four parliamentary seats in 2019. Accordingly, Kumar concludes, 'the Modi wave bypassed Punjab, the AAP became history and Punjab limped back to bipolar politics' between the Congress and Akali Dal–BJP alliance.[40]

CONCLUSION

A number of questions remain after this overview of the 2019 elections and some highlights from our 20 chapters. What will be the continuing impact of a popular leader and his apparently increasingly dominant political party and alliance? Will Hindu nationalism be a focus for uniting India harmoniously or will Kashmir and basic questions of who is or who can become a citizen become more divisive? Will Rahul Gandhi or other leadership revive the Indian National Congress and what are the implications for dynastic politics throughout India? To what extent will India's democratic infrastructure be harnessed to *vikas* developmental goals in a cooperative manner? Or will education, the judiciary, Election Commission, the media and other bulwarks of civil society be further compromised? How does the economy factor into the future electoral success of Prime Minister Narendra Modi and his chief lieutenant and Home Minister Amit Shah?

Table I.2 *General Election to Lok Sabha Result 2019*

Result Status			
Status Known for 542 out of 542 Constituencies			
Party	Won	Leading	Total
Aam Aadmi Party	1	0	1
AJSU Party	1	0	1
All India Anna Dravida Munnetra Kazhagam	1	0	1
All India Majlis-E-Ittehadul Muslimeen	2	0	2
All India Trinamool Congress	22	0	22
All India United Democratic Front	1	0	1
Bahujan Samaj Party	10	0	10
Bharatiya Janata Party	303	0	303
Biju Janata Dal	12	0	12
Communist Party of India	2	0	2
Communist Party of India (Marxist)	3	0	3
Dravida Munnetra Kazhagam	23	0	23
Indian National Congress	52	0	52
Indian Union Muslim League	3	0	3
Jammu & Kashmir National Conference	3	0	3
Janata Dal (Secular)	1	0	1
Janata Dal (United)	16	0	16

(Continued)

Table I.2 *(Continued)*

Result Status			
Status Known for 542 out of 542 Constituencies			
Party	Won	Leading	Total
Jharkhand Mukti Morcha	1	0	1
Kerala Congress (M)	1	0	1
Lok Janshakti Party	6	0	6
Mizo National Front	1	0	1
Naga People's Front	1	0	1
National People's Party	1	0	1
Nationalist Congress Party	5	0	5
Nationalist Democratic Progressive Party	1	0	1
Revolutionary Socialist Party	1	0	1
Samajwadi Party	5	0	5
Shiromani Akali Dal	2	0	2
Shiv Sena	18	0	18
Sikkim Krantikari Morcha	1	0	1
Telangana Rashtra Samithi	9	0	9
Telugu Desam	3	0	3
Yuvajana Sramika Rythu Congress Party	22	0	22
Other[41]	8	0	8
Total	542	0	542
All Party[42]			

NOTES

1. See Chapter 3, 'Amazing Dimensions of Managing the Biggest Election in World History', by S. Y. Quraishi (former CEC [2014]).
2. See Chapter 1, Walter Andersen, 'Bharatiya Janata Party: Consolidating Power', in this book.
3. Kaushik Deka, 'A Losing Hand', *India Today* (Election Issue, 2019, 3 June), 28–31, especially p. 29 where '10 Reasons for the Grand Debacle' are explained.

4. Paul Wallace, 'Single Party and Strong Leadership (BJP)' in *India's 2014 Elections: A Modi-Led BJP Sweep*, ed. Paul Wallace (New Delhi: SAGE Publications, 2015), 12.
5. *The Print* (2019, 30 July).
6. Private sources within India during post-election discussions during May–June 2019 and subsequent correspondence.
7. *See Chapter 20, 'Politics of Identity, Regionalism and the BJP: A Synoptic View from North-East India', by Rajesh Dev.*
8. Sudha Pai and Sajjan Kumar provide the background of the alliance formed against the BJP in Uttar Pradesh and explain why it did not succeed in Chapter 7 of this book.
9. Avjit Ghosh, 'Why Media Missed Out on a Bigger TsuNaMo', *The Times of India* (2019, 24 May 24), 22.
10. See examples of fake news in Chapter 6, Devika Malik and Pallavi Bedi's 'Election News 2019: Free, Fair and Fake? Examining Trends in Misinformation around Indian National Polls', of this book.
11. Ameya Karve and Divya Patil, 'Indian Household Debt after Unemployment Rose to a 45-Year High', *The Print* (2019, 29 August).
12. *The Economist*, 'Meager Fare' (2019, 29 August). Available at https://www.economist.com/finance-and-economics/2019/08/31/indias-government-is-scrambling-to-revive-the-economy?cid1=cust/ednew/n/bl/n/2019/08/29n/owned/n/n/nwl/n/n/NA/299863/n (accessed 29 August 2019).
13. Naidu 'undertook a tour of state capitals to sew up' an alliance between 'regional parties and Congress...' (*The Times of India*, 'TsuNaMo 2.0 Hits Mamata & Naidu' [2019, 24 May]), 11.
14. S. Nagesh Kumar, 'Chief Ministers N. Chandrababu Naidu of Andhra Pradesh and K Chandrasekhara Rao of Telangana, who nursed ambitions of playing a key role in the formation of the next government, are humbled by the people's verdict' (*Frontline* [Election Special], 2019, 7 June), 82.
15. Srinivasulu, in his conclusion in Chapter 15, points out that Naidu could not 'arouse the Andhra identity as an electoral issue...partly because of its electoral opponent YSRCP being another regional party'. He provides a detailed analysis of both states.
16. Swapan Dasgupta, 'A Profound Transformation in Bengal', *The Telegraph* (2019, 30 May). Available at https://www.telegraphindia.com/opinion/post-election-data-indicates-a-transformation-in-west-bengal-with-regard-to-the-bjp-and-hindutva/cid/1691461 (accessed on 31 May 2019). Sriroop Chaudhuri provides detailed coverage on West Bengal in Chapter 13 of this book.
17. Jawhar Sircar, 'There Is Still Some Hope Left for Secularism in Bengal', *Ananda Bazar Patrika* (Bengali edition, 2019, 22 July). Also, see Nilanjan Mukhopadhyay, 'Will Bengal Be Narendra Modi's Launch Pad for Inclusive Politics?' *Blomage* (2019, 6 June). Available at http://www.blomage.com/

politics/will-bengal-be-narendra-modis-launch-pad-for-inclusive-politics/1 (accessed on 9 June 2019).

18. Available at https://en.wikipedia.org/wiki/Jaish-e-Mohammed (accessed on 17 September 2019).
19. Avinash Kumar in his chapter on Madhya Pradesh in this book. Also, see the chapters by Walter Andersen on the BJP, Sumit Ganguly on Foreign Policy, Sudha Pai on Uttar Pradesh and Reeta Tremblay on Jammu and Kashmir for more details and analysis.
20. Swansy Afonso, 'Modi's Popularity Back to Peak Levels on Air Strike, Survey Says', *Bloomberg* (2019, 6 April). Available at https://news.yahoo.com/modi-apos-popularity-back-peak-042823084.html (accessed on 24 July 2019).
21. *The Times of India*, 'Polls Over, Modi Pledges to Forget Bitterness, Calls for Consensus', *The Times of India* (2019, 24 May), 22.
22. See the chapters in this book by Akhil Ranjan Dutta, 'Assam Polls: The Hindutva Wave', and by Rajesh Dev, 'Politics of Identity, Regionalism and the BJP: A Synoptic View from North-East India'.
23. *The Hindu*, 'Citizenship, Figured: On Assam NRC Final List' (Editorial, 2019, 2 September). Available at https://www.thehindu.com/opinion/editorial/citizenship-figured/article29316557.ece?homepage=true (accessed on 2 September 2019).
24. Praveen Donthi, 'The Liberals Who Loved Modi', *The Caravan* (2019, 16 May). Available at https://caravanmagazine.in/politics/the-liberals-who-loved-modi (accessed on 2 June 2019).
25. Ibid.
26. Nistula Hebbar, 'Narendra Modi 2.0: Not the End of Secularism, says U.S. Scholar Walter Andersen', *The Hindu* (2019, 1 June). Available at https://www.thehindu.com/profile/author/Nistula-Hebbar-205/ (accessed on 3 June 2019).
27. Over 2,000 merchants, elected representatives and students were detained as thousands of soldiers reinforced the already militarized Srinagar. Some were reported to have been flown in 'secret flights' to cities in Uttar Pradesh. Jeffrey Gettleman, 'Kashmir Is Silent as a Graveyard after India Seizes Leaders', *The New York Times* (2019, 24 August 24), A4. Another article by Jeffrey Gettleman, with Hari Kumar, combined the citizenship issue in Assam with the actions in Kashmir stating that Prime Minister Modi is pushing the 'most forceful and divisive Hindu nationalist agenda ever attempted in India', so as to 'fundamentally reconfigure the concept of Indian identity'. 'Making India More Hindu, One Test at a Time', *The New York Times* (2019, 18 August), A1.
28. Sumit Ganguly, 'Modi Crosses the Rubicon in Kashmir', *Foreign Affairs* (2019, 8 August).
29. Ajai Sahni, 'J&K: A New Reality', *SAIR Weekly Assessments & Briefings* 18, no. 7 (2019, 12 August).

30. See Chapter 5 'Political Accountability and Organized Public Action in India: Making Power Answer to People' by Jyotirindra Dasgupta and Anshu N. Chatterjee.
31. See Chapter 4, 'Staking Gender Equality: The Electoral Dynamics of Identity and Rights' by Rainuka Dagar.
32. See Chapter 16, 'Karnataka: BJP's Spectacular Victory over the Congress and JD(S)', by Shivaputra S. Patagundi and Prakash Desai.
33. See Chapter 15.
34. See Chapter 14, 'Biju Janata Dal's Fifth Term in Odisha', by Pradeep Nayak.
35. See Chapter 17, 'Tamil Nadu: Political Pluralism and Party System Changes', by C. Manikandan and Andrew Wyatt.
36. Ibid.
37. See Chapter 18 'Kerala: The Exception That Proves the Rule?' by James Chiriyankandath.
38. Ibid.
39. M. J. Akbar without qualification asserts that 'In Punjab Congress has won only because of Captain Amarinder Singh'. M. J. Akbar, 'The Price of a Wink: A Dynasty That Once Sprinkled Stardust Has Been Turned into Sawdust', *Open* (2019, 24 May), 14.
40. See Chapter 8, 'Claims of Alternative Politics of AAP: Wither? Why? Punjab and the 2019 Elections', by Pramod Kumar.
41. Available at https://results.eci.gov.in/pc/en/partywise/other.htm (accessed on 17 September 2019).
42. Available at https://results.eci.gov.in/pc/en/partywise/allparty.htm (accessed on 17 September 2019).

PART I

Thematic Studies

Chapter 1

Bharatiya Janata Party

Consolidating Power

Walter Korfitz Andersen

The Hindu nationalist Bharatiya Janata Party (BJP) won a second major national victory in a row in the 2019 parliamentary elections, which could signal the emergence of a Hindu-centric inflection point in Indian affairs. This development may also portend Right-wing nationalist domination of Indian politics for years to come, a mirror inverse of the political pre-eminence the Congress party enjoyed during the five decades following Indian independence. The Congress—now with just 52 of 543 elected seats—is no longer a national rival, and the various regional parties in 2019 again demonstrated their inability to form a united opposition. The BJP meanwhile continued to enlarge its presence in the east against those same disparate regional parties and has embarked with some apparent success on superimposing its Hindutva ideology onto regional narratives.[1] Its power duo of Prime Minister Narendra Modi and party President Amit Shah are committed to a similar process in the south, where the party is presently weak but where it can utilize the ubiquitous presence of its ideological precursor, the Rashtriya Swayamsevak Sangh (RSS), as well as the Sangh's dozens of affiliated organizations, which penetrate a broad swath of Indian society.

The elections underscore Shah's critical role in the party's consolidation of power: it was the centralized party structure that he shaped which led to such strident electoral gains throughout the entire nation. The campaign also demonstrated Modi's virtually complete trust in Shah to the extent that Shah is now effectively the prime minister's deputy in all but title. He has been a confidante of Modi for the past 30 years and helped manage the prime minister's rise to power first in Gujarat and then at the national level. Shah was at the prime minister's side at virtually every post-election event and was appointed to the powerful cabinet post of home minister in the wake of the elections.[2] This cabinet position will give Shah a decisive voice in shaping a concerted approach to terrorism, as well as trying to stabilize domestic unrest in such states as Jammu and Kashmir, issues that were at the forefront of the BJP's parliamentary campaign. An important component of the plan regarding Jammu and Kashmir was to implement the BJP manifesto's promises to do away with that state's special constitutional provisions (Articles 370 and 35 A)—the former providing a measure of autonomy to the state of Jammu and Kashmir and the latter limiting property rights to 'permanent residents' of that Muslim-majority state.[3] Shah introduced legislation in the Rajya Sabha (5 August 2019) and the Lok Sabha (6 August 2019) that carried out the campaign pledges on Kashmir. The legislation effectively scrapped Articles 370 and 35A, and was passed by large margins in both houses with the support of several opposition parties. In addition, the state was divided into two union territories (Jammu and Kashmir, and Ladakh).

Shah in addition is the only Member of Parliament to sit on all eight cabinet committees, and he is also an ex officio member of the NITI Aayog public think tank, which is tasked to provide strategies for India's development with a focus on economic growth.[4] Underscoring Shah's continued power in the party's organizational affairs was the 17 June 2019 announcement following a meeting of the BJP's Parliamentary Board that the party would have a working acting president, MP J. P. Nadda, presumably with Shah continuing to play a guiding role in the party's affairs, at least until important state assembly elections in late 2019.[5]

The continued centralization of power on policy is also evident by Modi's elevation of people he knows and trusts to prominent positions, a seeming effort to create something akin to the US Presidential

Cabinet. Thus, he brought in a brilliant foreign service officer and former External Affairs Secretary, Subrahmanyam Jaishankar, as the Minister for External Affairs, and then elevated his National Security Advisor Ajit Doval to cabinet rank; also, he elevated two key members of the powerful Prime Minister's Office (PMO) who had served him in Gujarat and later in New Delhi, principal secretary to the Prime Minister Nripendra Misra, and Pramod Kumar Misra, the additional principal secretary.[6]

THE BJP EXCEEDS ITS OWN ELECTORAL EXPECTATIONS

Shah built the BJP's parliamentary campaign around Modi, and the decision to make it a referendum on Modi and his government resonated very well with voters, who registered the highest turnout ever at slightly more than 67 per cent of some 900 million eligible voters. The BJP was victorious in 303 of the 437 parliamentary constituencies it contested (of a total of 543 seats), a significant improvement over the 282 seats won in 2014—all while improving its popular vote share from 31.3 to 37.5 per cent. Its National Democratic Alliance (NDA) partners won another 50 seats, bringing the NDA seat total to 353 (vs 336 in 2014), and the NDA popular vote total to about 45 per cent (vs 38.5% in 2014). Of the BJP's 303 seats, 224 were won by more than 50 per cent of the votes.[7] An analysis of results reveal that the BJP's support transcended divisions of caste, education, urban/rural habitation and income, though it fell far behind the opposition in winning the votes of Muslims, India's largest religious minority. One reputable poll estimated the party won only around 8 per cent of the Muslim vote, about the same as in 2014.[8] Contrary to much speculation, however, its support among Dalits increased further, from 24 per cent in 2014 to 34 per cent in 2019, as did its increased support from the higher reaches of the Other Backward Classes (OBC), as well as among 18–25 years old voters, whose share for the BJP went from 34 per cent in 2014 to 41 per cent in 2019.[9] In addition, the disparity between the party's urban and rural constituencies declined from 8.9 per cent in 2014 to only 3.5 per cent in 2019.[10]

The opposition played into the hands of the NDA by also focusing their campaign rhetoric on Modi.[11] The BJP retained a solid hold on the populous Hindi-speaking centre of the country, especially in Uttar Pradesh, which sends 80 Members to the Parliament. The BJP won 62 seats there and increased its percentage of the popular votes in the state by 8 per cent to 49.6 per cent. Moreover, it established a strong presence against the ruling regional parties of the east: in West Bengal, it went from 2 to 18 of 42 seats, with 40 per cent of the popular votes; in Odisha, it went from 1 to 8 of 21 seats, with 38 per cent of the popular votes.

The one area of the country where it registered very poorly was in the Dravidian-speaking south, except for the state of Karnataka and, to a certain extent, Telangana. While there was widespread grumbling across the country about the Modi government's relatively poor record on job creation—an issue at the top of many surveys of voter concerns, an analysis of the votes indicates that the voters, especially the aspirational youth, still trusted Modi eventually to produce favourable results.[12] In addition, the government's vigorous response to the February 2019 terrorist attacks in Kashmir by attacking a terrorist base within Pakistan added national security and decisive leadership to the BJP's campaign themes. Layered over this were Hindu-centric themes, like effectively denying Muslims migrants citizenship in the National Register of Citizens, while providing citizenship to Hindu, Sikh and Buddhist migrants. The BJP also leveraged religious themes, such as Modi meditating for 17 hours at Kedarnath Cave, a popular Hindu pilgrimage site in the Indian state of Uttarakhand.

A significant advantage for the BJP in the 2019 campaign was its ability to raise far more money than its main opposition, the Congress party and the various regional parties.[13] Data from Facebook's Ad Library reports that the BJP between February and April 2019 spent almost 10 times as much as the Congress on political ads on social media platforms like WhatsApp.[14] According to the Association for Democratic Reforms (ADR), which monitors the financial assets of the major political parties, its most recent figures for the 2017–2018 fiscal year shows BJP's income from all sources had a comparable advantage, with the BJP collecting 1,027.34 crore rupees in the fiscal year to the Congress' 199.15 crore (about 140,000 dollars to the crore in 2019).[15]

A SCARE

Up to mid-2018, the BJP's return to power despite some setbacks seemed a foregone conclusion. The party appeared to be on the verge of evolving into the hegemonic political power once exemplified by the Congress. The only early significant setbacks were the loss of the Delhi Legislative Assembly in February 2015[16] and the loss of the Bihar Assembly in the same year to a coalition whose victory was assured by the defection of former BJP ally, the Janata Dal (United), to the opposition.[17] These were warning signals of more challenges to come in the next year. The BJP's lacklustre performance in the December 2017 assembly votes in Modi's own state of Gujarat was especially disquieting. While it was their sixth straight victory in the state, the BJP won only 99 seats in the 182-member assembly, a loss of 16, all of which went to Congress, giving it a total of 77 seats. Perhaps reflecting farmer grievances, the major losses were in rural areas.[18] Discontent over lack of jobs among the large population below age 35 may also have translated into a BJP decline in urban areas as well.[19] Further insecurity regarding parliamentary prospects in 2019 was precipitated by the loss of two Lok Sabha by-elections in the critical state of Uttar Pradesh, where the BJP had won 71 of 80 seats in 2014. Especially disconcerting was the loss of the Gorakhpur district in the eastern part of the state that had long been represented by the BJP Chief Minister of Uttar Pradesh, the Hindu religious figure, Yogi Adityanath.

State assembly elections in May 2018 in the large southern state of Karnataka was also a disappointment. The BJP, despite emerging as the largest party (104 of 224 assembly seats) and hoping to regain the state it lost in 2013, came in second to a Congress-led coalition in which the Congress won 78 seats and its ally, the Janata Dal (Secular) won 42.[20] But the BJP's loss to the Congress in three Hindi-speaking state assembly elections (Chhattisgarh, Madhya Pradesh and Rajasthan) in December 2018 aroused major concerns in the BJP and revived hopes in the Congress that it could (with electoral partners) seriously challenge the BJP in the 2019 parliamentary elections only months away by appealing to farmer discontent and a poor job creation record of the Modi government.[21] While these grievances may have adversely affected the BJP in local elections, they do not appear to have worked against the party nationally in 2019 and polling data suggest that it was confidence in Modi that prompted even the jobless to vote for the BJP.[22]

REGAINING CONFIDENCE

The BJP, thus, seemed to face a significant challenge nationally as the election year opened. Opinion polls in January–February 2019 gave the BJP and its allies between 225 and 242, well short of the required 272 seats. Those polls showed the Congress with 147–180 seats and others with 140–160 seats.[23] Much would therefore depend on alliances that the Congress could negotiate, and talks between the Congress and other parties collapsed in West Bengal, Uttar Pradesh and Delhi while the BJP was able to maintain critical poll alliances in Bihar and Maharashtra. One reputable poll noted that for the first time since coming to power, Modi's support in mid-2018 had dropped below 50 per cent to 49 per cent, a drop of 4 per cent in January 2018 and a drop of 16 per cent from Modi's peak support level in January 2016.[24] One factor in this fall may have been related to the late 2016 demonetization decision that was a blow to a cash-dependent economy.

Yet, polls taken in March, a month before the polling began, show a significant improvement in the party's popularity, with its likely victories up some 30 seats from polls early in 2019, now showing a range from 264–291 seats.[25] Polls at that time also show a rising popularity of Prime Minister Modi. In the wake of the Indian retaliation for the 14 February 2019 terrorist attack, two reputable polls show that support for Modi increased 7 per cent to 52 per cent nationally.[26] Perhaps most welcome by the BJP is that approval of Modi's governance in pre-election polls was over 60 per cent in the three northern Hindi-speaking states lost to the Congress in December 2019: Chhattisgarh, Madhya Pradesh and Rajasthan.[27] In those states, the BJP won handily in the 2019 parliamentary elections, winning 9 of 11 seats in Chhattisgarh, 24 of 25 in Rajasthan and 28 of 29 in Madhya Pradesh. The prize, of course, was Uttar Pradesh where it trounced an opposition alliance by winning 62 of 80 seats in India's most populous state, only 9 seats less than in 2014.

Three decisions made by the Modi government in early months of 2019 seem to have played a significant role in mobilizing additional support for his party. First was the decision to provide assistance that would benefit the poor from any caste who did not fit into any reserved category. Second was the decision to transfer 6,000 rupees annually to the bank accounts of the marginal farmers—and a promise in the party manifesto to eventually extend this benefit to all the farmers. Third was the air strikes against a terrorist facility inside Pakistan that were ordered on 26 February 2019 following the 4 February 2019 terrorist attacks on Indian security forces killing 40 in the Pulwama district of Kashmir.[28] The BJP manifesto makes especially strong appeals to security issues and, by extension, to nationalism, including specifically Hindu nationalism. Security and nationalism were frequently used themes in the prime minister's speeches during the campaign to underscore his firm policy on security.

Still another long-term electoral factor was the Modi government's increasing focus on delivery of social welfare schemes to the poor, and reminding the recipients during the campaign of the government's help to them.[29] Modi and Shah in their victory speeches, apparently realizing the electoral importance of poverty alleviation, announced that it would be the focus of the next five years.[30] A senior BJP figure told journalist Sheela Bhatt that 'serving the poor is our project for the next 25 years'.[31] In line with this project, the Modi government's 2019 budget emphasizes continuing and expanding welfare schemes.[32] An advantage in this approach is that it gets above explicit and contentious appeals to caste and religion.

THE RSS WORKS FOR MODI AND THE BJP

The RSS, India's largest NGO and the Hindu nationalist ideological godfather of the BJP, wants the BJP to remain in power in large part because political power provides its many affiliates working in such fields as education, universities, industries and the Hindu religious establishment access to a government that plays a pervasive role in what they do. The RSS also provides the organizational structure to build the party in places where it is now weak, such as in the southern states of Andhra Pradesh, Kerala and Tamil Nadu. In a separate research for a book on the RSS, senior RSS figures told us that the organization would not likely go 'all out' for the party in 2019 as it did in 1977 and 2014 when it feared that the Congress party would impose restrictions on its activities.[33]

However, as challenges to continued BJP rule mounted in late 2018, its leaders spoke out more strongly for its members to bring out the votes for the party. This was reflected in comments of its leader, Mohan Bhagwat, in a series of open discussions with the public in September 2018 at New Delhi. The RSS' 2018 Vijayadashami speech, an occasion used to announce the group's goals for the next year, avoided the populist criticism of the Modi government reflected in its 2017 speech and called rather for bringing out the votes. On the eve of elections in March 2019, the Pratinidhi Sabha—the 'parliament' of the RSS—concluded with a speech by Suresh Joshi, its general secretary, encouraging the delegates from the RSS and its affiliated organizations to get out the votes.[34] Yet a cautionary note was expressed by Seshadri Chari—former editor of the RSS' English language weekly, *Organiser*—when he wrote in a post-poll article that Shah is a powerful 'deputy Prime Minister' who 'hits where it hurts' and cited the cautionary advice of the RSS Head Mohan Bhagwat that those elected in a democracy should not 'misuse' their power.[35] Bhagwat and other senior RSS officials have frequently spoken out against a 'cult of personality' in the BJP.

FUTURE TRENDS AND CHALLENGES

Modi and Shah after the 2014 victory adroitly shifted the BJP's image from that of an upper caste elite party focused on economic development to one that is more inclusive and addresses the needs of the poor through a range of welfare programmes. This tactic enabled Modi and Shah to expand significantly the party's voter base to mobilize support from the so-called OBC and Dalits, and enabled it to achieve an electoral landslide. Despite its recent electoral successes, however, the BJP faces major challenges that, if not addressed, could undermine its long-time political prospects and its odds of evolution into a national umbrella party like the role once occupied by the Congress.

Perhaps the BJP's most significant challenge is whether its Hindutva ideology is sufficiently flexible to produce policies that lead to faster economic growth as well as greater social cohesion. The latter would require policies that restrain the anti-Muslim and anti-Christian intolerance of the radical right, especially on such cultural issues as beef consumption. One possible handle to this might be to build on the essentially equalitarian underpinning of its ideology, which is based on the writings of the party's major ideologue, Deendayal Upadhyaya.[36] Early signs are hopeful, as the prime minister has publicly condemned expressions of intolerance by some BJP politicians.

The achievement of its economic goals, meanwhile, has been challenged by the slowing of the economy, both internationally and domestically. The 2018–2019 Economic Survey of India sets a goal of consistent, investment-driven 8 per cent growth to achieve the Modi government's vision of a five trillion-dollar economy by 2024.[37] Making the task more difficult, however, are disagreements within the larger Sangh family on how to achieve this economic growth. For example, a large part of the RSS family (such as its labour affiliate) is opposed to foreign investment. Several of them in addition have an economically populist orientation focused on expansive social welfare programmes that could reduce available funds for development. The Modi government on the other hand looks favourably on foreign investment as it seeks to meet the demand for creating jobs at a faster pace. The RSS will almost certainly play a key role on this issue (and others) as it seeks to mediate the differences among its member organizations. In doing so, it will need to balance sometimes conflicting demands of populism and development.

NOTES

1. For an analysis of this Hindutva superimposition, see Suhas Palshikar, 'Post-Poll Survey: The BJP's "Act East" Moment', *The Hindu* (2019, 28 May). Available at https://www.thehindu.com/elections/lok-sabha-2019/the-bjps-act-east-moment/article27266661.ece (accessed on 17 June 2019).
2. For a very good analysis of the close coordination between Narendra Modi and Amit Shah on political issues, see the analysis of Sheela Bhatt (who BJP sources tell me is the best informed journalist on the inner workings of the

BJP): 'Modi–Shah's Political Genius Is in Reading Voters Correctly', *The Sunday Guardian* (2019, 8 June). Available at https://www.sundayguardianlive.com/news/modi-shahs-political-genius-reading-voters-correctly (accessed on 19 June 2019).

3. See discussion of Shah's likely goals as home minister dealing with such issues as Kashmir in: Utpal Kumar, 'Amit Shah Gears Up to Crack the Big Kashmir Puzzle', *The Sunday Guardian* (2019, 8 June). Available at https://www.sundayguardianlive.com/news/amit-shah-gears-crack-big-kashmir-puzzle (accessed on 18 June 2019).
4. For report of the composition of the cabinet committees, see NDTV report at https://www.ndtv.com/india-news/key-cabinet-panels-revamped-amit-shah-part-of-all-rajnath-singh-in-2–2048748 (accessed on 26 June 2019). Only the prime minister and Shah are members of the important Appointments Committee. Rajnath Singh is a member of six cabinet committees, but is not on the key Cabinet Committee on Political Affairs as of this draft.
5. See analysis of this appointment in 'JP Nadda Appointed Working President', *India Today* (2019, 17 June). Available at https://www.indiatoday.in/india/video/jp-nadda-appointed-bjp-working-president-1550801–2019–06-17 (accessed on 19 June 2019).
6. For an excellent review of Modi's presidential style of governance, see Shekhar Gupta, 'Why the New Modi Model Is the Old Gujarat Model Raised to the Power of 3 Super-Bureaucrats', *The Print* (2019, 15 June). Available at https://theprint.in/national-interest/why-the-new-modi-model-is-the-old-gujarat-model-raised-to-the-power-of-3-super-bureaucrats/250297/ (accessed on 30 June 2019).
7. Figures from Centre for the Study of Developing Societies (CSDS) post-poll data in Sanjay Kumar, 'Here's How BJP Earned the Massive Mandate: Explained in Numbers', *The Economic Times* (2019, 28 May). Available at https://economictimes.indiatimes.com/news/elections/lok-sabha/india/heres-how-bjp-earned-massive-mandate-explained-in-numbers/articleshow/69529857.cms (accessed on 5 July 2019).
8. Ibid.
9. Sanjay Kumar and Pranav Gupta review findings of Lokniti centre post-poll voter surveys in 'Where Did the BJP Get Its Votes from in 2019?' *LiveMint* (2019, 3 June). Available at https://www.livemint.com/politics/news/where-did-the-bjp-get-its-votes-from-in-2019–1559547933995.html (accessed on 5 July 2019).
10. Ibid.
11. A post-poll CSDS-Lokniti post-poll survey reports that about a quarter of the BJP's voters in the critical state of Uttar Pradesh would not have voted for BJP candidates if Modi were not in charge of the party. See discussion of poll in: Mirza Asmer Beg, Shashikant Pandey and Sudhir Kare, 'Post Poll Survey: Why Uttar Pradesh's Mahagathbandhan Failed', *The Hindu* (2019, 26 May). Available at http://binj.in/lifestyle/

post-poll-survey-why-uttar-pradeshs-mahagathbandhan-failed/ (accessed on 21 June 2019).

12. Coomi Kapoor, a consulting editor of the *Indian Express*, in trips to Haryana and western Uttar Pradesh during the campaign, wrote that the majority of her interlocutors saw this as a presidential election in which people talked of support for Prime Minister Modi, and not the BJP or a particular candidate: 'Unseeing the Wave: When It Comes to Elections, Experts and Politicians Tend to Wear Blinkers', *The Indian Express* (2019, 22 May). Available at https://indianexpress.com/article/opinion/columns/lok-sabha-election-results-narendra-modi-exit-polls-bjp-congress-rahul-gandhi-5741253/ (accessed on 25 September 2019).
13. For a comparison of the financial advantage of the BJP over the Congress over the past several years, see Bibhudatta Pradhan, Archana Chaudhary and Abhijit Roy Chowdhury, 'India's Opposition Party Running out of Cash', *Bloomberg* (2018, 23 May). Available at https://www.bloomberg.com/news/articles/2018–05-22/empty-coffers-hinder-india-congress-party-s-plans-to-topple-modi (accessed on 16 March 2019).
14. Amrita Madhukalya, 'Who's Creating WhatsApp Buzz This Election Season?' *Hindustan Times* (2019, 12 May). Available at https://www.hindustantimes.com/lok-sabha-elections/who-s-creating-whatsapp-buzz-this-election-season/story-NAewnMqSCqZlxtGlaelDhO.html (accessed on 17 September 2019).
15. The report of political party financial assets from the Association for Democratic Reforms, 'Analysis of Findings of National Parties: FY 2017–18' is available at https://adrindia.org/node?page=0%2C0%2C0%2C0%2C0%2C0%2C1 (accessed on 17 March 2019).
16. The BJP, having won all 7 parliamentary seats in Delhi's parliamentary contests in 2014, was confident it would again do well in the assembly polls.
17. Nitish Kumar, leader of the Janata Dal (United), defected from the BJP-led NDA prior to the 2014 parliamentary elections due to the BJP's choice of Narendra Modi as putative prime minister. The BJP subsequently lost to an opposition coalition in the 2015 assembly elections that included Kumar's party, but his relations with alliance partners were contentious and he rejoined the NDA in 2017. Bowing to what it thought were electoral compulsions, the BJP agreed to a 17–17 share with the Janata Dal (United) and the remaining 6 to the Lok Jana Shakti party, a decision that reportedly rankled some BJP politicians. For an analysis of the changing dynamics of Bihar politics, see: *The Indian Express*, 'Explained: The Story That Nitish–Modi Picture Patna Tells' (2019, 3 March). Available at https://indianexpress.com/article/explained/nitish-kumar-narendra-modi-bihar-nda-bjp-jdu-5609149/ (accessed on 30 April 2019).
18. Despite the periodic farmer protests throughout the country, data by the CSDS-Lokniti post-poll survey revealed that 68 per cent of the farmers were found to be satisfied with the performance of the Modi government; of those reporting agricultures as their main occupation, 39 per cent voted for the BJP.

Amrit Prakash Pandey and Manesh Rana, 'Post-Poll Survey: Farmers' Issues Were Not Centre Stage', *The Hindu* (2019, 27 May). Available at https://www.thehindu.com/elections/lok-sabha-2019/farmers-issues-were-not-centre-stage/ (accessed on 26 June 2019).

19. As in the case of the farmers, the CSDS-Lokniti poll found that the BJP was favoured among voters below age 35 more so than in any other age category. Jyoti Mishra and Amrit Negi, 'Post-Poll Survey: BJP, the Most Preferred Party of Young India', *The Hindu* (2019, 29 May). Available at https://www.thehindu.com/specials/the-hindu-csds-lokniti-post-poll-survey/article27259339.ece (accessed on 25 June 2019).
20. In those elections, the Congress, which had been the ruling party, lost 42 seats, but they were able to form a coalition with the Janata Dal (Secular) and win a narrow majority. They also had slightly more popular votes than the BJP.
21. The elections were, however, quite close in Rajasthan and Madhya Pradesh, and in the latter the BJP even won more popular votes than the Congress.
22. See poll results in: Pandey and Rana, 'Post-Poll Survey', and Mishra and Negi, 'Post-Poll Survey'.
23. A compilation of polls taken in January through March 2019 can be found in: LokSabhaElections.in, 'Latest Opinion Polls and Surveys Lok Sabha Election 2019'. Available at https://www.loksabhaelections.in/ (accessed on 2 April 2019).
24. The polling referred to here comes from *India Today*'s periodic 'Mood of the Nation' surveys. A comprehensive analysis of these surveys is by Arviral Virk, 'For the First Time, Modi's Popularity Rating Slips Below 50%', *The Quint* (2018, 20 August). Available at https://www.thequint.com/news/politics/india-today-mood-of-nation-poll-narendra-modi-declining-popularity (accessed on 30 April 2019).
25. LokSabhaElections.in, 'Latest Opinion Polls and Surveys Lok Sabha Election 2019'.
26. The results of the two polls, VMR and Times Now, conducted between 5 February and 21 February 2019, are analysed by Kat Hopps, 'India Heads to Polls—Modi Popularity Soars as 7 Phase Begins', *Express* (2019, 12 March). Available at https://www.express.co.uk/news/world/1098493/india-election-2019-polls-latest-narendra-modi-indian-election-commission (accessed on 15 April 2019).
27. Statistics collected by CVoter and analysed by Aditya Menon, 'PM Modi Least Liked in South of India and Punjab: Popularity Just 2% in TN', *Bloomberg/Quint* (2019, 22 March). Available at www.bloombergquint.com/politics/pm-modi-most-disliked-in-south-india-tamil-nadu-kerala-punjab-lok-sabha-polls-2019 (accessed on 4 April 2019).
28. A comprehensive discussion of the impact of these issues on the campaign in: Swansy Afonso, 'Modi's Popularity Back to Peak Levels on Air Strike, Survey Says', *Bloomberg* (2019, 6 April). Available at https://news.yahoo.com/modi-apos-popularity-back-peak-042823084.html (accessed on 23 April 2019). The

article is based on a poll conducted by the Lokniti research programme at the CSDS from 24 March to 31 March 2019.

29. An excellent argument on the electoral importance of efficient welfare programmes is in: Rahul Verma and Pranav Gupta, 'Scale of BJP's Massive Victory Can't Solely Be Attributed to National Security and Polarization', *The Print* (2019, 24 May). Available at https://theprint.in/opinion/scale-of-bjps-massive-2019-victory-cant-solely-be-attributed-to-national-security-polarisation/239936/ (accessed on 30 June 2019).
30. Sheela Bhatt, 'BJP Set to Transform into Garib's Janata Party', *The Sunday Guardian* (2019, 25 May). Available at https://www.sundayguardianlive.com/news/bjp-set-transform-garibs-janata-party (accessed on 8 June 2019).
31. Ibid.
32. For an analysis of the 2019 budget's focus on welfare and job creation, see Press Trust of India, 'Budget 2019: Fiscal Goals to Welfare, DBS Lauds Mix of Continuity, Change', *Business Standard* (2019, 6 July). Available at https://www.business-standard.com/article/pti-stories/india-s-2019–20-budget-mixes-continuity-with-winds-of-change-says-dbs-119070600119_1.html (accessed on 7 July 2019).
33. See our report of interviews on this subject with senior RSS officials in Walter K. Andersen and Shridhar D. Damle, *The RSS: A View to the Inside* (Gurgaon: Penguin Viking, 2018), Chapter 1.
34. RSS General Secretary Joshi focused on this issue during his press briefing at the end of this yearly session. Available at rss.org/Encyc/2019/3/10/ABPS-press-briefing-by-RSS-sarkaryavah.html (accessed on 18 June 2019).
35. Seshadri Chari, a full-time RSS worker and formerly editor of the RSS weekly *Organiser*, wrote an unusually frank opinion piece on the new government in 'Amit Shah Is the Prime Minister in Modi Cabinet and He Hits Where It Hurts', *The Print* (2019, 7 June). Available at http://theprint.im/opinion/amit-shah-cabinet-he-hits-whee-it-hurts/246899/ (accessed on 18 June 2019).
36. Deendayal Upadhyaya (1916–1968) in his book *Integral Humanism* (Delhi: Navchetan Press, 1968) provided the intellectual basis for the RSS' version of Hindutva, grounding his analysis in a uniquely Indian sense of identity that reflected the subcontinent's religious and cultural heritage and called for social equality. Upadhyaya was a full-time RSS worker who was seconded in the early 1950s to the RSS' political affiliate, the Bharatiya Jana Sangh, predecessor of the BJP, to lend it organizational shape; he later became its general secretary and president.
37. An analysis of the Modi government's economic goals is in: *Business Standard*, 'Economic Survey of India 2019' (2019, 4 July). Available at https://www.business-standard.com/budget/article/economic-survey-2019-economy-expected-to-rebound-fy20-growth-pegged-at-7–119070400459_1.html (accessed on 5 July 2019).

Chapter 2

Foreign Policy and the 2019 Indian National Elections

Sumit Ganguly

Foreign policy issues, rarely, if ever, have shaped India's national electoral outcomes. India's 2019 elections are an exception as foreign policy reinforced the ruling party's strong leadership and thus the electoral outcome. In the past, it seldom exercised a significant role. They have, at most, barring rare circumstances, played a limited role in influencing national electoral results. For example, it can be argued that in the 1980s, India's involvement in the Sri Lankan Civil War had some impact on national electoral outcomes. In particular, a female suicide bomber, belonging to the Liberation Tigers of Tamil Eelam (LTTE) was responsible for the assassination of Prime Minister Rajiv Gandhi during the 1991 election campaign. His death played some role in highlighting India's infelicitous military intervention in Sri Lanka and thereby had some impact on the outcome of the election.

That said, in considerable apart, foreign and security policy issues, have long remained the preserve of India's political elite. Few individuals in the parliament have any particular expertise in these matters and even fewer of their constituents pay much heed to foreign and security policy concerns on a routine basis. Instead socio-economic issues, more often than not, play a critical role in determining Indian electoral outcomes. Not surprisingly, few of India's parliamentarians find it necessary to devote substantial time and attention to foreign policy issues unless they have a particular personal interest in the subject.

Despite the low salience of foreign policy issues in Indian national elections, they probably played a non-inconsequential role in the 19th General Elections. Some part of the Bharatiya Janata Party (BJP) sweep of the elections (especially in northern India) with a resounding win of 303 out of a possible 543 seats in India's parliament can be attributed to foreign and security policy choices. With its allies in the National Democratic Alliance (NDA), the BJP-governing alliance rises to a dominant total of 354 seats.

CENTRAL ARGUMENT

This chapter argues that, in all likelihood, the framing of a terrorist attack in the troubled Indian-controlled portion of the disputed state of Jammu and Kashmir played a significant role in the election. The attack was the work of a Pakistan-based terrorist organization, the Jaish-e-Mohammed (JeM), which had been previously responsible for a spate of other dramatic attacks in Kashmir and elsewhere. On this occasion, the JeM attacked a convoy of the Central Reserve Police Force (CRPF) convoy in Pulwama on 14 February killing 40 personnel.[1] The incident only added to the woes of a state that was wracked with widespread political instability and violence.

The Modi regime not only carried out a retaliatory attack in the wake of this incident but actually permitted the Indian Air Force (IAF) to strike a target at Balakot within Pakistan. This episode involved the first use of the IAF to cross the international boundary since the 1971 war. The efficacy of this action, however, remains the subject of a spirited debate.[2]

Furthermore, this chapter will also focus on how Pakistani authorities portrayed the incident and its aftermath. The Pakistani accounts, to no particular surprise, differed in considerable measure from those in the Indian media. Finally, the chapter will conclude with a brief extrapolation of the significance that the Modi regime attaches to its foreign policy endeavours.

THE MEDIUM AND THE MESSAGE

In the immediate aftermath of the attack, the Modi regime made extraordinarily adroit use of the electronic media to highlight India's putatively robust response to Pakistan's continued dalliance with terror. In making this argument, the regime very skilfully sought to portray itself as forthright, muscular and unafraid-to-use force to defend India's national security interests. In fact, it can be argued that faced with rising unemployment, a sagging economy and declining foreign investment, the Pulwama attack provided Modi an opportunity to burnish his national security credentials and one that he wasted little time in seizing.[3]

Based upon a Reuters poll conducted shortly after the military action, there is evidence that following the IAF strike the BJP saw a distinct uptick in its electoral fortunes.[4] It is to the credit of Prime Minister Modi and his party's deft public relations apparatus that even a retaliatory Pakistani air attack and the shooting down of an aging Indian MiG-21 Bison, along with the capture (and subsequent release) of its pilot, Wing Commander Abhinandan Varthaman, did not dampen enthusiasm for the ruling party. Indeed, some analysts argued that India's actions underscored that Modi was a 'decisive leader'.[5] The shooting down of this aircraft and the capture of its pilot should have been seen as a humiliation for the IAF. Instead the public relations campaign focused on his quick release and thereby framed the outcome as a victory for Indian diplomacy.

There is also some anecdotal evidence that suggests how Modi's actions resonated beyond the elite circles. One report cited an unemployed engineer in the critical state of Madhya Pradesh as saying that 'Who else can I vote for? Nobody else can fix India *or protect us from Pakistan…Look at how he made Pakistan pay for Pulwama*' (emphasis added). Others apparently echoed this sentiment arguing that 'He went inside Pakistan and taught them a lesson. He brought Abhinandan back in a day'.[6]

THE USES OF SOCIAL MEDIA

It is important to demonstrate that the electoral support that the Pulwama attack and its aftermath generated did not ensue of its own accord. Instead it appears that it was the result of a carefully orchestrated and relentless social media campaign on the part of the Modi electoral machine. The extremely deft use of messages on Facebook and WhatsApp, which praised the prime minister for his apparently fearless leadership, no doubt played a vital role in shaping public opinion.[7] On the other hand, the principal opposition party, the Indian National Congress, proved to be far less adept in its use of social media even as it faced this onslaught from the ruling party. Rahul Gandhi, the party president, could not find any adroit strategy to counter the social media barrage from Modi and his associates.

THE ROLE OF THE ELECTRONIC MEDIA

Other forces also worked to the advantage of the ruling regime. The vast majority of India's television news channels also contributed to the particular framing of the Pulwama attack and India's military response to it. A number of analyses have concluded that the electronic media, in large part, helped frame the issue in highly propagandistic, jingoistic and pro-regime terms. The largely uncritical and highly favourable coverage of the response to the terrorist incident probably swayed a segment of the electorate. In any case, these reports effectively drowned out any critical discussion of other issues that had surfaced in the spring of 2019 most notably allegations of corruption in the acquisition of the Rafale fighter aircraft from France.[8]

These charges stemmed, in considerable part, from Modi's decision to abruptly purchase 36 aircraft 'off the shelf' when on a visit to France in 2016 instead of the 126 that the previous Congress-led United Progressive Alliance (UPA) government had agreed to purchase. The decision became even more controversial as an agreement was also reached between Reliance Industries, an Indian industrial conglomerate, and Dassault Aviation, the manufacturer of the aircraft, for a substantial investment in India. The choice of Reliance as the partner stirred the controversy because its scion, Anil Ambani, is widely believed to be close to Modi.

The Congress sought to portray this episode as an evidence of corruption against a regime that had touted its credentials as being free from any such taint. Rahul Gandhi led the charge in the parliament arguing that the Modi regime had 'dishonored the blood of our martyred soldiers' and had 'betrayed India's soul'.[9] Despite these sharp attacks, they appeared to have little resonance with India's electorate.

A VIEW FROM ISLAMABAD

How were the Pulwama attack and the events that followed discussed in the Pakistani press? At the outset, Prime Minister Imran Khan in a video message asserted that Pakistan would address India's concerns about the attack if it could provide 'actionable evidence'.[10] Not surprisingly, the Pakistani press did not accept the Indian allegation that JeM was responsible for the attack on the CRPF convoy. In this context, it needs to be borne in mind that an organization that enjoys the patronage of the overweening Inter-Services Intelligence Directorate (ISI-D) cannot be subject to widespread criticism in the Pakistani media.[11]

More to the point, it quite predictably referred to the incident having taken place in 'Indian occupied Kashmir' and alluded to the quest for 'self-determination' on the part of the Kashmiris.[12] Some Pakistani newspapers, most notably *The Nation*, went further. One report in *The Nation* which referred to the bombing as a 'valiant' act generated much resentment and anger in India.[13]

As discussed earlier, India carried out a retaliatory air attack on Balakot which it deemed to be a terrorist training camp. Pakistani officialdom claimed that while the strike did take place, the location had no terrorist training facilities and that the Indian airstrikes had destroyed a forested area. It also dismissed the Indian claims that a large number of terrorists had been killed as 'reckless, self-serving and fictitious'. Furthermore, it accused India of 'ecoterrorism' and threatened to lodge a complaint to the United Nations.[14]

Not long after the Indian attack on Balakot, Pakistan carried out a counter-retaliatory strike outside the city of Srinagar in Indian-controlled Kashmir. As the IAF intercepted the Pakistan Air Force aircraft, an aging Indian MiG-21 Bison aircraft was shot down over Pakistan territory with the pilot bailing out. Subsequently, Pakistan, with considerable fanfare, released the Indian pilot who had suffered minor injuries. While Pakistan portrayed his release as an act of magnanimity, Modi's government sought to portray it as a victory for Indian diplomacy.

The differences in how the two sides saw the incident and followed its wake remain stark. Long after the initial incident, India's retaliation in Balakot and after Pakistan's counter-retaliation, Khan continued to assert that the Pulwama attack was 'indigenous'.[15]

INDIAN FOREIGN POLICY AFTER THE ELECTION

There is little or no question given the ideological proclivities of this regime that it will devote a substantial amount of its energies to domestic policy issues. However, given Prime Minister Modi's track record during his first term, it is reasonable to surmise that he will not neglect foreign policy. Indeed, at his inauguration, he made it a point to invite the leaders of the Bay of Bengal Initiative for Multi-Sectoral Technical and Economic Cooperation (BIMSTEC) to attend. It is worth noting that neither Pakistan nor the People's Republic of China (PRC) are members of this entity.

It is more than evident that the second Modi regime is unlikely to try and improve relations with Pakistan unless it perceives that the country has abandoned or at least curtailed its involvement with terror. Depicting Pakistan as an aggressor and as a state that is fundamentally inimical to India's national security interests clearly worked well for the regime in the elections.

Furthermore, following the decision on 5 August 2019 to dispense with Kashmir's special status in the Indian union through an abrogation of Article 370 of the Indian Constitution, relations with Pakistan are now bound to become more fraught.[16] In the wake of New

Delhi's announcement, Pakistan asked the Indian high commissioner to Islamabad to leave, snapped train links, ended all trade relations and ended access to Indian civilian aircraft over Pakistani airspace. It is hard to visualize how bilateral relations could possibly improve in the foreseeable future.

It faces a more vexed choice when dealing with the PRC. There is little or no question that it sees the PRC as a long-term threat. The new Minister for External Affairs Subrahmanyam Jaishankar, who was an ambassador to the PRC, has few illusions about the growth of the PRC's military capabilities and the consequent threat they pose for India. Yet there are few political dividends at the hustings in adopting an entirely hard-line stance towards the PRC. Accordingly, it seems reasonable to surmise that the regime will pursue a policy that is firm but not provocative in dealing with India's behemoth neighbour.

A final challenge that India will face involves its relations with the USA in the context of its own policies towards Iran and Afghanistan. Relations with both states are crucial for India. While under American pressure it has ended its oil purchases from Iran, it cannot entirely abandon its ties with the country. It has a significant investment in the port of Chabahar and also needs to remain on good terms with the country to ensure the quiescence of its own substantial Shia population.

In a similar vein, it can ill-afford to walk away from its substantial economic, political and diplomatic investments in Afghanistan. With President Trump's stated intention of extricating the USA from Afghanistan, even it if means granting Pakistan considerable leeway in the country, India may well find itself in a real quandary. On the one hand, it can ill-afford to antagonize the USA given the very real improvements that have taken place in the relationship in the last two decades. Yet it cannot willingly acquiesce in seeing Pakistan acquire carte blanche in the country's internal affairs. Such an outcome could see a return to the days of the Taliban-dominated regime when Afghanistan had become a staging ground for Pakistan-sponsored terrorists' intent on wreaking havoc in India.[17]

As President Trump sought to elicit Pakistan's cooperation to divest the USA from Afghanistan, he created an important controversy with

India. Very possibly at the urging of Imran Khan, he quite abruptly offered to mediate the Kashmir dispute. To compound matters, he claimed that Prime Minister Modi had suggested that he might serve as a mediator. Within hours, the Indian Ministry of External Affairs categorically denied that Modi had proffered any such suggestion. More to the point, it reiterated India's long-standing position following the Simla (Shimla) agreement of 1972 that any negotiations involving the dispute must be strictly bilateral.[18]

Even though the Indian public evinces no routine interest in foreign policy issues, significant setbacks on any of these fronts could enhance the salience of foreign policy in the next General Elections. Consequently, the regime's ability to tackle these challenges could make a difference, if again only at the margins, in the next national polls.

NOTES

1. Maria Abi-Habib, Sameer Yasir and Hari Kumar, 'India Blames Pakistan for Attack in Kashmir, Promises a Response', *The New York Times* (2019, 15 February).
2. Marcus Hellyer, Nathan Ruser and Aakriti Bachawat, 'India's Balakot Airstrike Shows How Hard Precision Bombing Is', *The National Interest* (2019, 27 May). Available at https://nationalinterest.org/blog/buzz/indias-balakot-airstrike-shows-how-hard-precision-bombing-49397 (accessed on 18 September 2019).
3. Satish Misra, 'Emerging Electoral Dynamics after Pulwama Tragedy', *Observer Research Foundation* (2019, 5 March). Available at https://www.orfonline.org/expert-speak/emerging-electoral-dynamics-after-pulwama-tragedy-48718/ (accessed on 18 September 2019).
4. Adam Withnall, 'Kashmir Tension: How Will Indian Voters Respond to Pakistan Airstrikes Ahead of Elections?' *The Independent* (2019, 26 February).
5. Michael Safi, Mehreen Zahra-Malik and Azhar Farooq, 'India Demands Safe Return of Pilot Shot Down by Pakistan over Kashmir', *The Guardian* (2019, 28 February).
6. Vivan Marwaha, 'The Secret behind Millennial Support for India's Modi', *The Washington Post* (2019, 24 May).
7. Ibid.
8. Suchitra Vijayan and Vasundhara Sirnate Drennan, 'After Pulwama, the Indian Media Proves It Is the BJP's Propaganda Machine', *The Washington Post* (2019, 4 March).
9. Iain Marlow, 'A Guide to the Controversy over Modi's French Fighter Jet Deal', *The Washington Post* (2018, 2 October).

10. *Dawn*, 'Pakistan Will Address Actionable Evidence If Shared By Delhi, Khan Tells India after Pulwama Attack' (2019, 19 February).
11. For the connection between the ISI-D and a range of terrorist organizations including the JeM, see S. Paul Kapur, *Jihad as Grand Strategy: Islamist Militancy, National Security and the Pakistani State* (New York, NY: Oxford University Press, 2016).
12. Akash Sriram, 'A War of Words? Conflicting Media Narratives between India and Pakistan', *The Diplomat* (2019, 8 March). Available at https://thediplomat.com/2019/03/a-war-of-words-conflicting-media-narratives-between-india-and-pakistan/ (accessed on 18 September 2019).
13. *India Today*, 'Janhvi Kapoor Slams Pakistan for Calling Pulwama Terror Attack a Fight for Freedom' (2019, 16 February). Available at https://www.indiatoday.in/movies/celebrities/story/janhvi-kapoor-slams-pakistan-daily-for-calling-pulwama-terror-attack-a-fight-for-freedom-1457626–2019–02-16 (accessed on 18 September 2019).
14. AFP-JIJI, 'Pakistan to Lodge "Eco-Terrorism" Complaint against India over Damage to Trees from Airstrikes', *The Japan Times* (2019, 2 May).
15. *The Week*, 'Pulwama Attack an "Indigenous" Incident, Pakistan Should Not Be Blamed: Imran' (2019, 24 July).
16. Sumit Ganguly, 'Modi Crosses the Rubicon in Kashmir', Foreign Affairs.com (2019, 8 August). Available at https://www.foreignaffairs.com/articles/india/2019–08-08/modi-crosses-rubicon-kashmir (accessed on 18 September 2019).
17. Michael Rubin, 'Winning in Afghanistan Requires Taking the Fight to Pakistan', *The National Interest* (2019, 3 June).
18. Rebecca Ratcliffe, 'Fury in India over Donald Trump's Kashmir Claims', *The Guardian* (2019, 23 July).

Chapter 3

Amazing Dimensions of Managing the Biggest Election in World History

S. Y. Quraishi

Voting is a civic sacrament.

—Theodore Hesburgh

In keeping with the well-established tradition, the 2019 General Elections to the 17th Lok Sabha broke its own record as the largest in history. Indian elections are eye candy of experts and media every five years because it tells the unparalleled story of an electorate larger than every continent, making history over a short period of a month.[1]

MIND-BLOWING LOGISTICS!

The enthusiastic Indian electorate thronged to a million polling stations to cast over 600 million votes.[2] A total of 2.33 million ballot units, 1.63 million control units and 1.74 million Voter Verifiable Paper Audit Trails (VVPATs) were used.[3] In order to transport men and materials throughout the country, airplanes, helicopters, boats, tractors, motorcycles, bullock carts, mules, elephants and camels were hired. Over 120 trains with 3,000 coaches, over 200,000 buses and thousands of cars worked with clockwork precision.[4] These numbers are stunning in comparison with the first General Elections. In 1952, about half of the electorate was eligible excluding Jammu and Kashmir out of a total population of 36.11 crore.[5] Separate boxes were used for each candidate.

Since then, we have come a long way from ballot boxes to paper ballots to electronic voting machines (EVMs), now equipped with VVPAT. Equal voting rights for men and women aged 21 were provided, unlike the USA or UK where it took over a century. Voting age was reduced to 18 in 1988.[6] The population has quadrupled, but the phases have reduced to a tenth! The 1952 elections were held in 68 phases over four months between 25 October 1951 and 21 February 1952 for 489 parliamentary seats. In comparison, the 2019 elections were held in seven phases from 11 April to 19 May 2019 for 543 seats.[7] While there were only 53 parties, the number is 2,354 now![8]

For conducting such a mammoth exercise, the Election Commission of India (ECI) borrowed 12 million polling staff from central and state government departments. They range from senior civil servants, police officers and engineers to schoolteachers, clerks, health care workers, etc.[9] They are solely answerable to the ECI during their deputation and their neutrality is non-negotiable. Although public sector banks and university employees are deployed to supplement the government servants, private sector employees are kept out by law. Over 2,000 election observers, all senior civil servants, from outside the states were appointed for overall monitoring, reinforced by about 75,000 videographers and photographers. They were assisted by 151,000 micro-observers assigned to each polling station for recording any wrongdoing at booths during voting.[10]

SCHEDULING MAMMOTH ELECTION

A complex web of factors comes into play while scheduling Indian elections. As often before, the ECI was criticized for the dates and number of phases. But one forgets that the ECI has to factor in weather, agricultural cycles, examinations, religious and social festivals, and law and order while finalizing election dates.[11] As sometimes in the past, the most important concern for the Commission was voters' security. The Commission deployed paramilitary forces and federal armed police. They are considered neutral because they are not deployed in home states. For two decades, all parties have been demanding that these forces be deployed in their constituencies, but since these forces are limited it necessitates rotation. It was reported that 270,000 paramilitary and 2 million state police was deployed in 2019.[12]

Elections can indeed be held on a single day, in one phase, provided adequate number of central armed police forces can be made available even if it needs raising more battalions. Additionally, if simultaneous elections are to be held as the ruling party has been suggesting, nearly 23 lakh EVMs and 25 lakh VVPAT units would be required. The total cost works out to be approximately ₹10,000 crore.[13] This is a small price to pay as the side effects of staggered elections are significant. While the Model Code of Conduct (MCC) is in force in a particular constituency, campaigns continue on social media and messaging apps such as WhatsApp. Even opinion/exit polls are circulated! It is almost impossible for the Commission to monitor these violations. If election happens on a single day, these issues will vanish.

REACHING EVERY INDIAN

In accordance with its motto 'No Voter to be Left Behind', the ECI left no stone unturned to reach every last voter. Election rules require that no Indian citizen should have to travel more than 2 km to vote,[14] regardless of terrain or weather. Hence, thousands of officials walked two–three days to reach polling stations otherwise inaccessible.[15] A booth was set up in Gir National Park in Gujarat for the Hindu priest of Banej temple to come and vote at a time of his choosing. In Arunachal Pradesh, out of 2,202 polling stations, 7 had less than 10 voters. Six brave and determined officials hiked for 300 miles to reach Malogam, where a lone woman, Sokela Tayang, is registered to vote.[16] As soon as she voted at 9.30 a.m. on 11 April, the polling booth recorded 100 per cent turnout! Since she was the lone voter, the secrecy of her vote could not be protected.

In Ladakh, a booth was set up at 4,327 m for 12 voters. Officials used oxygen tanks to reach Anlay Pho, a village 4,500 m above the sea level. In Andaman and Nicobar Islands, officials braved swamps infested with crocodiles and sea snakes, travelling in tribal boats, to reach a handful of voters.[17] This is the Commission's grand promise to our people, equality of opportunity in the land of diversity.

REVOLUTIONIZING PARTICIPATION—THE SVEEP WAY

The political scientist Larry Sabato once remarked that every election is determined by people who show up. Although election management bodies (EMBs) focus on conducting elections, they neglect awareness. Voter education has become integral for ECI efforts since launching Systematic Voters' Education and Electoral Participation (SVEEP) in 2009.[18] Ever since the first National Voters' Day (NVD) was celebrated in 2010 with the theme 'Greater Participation for a Stronger Democracy', there has been no looking back. The SVEEP division rolled out comprehensive outreach and multimedia campaigns aimed at filling gaps in information, motivation and facilitation.[19] NVD is celebrated all over the country right from the national level down to each polling station where new voters are felicitated with a badge carrying the logo 'Proud to be a Voter-Ready to Vote', administered the pledge and handed over their Elector Photo Identity Cards (EPICs).[20]

In 2018, the event witnessed the felicitation of Champions of the National Elections Quiz, the largest elections quiz in the world with 1.35 million students of 9th–12th standard from 38,000 schools across India.[21] In 2019, chief election commissioners (CECs) and senior officials from Bangladesh, Bhutan, Kazakhstan, the Maldives, Russia and Sri Lanka graced the occasion.[22] Campaigns on ethical voting; literacy clubs for embassies, armed forces, colleges, rural and tribal areas; social media campaigns for poll reminders; campaigns such as the #JetSetVote[23] had been employed. National- and state-level icons such as late President A. P. J. Abdul Kalam, M. S. Dhoni (cricketer), Aamir Khan (Bollywood actor), Prahlad Singh Tipaniya (folk singer), Cheteshwar Pujara (cricketer), Gopinath Muthukad (magician) and

Abhinav Bindra (shooter), among others, have inspired people with their star power.[24] Famous folk singers Malini Awasthi and Sharda Devi from UP and Bihar motivated millions of female voters.[25] Stalwarts such as M. C. Mary Kom (boxing), Saina Nehwal (badminton), Apurvi Chandela (shooter), Dipa Karmakar (gymnastics), Ankita Raina (tennis), Kiran Parmar (kabaddi) and Daxa Patel (Bharatanatyam) have used their star power to motivate women and youth.[26]

As a result, new records were set in voter turnout.[27] As compared to 66.4 per cent in 2014, 67.38 per cent voted in 2019, the highest ever in India's electoral history.[28] This seems like a marginal change, but is stunning considering that 86 million new voters were added since 2014 alone![29] According to the Consolidated Voter Turnout Data of the ECI,[30] women outnumbered men in Andhra Pradesh, Arunachal Pradesh, Bihar, Daman and Diu, Himachal Pradesh, Kerala, Lakshadweep, Manipur, Meghalaya, Mizoram, Puducherry, Tamil Nadu and Uttarakhand. The difference was just 0.07 per cent overall, the lowest in any election (Figure 3.1).

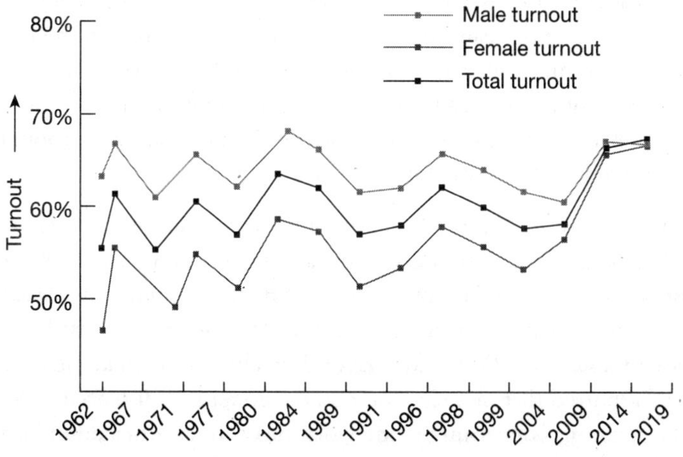

Figure 3.1 *Gender-Wise Participation in General Elections, 1962–2019*

Source: Scroll.in, Trivedi Centre for Political Data.[31]

THE ECI UNDER ATTACK

The Commission and 12 million polling staff deserve enormous praise and admiration for their accomplishments. But what was to be celebrated as the festival of democracy and a subject of national pride was mired in controversies. From the days of its inception under Sukumar Sen till recently,[32] while the ECI has been lauded for conducting free and fair elections, the response was mixed this time. It was painful to watch the Commission coming under attack for what was described as 'pusillanimous'[33] response to repeated violations of the MCC, especially by the ruling party. A string of avoidable controversies started with PM's 27 March announcement of India's first anti-satellite (ASAT) test.[34] In the past, such announcements have been made by the Defence Research & Development Organisation (DRDO). But the Commission ruled that it was not a violation.

The launch of NaMo TV without licence, a biopic on the PM's life, a web series 'Modi: A Common Man's Journey', all came under scanner.[35] The Supreme Court of India had to intervene on six different occasions to question the Commission. This is fraught with risk which is not being realized, because Article 329 has barred the courts from intervening once the election process has started.[36] Now the doors have been opened for the court's intervention. The Court was unconvinced by the ECI's submission on 15 April that it was 'toothless' and 'powerless' to act on hate speeches.[37]

In response to Court's deadline of 6 May to act on complaints of Code violations, the Commission debarred many politicians from campaigning for up to 3 days by invoking Article 324, which was widely appreciated.[38] But when it came to the PM and BJP president (now home minister), the ECI hastily gave 'clean chits' to them in each case.[39] It was reported that one election commissioner had dissented in 5 out of 11 decisions concerning Code violations.[40] In case of a difference of opinion within the poll panel, decisions are taken by a majority vote. But dissent is a healthy sign of objective deliberation within a constitutional body. His demand for his dissenting note to be made public was worthy of positive consideration. But the Commission rejected it, with the CEC saying his dissent was 'avoidable' during elections.[41]

As in the past, aspersions were also cast on the EVM–VVPAT arrangement. I would like to reiterate that every opposition party maligns it without any concrete evidence, and then comes to power with the same machines! Having said that, the Commission's refusal to engage did not help in assuaging the scepticism of the political parties and the general public. According to the ECI, tallying VVPAT slips with EVM count one per Assembly constituency was based on scientific methodology endorsed by the Indian Statistical Institute.[42] But as many as 21 opposition parties approached the Supreme Court, which advised the Commission to increase the counting to 5 VVPATs per Assembly segment, citing 'better voter confidence and credibility of electoral process'.[43] The opposition made two more demands: one, the five VVPAT machines must be counted in the beginning and two, in the event of a mismatch, all machines in the Assembly segment must be counted. The Commission rejected these as unfeasible.[44]

That the system is foolproof was demonstrated in this election. Physical verification of VVPAT slips with EVM count was done across 20,695 polling stations before declaration of results as per Court orders, and no mismatch was detected according to the ECI. This goes on to show that EVM–VVPAT is the final solution. The issue is of trust deficit which can only be tackled by open-minded discussions. This controversy has refused to die down even after the elections are long over, with a high-pitched demand to return to ballot papers. Instead of returning to days of ballot papers which were fraught with stuffing of ballot boxes by booth capturers, thousands of invalid votes, etc., let us see if a consensus can be built on the EVM/VVPAT arrangement by tweaking the system. Several parties are demanding counting a larger VVPAT audit, from 30 per cent to 50 per cent to 100 per cent. The ECI's concern is that it would take several days, which many dispute.

I would like to offer a via media; instead of counting EVMs, count 100 per cent VVPAT slips. This will reduce the time taken and will be almost similar to counting paper ballots, which will serve to satisfy parties doubtful about EVMs. This way, EVMs are not abandoned and continue to play the most critical role for which these are designed. This will put all controversies about EVM manipulation behind us and end the demand for return to the ballot papers.

RESTORING THE GLORY

Reputation takes years to build, but minutes to get demolished. One hopes that the erosion of Commission's reputation is a temporary aberration. Some systemic electoral reforms are urgently needed to restore the public faith in the institution. The Law Commission's 255th report recommended a collegium for appointing the poll panel (the CEC as well as the ECs), consisting of the PM, the Leader of the Opposition and the Chief Justice of India (CJI).[45] Political stalwarts such as L. K. Advani and former CECs B. B. Tandon, N. Gopalaswami and I have backed the idea even while in office. But it seems to have fallen on deaf ears of the successive governments. A public interest litigation was filed in the Supreme Court in 2015 regarding the same.[46] In 2017, a bench comprising CJI J. S. Khehar and Justice D. Y. Chandrachud questioned the government regarding absence of any law on the matter even after seven decades.[47] The Court took up the case again in 2018 and referred it to a five-judge Constitution bench, which is yet to be constituted. Why doesn't the judiciary realize the urgency of this critical issue?

As discussed earlier, the ECI's reputation suffered because, by its own admission, it was 'toothless' to rein in recalcitrant political parties. This has led to the resurrection of an old debate about whether MCC should be made into law. This amounts to transferring the model code from the ECI to the judiciary. In my opinion, transferring the Commission's power to the judiciary would destroy the purpose, if nothing else, for delay in decision-making. This solution is often proposed by people stung by MCC's moral force!

While the debate between the legal and moral force of the MCC continues, an anecdote from May 2012 by-election to Goa's Cortalim constituency is worth recalling. The Late Goa CM Manohar Parrikar planned to induct a candidate into his council of ministers. The ECI 'advised' Parrikar to defer it, but he forcefully argued that it was his constitutional right. I admitted that although it was indeed his constitutional right, it was an 'advice' in the interest of level playing field. He not only accepted the advice but remarked that he *bows to the moral authority of the model code of conduct, which should take precedence over his constitutional right*. What an outstanding example of statesmanship![48] Such stellar examples are few and far between. The real cure lies in empowering the Commission to deregister political parties for gross violations of the MCC and other electoral provisions. Presently, despite being the registering authority under Section 29A of the Representation of the People Act, 1951 (RP Act, 1951),[49] it cannot deregister them even for the gravest of violations. The Commission has been seeking this reform for over 20 years, with no success.[50]

MONEY, MEDIA, MAFIA

The crippling effect of money power was on full display in 2019. The Commission seized nearly ₹1,300 crore worth of drugs/narcotics, cash (₹839 crore), liquor (worth ₹294 crore), gold/silver (valued around ₹986 crore) and freebies/items worth ₹58 crores, totalling ₹3,500 crores. Tamil Nadu (₹952 crore), Gujarat (₹553.76 crore), Delhi (₹430.39 crore), Punjab (₹286.41 crore) and Andhra Pradesh (₹232.02 crore) topped the list. The main cause for worry is the proportion of drugs/narcotics seizures, with Gujarat (almost ₹524.35) crore dislodging Punjab.[51]

In my book, *An Undocumented Wonder: The Making of the Great Indian Election*, I have provided a checklist of 40 modus operandi[52] of political parties/candidates using illegal money in elections. 'Distribution of liquor, drugs and poppy husk' is the penultimate item on the list. It is horrifying that it has graduated to the top three in 2019.[53] According to the Centre for Media Studies Report released in June 2019,[54] nearly ₹100 crores were spent per constituency and ₹700 per voter. Report estimates the total campaign and management cost of elections at a whopping ₹55,000–60,000 crores, dwarfing others before it nationally and internationally![55]

Another controversy which raised a storm was the electoral bonds which tipped the scales in favour of the ruling party. These bonds have not found many backers ever since they were introduced. Former CECs Nasim Zaidi and O. P. Rawat publicly expressed concern while in office,[56] which seem to have fallen on deaf ears. Millions can now be freely paid by companies and the source need not be declared to the Commission. This is the institutionalization and legalization of crony capitalism. Additionally, the cap on donations, which used to be

7.5 per cent of the average three-year profits, has now been removed. Now 100 per cent of the profits can be donated to any party. This is a recipe for disaster as shell companies can now exist solely to fund political parties.[57]

To make matters worse, the Foreign Contribution (Regulation) Act (FCRA), 2010, now exempts political parties from the scrutiny of foreign funds received by them. The amendment makes it legal for political parties to receive funding from foreign donors, that too with 42 years retrospective effect! Unsurprisingly, the worst nightmares of political funding have been realized. It was reported that the sale just before elections surged by 62 per cent to over 1,700 crore in 2019. The ruling party received 95 per cent of total donations from the sale of these bonds.[58] A whopping 99.8 per cent of the total bonds sold were in denominations of ₹10 lakh and ₹1 crore,[59] which shows that corporations are purchasing these bonds, not the common man.

The crippling influence of money and muscle power has led to the strengthening of a nexus between politicians, business houses and media. These illegal operations have become 'organized', involving advertising agencies and public relations firms, besides journalists, managers and owners of media houses.[60] Good examples are opinion and exit polls which dominate the news cycle, followed by channels either taking credit for accurate predictions or trying to justify their margins of error! All parties have opposed polls at one point or another, except when they are shown as winning. A sting operation called 'Operation Prime Minister' by the News Express TV channel during the 2014 election revealed that in exchange for money, polling companies were willing to manipulate the results by tinkering with sample size, margin of error and even deleting the negative samples![61]

It is being asserted that most exit polls were stunningly accurate this time. But regardless of their content or accuracy, both the conduct and dissemination of exit polls is banned since 2008 under 126A of the RP Act, 1951.[62] How can these polls be disseminated, when the conduct itself is banned? Media houses competed with each other to openly flout these rules yet again.

As for opinion polls, even if a single voter succumbs to the band-wagon effect (cheated into believing that 'X' is winning) and changes his/her preference, damage is done. Moreover, if these polls don't make any difference, why are political parties willing to splurge on them?[63] I have long been of the view that both opinion and exit polls belong to entertainment channels, not news!

My solution to curbing money power is state funding of political parties (not elections).[64] It is important to understand the distinction between state funding of elections and political parties, and why I endorse the former. Instead of funding candidates, parties can be funded post-election based on their performance. We could, for instance, agree that for every vote obtained, ₹100 be given. Since the number of votes polled cannot be fudged, reimbursement based on the votes polled would be accurate. No extortion, bribes or quid pro quo. Private donations will be totally banned. The party accounts will be subject to audit by the Comptroller and Auditor General. This system has successfully worked in a number of Western democracies.[65]

These proposals have been discussed since the past two decades. But how will the Parliament legislate in the national interest when it is occupied by criminals? According to a report by the Association for Democratic Reforms, an astonishing 43 per cent of the newly elected Lok Sabha MPs have criminal cases against them.[66] This figure was 30 per cent in 2009 and 34 per cent in 2014, showing a phenomenal jump in 2019. This means that the number of people with heinous cases has more than doubled since 2009. These cases range from rape, dacoity, murder, culpable homicide, criminal intimidation, trespassing and kidnapping.

Unfortunately, the September 2018 verdict of the Supreme Court on the matter was a lost chance. Even though the Commission has been expressing its helplessness and crying itself hoarse for decades, the Supreme Court proceeded to throw the ball back in the ECI's court![67] The Parliament is obliged to make a law on the matter according to Article 102(1) of the Constitution,[68] but if history is anything to go by, that is unlikely to happen. After all, why will a parliament full of people with criminal charges legislate against their own self-interest? Judicial activism was required on the matter, as the doctrine of separation of powers has to be seen in the light of checks and balances.

A WELCOME DEBATE

It was encouraging to witness the broad agreement on the need for reform in a short duration discussion in Rajya Sabha held on electoral reforms on 3 July in the wake of the latest election.[69] A diverse set of opinions was expressed related to appointment process of the poll panel, social media and fake news, simultaneous elections, provision for universal electoral roll for all three levels of governance and proportional representation. What was historic was a demand for choosing a 'national government' for the duration of elections for nullifying the ruling party influence.[70] Historically, such a demand was never made as the ECI's neutrality was supposed to be playing that role. This shows the gravity of the situation.

I have been a consistent advocate of a number of these reform proposals. Apart from the aforementioned collegium and state funding of political parties, capping the expenditure of political parties, gender representation in legislatures, proportional representation for Lok Sabha and strengthening the IT Act, 2000, to effectively deal with social media transgressions are some of the points from a long list. It remains to be seen whether the political class shall translate rhetoric into action.

Every time they happen, the great Indian election is a moment of pride for the 1.3 billion of us. As we inch towards becoming the world's most populous country, we can only become fit for the future when our representatives legislate in the national interest. Our constitution provides the ECI with a massive constitutional mandate and it is urgent that its sanctity is cherished and preserved. A consensus must be built to undertake electoral reforms to preserve the credibility, freeness and fairness of the process. I remain an ardent optimist that the 17th Lok Sabha shall take it upon itself to enable the world's largest democracy to become the world's greatest.

NOTES

1. The GE 2019 happened between 11 April and 19 May in seven phases.
2. The total turnout was 67.38 per cent out of the 900 million registered voters.
3. Available at https://www.thequint.com/voices/opinion/ex-chief-election-commissioner-answers-queries-2019-lok-sabha-polls (accessed on 8 June 2019).
4. Available at https://doc-research.org/2019/05/the-scale-of-the-indian-elections/ (accessed on 24 July 2019).
5. The Census of India, 1951. Available at http://censusindia.gov.in/Census_Data_2001/India_at_glance/variation.aspx (accessed on 8 June 2019).
6. The Constitution (61st Amendment) Act, 1988. Available at https://en.wikipedia.org/wiki/Sixty-first_Amendment_of_the_Constitution_of_India (accessed on 9 June 2019).
7. Available at https://www.news18.com/news/india/great-indian-elections-1951–2019-the-story-of-how-90-crore-voters-make-and-break-history-2062747.html (accessed on 9 June 2019).
8. Available at https://www.news18.com/news/india/great-indian-elections-1951–2019-the-story-of-how-90-crore-voters-make-and-break-history-2062747.html (accessed on 9 June 2019).
9. Available at https://www.nytimes.com/2019/04/25/opinion/india-elections.html (accessed on 9 June 2019).
10. Available at https://scroll.in/article/918524/behind-indias-election-are-five-million-workers-this-series-brings-you-their-stories (accessed on 24 July 2019).
11. Available at https://www.nytimes.com/2019/04/25/opinion/india-elections.html (accessed on 9 June 2019).
12. Available at https://www.thehindubusinessline.com/news/elections/lok-sabha-polls-27-lakh-paramilitary-20-lakh-state-police-deployed/article26971665.ece (accessed on 10 June 2019).
13. Available at https://economictimes.indiatimes.com/news/politics-and-nation/law-ministry-flags-concerns-on-simultaneous-polls/articleshow/64754070.cms?from=mdr (accessed on 24 July 2019).
14. The Conduct of Election Rules, 1961. Available at http://legislative.gov.in/sites/default/files/%282%29%20THE%20CONDUCT%20OF%20ELECTION%20RULES%2C%201961.pdf (accessed on 10 June 2019).
15. Available at https://m.dailyhunt.in/news/india/english/news+bharati-epaper-newsbhar/nationalvotersday+commitment+of+no+voter+to+be+left+behind-newsid-107169754 (accessed on 11 June 2019).
16. Available at http://www.newindianexpress.com/nation/2019/apr/13/lions-crocodiles-and-sea-snakes-tales-of-reaching-indias-remotest-voters-1963923.html (accessed on 9 June 2019).

17. Available at https://www.thehindu.com/news/cities/Coimbatore/tough-trek-to-jarugumalai-for-polling-officials/article26867874.ece (accessed on 24 July 2019).
18. Available at https://eci.gov.in/sveep/ (accessed on 9 June 2019).
19. S. Y. Quraishi, *Participation Revolution with Voter Education. The Great March of Democracy-Seven Decades of India's Elections* (New Delhi: Penguin Random House India, 2019), 111–121.
20. Available at https://ecisveep.nic.in/articles.html/national-voters-day/ (accessed on 29 July 2019).
21. Available at https://eci.gov.in/files/file/9306–9th-national-voters%E2%80%99-day-to-be-celebrated-on-25th-january-2019/ (accessed on 24 July 2019).
22. Available at https://eci.gov.in/files/file/9306–9th-national-voters%E2%80%99-day-to-be-celebrated-on-25th-january-2019/ (accessed on 24 July 2019).
23. Available at https://www.youthkiawaaz.com/jetsetvote/ (accessed on 10 June 2019).
24. Available at http://sveepdigitallibrary.nic.in/Sveep_data/VoiceIndia-Jan2018.pdf (accessed on 13 July 2019).
25. Available at https://ecisveep.nic.in/approach/national-regional-icons/ (accessed on 11 June 2019).
26. Available at https://www.youthkiawaaz.com/2019/02/dr-s-y-quraishis-the-great-march-of-democracy-decodes-the-process-of-self-governance/ (accessed on 23 July 2019).
27. Available at https://en.wikipedia.org/wiki/2014_Indian_general_election (accessed on 9 June 2019).
28. According to the voter turnout numbers released by the ECI on 4 June 2019, approximately 613.14 million voted out of approximately 910 million. Available at https://eci.gov.in/files/file/9997-reconciled-consolidated-voter-turnout-data-of-lok-sabha-2019/ (accessed on 9 June 2019).
29. Available at https://en.wikipedia.org/wiki/2014_Indian_general_election (accessed on 9 June 2019).
30. Available at https://eci.gov.in/files/file/9997-reconciled-consolidated-voter-turnout-data-of-lok-sabha-2019/ (accessed on 19 July 2019).
31. Available at https://scroll.in/article/924965/verdict-2019-in-charts-and-maps-more-voters-turned-out-than-ever-before-more-parties-contested (accessed on 24 July 2019).
32. List of Chief Election Commissioners of India. Available at https://en.wikipedia.org/wiki/Chief_Election_Commissioner_of_India (accessed on 15 July 2019).
33. Available at https://thewire.in/politics/retired-civil-servants-letter-president-ec-crisis-of-credibility (accessed on 15 June 2019).
34. Available at https://www.ndtv.com/india-news/pm-modis-mission-shakti-speech-didnt-violate-model-code-of-conduct-election-commission-2014950 (accessed on 15 July 2019).

35. Available at https://www.daijiworld.com/news/newsDisplay.aspx?newsID=576585 (accessed on 15 July 2019).
36. Available at https://indiankanoon.org/doc/1797219/ (accessed on 11 June 2019).
37. Available at https://caravandaily.com/sc-asks-ec-to-explain-its-inaction-against-hate-speech/ (accessed on 9 June 2019).
38. Available at https://www.indiatoday.in/elections/lok-sabha-2019/story/mayawati-adityanath-election-commission-ban-election-campaign-1502229–2019–04-15 (accessed on 9 June 2019).
39. Available at https://www.thehindu.com/opinion/op-ed/its-time-to-take-stock-of-the-electoral-process/article27239174.ece (accessed on 15 July 2019).
40. Available at https://scroll.in/latest/924181/ec-rift-ashok-lavasa-defends-his-right-to-dissent-says-minority-view-must-be-part-of-final-order (accessed on 16 July 2019).
41. Available at https://economictimes.indiatimes.com/news/elections/lok-sabha/india/silence-difficult-but-more-desirable-to-see-through-poll-process-cec-on-lavasas-public-dissent/articleshow/69562361.cms (accessed on 16 July 2019).
42. Available at https://www.hindustantimes.com/lok-sabha-elections/election-commission-gets-isi-report-on-counting-vvpat-slips-decision-soon/story-bv7G6HxcxcKSWL3FwEs06M.html (accessed on 12 June 2019).
43. Available at https://www.business-standard.com/article/pti-stories/sc-directs-ec-to-increase-matching-of-vvpat-slips-to-5-booths-per-assembly-segment-119040800631_1.html (accessed on 12 June 2019).
44. Available at https://www.indiatoday.in/elections/lok-sabha-2019/story/election-commission-opposition-vvpats-1531801–2019–05-22 (accessed on 10 June 2019).
45. Available at http://lawcommissionofindia.nic.in/reports/Report255.pdf (accessed on 10 June 2019).
46. Available at https://www.livelaw.in/no-transparent-procedure-appointing-cec-election-commissioners-sc-centre/ (accessed on 10 June 2019).
47. Available at https://economictimes.indiatimes.com/news/politics-and-nation/supreme-court-questions-centre-on-enabling-law-on-appointment-of-cec-ecs/articleshow/59459851.cms?from=mdr (accessed on 24 July 2019).

    A bench comprising Chief Justice J. S. Khehar and Justice D. Y. Chandrachud said that Article 324 of the Constitution provides that the appointments of the CEC and the ECs be made as per the enabling law, but the law has not been enacted so far.
48. Available at https://www.organiser.org/Encyc/2019/4/30/Assert-the-Moral-Power.html (accessed on 10 June 2019).
49. Available at https://eci.gov.in/files/file/9431-registration-of-political-parties-under-section-29a-of-the-representation-of-the-people-act-1951-%E2%80%93-public-notice-period-%E2%80%93-regarding/ (accessed on 23 July 2019).

50. Available at https://eci.gov.in/files/file/9431-registration-of-political-parties-under-section-29a-of-the-representation-of-the-people-act-1951-%E2%80%93-public-notice-period-%E2%80%93-regarding/ (accessed on 10 June 2019).
51. Available at https://www.tribuneindia.com/news/comment/gujarat-dislodges-punjab/775997.html (accessed on 17 July 2019).
52. S. Y. Quraishi, *An Undocumented Wonder: The Making of the Great Indian Election* (New Delhi: Rainlight Rupa, 2014), 265.
53. Available at https://www.tribuneindia.com/news/comment/gujarat-dislodges-punjab/775997.html (accessed on 12 June 2019).
54. Available at https://www.mediavigil.com/wp-content/uploads/2019/06/CMS-Report_31May2019_final.pdf (accessed on 24 July 2019).
55. Available at https://scroll.in/latest/925882/bjp-spent-nearly-45-or-rs-27000-crore-of-total-expenditure-for-2019-lok-sabha-polls-report (accessed on 11 June 2019).
56. Available at https://www.dnaindia.com/analysis/column-undermining-accountability-2726801 (accessed on 29 July 2019).
57. The ECI has pointed out that 'this opens up the possibility of shell companies being set up for the sole purpose of making donations to political parties'.
58. Available at https://www.business-standard.com/article/current-affairs/ruling-bjp-bags-95-of-funds-why-there-s-an-uproar-over-electoral-bonds-119040500309_1.html (accessed on 27 July 2019).
59. Available at https://www.ndtv.com/india-news/general-elections-2019–99-8-electoral-bonds-sold-were-of-highest-denominations-says-rti-2023120 (accessed on 28 July 2019).
60. S. Y. Quraishi, *An Undocumented Wonder*, 259.
61. Available at https://www.youtube.com/watch?v=IDLld_f7-Po (accessed on 11 June 2019).
62. Available at https://eci.gov.in/files/file/9833-media-coverage-during-the-period-referred-to-in-section-126-a-of-rp-act-1951-%E2%80%93-violations-%E2%80%93-regarding/ (accessed on 12 June 2019).
63. Available at https://www.thequint.com/voices/opinion/opinion-and-exit-polls-are-okay-if-their-integrity-is-beyond-doubt-supreme-court-election-commission (accessed on 12 June 2019).
64. Available at https://www.thehindu.com/opinion/op-ed/Should-elections-be-state-funded-writes-yogendra-yadav-Manish-Tewari-S.Y.-Quraishi/article17314365.ece (accessed on 11 June 2019).
65. Available at https://www.orfonline.org/research/towards-public-financing-elections-political-parties-india-lessons-global-experiences/ (accessed on 23 July 2019).
66. Available at https://www.thehindu.com/elections/lok-sabha-2019/43-newly-elected-lok-sabha-mps-have-criminal-record-adr/article27253649.ece (accessed on 29 July 2019).

67. Available at https://indianexpress.com/article/opinion/columns/criminal-isation-of-politics-politicians-corruption-dipak-misra-supreme-court-lost-chance-5378611/ (accessed on 28 July 2019).
68. Available at https://indiankanoon.org/doc/964829/ (accessed on 29 July 2019).
69. Available at https://www.thehindu.com/opinion/lead/a-welcome-debate-on-electoral-reforms/article28391880.ece (accessed on 18 July 2019).
70. Raised by Ram Gopal Yadav of the Samajwadi Party in Rajya Sabha on 3 July 2019 during the short duration discussions on electoral reforms. The motion was moved by Derek O'Brien of the All India Trinamool Congress party.

Chapter 4

Staking Gender Equality

The Electoral Dynamics of Identity and Rights

Rainuka Dagar

Gender equality has remained outside the domain of electoral politics in India. Select issues have provoked electoral commitment, such as women safety being made an indicator of governance in 2014. The 2019 elections are a deviation with women rights more extensively raised. The specific interests of women, their conditions of discrimination and violence, the unequal relations of power between men and women are well expounded in the corridors of activism and rights movements. Less articulated are these conversations in public, even more so in the mandate for governance that political parties seek in Indian democracy. The struggle for gender equality in a diversely patriarchal society with economic, cultural and religious differences impacts the power equations variously and in combination with different axis of power. The sexual abuse of Scheduled Caste (SC) women is built into the historical relations of land owning and labouring populations that is different from the sexual harassment at urban work spaces or the family economy of female prostitution practised by the *Bedia* tribe in central India or the abuse of the LGBTQ+ groups. Such multifarious discriminations within religious and cultural tensions remain a potential leverage for identity politics.

The electoral campaign was set to a discourse of national security, development and accountable governance in the backdrop of identity politics. If 'democracy is government by Discussion',[1] how are the perspectives from the specificities of gender conditions expressed and merged in different political persuasions to shape policy? This discussion explores how gender rights in an assertive multicultural society with discordant interests steeped in cultural and social relational norms and values of patriarchy were negotiated across political contingencies of an election campaign. The first section provides an overview of gender representation of voters, candidates and elected members. The second analyses the electoral and peoples' agenda on gender equality followed by a discussion of how women rights and empowerment, core dimensions of gender equality, pan out in the electoral politics of the 2019 Lok Sabha.

GENDER REPRESENTATION: AN OVERVIEW

Voter participation in the electoral process was unparalleled with the highest ever electoral turnout (67.36%) for the 2019 Lok Sabha. The participation level was above the global average of 66 per cent that records minor differences between men and women.[2] In India, women were part of this large turnout, continuing the trend of rising political interest to form an increasing proportion of the total voters. They constituted 47.95 per cent of the total voters in India, docking a rise of nearly 1 per cent from the previous Lok Sabha elections in 2014. For the first time, the proportion of voters from the registered voters in both men and women was similar—with the women voters decreasing the gap to a nominal 0.07 per cent (Table 4.1).

The proportion of registered women voters to women citizens, however, continues to lag behind that of their male counterparts. Time, poverty, imbalanced sex ratios and relative inaccess to public services and spaces factor in to dampen women's presence in the electoral rolls and in voting percentages. Women outnumbered the male voters in 9 states and UTs (lower than the 16 in 2014), all of which were outside the ambit of the classical patriarchal belt. These included four in the north-east, three in the south and two coastal UTs.

Table 4.1 *Gender-Wise Participation in Lok Sabha Election, 1951–2019*

Election Year	Contestants			Elected		Registered Elector over Total Registered Elector (%)		Votes Polled over Total Votes Polled (%)		Votes Polled over Registered Elector (%)	
	Men	Women	Other	Men Elected over Total Seat (%)	Women Elected over Total Seats (%)	Men	Women	Men	Women	Men	Women
(1)	(2)	(3)	(4)	(5)	(6)	(7)	(8)	(9)	(10)	(11)	(12)
1951						55	45				
1957	1,472 (97.04)	45 (2.96)		467 (94.53)	22 (5.47)	52.8	47.2	61.7	38.3		
1962	1,919 (96.68)	66 (3.32)		463 (93.72)	31 (6.28)	52.7	47.3	60.2	39.8	63.31	46.6
1967	2,302 (97.13)	67 (2.83)		491 (94.42)	29 (5.58)	52	48	56.6	43.4	66.63	55.5
1971	2,686 (97.00)	83 (3.00)		494 (95.37)	24 (4.63)	52.3	47.7	57.7	42.3	60.9	49.1
1977	2,369 (97.13)	70 (2.87)		523 (96.49)	19 (3.51)	52	48	56.4	43.6	65.62	54.9

1980	4487 (96.93)	142 (3.07)	501 (94.71)	28 (5.29)	52.1	47.9	56.9	43.1	62.16	51.2
1984	5,320 (96.85)	173 (3.15)	498 (92.10)	43 (7.95)	51.8	48.2	55.6	44.4	68.170	58.6
1985	171 (95.00)	9 (5.00)	26 (96.29)	1 (3.07)	54.3	45.7	51.8	48.1	72.6	71.4
1989	5,962 (96.79)	198 (3.21)	501 (94.53)	29 (5.47)	52.5	47.5	56.1	43.9	66.13	57.3
1991	8,668 (96.37)	326 (3.62)	484 (92.89)	37 (7.10)	52.5	47.5	57	43	61.58	51.3
1992	65 (96.37)	2 (2.98)	11 (84.61)	2 (15.38)	54.1	45.9	59.8	40.2	26.45	21
1996	13353 (95.71)	599 (4.29)	495 (92.52)	40 (7.48)	52.3	47.7	56	44	62.06	53.4
1998	4,476 (94.23)	274 (5.77)	505 (92.15)	43 (7.85)	52.3	47.7	55.6	44.4	65.86	57.7

(Continued)

Table 4.1 *(Contiuned)*

Election Year	Contestants			Elected		Registered Elector over Total Registered Elector (%)		Votes Polled over Total Votes Polled (%)		Votes Polled over Registered Elector (%)	
	Men	Women	Other	Men Elected over Total Seat (%)	Women Elected over Total Seats (%)	Men	Women	Men	Women	Men	Women
(1)	(2)	(3)	(4)	(5)	(6)	(7)	(8)	(9)	(10)	(11)	(12)
1999	4364 (93.89)	284 (6.11)		497 (91.03)	49 (8.97)	52.3	47.7	55.7	44.3	63.96	55.6
2004	5,080 (93.47)	355 (6.53)		500 (92.08)	43 (7.92)	52	48	55.6	44.4	61.66	53.6
2009	7514 (93.11)	556 (6.89)		484 (89.13)	59 (10.87)	52.3	47.7	54.2	45.8	60.20	55.8
2014	7,577 (91.83)	668 (8.10)	6 (0.07)	481 (88.58)	62 (11.42)	52.4	47.6	53	47	67.09	65.6
2019	7,298 (90.92)	724 (9.02)	4 (0.04)	465 (85.63)	78 (14.36)	51.94	48.00	51.66	47.95	67.98	68.17

Source: Computed from the Election Commission of India Statistical Reports of Lok Sabha Elections for the Years 1951, 1957, 1962, 1967, 1971, 1977, 1980, 1984, 1985, 1989, 1991, 1992, 1996, 1998, 1999, 2004, 2009, 2014 and 2019. https://eci.gov.in/statistical-report/election-results/ (accessed on 14 August 2019).

Participation in the democratic process was encouraged by awareness campaigns urging citizens to register and exercise their right to vote. These promotions were not limited to the Election Commission of India (ECI) or the government, but included corporate India, NGOs and political parties. Women formed a specific group that was wooed and it would appear that political messages rousing women's interest to participate in the democratic process did reach out, if voter turnout is an indicator. 'Identity-based targeting' of women as a social group, as defined by Holman, were a feature of advertisement campaigns.[3] They gave visibility and recognition to women's equal status as voters, presenting them as an inclusive section of the population. Modi's *Main Bhi Chowkidar* (political watch person) campaign by the BJP projected women as an assertive political agent on issues raised by the party such as development, corruption, cleanliness and education, staking citizen accountability in governance and development programmes. One linked cleanliness of the house to clean governance, another the convenience of a toilet in the house for a physically incapacitated mother shaming a son to vote. The campaign mobilizing voters was reported to be a huge success on social media platforms.[4] There were no advertisements without women, but there were women-only clips highlighting their relevance as voters to the party.[5]

Women continued to inch into electoral politics with a growing number of candidates and elected representatives. The LGBTQ+ community recognized by the ECI in 2014 also registered their identity in the electoral process showing 0.04 per cent contested elections.

The 1.3 per cent number of female candidates per constituency was a marginal rise over 1.2 per cent in the previous election, though much restricted in agency and participation in comparison to men for whom the number was 13.4 per cent (Table 4.2). Women candidature was boosted by reservation in ticket distribution by two parties based in eastern India: the All India Trinamool Congress (AITC) led by a women leader which reserved 40 per cent for women candidates, and one-third reservations by state party Biju Janata Dal (BJD). This exemplar initiative took the overall allocation for women candidates by state-based parties to 10.3 per cent and slightly higher for the national parties at 12.5 per cent. A record number of 724 women entered as

Table 4.2 *Availability of Women Candidates per Constituency, 1962–2019 Lok Sabha Elections*

Year	No. of Males Candidates	No. of Females Candidates	No. of Parliament Constituencies	No. of Males Candidates per Constituency	No. of Female Candidates per Constituency
1962	1,919	66	494	3.88	0.13
1967	2,302	67	520	4.43	0.13
1971	2,686	83	518	5.19	0.16
1977	2,369	70	542	4.37	0.13
1980	4,487	142	529	8.48	0.27
1984	5,320	173	541	10.35	0.34
1985	71	9	27	6.33	0.33
1989	5,962	198	529	11.27	0.37
1991	8,420	329	534	15.77	0.62
1992	65	2	13	5.00	0.15
1996	13,353	599	543	24.59	1.10
1998	4,476	274	543	8.24	0.50
1999	4,364	284	543	8.03	0.52
2004	5,080	355	543	9.36	0.65
2009	7,514	556	543	13.84	1.02
2014	7,577	668	543	13.95	1.25
2019	7,298	724	543	13.44	1.33

Source: Computed from Election Commission of India Statistical Reports of Lok Sabha Elections for the Years 1962, 1967, 1971, 1977, 1980, 1984, 1985, 1989, 1991, 1992, 1996, 1998, 1999, 2004, 2009, 2014 and 2019.

candidates comprising 9.02 per cent of the contestants; a per cent more than in 2014.

As Members of Parliament (MP), they had the highest numbers (78) ever, representing 14.36 per cent of the legislature. Women's limited presence in the electoral fray was matched by their membership in the governing council of political parties. The range of women office-bearers falls below 17 per cent with the state-based BJD recording the highest per cent at 16.6. The BJP had 15.5 per cent, the Communist Party of India (Marxist) (CPI[M]) 11.7 per cent in the politburo, the AITC 13.6 per cent and the Congress 10.9 per cent. Women's lean leadership provided presence in party campaigning accounting for 12.5 per cent (BJP), 10 per cent (Congress) and 5 per cent of the Samajwadi Party star campaigners.[6] The disproportionate numbers of women in public spaces were mirrored in the office-bearers of the ECI, who with 7 of the 74 members formed 9.45 per cent of the administrators, in what the election commissioner called the 'largest festival of democracy'.[7]

Women's numbers in the Indian legislature falls well short of both the global average of 24.3 per cent[8] and from the one-third critical mass widely acknowledged as change initiating.

Strategies to bridge the gap in political inequalities have long evolved from the right to vote to a more substantive participation[9] making room for debates on other identities and perspectives, as argued by Iris Young.[10]

The plurality of perspectives gets bound when representatives are part of the politics of patronage riding into power on family bastions and interests. Indian politics is cast in dynastic succession with scholars' capturing differing numbers while endorsing the trend.[11] The dynast is categorized as a MP who has had a relative serving an elected mandate or as representative of a political party's governance council. In 2019, 31.8 per cent of the elected representatives are dynasts, up from 13.40 per cent in 2014. Women dynasts (60.2%) were more than double that of men (28%) in 2019, up from 31.2 per cent in 2014, while male numbers rose from 11.02 per cent in 2014. Another group of 'elites' categorized as MPs, who were film stars, singers, media stars or leading professionals/industrialists, comprised 13.25 per cent of the total members in 2019, with women leaders at 15.38 per cent (Table 4.3).

Table 4.3 *National and Female-Headed Party-Wise Background of Elected Candidates for 2009, 2014 and 2019 Lok Sabha Elections*

Background	Type	Party	2009			2014			2019		
			M	F	T	M	F	T	M	F	T
Elite	National parties	BJP	3	1	4	42	4	46	28	8	36
		BSP	–	–	–	–	–	–	2	1	3
		CPM	–	–	–	1	1	2	1	–	1
		INC	15	5	20	6	–	6	4	–	4
		NCP	–	–	–	2	–	2	1	0	1
	Female headed	AIADMK	–	–	–	–	–				
		AITC	3	–	3	6	4	10	7	3	10
	Others		7	2	9	19	2	21	17	0	17
	Total		**28 (5.77)**	**8 (13.79)**	**36 (6.62)**	**76 (15.8)**	**11 (17.74)**	**87 (16.21)**	**60 (12.9)**	**11 (15.38)**	**71 (13.25)**
Dynasts	National parties	BJP	12	3	15	19	5	24	61	22	83
		BSP	4	4	8	–	–	–	3	1	4
		CPM	3	1	4	1	–	1	–	–	–
		INC	45	12	57	8	4	12	21	6	27
		NCP	4	2	6	–	1	1	1	0	1

	Female headed	AIADMK	–	–	–	2	–	2	0	1	1
		AITC	2	1	3	2	4	6	1	5	6
	Others		25	5	30	21	6	27	42	12	54
	Total		**95 (19.59)**	**28 (48.28)**	**123 (22.65)**	**53 (11.02)**	**20 (32.26)**	**73 (13.44)**	**129 (27.7)**	**47 (60.2)**	**176 (32.4)**
Others	National parties	BJP	88	9	97	191	21	212	172	10	182
		BSP	13		13	–	–	–	3	0	3
		CPM	11		11	6	–	6	2	0	2
		INC	123	6	129	26	–	26	21	3	24
		NCP	3		3	3	–	3	2	0	2
	Female headed	AIADMK	9		9	31	4	35	–	–	–
		AITC	10	3	13	15	3	18	5	1	6
	Others		104	5	108	80	3	83	71	6	77
	Total		**361 (74.58)**	**23 (38.98)**	**384 (70.71)**	**352 (73.18)**	**31 (50)**	**383 (70.53)**	**276 (58.9)**	**20 (25.6)**	**296 (54.5)**
Grand Total			**484 (100.0)**	**59 (100.0)**	**543 (100.0)**	**481 (100.0)**	**62 (100.0)**	**543 (100.0)**	**465 (85.63)**	**78 (14.36)**	**543 (100)**

Source: Background of elected candidates' compiled from net searches in 2014 and 2019.

Clearly, the winnability of candidates, particularly so for women, stems from a family reservoir of political power.

It was a dynast network that gave rise to women leaders, but the question of women's interests being expressed in the gender discourse during the electoral campaigning is explored in the next section.

GENDER IN THE ELECTORAL AGENDA

Ideological persuasions on gender equality have been gathered through the process of agenda setting by political parties in their manifestos, leader's subsequent articulations in public speeches to influence voters and a people's agenda from citizens sampled from five states. A survey of Assam, Haryana, Maharashtra, Meghalaya and Punjab was conducted in 2019 prior to the announcement of elections. Equal male female citizens were randomly selected from a village and a town in 9 districts of 5 states of India to represent different socio-economic variations of caste, religion, income and age.

Policy attention to women rights in the manifestoes of all national and state parties continued to expand from the traditional welfarist measures of health care, education and protection from crimes to stated preferences for economic empowerment and political reservation. Women rights were articulated from different political standpoints. CPI(M) addressed maternal health and equal remuneration as part of women worker rights, pledging new legislation for domestic and house workers. Crimes against women (CAW) were promised effective and fast-track justice, protective legislation for 'so-called honour' crimes and from criminalization of triple talaq.[12]

For the BJP, women health care and CAW were framed to ensure a dignified life for women. It focused on women-led development, with a road map for women workforce and financial empowerment. It promised to legislate criminalization of triple talaq and enact the uniform civil code (UCC) which has been part of all its manifestos and Right-wing Hindu ideology.[13] The Congress, in addition to basic facilities, emphasized women reservation in central government, more jobs in municipalities and 33 per cent reservations in the police force.

The Congress was the only party that acknowledged the rights of the LGBTQIA+ community, promising equality and protection to people of different sexual identities.[14]

Political parties' election programmes for women's rights resonated with citizen expectations. Respondents cited women's empowerment, detailed variously from principles of equality, women safety, financial autonomy and basic development facilities. Concern for women rights was found to be the highest in Maharashtra (45%), followed by Punjab (24%), Haryana (17%), Assam (11%) and Meghalaya (9.6%) which citizens expected their elected legislator to pursue (Table 4.4). Women's safety was the foremost issue across all states, in both men and women respondents. Subsequent preferences varied by state and gender, with women empowerment in Maharashtra, girl education in Punjab and equality in Assam cited as a second concern. Girl child schemes, violence such as acid attacks and female foeticide, transport facilities for working women, work-from-home job opportunities and increased pensions for widows were other mentions. Scant numbers had an opinion on the government's past performance on women's rights and less than 7.5 per cent (with Maharashtra the highest) opined raising the issue by a candidate or party would affect their choice of vote (Table 4.5).

Women's rights were not a priority policy concern with citizens, leaving political parties to be the 'mediating institutions' to bring them into the fold of democratic political processes.[15] The question being when do political parties respond to women's rights? The next section explores the gendered context of the campaign.

GENDER RIGHTS ON THE CAMPAIGN TRAIL

The electoral campaign of political parties is explored to decode the organized and repeated effort seeking to influence voting decisions involving social relations in context to gender equality. Bordieu, arguing for the importance of language in political discourse and its impact, underlines 'it is not the language itself which has wider ramifications but rather (the) consequence of (a) powerful person using the language to achieve some goal'.[16] Speeches of select political party leaders were

Table 4.4 *Respondents' Opinions on Women Rights Issues They Want Addressed by Their Elected Representatives*

States	Assam			Haryana			Maharashtra			Meghalaya			Punjab		
Sex	Female	Male	Total	Female	Male	Total	Female	Male	Total	Female	Male	Total	Female	Male	Total
Total	N=122	N=127	N=249	N=195	N=185	N=380	N=105	N=95	N=200	N=104	N=106	N=210	N=260	N=268	N=528
Schemes for girls	0.8	0	0.4	0.5	0.5	0.5	1	0	0.5	0	0.9	0.5	0.4	0.7	0.6
Male–female equality	2.5	0	1.2	0.5	1.6	1.1	7.6	3.2	5.5	0	0	0	1.2	4.9	3
Education of girls	0.8	0.8	0.7	1	1.6	1.3	4.8	2.1	3.5	0	0	0	11.2	14.6	12.9
Women empowerment	2.5	1.6	2	7.7	3.8	5.8	19	16.8	18	0	1.9	1	5.4	1.9	3.6
Others	2.5	0	1.2	4.1	5.4	4.7	8.6	7.4	8	6.7	0	3.3	5.4	10.4	8
Mentioned at least one	18.9	4	11.3	20.5	14.0	17.1	42.9	47.5	45	12.5	6.7	9.6	25.3	24.2	24

Source: Field survey January–February 2019.
Note: Due to multiple responses, the sum of all is not equal to the total number.

Table 4.5 *Respondents' Perception Is on Women Empowerment*

States	Assam			Haryana			Maharashtra			Meghalaya			Punjab		
Sex	Female	Male	Total	Female	Male	Total	Female	Male	Total	Female	Male	Total	Female	Male	Total
Total	N=122	N=127	N=249	N=195	N=185	N=380	N=105	N=95	N=200	N=104	N=106	N=210	N=260	N=268	N=528
Modi government has delivered on women empowerment	0	0.8	0.4	16.9	5.9	11.6	2.9	4.2	3.5	1.9	0	1	9.6	10.8	10.2
Modi government has not delivered on women empowerment	10.7	15	12.9	23.6	17.8	20.8	29.5	20	25	2.9	9.4	6.2	10	8.2	9.1
Women empowerment a consideration in choice of party/candidate	2.4	2.3	2.4	5	2	3.8	9.5	5.3	7.5	6.8	1.8	4.2	4.6	2.9	3.7

Source: Field survey January–February 2019.
Note: Due to multiple responses, the sum of all is not equal to the total number.

accessed to map the gender campaign messages—these being Narendra Modi (BJP), Rahul Gandhi (INC) and Mamata Banerjee (AITC). The BJP and INC formed the leaders of National Democratic Alliance (NDA) and United Progressive Alliance (UPA) coalitions and Banerjee was selected as a women leader with a party that gave the highest nomination to women candidates.

The agenda of the electoral arena was set by the BJP with women entitlements and rights raised in 69 per cent of Modi's speeches. Additionally, using gendered and masculine language of national security was part of 78 per cent of his public rallies (Table 4.6). Two simultaneous discourses on women's rights were conducted during the elections. One pertained to development-related women needs which can be classified as being inclusive, directed at practical gender needs (PGN) and having support across the political spectrum, as mentioned in the manifestos. PGN relate to the responsibilities rising from traditional gender division of labour. In the elections, these referred to the inadequacies of living conditions such as lack of access to drinking water, smokeless cooking option of gas, sanitation and toilets, and maternal and child health. Promises extended to facilities and schemes for women's economic upliftment—such as employment opportunities, skill development, access to funds and bank accounts.

Candidates made promises for economic and income-related provisions for women, particularly young, rural and SC/ST populations as relevant to the nature of inaccess and site of speech. The INC leader only mentioned economic schemes for women in his election speeches. The main scheme Banerjee listed was a health card for families under the woman's name (16.8%), followed by girl schemes such as education, insurance (11.2%) and widow pension and welfare measures (10.1%). In addition to economic schemes (12.6%), Modi promised provisions for maternal health, child immunization, nutrition, well-being centres, smokeless cooking gas, electricity, cleanliness, and toilet and water facilities (45.2%); women were assured safety and protection against rape in 33 per cent of Modi's speeches. The missing girl child, a flagship programme of his government, was barely mentioned (3.7%).

A second narrative revolved around identity politics with three hegemonies—majority–minority religion, dominant–SC castes and

Table 4.6 *Indicators and Patterns of Gender-Based References in Speeches of Select Leaders, 2019 Lok Sabha*

		Rahul Gandhi	Narendra Modi	Mamata Banerjee
		N=29	N=106	N=89
1	Practical gender needs (water, cooking gas, toilets, cleanliness campaign to improve women conditions, maternal and child health facilities)	–	48 (45.28)	15 (16.8)
2	Economic empowerment for women	9 (31.03)	13 (12.26)	1 (1.2)
3	Women role models	–	3 (2.83)	–
4	Women safety	–	35 (33)	–
5	Muslim women rights (triple talaq/*nikah halala*/JK women's conditional transfer of property rights)	–	18 (16.98)	–
6	Gendered and masculine language of national security	–	83 (78.30)	–
7	Schemes for girls	–	4 (3.77)	10 (11.2)
8	Women welfares	–		9 (10.1)

Source: Contents Analysis of Campaign Speeches between 11 March 2019 and 16 May 2019.
Note: Parenthesis contain the percentages.

male–female positioning pursued simultaneously and advantageously for mobilizing political support. A fault line was the Muslim women's rights, centred around criminalization of triple talaq, instant divorce by a Muslim man, a form of Islamic divorce practised in India. The issue was contentious in the nature of reforms suggested and in the singling out of Muslim personal law rather than the violative aspect of the practice which had wide agreement in political parties, civil society and Muslim women's rights groups.[17] Also articulated was the discrimination against women rights in passing inherited property to their children if married outside the state (a reference to Article 35A of the Constitution applicable in Muslim majority Jammu and Kashmir). PM Modi sought votes to 'protect the Muslim sisters from triple talaq, promised to legislate against it and vowed that in spite of efforts of opposition parties daughters will get justice'. He informed Muslim women voters that in many Muslim countries the practice has been discontinued and 'we in India also want to give Muslim women the same rights'.[18] This assurance was a significant part of his campaign repeated in 17 per cent of his speeches (Table 4.6) in sites of large Muslim populations as in Bihar, West Bengal and Uttar Pradesh.

The BJP had a contrasting position for a discriminatory Hindu religious practice of disallowing women of menstruating age to pray at the Sabrimala temple in Kerala. A civil society-led national campaign won a Supreme Court order that termed the practice discriminatory and unconstitutional while overturning the high court verdict. In spite of the judgement and a gender-equality supportive Left government in the state, women's entry could not be ensured. The BJP reinforced the Sabrimala traditions in its manifestoes as a protection of cultural heritage supporting protest against the Supreme Court verdict. The INC in disagreement with the Supreme Court ruling demanded that the state government file a review petition.

In two election rallies in the region, Modi promised to protect the Sabrimala tradition stating, 'as long as there is BJP none can destroy your faith'.[19] The CPI(M) complaining to the ECI about the campaign atmosphere being in violation of the model code of conduct wanted a ban to further references to the temple.[20] The Sabrimala issue has been termed as the BJPs 'Biggest expansion in the state over the six months'.[21] The party failed to win any seat, marginally improved its vote share to 12.93 per cent from 10.85 per cent in 2014 and succeeded in polarizing the campaign.[22]

The other discourse in identity politics was located in the gendered construction of masculinities, drawing meaning from a cultural repertoire to make claims for national security. The weave of a gendered language of power and violence was articulated in 78 per cent of Modi's speeches. The appeal 'press the button of the lotus (BJP symbol) thinking you are pressing the trigger pointed at a terrorist'[23] was cushioned with the concepts of honour, protection and courage: 'we are not the ones to fear but preserve', 'ahead of fear is... democracy' (ad-libbed to a famous soda campaign), the soldiers were referred to as ideal sons—'the nation is giving a standing ovation to our sons' and women glorified as 'brave mothers of our soldiers'. The gendered 'rhetorical manoeuvres' of national security were framed as essential Hindu values.[24] 'The land of 5 *Dhams*—the 5th *Dham* is a soldier *Dham'* referring to the army academy in Uttarakhand (*Dham* is a Hindu religious pilgrimage for *moksha*—eternal salvation).[25] 'Followers of Mother *Kali* live in fear', 'if our God is butter eating, plays the flute, he also has the *Sudarshan chakra*'[26]—an indestructible spiritual weapon. Association and meanings were constructed using gendered metaphors framed in religious and cultural values within a development and governance discourse to legitimize and broaden the political authority of the party.

THE INSTRUMENTALITY OF GENDER RIGHTS

A strategic narrative of power constructing an imagery of hegemonic, decisive and governance-delivering politics was weaved into the meaning of women's rights, equality and practices of gender relations. The rights discourse on distribution of development facilities to women as a disadvantaged group along the intersectionalties of caste, income and region were highlighted. This narrative found common cause across the political spectrum, with the BJP integrating the 'practical gender needs' that alleviate women's daily drudgery into speeches, advertising campaigns and interviews of its star campaigners. The other parties made few references to women, focusing on financial incentives.

Congress President Rahul Gandhi announced a welfare scheme repeatedly (31%) to inform women that money would come to their bank accounts under the Nyuntam Aay Yojana (NYAY) scheme; Mamata Banerjee spoke of a homestay tourism scheme and distribution of chicken and goats to women for their empowerment.[27] Facilities related to home and childcare were mentioned, neither linked to the specific conditions of women or integrated into the central political message of the party to remain as a listing of ad hoc initiatives. In contrast, Modi highlighted the drudgery and plight of poor women as a group, identifying himself with their impoverishment, 'my caste is poverty'. He combined all poor women irrespective of caste religion or region, aligning himself as 'sensitive to the plight of my sisters' to reach out to poor women. As a respondent mentioned, 'Modi has given us gas, care in hospitals for our deliveries, we will vote for him'.

Aside from the reach to poor women, the BJP adopted a targeted approach on women's rights, differentiated on religion and caste. The specificity of Muslim women's plight under triple talaq was positioned against a discriminatory practice of some Muslim populations—the Indian Muslims. Underlining that the practice was abolished in many Muslim countries, the BJP announced it was not targeting Muslims per se. The experience of Muslim women made it an 'immediate reality'[28] for them and presenting Muslims as a heterogeneous group allowed BJP to seek votes from Muslim women.[29] The issue in the backdrop of improved facilities such as drinking water, housing, toilets and pensions made voting for the BJP a viable choice.[30] As one respondent put it 'The Modi Government is good—we have made a toilet, the poor are getting houses and he has thought of our plight (triple talaq)'.

In contrast, the practised violations against Hindu women falling in a domain other than the personal laws, what the Supreme Court called 'discriminatory exclusion' to worship at the Sabrimala temple, were positioned as an issue of faith and culture rather than a discrimination against women. It avoided pitting Hindu women against a 'Hindu patriarchy'; an approach followed for Muslim women. It avoided equating Hindu and Muslim religions as both selectively unfair to women. A simultaneous hegemony of unequal rights between men and women, and between the majority and minority community was promoted. The approach did not destabilize the traditional Hindu vote bank of the party and by placing it as a cultural issue, rather than a denial of women's rights, the party appealed to women voters for improving their daily living conditions and the promise of physical safety.

A third approach focusing on women's dignity was followed for the SC population. It appealed to the group by highlighting facilities of toilets aimed at the poor that safeguarded the women from sexual abuse and the embarrassment of open defecation. No direct call was made to the SCs but the repeated sanitation and toilet campaign reached out to those affected by lack of earlier facilities and as a metaphor to the historically marginalized, those 'polluted' by their work of scavenging and cleaning the night soil. That PM Modi washed the feet of the untouchables (gesture of esteem in Indian culture) in recognition of their contribution as sweepers, as part of the cleanliness campaign at the Kumbh Mela, site for Hindu worshipers and the world's largest congregation, in February prior to the elections was mentioned in his campaign.[31] It generated sentiments as put across by a woman SC respondent, 'we could never imagine our PM would wash the feet of sweepers—he has respected us like no other'. The SC were courted with an entitlement to dignity rather than identity. It was made without a collectivist claim or visibly disturbing the vote bank politics seemingly a Mayawati bastion.[32] Women entitlements provided a channel to garner SC votes.

In the same vein, the delay in lodging an FIR in the rape of a Dalit girl in Alwar, Rajasthan, a Congress-ruled state, was highlighted by Modi. He repeatedly called out to Mayawati, the BSP leader, 'UP dalit girls are asking their leader why are you supporting a government that violates us?'[33] Unlike the BJP, opposition parties could not rally to hold the BJP state government in Uttar Pradesh to account over a minor's rape in Unnao in which a BJP state legislator was the accused with two charge sheets filed. He was thrown out of the party, only post the elections as the case proceedings moved to the Supreme Court. Opposition parties were unable to spear a campaign during the elections that was apprehended by the BJP of being potentially disastrous electorally.[34] The violation of women acquired meaning with context rather than a democratic mandate for human rights or gender justice.

It was the BJP who highlighted women entitlements and rights into their political campaign, but as a strategy of political gain rather than a promotion of democratic rights.

CONCLUSION

The legitimate claim of women interests in democratic governance is yet to be consolidated. The representation of women as voters, candidates and elected MP has been increasing, but in small numbers. Women leaders fall well short of a critical mass in numbers to make them 'isolated and constrained'[35] in advancing gender equality. More so with the majority being 'dynasts', a part of political families, rather than independently evolved voices for 'women interests' or promoting deliberative democracy from different perspectives.

The demand for women rights or parity does not form a significant part of the electorate consideration. Citizens were concerned for women rights such as safety and economic empowerment but it had little influence in their voting decisions. It appears democratizing and gendering the polity is not part of a political consciousness in India.

Women, however, were targeted by some political parties as a vote group. The reservations for women candidates by the AITC and the BJD, and the integration of women entitlements into their political campaign by the BJP were both moves sought to capture women's votes. One, with the politics of presence and the other with improved conditions of living faced by poor women.

For the first time, the electoral discourse mainstreamed women interests, albeit with a focus on providing the basic facilities that women traditional roles demand—the practical entitlements that do not disturb the existing gender power relations or other axis of power in which gender relations are practised. Policy prescriptions called for women-led development with no resolutions for the subsequent double-day burden or the politics of the care economy. The discourse privileged a divisive multiculturalism over women's rights. The appropriation of patriarchal language and masculine symbols of power to promote a nationalist doctrine of supremacy and the dichotomous stand on women and religious/cultural rights reinforced and justified unequal power relations. Political parties did seek to mobilize women voters but approached gender constructs from their ideological prisms and situational calculations.

Basic rights and protections, as Phillips notes, offer women the most immediate gains while gender inequalities and the reframing of the power relations remain seemingly intangible though fundamental to democracy.[36] In India, raising democratic consciousness for participatory gender equal polity remains a challenge, and poised to grow given the thrust to identity politics.

NOTES

1. Amartya K. Sen, *The Idea of Justice* (Cambridge, MA: Belknap Press, 2009), 324.
2. Abdurashid Solijonov, *Voter Turnout Trends around the World* (Stockholm: International Institute for Democracy and Electoral Assistance, 2016).
3. Mirya R. Holman, Monica C. Schneider and Podel, 'Gender Targeting in Political Advertisement', *Political Research Quarterly* 68, no. 4 (2015): 816–829.
4. *The Economic Times*, 'BJP's Chowkidar Campaign a Hit on Social Media'. Available at https://economictimes.indiatimes.com/news/elections/lok-sabha/india/bjps-chowkidar-campaign-a-hit-on-social-media/articleshow/68737131.cms (accessed on 20 July 2019).
5. As noted on NaMo TV viewing between 9 a.m. and 6 p.m. on 8 April 2019.
6. Computed from the ECI's website.
7. Ibid.
8. Inter-Parliamentary Union, *Women in National Parliaments*. Available at http://www.ipu.org/wmne/world.htm (accessed on 24 July 2019).
9. Anne Phillips, *The Politics of Presence* (Oxford: Oxford University Press, 1995).
10. Iris Marion Young, *Inclusion and Democracy* (Oxford: Oxford University Press, 2000).
11. Kanchan Chandra, *Democratic Dynasties: States, Party and Family in Contemporary Indian Politics* (New Delhi: Cambridge University Press, 2016); Christophe Jaffrelot and Gilles Verniers, 'Explained Why So Many MPs are Dynast's', *The Indian Express* (2019, 27 May).
12. Communist Party of India (Marxist), *Election Manifesto 17th Lok Sabha* (2019).
13. Bhartiya Janta Party, *Bhartiya Janta Party Sanklap Patra, Lok Sabha 2019* (New Delhi: Bhartiya Janta Party, 2019).
14. India National Congress, *INC Manifesto 2019* (New Delhi: India National Congress, 2019).
15. Christina Wolbrecht, Alivin Tillery, Peri Arnold and Rodney Hero, *The Politics of Democratic Inclusion* (Philadelphia, PA: Temple University Press, 2005).
16. Pierre Bourdieu, *Language and Symbolic Power* (Cambridge, MA: Harvard University Press, 1991), 188.
17. Anindita Chakrabarti and Suchandra Ghosh, 'Judicial Reform vs Adjudication of Personal Law: View from a Muslim Ghetto in Kanpur', *Economic & Political Weekly* 52, no. 49 (2019, 9 December): 12.
18. Narendra Modi, *Public Rally* (Aurai, Bhadoli, Uttar Pradesh, 2019, 5 May).
19. Narendra Modi, *Public Speech* (Ramanathapuram, Tamil Nadu and Bangalore, Karnataka, 2019, 13 April).

20. *Deccan Herald,* 'CPM Wants Action against Modi for Sabrimal Remarks' (2019, 16 April).
21. *Livemint,* 'BJP Fails to Take Advantage of Sabrimal Row' (2019, 23 May). Available at https://www.livemint.com/elections/lok-sabha-elections/bjp-fails-to-take-advantage-of-sabarimala-row-1558605841095.html (accessed on July 24, 2019).
22. *The Hindu*, 'Election Results 2019: Sabrimal Might Have Worked in Favour of Congress in Kerala' (2019, 24 May).
23. Narendra Modi, *Public Rally* (Kargoal, Madhya Pardesh, 2019, 17 May).
24. Saba Gul Khattak, 'Security Discourses and the State in Pakistan', *Alternatives* 21 (1996): 341.
25. Narendra Modi, *Public Rally* (Rudrapur, Uttarakhand, 2019, 28 March).
26. Narendra Modi, *Public Rally* (Paliganj, Patna, Bihar, 2019, 15 May).
27. Mamata Banerjee, *Public Rally* (Namkhana, West Bengal, 2019, 13 May).
28. See V. L. Allen, *Social Analysis: A Marxist Critique and Alternative* (London: Longman, 1975) for a formulation of the immediate reality blurring the larger social condition.
29. *Deccan Herald,* 'Triple Talaq Debate Divides Women and Men in Western UP' (2019, 3 April). Available at https://www.deccanherald.com/national/national-politics/triple-talaq-debate-divides-women-and-men-in-western-up-726702.html (accessed on July 24, 2019).
30. Abhay Mohan Jha, 'Muslim Women Favoured Modi on Triple Talaq Issue', *Times of India* (2019, 25 May). Available at https://timesofindia.indiatimes.com/city/patna/muslim-women-favoured-modi-on-triple-talaq-issue/articleshow/69488698.cms (accessed on July 24, 2019).
31. Narendra Modi, *Public Rally* (Deoria, Uttar Pradesh, 2019, 12 May).
32. *Livemint*, 'Ten Charts That Explain 2019 Lok Sabha Verdict' (2019, 24 May). Available at https://www.livemint.com/elections/lok-sabha-elections/ten-charts-that-explain-the-2019-lok-sabha-verdict-1558636775444.html (accessed on June 14, 2019).
33. Narendra Modi, *Public Rally* (Kushinagar, Uttar Pradesh, 2019, 12 May).
34. *The Financial Express*, 'Unnao Rape Case Hurting BJP's Reputation, May Ruin Modi's Prospects in 2019 Election, Says Party Spokesperson' (2018, 12 April).
35. Shirin M. Rai and Carole Spary, *Performing Representation: Women Members in the Indian Parliament* (Oxford: Oxford University Press, 2019), 290.
36. Anne Phillips, *Democratizing against the Grain* (LSE Research Online, 2018 June [Cited 22 July 2019]). Available at http://eprints.lse.ac.uk/88161/ (accessed on 19 September 2019).

Chapter 5

Political Accountability and Organized Public Action in India

Making Power Answer to People

Jyotirindra Dasgupta and Anshu N. Chatterjee

Parliamentary electoral system in a country like India offers too large a context to seriously consider the voices and aspirations of participating citizens. Fortunately, the political system of representation offers ways of connecting the people with their representatives. These connections imply processes of authorization and accountability that constitute the basic foundations of the democratic system and its legitimation in the national community.[1] Representatives are authorized by constituents to accomplish particular political objectives within a reasonable frame of time. They are also held to account to those who he/she represents in order to meet expected rules of democratic legitimation. However, comparative studies indicate that instances of accountability in most parts of the democratic world tend to be weaker than those of authorization.

RESPONSIVENESS AND ACCOUNTABILITY

We will discuss some problems of responsiveness and accountability with special reference to the inter-election years after 2014 beginning first with a focus on the electoral agenda.[2] We also look at the relevant politics of policy processing and responsiveness. If the responsiveness turned out to be less than expected, what modes of accountability were available? In case of absence of processes to hold representatives to account, what options were available? To what extent was there room for unorthodox public action calling for civil society organizations to offer alternatives? Calling authorities to account for their role and actions assumes that the constituents share critical norms of deliberation. How evident were such norms?

It is noted that the concept of accountability is more demanding than that of responsiveness or answerability. Responsiveness may refer to a government's or any public institutions' willingness to align policies in favour of the expressed preferences of the people.[3] Accountability, however, implies holding specific authorities and policy implementing officials responsible for specific policy processes and products.[4] It may accompany appropriate sanctions. In fact, elections may turn out to be major, though delayed, sanctions that may strengthen prospects of political accountability.

Representation is a complex process that need not be limited to a simple notion of reflecting and processing a voter's interest. Besides interest, which is subject to many interpretations, there are other important aspects like opinions or social affinities and cultural perspectives of the citizens that need to be inducted into representational processes.[5] These processes get more complicated because it is political parties that provide coordinated platform for representation.[6]

MANDATE AND RESPONSE

Two successive Lok Sabha elections in 2014 and 2019 show relatively clear road maps of political preferences of parties indicating recent patterns of popular political inclination. For our purpose, these elections and the intervening years offer evidence regarding what the voters authorized in the form of party programmes and what policy products followed. We also examine the ruling agenda, its implementation and its consequent responsiveness to the citizens. They also lead to the problems of probing into accountability issues. We then focus on the modes of expressing grievances and ways of seeking redress that include insurgent supplements to conventional political struggles.[7]

For a brief sense of the new ruling leadership's interpretation of the mandate from the electorate in 2014, we turn to some promises made in the first session of both Houses of the Parliament after the elections to the 16th Lok Sabha.[8] Whenever necessary, we glean additional evidence from the Bharatiya Janata Party (BJP)'s literature.[9] The mandate translated in general terms of policies for 'development through good governance'. There was a sense of continuity with prior developmental history. However, a marked emphasis on 'strong willpower' to accelerate the pursuit of 'public interest', especially in the areas of poverty alleviation, community asset creation and infrastructural improvement, was clearly evident.

BENEFIT EXPANSION

The agenda attends to some primary amenities and services for the poor that were never offered before. A party best known for its religious concerns and sacred symbolism succeeded in turning the nation's gaze to the continuing neglect of elementary facilities of toilets, household provisions or other necessities of livelihood. Women, in particular, were impressed by the fact that their unhealthy smoke-filled cooking areas in poor homes finally received attention at the national policy level. Such programmes and projects conducted with reasonable pace of delivery and efficiency, apparently, earned the BJP spectacular political rewards during the 2019 Lok Sabha elections.[10] A selected few are noted here. Nearly seven decades after 1947, the sanitary situation for close to half of the population remained abysmally poor. '... by 2014, around 100 million rural and about 10 million urban households in India were without sanitary toilet....'[11] The Swachh Bharat Mission (SBM) was inaugurated in 2014 to realize universal sanitation coverage by the end of 2019. During the four years, more than 99 per cent of rural India was claimed to be covered, a project involving community participation.

The blessings of the beneficiaries turned into political benefit for Prime Minister Narendra Modi. His modest social origin presumed to resonate with the masses, particularly at miserable social margins. Women in poor rural homes discovered a national leader who personally advocated reforms that were likely to benefit them the most. Bringing sanitation facilities at home afforded them an aspect of dignity that they had missed. The new facilities enabled progressive eliminations of gender disparity through the construction of gender-specific toilets in public areas such as schools, roads and parks. They helped increase the enrolment ratio of girls in schools by improving health and hygiene standards.[12] Burning wood for cooking in poor households is an age-old source of pollution for women. The Modi regime offered an escape by providing access for millions of poor homes in the form of affordable gas cylinders.

Several other benefit-oriented schemes and programmes were targeted to gain the assent from a wide range of population. The agenda of 2014 promised universal household electrification, financial inclusion of the poor through access to banking facilities, support for micro-enterprises, health plans, housing subsidies and various insurance arrangements.[13] The financial inclusion scheme alone claimed to bring banking facilities to nearly 350 million people as well as a marked improvement in the disbursement system deployed after 2014. The impressive last mile delivery system and expanded direct benefit transfer (DBT) processes set the Modi regime schemes apart from their predecessors.[14] Voters noticed and the ground was paved for the ruling party's positive connections with the sentiments of citizens in large numbers and diverse social bases.[15]

Despite the overall improvements in the implementation of many of these programmes, the disconcerting lineage of patterns of leakages, diversion and abuse affecting the intended receiver could not be wished away. The complex delivery system of the central government schemes that are generally filtered through state, district- and village-level authorities create barriers to implementation.[16] Local notables, including party functionaries, are not always eager to let the delivery system follow proper rules. We will discuss some of these issues later.

SUBDUED SUPPLY

When benefits expand in a poor country, there are the basic issues of paying for them. The election agenda of the BJP promised elaborate programmes of 'economic revival' including renewed energy for growth, investment, employment and social justice in order to build a 'globally competitive economy'.[17] It pledged to offer an aspirational programme of production to serve the 'inspired people' to pursue the ideal of *Shrestha Bharat* (best India).[18] However, the economic accomplishments of the new government despite a strong mandate in 2014 proved to be less than expected. The GDP growth rate of 8 per cent in 2015 declined to 6.8 per cent in 2018. The supply side of the economy indicated a similar trend. Gross value added (GVA) at constant basic prices, reflecting the production side of the economy, registered a change from 8 per cent to 6.6 per cent.[19] From 2016–2017 to 2018–2019, real growth in agriculture and industry, respectively, declined from 6.3 per cent to 2.9 per cent and 7.7 per cent to 6.9 per cent.[20]

Reasons for concerns about the economy and what it means for the poor increases when the employment situation during the inter-election period is considered. Here, the official data received criticism because of lack of consistency in reporting the distressing rise of unemployment in the country. According to one official report, the rate of unemployment increased from 4.9 per cent in 2014–2015 to 6.1 per cent in 2017–2018.[21] An Organisation for Economic Co-operation and Development survey of Indian economy indicated that nearly 31 per cent of youth in India around 2015 were not 'engaged in any purposeful activity'.[22] The female unemployment rate was higher. The reported unemployment rate disguised a much higher rate of underemployment.

By 2017, the situation worsened due to the imposition of a policy of demonetization which reduced labour participation rates. It is estimated that about 1.5 million jobs were lost during the first four months of 2017.[23] The regime must have worried that the rate of unemployment among the educated, including the graduates and above at 28.2 per cent, was the highest since the beginning of the century.[24] These are discouraging developments, despite the fact that deceleration of an economy with a high growth rate, reasonably low inflation rate and other marks of resilience, need not necessarily sound ominous.

POLICY, PROCEDURE AND CIVIC PERSPECTIVES

The comfortable majority earned by the BJP in the 2014 elections, along with a reputation for an elaborate organizational structure, encouraged it to pursue political consolidation during the following years. While pursuing the productive and distributive policies of the mandate, the leaders headed by Modi tried to blend their Hindu nationalist notions of solidarity with functional concepts of development and welfare. A skilful marketing of a strong, socially concerned and culturally empathic brand of 'charisma' helped build a gilded image for Modi.[25]

Thus, public perception of the quality of policy products was not necessarily limited to their intrinsic worth. In some cases, their evaluation was aided by the symbolic value of the image of the leader dominating the government and the party. The implication of symbolism in policy analysis can be easily misinterpreted. As it is discussed in organization theory, symbols are not necessarily devices of the powerful for confusing the weak. They can be seen as instruments of interpretive order deployed for reducing ambiguities of political life.[26] The BJP's 2014 election manifesto and Modi's political style during the years of consolidation of power appeared to separate the promotion of the symbols of inclusive political solidarity of a federalized nation from that of an exclusive religion-based nationalism derived from a selected formulation of Hinduism or Hinduness.[27]

No explicit reference to Hindu nationalism appeared in the 2014 document. Given India's long history of democratization based on secular inclusion, the party strategically aligned with a constitutionally grounded ideal of wide solidarity to seek the assent of citizens across regions and cultures.[28] The party made careful attempts to demonstrate deference for constitutional procedures and transparent policies for inclusion. A preference for cosmopolitan inclination impressed on the agenda and on the political style of the prime minister. How did all this symbolism and policy pursuit work during the five consolidating years? What did the citizens make of the transition's record? The party promised an accountable system. What could the citizens do to test that promise in practice?

These are complex questions to which we can reach approximate answers on the bases of emerging evidence from a variety of sources. A general test of political accountability may suggest that the 2019 parliamentary elections offered a positive verdict both on the performance record of the transition and the party's agenda for the future. But the voter needs to be analysed in the context in which a citizen articulated evaluation in daily life. Political representation is a highly differentiated process involving many aspects that unfortunately tend to be mixed in a composite vote. What the citizen wants to communicate to the representatives in terms of productive interests, redistributive benefits or expectations regarding cultural, religious, ethnic and other modes of recognition calls for elaboration.

Political accountability intimations registered once in five years, cast in the context of a nationally exciting election day, cannot capture the disaggregated sensibilities expressed over the course of a long transition. Also, the retrospective power of the electoral process to hold a ruling authority to account at any level of politics need not be underestimated. The BJP's national test in 2019 was preceded by three important state-level election losses in 2018. Again, by 2019, parliamentary elections turned the tide in its favour in the same states. What accountability messages do such electoral voice carry? Perhaps they may suggest the importance of other short-term possibilities of calling authorities either to account, or at least to respond to, citizens' urgent concerns.

For example, what did the BJP's concept of *Ek Bharat, Shrestha Bharat* (one India, best India) imply to those segments of India where strong scepticism, if not reservation, prevailed long before the party captured national power?[29] In fact, the big majority of the BJP attained in the 2019 parliamentary election and the nationalist rhetoric of the leaders created a fear of majoritarian moves to impede or suppress regional autonomy or aspirations.[30] Ideas of majoritarian nationalism seemed to be especially dangerous in the context of the party's cultural socialization policies pursued to promote religious and patriotic themes in different spheres of public life. Persistent attempts to promote greetings and slogans aligned with Hindu symbols with references to Sri Ram, Bharat Mata and others, and sometimes forcing minorities or even unwilling Hindus from the non-Hindi speaking people have injected new elements of distress in the national political life.[31] The drastic intervention to change the status of Jammu and Kashmir, and to reorganize the area in 2019 soon after the election, proved that the fears were not unfounded. Multicultural India nervously watched the unilateral zest of the ruling party, wondering which region or culture may be the next target.

The BJP agenda promised transparency and accountability. How would the concerned regions and their citizens make sure that the integral nationalists riding majority waves will realize that citizenship in a multicultural country may involve a variation in relative affinity to the concepts of nation and region? Is such wide variation compatible with integral nationalism? How did Indian citizens report their own responses on these issues during the inter-election years? A survey of 12 states conducted in 2018 offers some interesting responses.[32]

The general finding of the survey is that there is almost a 'clear and equal divide across numbers of respondents who identify themselves as more regional, more national and also feel both equally'. In Delhi, Uttarakhand and Uttar Pradesh, responses tend to be highly national, just as the number are heavily skewed in favour of regional allegiance in the cases of Jammu and Kashmir, Tamil Nadu and Nagaland. In states such as Punjab, Kerala and Assam, responses reveal affinity to both regional and national identities.[33] There is also internal variation within each state according to rural and urban settings. Generally, urban residents tend to feel more national; though in Jammu and Kashmir, urban respondents display a higher regional affinity compared to their rural counterparts. In Jammu and Kashmir, 81 per cent urban residents felt close to regional identity as compared to 64 per cent of their rural counterparts.[34] What measure of significance do these pictures of complex distribution of national and regional sentiments carry to the proponents of assimilative integration?

ACCOUNTING AND THE PARLIAMENT

Citizens can hold authorities to account in many ways. They can probe policy processes by demanding access to pertinent information. Armed with a right to information (RTI), they can scrutinize procedures and policies, and their compliance with the publicly stated objectives. Many of these endeavours may not succeed in imposing sanctions. But simply the impact of investigative pressures, adverse media campaigns, shaming effects on officials and transparency gains can be highly rewarding. Civic initiatives for accountability may be facilitated by a community's sense of trust for the relevant institutions or offices or actors. A brief note on different levels of such trust in India during our inter-election years is in order.

From the vantage point of interest in accountability, the most positive response of the citizens was reserved for the Supreme Court, while political parties scored the lowest levels of public trust. The 2018 report, cited earlier, suggests that a reasonably high level of trust was enjoyed by the Parliament, the Election Commission of India and gram panchayat.[35] As explained later, given the small scale and proximity to the people, the panchayat level of political operation appears to provide a better context to study political accountability than elsewhere.

Be that as it may, the Parliament's place in any study of accountability in India remains important for a number of reasons. Besides passing bills, key role of the Parliament is to hold the government accountable. The composition of the 17th Lok Sabha may raise many questions regarding the fairness of participation rates of important segments of population. Women still comprise only 14.4 per cent of the total of 542 members.[36] Though the caste composition has improved in favour of the disadvantaged segments, Muslim representation remains low in general and totally absent in the BJP. Most of the Lok Sabha members are millionaires and 39 per cent of the BJP winners have criminal cases against them.[37] Modi repeatedly promised to '...rid Parliament of criminals...' but the party keeps increasing their participation, if not prominence, in the Lok Sabha.[38]

The 16th Lok Sabha was busier than its predecessor. It worked for 20 per cent more hours than the previous one and it spent 13 per cent of its time on question hour which normally affords opportunity to hold the government accountable.[39] Short duration discussions and calling attention motions also served similar purpose. While this Lok Sabha's performance on these matters appeared to be better than that of the UPA-dominated predecessor, a significantly lower proportion of bills introduced were referred to committees. However, the expedited discussions, aided by a comfortable majority, offered the possibility of compromise on accountability. Committees offer scrutiny in a more exhaustive and objective manner and frequently provide opportunity for engaging with relevant stakeholders and experts.[40] But the BJP leaders chose to send only 25 per cent of the new bills to committees, as compared to 71 per cent of those in the case of the 15th Lok Sabha.[41]

Some of the committees, including the financial ones, follow a long tradition of working without much concern for party whips. Consensual reports based on support across parties have not been unusual. Senior opposition MPs have chaired important committees.[42] Healthy conventions, though not without exception, have enjoyed cumulative growth. A strategy of hasty rejection of such parliamentary tradition may already carry disconcerting signals for accountability. At least, the 16th Lok Sabha had to take into account the fact that it lacked the assurance of majority support in the Upper House (Rajya Sabha). By the middle of 2019, the scope of resistance from the Rajya Sabha declined. The march of a Modi majority, as the brash move to revoke Article 370 demonstrated, is now too assured to make Indian democracy stay untroubled.

CIVIC OPTIONS

As noted earlier, citizens in India feel that they can trust other institutions besides the Parliament to aid and assist processes of accountability, transparency and fair procedure in public life. Institutions such as the Supreme Court and the Election Commission of India enjoy general confidence for their role in working for the people's interests when powerful authorities fail them. Civil society organizations also play a crucial role in cleaning up the election processes. In fact, important initiative for electoral reforms were led by Jayaprakash Narayan in 1974 and later.[43]

For many years, the reform ideas did not find favour in the earlier policy circles. However, after 1999, the Association for Democratic Reforms (ADR) steadily pursued legal action to eventually gain strong support from the Supreme Court to authorize the Election Commission of India to clean up the polls. The combination of efforts of civic organizations, such as the ADR, Common Cause, Mazdoor Kisan Shakti Sangathan (MKSS), and constitutionally authorized institutions, such as the Supreme Court and the Election Commission of India, has contributed an institutionalized system of accountability of surprising durability. Since the turn of this century, the ability to publicize criminal antecedents of candidates and details of their assets, and to disqualify convicted legislators as well as prevent them from contesting elections, have earned the electoral authority an enviable status.[44] The way the Election Commission of India imposed the Model Code of Conduct in some disturbed areas during the elections of 2019 came as a pleasant surprise to many observers.

The Supreme Court's role in supporting accountability covers an extensive and highly innovative ground. We limit ourselves to a few comments on the record of judicial activism and its use of public interest litigation.[45] The latter, according to the Supreme Court, implies collaborative effort of the petitioner, public authority and the Supreme Court to realize rights and benefits 'conferred upon the vulnerable sections of the community and to reach social justice to them'.[46] It offers a new dimension of public action connecting citizens with government. The prestige of the Supreme Court adds a new element of strength to the voice of the citizens at social margin. Also, the accompanying media publicity augments the voice in the public space. The contribution of judicial activism to the fields of human rights, environmental issues, liberation of bonded labourers and releasing illegally held prisoners has immensely strengthened the case for accountability.[47] It also added to the prestige of the judiciary.

Perhaps, the most effective aids to accountability systems serving the disadvantaged population were provided by a set of rights-based legislations from the turn of this century. The RTI movement set an example for Right to Employment, Right to Education, Forest Rights Act and others that initiated new approaches to development in India.[48] The exemplary role of the RTI Act of 2005 was made possible because of a fortunate collaboration of many civic associations, judicial authorities and policy planners. How village-level organizations with skilful support from dedicated urban activists can make a difference in developmental policy processes was evident in the story of the RTI. According to a leader of the MKSS which played a critical role, it has 'made it possible for every citizen to use it to access every other right'.[49] By 2016, about a total of 1.75 crore RTI applications were filed by users.

The National Advisory Council (NAC) needs special mention in the context of the evolution of the RTI and the Right to Employment. The UPA administration created it as a semi-official consultative body to aid policy processes pertaining to development and welfare.[50] Besides officials, this body invited civil society leaders, academic scholars and retired administrative personnel. Serious and effective collaboration of ruling party leaders like Sonia Gandhi and civic association leaders like Aruna Roy offered a rare opportunity for regular interaction across political lines. Our study of policy processes of the BJP-led rule since 2014, however, indicates a reversal of such inclination for interaction or cooperation.

A major contribution of civic groups like the MKSS to accountability processes consisted of the practices of social auditing conducted in the highly accessible context of rural public hearing. Social auditing practices like Jansunwai since 1996, as practised by the MKSS in Rajasthan or elsewhere, helped expose corruption, irregularities and inefficient delivery mechanisms. The conduct of audit at close rural contexts afforded a new opportunity for directly holding authorities to account and to seek redress for the people who were most affected or were intended beneficiaries of schemes likes National Rural Employment Guarantee (NREGA) Act of 2005.[51] It required considerable courage for a villager to face a powerful adversary and to present convincing evidence in a risky communicative situation. Such a vivid exercise of accountability operation would be impossible to obtain in all the kinds of larger contexts that we have discussed earlier.

RIGHTS AND REVERSAL

Confrontation to combat corruption involved in benefit programmes or productive projects may also call for organized political mobilization, particularly when no redress is available through meetings or hearings. NREGA reports indicate that new opportunities for labour organizations fighting for the rights of agricultural workers were explored in different parts of India. Organizations such as the New Trade Union Initiative of New Delhi, Grameen Mazdoor Sabha of Gujarat or Grameen Coolie Karmikara Sangathan in Karnataka have engaged in effective protest campaigns.[52] When negotiations did not pay, they marched to the local authorities and sought to apply accountability norms through collective action. Passive participants in organized projects have demonstrated time and again that their transformation potential cannot be underestimated. The experience of one mode of organized participation can change into a more radical version if an altered context calls for it.

Rights are not gifts; they are hard-earned resources for the citizens in a democracy. For every right mentioned earlier, there is a long history of gaining them as a result of persistent endeavour made by dedicated civic associations. Political parties are not prominent players, especially when they are in or close to power. During the inter-election period that we have concentrated on, the BJP as the ruling party has taken more interest in reducing the importance of rights than actually strengthening them. Most recently, in 2019, they rushed through an amendment to the RTI in order to reduce the autonomy of the implementing authority relative to the powers of the executive. The amendment undermined the independence of the RTI by placing tenure and salary decision at the central and state level in the hands of central authorities. The vote was 218 versus 79 in July 2019. The opposition could only walk out. The task of organizing protest out in the street was left to the National Campaign for People's Right to Information (NCPRI).

Independent institutions to serve the people to ensuring proper investigation and prosecution into allegations of corruption against public servants have not been encouraged since 2014. The Lokpal and Lokayuktas Act of 2013 received presidential assent in 2014. It took more than five years after the law was enacted for the state to appoint the chairperson and members of the Lokpal, who then would function as an independent anti-corruption ombudsman. However, in 2016, even before the Lokpal was functional, '...amendments were made to weaken key provisions of the legislation relating to asset disclosures by public servants'.[53] The government was careless. The mass media did not make much of it. Parties displayed no interest; not even those that claimed a reputation for detecting thieves (*chor*). Only civic associations such as Satark Nagrik Sangathan and the NCPRI continued their usual vigilance.

TORMENT OF MAJORITY

When rights recede, the citizens who voted for the BJP in two successive national elections should worry about the fate of the mandate. Did democracy fail them? Is a majoritarian machine going to reverse all the gains in accountability that we have described earlier? Was Modi's promise of wide band national solidarity combined with aspirational developmentalism simply an electoral cover for a monolithic mix of religious nationalism and elitist industrialization? Is all the political capital built over seven decades for trusted institutions such as the Election Commission of India, the Supreme Court, the Parliament and others going to give way to some devotional symbols designed to destroy dissent and diversity? Can Modi afford to lose the expanding areas of support that he recently gained from unexpected areas outside the north and the west of the country due to promises of aspirational changes?

In fact, the local BJP, in confronting West Bengal's ruling party, earned considerable success in fighting corruption by promoting an anti 'cut' money (kickbacks) campaign. This was an organized direct action by village population to force corrupt officials or leaders to surrender ill-gotten money back to the victims in contexts of public shaming.[54] Given this new entry into insurgent action to support accountability, it should not be easy to reconcile this radicalism with the national-level mandate's retreat from citizen's rights.

These new areas of support, for example, in West Bengal, are not compatible with hard-line Hindu nationalism. Will wider national bases founded on secular symbols of solidarity and inclusionary development serve Modi's charisma better than majoritarian religiosity? The 2019 elections in West Bengal demonstrated unexpectedly high support for the BJP from the Dalit and the tribal people.[55] All this may promise new avenues of dispensing with the fear of losing old support. The choices made in this regard may be critical for the future of India's democratization.

NOTES

1. Iris Marion Young, *Inclusion and Democracy* (New York, NY: Oxford University Press, 2000), 128.
2. Here, we use the notion of agenda as Robert A. Dahl does in his analysis of democratic process. See his *On Democracy* (New Haven, CT: Yale University Press, 1998), 38.
3. See Bernard Manin and Adam Przeworski, 'Introduction', in *Democracy, Accountability, and Representation*, ed. Bernard Manin and Adam Przeworski (Cambridge: Cambridge University Press, 1999), 9.
4. See John Dunn, 'Situating Democratic Political Accountability', in *Democracy, Accountability, and Representation*, ed. Bernard Manin and Adam Przeworski (Cambridge: Cambridge University Press, 1999), 330; and David Held, *Models of Democracy* (Palo Alto, CA: Stanford University Press, 1987), 283–284.
5. For differentiated modes of representation, see Young, *Inclusion and Democracy,* 133–141. For the concepts of 'intentions', its variability and role in institutional processes, see James March and Johan P. Olsen, *Rediscovering Institutions, The Organizational Basis of Politics* (New York, NY: The Free Press), 65–67.
6. According to Max Weber, parliamentary system involves 'voluntaristic intervention' of the parties. See his *Economy and Society*, vol. 1. (Berkeley, CA: University of California Press, 1978), 294.
7. The reference to insurgence indicates action that may appear to transgress the normal codes of constitutionality. See S. Dryzek, *Deliberative Democracy and Beyond* (Oxford: Oxford University Press, 2000), 85.
8. See the 'Address by the President of India, Pranab Mukherjee to Parliament' (New Delhi: Central Hall of the Parliament, 2014, 9 June).
9. For example, *BJP Election Manifesto 2014* and other publications including news communications.

10. Uday Mahurkar, 'Modi, Shah Reign Again', *India Today* (2019, 3 June), 16.
11. Government of India, *Economic Survey 2018–2019*, vol. 1 (New Delhi: Government of India, July 2019), 148.
12. Ibid., 160.
13. For details, see Vivasvan Shastri and Yesha Bhatt, *Reforming Lives, Rebuilding Economy* (New Delhi: Prabhat Prakashan, 2018).
14. Mahurkar, 'Modi, Shah Reign Again', 18–19. This report says that the DBT system used by the previous regime, United Progressive Alliance (UPA), was designed to reach 250 million people, while the Modi DBT was to serve 550 million people (p. 19).
15. According to the reports, some minority voters appreciative of the benefits probably chose to stay home and not strengthen the opposition. Mahurkar, 'Modi, Shah Reign Again', 18.
16. See, for example, Simon Chauchard, *Why Representation Matters* (Cambridge: Cambridge University Press, 2017), 70.
17. See *BJP Election Manifesto 2014*, 1–7.
18. Ibid., 1.
19. Government of India, *Economic Survey, 2018–2019,* vol. 2 (New Delhi: Government of India), 2 and 17.
20. Ibid., 18.
21. Ibid., 1.
22. See Narasimhan Srinivasan and Girija Srinivasan, *State of India's Livelihood Report 2017* (New Delhi: SAGE Publications, 2018), 125–126. The OECD report cited was dated 2017.
23. See details including the findings of Centre for Monitoring Indian Economy (CMIE) in Srinivasan and Srinivasan, *State of India's Livelihood Report 2017*, 126–127.
24. See Paaritosh Nath, 'Employment Scenario and the Reservation Policy', *Economic & Political Weekly* 54, no. 19 (2019): 58.
25. Max Weber's concept of charisma is rather complex; it refers to a personality considered '…extraordinary and treated as endowed with supernatural, superhuman, or at least specifically exceptional powers or qualities'. See Weber, *Economy and Society*, 241–242 and passim.
26. March and Olsen, *Rediscovering Institutions,* 48–49.
27. *BJP Election Manifesto 2014*. Note the emphasis on the 'Model of national development, which is driven by the states…' (p. 2); and on India 'without exclusion, without exception' (p. 3).
28. For a discussion of constitutionality grounded solidarity serving as a basis for a cosmopolitan, as opposed to ethnocentric, national bond, see Jurgen Habermas, *The Inclusion of the Other, Studies in Political Theory* (Cambridge, MA: The MIT Press, 1998), 118–119.
29. See *BJP Election Manifesto 2014*, 1–7.
30. A good discussion of the reasons of rising fear is offered in Suhas Palshikar, 'Towards Hegemony, BJP beyond Electoral Dominance', *Economic & Political Weekly* 53, no. 33 (2018): 36–42.

31. Ibid., 38.
32. See Azim Premji University and CSDS-Lokniti, *Politics and Society between Elections* (Bengaluru: CSDS-Lokniti and Azim Premji University, 2018).
33. Ibid., 115.
34. Ibid., 116.
35. See Azim Premji University and CSDS-Lokniti, *Politics and Society between Elections*, 197–198. In terms of levels of trust, the army scored 80 per cent, the Supreme Court 69 per cent, the Election Commission of India 42 per cent with the Parliament being close.
36. Ajit Kumar Jha, 'Changing Face of the Legislature', *India Today* (2019, 17 June).
37. Ibid.
38. See the story of promise and non-performance on the criminalization issue in Milan Vaishnav, *When Crime Pays* (New Haven, CT: Yale University Press, 2017), 282–283. Many of the suspected MPs were included into Modi's first cabinet (p. 283).
39. PRS Legislative Research, *Vital Stats, Functioning of the 16th Lok Sabha* (New Delhi: PRS Legislative Research, 2019), 1–3.
40. M. R. Madhavan, 'Parliament', in *Rethinking Public Institutions in India*, ed. Devesh Kapur, Pratap Bhanu Mehta and Milan Vaishnav (New Delhi: Oxford University Press, 2017), 88–95.
41. PRS Legislative Research, *Vital Stats*, 2.
42. Madhavan, 'Parliament', 95.
43. Jagdeep S. Chhokar, 'Civil Society in Elections in India', in *The Great March of Democracy*, ed. S. Y. Quraishi, 154–155.
44. The details can be found in *ADR Handbook* (2019). Also, see E. Sridharan and Milan Vaishnav, 'Election Commission of India', in *Rethinking Public Institutions in India*, ed. Devesh Kapur, Pratap Bhanu Mehta and Milan Vaishnav (New Delhi: Oxford University Press, 2017), 417–463.
45. For a background of the role of the Supreme Court, See Madhav Khosla and Ananth Padmanabhan, 'The Supreme Court', in *Rethinking Public Institutions in India*, ed. Devesh Kapur, Pratap Bhanu Mehta and Milan Vaishnav (New Delhi: Oxford University Press, 2017), 104–138.
46. Shyam Divan, 'Public Interest Litigation', in *The Oxford Handbook of the Indian Constitution*, ed. Sujit Choudhry, Madhav Khosla and Pratap Bhanu Mehta (New Delhi: Oxford University Press, 2016), 664, 667.
47. Ibid., 679.
48. Sudhir Naib, *The Right to Information in India* (New Delhi: Oxford University Press, 2013), xiii.
49. Aruna Roy (with MKSS collective), *The RTI Story* (New Delhi: Roli Books, 2018), 23.
50. Rob Jenkins and James Manor, *Politics and the Right to Work* (London: Hurst, 2017), 42–43.
51. Amitabh Mukhopadhay, 'Foregrounding Financial Accountability in Governance', in ed. Devesh Kapur, Pratap Bhanu Mehta and Milan Vaishnav

(New Delhi: Oxford University Press, 2017), 328. See Roy, *The RTI Story*, 95–124 and *passim*.

52. Jenkins and Manor, *Politics and the Right to Work*, 230.
53. Anjali Bhardwaj and Amrita Johri, 'Undermining the Lokpal', *Economic & Political Weekly* 54, no. 18 (2019): 14.
54. Romita Datta, 'Counting the Cost of Cut Money', *India Today* (2019, 5 July).
55. Jyotiprasad Chatterjee and Suprio Basu, 'A New Trajectory of Politics in West Bengal', *Economic & Political Weekly* 54, no. 31 (2019): 16–19.

Chapter 6

Election News 2019

Free, Fair and Fake? Examining Trends in Misinformation around Indian National Polls

Pallava Bedi and Devika Malik

INTRODUCTION

As India prepared for what is one of the largest exercises in electoral democracy in the world, two things were clear: fake news was intended to impact election outcomes elsewhere in the world and back home in India the wide proliferation of unverifiable messages through various media were coinciding with extreme polarization of public discourse and even societal violence.

In the USA, Congress and the FBI had concluded this even though it was hard to establish the causal impact it had or the size of any correlated impact. We had seen social media being weaponized across the world to deliver polarizing, violence-inducing messaging in the USA, Kenya, Brazil and at home in India. Given how ubiquitous the term fake news had come to be, it was perceived as the foremost threat to the integrity of the colossal democratic process India was about to undertake.

In this chapter, we attempt first to determine what 'fake news' looks like in the Indian context. We do this by looking at how some definitions of the term and other associated information phenomena have evolved, and which one best describes those in the Indian context. Additionally, we attempt to analyse the narratives that drive the proliferation of the fake news phenomenon in India and how they relate to the elections. By way of research methodology, we rely on existing scholarship on the lexicon of fake news by First Draft who have led the academic effort to understand the 'information disorder'. We draw on the BBC's research on information-sharing behaviour of the Indian consumer to highlight trends that pave the way for fake news proliferation ahead of polls. Research by the MIT published by the *Hindustan Times* is also instructive in understanding the strategic power of the social media that political parties in India have been alive to ahead of elections and how they get organized in the effort to popularize fake news.

To supplement our review of existing literature, we conducted interviews with Indian media and observers including senior editor and former media advisor to the prime minister, Mr Pankaj Pachauri, as well as fact-checkers Rakesh Dubbudu of Factly and Sagar Kaul of MetaFact.

This chapter does not seek to estimate the impact that fake news may have had on electoral outcomes but the character and extent of such messaging that we know to have been intended to impact voter behaviour. We also don't focus on the medium for proliferation of fake news. Before we get to any meaningful analysis of the role that fake news has played in the recently concluded national elections in India, it is useful to deconstruct the new taxonomy of the term itself.

The term *fake news* has become part of common parlance as a catch-all for any information circulated through the plethora of news and non-news media that lacks accuracy, credibility or integrity. This non-specific understanding of the term is reflected in Wikipedia's definition of fake news:

> Fake news, also known as junk news or pseudo-news, is a type of yellow journalism or propaganda that consists of deliberate disinformation or hoaxes spread via traditional news media (print and broadcast) or online social media. The false information is often caused by reporters paying

> sources for stories, an unethical practice called checkbook journalism. Digital news has brought back and increased the usage of fake news, or yellow journalism. The news is then often reverberated as misinformation in social media but occasionally finds its way to the mainstream media as well.[1]

During the course of our research on India, we encountered a lack of definitional rigour. Senior journalists and commentators frequently cited examples of political parties/movements rallying accusations against other parties/leaders based on what they deemed unsubstantiated claims. Does such messaging through offline media such as flyers, placards and speeches or media reporting on such a movement constitute fake news? Many observers of the 1984 anti-Sikh riots in Delhi have documented rumour-mongering that incited violence. Does such rumour-mongering qualify as fake news? Does this change if the rumours originated/circulated deliberately or organically?

As researchers such as Claire Wardle, Ethan Zuckerman, Danah Boyd and Caroline Jack and journalists like the *Washington Post*'s Margaret Sullivan have argued, the term 'fake news' does not adequately convey the complex phenomena of misinformation and disinformation. As Zuckerman states, 'It's a vague and ambiguous term that spans everything from false balance (actual news that doesn't deserve our attention), propaganda (weaponized speech designed to support one party over another), and disinformation (information designed to sow doubt and increase mistrust in institutions)'.

Much of the discourse on 'fake news' conflates three notions: misinformation, disinformation and mal-information. Some researchers not only distinguish messages that are true from those that are false but also messages that are created, produced or distributed by 'agents' who intend to do harm from those that are not.

Disinformation: Information that is false and deliberately created to harm a person, social group, organization or country.

Misinformation: Information that is false, but not created with the intention of causing harm.

Mal-information: Information, that is based on reality, used to inflict harm on a person, organization or country.

In 'Fake News. It's Complicated',[2] Wardle outlines seven types of misinformation and disinformation, revealing the wide spectrum of problematic content online, from satire and parody (which, while a form of art, can become misinformation when audiences misinterpret the message) to full-blown fabricated content.[3] However, classifying 'fake news' by the intent into misinformation, disinformation and malinformation seems problematic as judging intent based on outcome is not always possible and this can and almost certainly does change along the content distribution chain.

Wardle et al. also review other few helpful definitions:

1. *Information (or influence) operations:* Actions taken by the governments or organized non-state actors to distort domestic or foreign political sentiment, most frequently to achieve a strategic and/or geopolitical outcome. These operations can use a combination of methods, such as false news, disinformation or networks of fake accounts, aimed at manipulating public opinion (false amplifiers).
2. *False news:* News articles that purport to be factual, but contain intentional misstatements of fact to arouse passions, attract viewership or deceive.
3. *False amplifiers:* Coordinated activity by inauthentic accounts that has the intent of manipulating political discussion (e.g., by discouraging specific parties from participating in discussion or amplifying sensationalistic voices over others).
4. *Disinformation:* Inaccurate or manipulated information/content that is spread intentionally. Disinformation is distinct from misinformation, which is the inadvertent or unintentional spread of inaccurate information without malicious intent.

For the purpose of this chapter, we define fake news as the intersection of mis/disinformation and the second category of false content that mimics news reporting in tonality, format and appearance. We also focus on messages that are designed and produced with an intent to mislead/polarize, even though the distribution and circulation might not always be with that intent. As such, we use the terms fake news, misinformation and disinformation interchangeably.

FAKE NEWS AND INDIA

The Internet subscribers in India increased from 22.86 million on 31 March 2012 to 636.79 million on 31 March 2019.[4] The proliferation of social media websites and the ubiquitous nature of instant messaging apps have led to them being regarded as the primary source of information/news. However, as per a report conducted by the Internet and Mobile Association of India (IAMAI) and Factly, newspapers still remain one of the top sources of information across different age groups.

It is also important to note that 'fake news' or misinformation is not a new phenomenon in India or elsewhere. 'Fake news' or propaganda campaigns to stir up hostilities or to create division in society, create a schism between the 'outsider' and the 'patriot' have been used throughout the 20th century. The two World Wars saw extensive use of propaganda to spread stories and information in an effort at image management and manipulation. The German Nazi Propaganda Minister Joseph Goebbels' efforts could certainly be regarded as a high tide in this phenomenon of the circulation and the institutionalization of fake news.[5]

India was not immune to these phenomena—there were several instances of 'fake news' or which at times may be better described as misinformation being circulated by mainstream newspapers as well as vernacular dailies. During the 1990 riots in Aligarh, the local newspapers published a story that a number of patients from the majority community were killed by Muslim doctors at a local hospital. It was subsequently established that this was false, but the damage had already been done,[6] culprits stopped the Gomti Express and killed them. The Press Council of India reprimanded the newspapers, but it was too late. The Press Council of India while analysing the role of the media during the 1990 clashes concluded that:

> There is little doubt that some influential sections of the Hindi press in UP and Bihar were guilty of gross irresponsibility and impropriety, offending the canons of journalistic ethics in promoting mass hysteria on the basis of rumour and speculation...They were guilty, in a few instances, of doctoring pictures (such as drawing prison bars on the

> photograph of an arrested mahant), fabricating casualty figures (for example, adding '1' before '15' to make '115' deaths) and incitement of violence and spreading disaffection among members of the armed forces and police, engendering communal hatred.[7]

In the aftermath of the Babri Masjid demolition and the riots that followed in Ayodhya, communal riots gripped Bhopal and Hindi newspapers were accused of fuelling the riots and spreading false information. Newspapers were accused of exaggerating the numbers of deaths and spreading rumours instead of verifiable news.[8] The then chief minister, in fact, issued an appeal which was printed in the newspapers to not fall for rumours.[9] During the 2002 Gujarat riots, two prominent Gujarat newspapers were accused of spreading false and inflammatory news and even when certain stories were denied as being true, there was no correction or clarification by the newspapers.

FAKE NEWS AND IMPACT ON US ELECTIONS AND BREXIT

A number of commentators suggested that Donald Trump would not have been elected president and Brexit results would not have gone in favour of the 'Leave' campaign had it not been for the influence of fake news. In the days immediately before and after the 2016 elections, 'people shared nearly as much "fake news"' as real news on Twitter.[10] The term fake news was ironically initially used by Donald Trump not against social media, but against mainstream media, namely CNN during the 2016 presidential campaign. However, the spread of fake news soon became a major public concern in the USA and thereafter in the subsequent elections in Brazil and France. The actual effects of fake news on the outcome of the 2016 US presidential elections have been questioned. There are divergent views on the subject, some analysts say that it is difficult to link misinformation or fake news with changes in an individual's voting habits.

An article published in the *Columbia Journalism Review* fears that the spread and influence of fake news have been overhyped. It states that fake news reached only a tiny proportion of the population before and during the 2016 elections. However, there have been other studies which have concluded that fake news or misinformation likely influenced the outcome of the 2016 elections in part because of its effect on undecided voters.[11]

Fake news was also a problem during the 2017 French presidential election; however, as per reports, the problem was not as severe as during the US elections. The BBC also worked with CrossCheck (a journalism project set up by First Draft) to verify and debunk fake stories.[12] In November 2018, the French Parliament passed a new law which empowers judges to issue orders seeking the immediate removal of 'fake news' during an election campaign. It also allows the French National Broadcasting Agency to suspend the licence of television channels controlled by a foreign state or under the influence of the state, if the channel is deliberately spreading false news likely to affect the sincerity of the ballot.[13]

NATIONALISM KEY DRIVER OF FAKE NEWS

The potency of fabricated news came into focus after the 2016 US presidential elections, where the focus has been on foreign-backed misinformation campaigns shaping elections and public discourse. In India, misinformation and fake news in the lead up to the 2019 Lok Sabha polls were 'Made in India'. However, the US experience trained a firm lens on Indian elections and any efforts to weaponize misinformation to sway election results.

In some sense, the fact that fake news in India did not surface in the context or midst of an election cycle makes it harder to draw a direct correlation—the themes that emerge from discourse analysis coincide with the key poll narratives of the main political camps. As the election period progresses, we see misinformation more blatantly buffeting and discrediting political candidates. As these trends peak around the polling months, another key trend in misinformation content is around the electoral process itself. Finally, post polls, while election-related content recedes, polarizing and anti-minority misinformation/fake news content continues to circulate.

Between 2014 and 2016, it had become commonplace to see forwarded messages celebrating international recognition for the Indian government. Interestingly, such rumours were often attributed to

UNESCO. In June 2016, fake news broke out across social media forums that the UN cultural agency had awarded Prime Minister Narendra Modi the title of best prime minister in the world. Another piece of news that travelled from e-mail to social media messenger platforms was that UNESCO had declared the Indian national anthem, Jana Gana Mana, the best in the world.

On November 2016, the Government of India announced the demonetization of all ₹500 and ₹1,000 banknotes. It also announced the issuance of new ₹500 and ₹2,000 banknotes in exchange for the demonetized banknotes. While the merits and efficacy of the policy were widely contested, fake news did the rounds that UNESCO declared new ₹2,000 note the best currency in the world. The rumours caught the eye of the BBC, which reported that 'thousands' of users of messaging apps had 'forwarded the message along with joyful emojis'. The messages were not limited to the aesthetics of the currency alone, further rumours surfaced that the new notes have a GPS chip to detect black money. And that new notes have radioactive ink. The fake news claimed that the Income Tax Department was using the isotope to trace large quantities of cash held at a particular spot. The Reserve Bank of India clarified that the new notes contain security features such as latent images, coloured strip security threads, watermarks, etc., but they do not have a chip installed as reported by *the Hindu*.

These examples attest to the eagerness of the Indian Internet user to believe and share even unverified news that promoted sentiments of national pride. In a study conducted by the BBC, looking at trends in fake news in India between 2015 and 2018, it was found that people share fake news for the following reasons:

- Sharing to verify within the network
- Sharing as a civic duty
- Sharing for community and nation-building
- Sharing as projection and expression of identity

Further, the most effective narratives that support the distribution of fake news content were found to be the following: overtly anti-majority discourse; Hindu power and superiority; preservation and revival: a related narrative—and associated messages—is more to do with the preservation and revival of ancient glories (usually Hindu), and progress and national pride. By 2017 and well into 2018, we saw these narratives acquire serious and sinister dimensions in what culminated as India's 'lynching epidemic'.

As the country kicked into election gear by 2018, religious nationalism had been cemented as the core emotive issue. Political parties ostensibly organized themselves for social media to be the primary front of political campaigning. Research studies as well as trends analysis by several fact-checking organizations point to an organized move to proliferate the Indian voter's media mindshare with political propaganda often manifesting itself in the form of fabricated news content.[14]

Social media analysts suggested that Right-wing networks are much more organized than those on the Left, pushing nationalistic fake stories further. Rakesh Dubbudu of fact-checking organization, Factly, concludes that states where BJP was not in contention saw different trends. Local fake news was far less organized, that is, regional parties were far less organized.

Based on a research published in the *Hindustan Times*,[15] 8 of the 10 most shared misleading images in pro-BJP messenger groups ahead of last year's state elections were about the Telangana manifesto, and the claims that Congress favoured only Muslims. According to a 2017 Lokniti-CSDS Mood of the Nation (MOTN) survey, around one-sixth of messaging app users in India said that they were members of a group started by a political leader or party. The study identified 693 pro-BJP groups; 156 pro-Congress and the rest voice support for various regional parties and religious groups. To be sure, it is not known how many of these groups are managed by the office-bearers of political parties.

As polling took off in March and April, misinformation was weaponized and disseminated in an aggressive, yet strategic, manner, in a bid to shape public opinion. After the verdict was declared on 23 May, the focus moved towards electronic voting machines (EVMs) and the integrity of the poll process, according to fact-checkers.[16]

MISINFORMATION CALLING ELECTORAL PROCESS TO QUESTION

During the run-up to the 2019 General Elections, there were widespread allegations of tampering of the EVM in favour of the BJP. A petition was also filed in the Supreme Court of India by 21 opposition party leaders seeking an increase in the Voter Verifiable Paper Audit Trail from one EVM to 50 per cent of EVMs per assembly constituency. The Supreme Court instead of increasing it to 50 per cent per assembly constituency directed the Election Commission of India to increase it to five EVMs per constituency.

In our interaction with Mr Pankaj Pachauri,[17] he stated that though there were numerous allegations of widespread tampering of EVM machines, most of them were found to be unsubstantiated and baseless. In March 2019, a video was widely circulated on social media claiming that the prime minister and Amit Shah, then president of the BJP and home minster following the elections, had hatched a conspiracy to store EVMs in a storeroom. Alt News, one of India's premier fact-checking websites, debunked the video and found it to be an old false video first circulated during the 2018 Madhya Pradesh state elections.[18]

Similarly, in 2017, a letter was circulated on social media purportedly written by the deputy election commissioner in Gandhinagar alleging that EVMs were being hacked in connivance with tech companies. Alt News was able to prove that the letter was fake and that there was no deputy commissioner by the name of the individual who allegedly wrote the said letter. During the General Elections, the Election Commission of India reported 154 instances of fake news or misinformation on social media platforms. All of this fake news reported by the Election Commission of India to social media platforms was about the Election Commission of India itself.[19]

The 2019 General Elections was not the first time that allegations of EVM tampering emerged. In 2009, senior BJP leader L. K. Advani, who was the Leader of the Opposition at that time, had demanded the reintroduction of ballot papers for the assembly elections in Maharashtra and three other states. That was the first time a mainstream political party had questioned EVMs. Advani demanded that, 'We should revert to ballot papers unless the Election Commission is able to ensure that

EVMs are foolproof and every possibility of their malfunctioning is taken care of'.[20] Once the BJP was in power, the tables were turned and now it was the turn of the opposition to claim tampering of EVMs and question the electoral process.

CONCLUSION

Our attempt in this chapter has been to define fake news and to analyse whether there is any causal link between fake news or propaganda and the election results. What we have found is that while fake news or misinformation is not exactly a new phenomenon as it has been around for several years. Whether it was rumour-mongering during the Babri Masjid demolition or during the 1984 riots, the extent and spread of propaganda-based news and misinformation is extensive.

For several months preceding the 2019 elections, fake news was used to create false perceptions about political candidates or specific groups of people, attempting to manipulate voter choices. In the run-up to the parliamentary elections, following the Pulwama attack and the strikes by the Indian Air Force in Balakot, there was a heightened sense of nationalism in the country and this nationalistic pride was used to develop and circulate several fake news stories across social media platforms. Such stories were also used to cement religious nationalism as a core emotive issue with the Indian citizens and to stoke up feelings of religious patriotism, especially among the Hindu community. In the midst of the elections, reports of EVM tampering and other stories soon emerged in an attempt to discredit the election process in mainstream media as well as on social media.

Surprisingly, following the declaration of the election results on 23 May, there has hardly been any research or study undertaken to analyse the extent of fake news during the election cycle and the causal relationship, if any, between fake news and the results of the election. In our interviews, we were often only presented with anecdotal evidence. We did not come across any substantive empirical data to conclusively prove or disprove this link. What we found was that while there was high consumption of fake news during this period, especially when it came to nationalism and the Indian army, little or no analysis has been undertaken to analyse the impact of the consumption of such fake news on the elections.

NOTES

1. https://en.wikipedia.org/wiki/Fake_news
2. C. Wardle, *Fake News. It's Complicated*, First Draft (2017, 16 February). Available at https://firstdraftnews.com/fakenews-complicated/ (accessed on 20 September 2019).
3. Claire Wardle and Hossein Derakhshan. *Information Disorder* (Strasbourg: Council of Europe, 2017).
4. Available at https://main.trai.gov.in/sites/default/files/PR_No.48of2019.pdf (accessed on 20 September 2019).
5. IAMAI and Factly, 'Countering Misinformation (Fake News) in India: Solution and Strategies'. IAMAI and Factly Report.
6. Available at https://shodhganga.inflibnet.ac.in/bitstream/10603/40546/14/17_chapter8.pdf (accessed on 20 September 2019).
7. Ibid.
8. Kakvi Kashif, *Fake News by Hindi Newspapers Fuelled 1992 Bhopal Riots, Killed 139 in Communal Clashes Following Babri Masjid Demolition*, Firstpost. Available at https://www.firstpost.com/india/fake-news-by-hindi-newspapers-fuelled-1992-bhopal-riots-killed-139-in-communal-clashes-following-babri-masjid-demolition-5683541.html (accessed on 1 August 2019).
9. Ibid.
10. Julie Posetti and Alice Matthews, 'A Short Guide to History of Fake News and Disinformation: A Learning Module for Journalists and Journalism Educators'. Available at https://www.icfj.org/sites/default/files/2018–07/A%20Short%20Guide%20to%20History%20of%20Fake%20News%20and%20Disinformation_ICFJ%20Final.pdf (accessed on 20 September 2019).
11. Jane Mayer, 'How Russia Helped Swing the Election for Trump' (2018, 24 September). Available at https://www.newyorker.com/magazine/2018/10/01/how-russia-helped-to-swing-the-election-for-trump (accessed on 20 September 2019).
12. Available at https://www.bbc.com/news/world-europe-39265777 (accessed on 20 September 2019).
13. Michael-Ross Fiorentino, 'France Passes Controversial "Fake News" Law'. Available at https://www.euronews.com/2018/11/22/france-passes-controversial-fake-news-law (accessed on 20 September 2019).
14. Available at https://qz.com/india/1599730/election-2019-congress-likes-facebook-over-whatsapp-in-kerala/ (accessed on 20 September 2019).

15. Available at https://www.hindustantimes.com/india-news/decoding-fact-free-world-of-whatsapp/story-LQ79X96OOKrGo7MHuW3TMP.html (accessed on 20 September 2019).
16. Available at https://www.altnews.in/may-2019-misinformation-weaponised-to-target-electoral-process-and-political-leaders/ (accessed on 20 September 2019).
17. Journalist and the Communication Advisor to the former Prime Minister Manmohan Singh.
18. Available at https://www.altnews.in/2018-mp-election-video-viral-as-bjp-and-election-commission-illegally-hoarding-evms/ (accessed on 20 September 2019).
19. Available at https://www.thequint.com/news/webqoof/election-commission-of-india-reported-154-fake-news-facebook-twitter-google (accessed on 20 September 2019).
20. Available at https://www.indiatoday.in/elections/story/the-many-claims-of-evm-tampering-in-india-1435638–2019–01-21 (accessed on 20 September 2019).

PART II

Analytical State Studies

A. Northern Cluster

Chapter 7

War of Perception, Brand Modi and Voters' Choice in Uttar Pradesh

Sudha Pai and Sajjan Kumar

In the 2019 national elections, the BJP has once again swept Uttar Pradesh (UP), pushing aside the much-anticipated SP–BSP–RLD *Mahagathbandhan* (alliance) and the Congress, which fresh from its success in three state assembly elections was viewed as having revitalized itself under the leadership of Rahul Gandhi. Although the BJP has gained fewer seats in UP, it has increased its vote share and gained support from all castes/classes. Its overall excellent performance in UP points to its continued dominance in the state; it has won a second consecutive victory since 2014, following the 2017 assembly elections. While the 2014 election attempted to establish right-wing rule in the country and in the key state of UP, in 2019 the attempt has been to consolidate the rule of the BJP.

Unlike the 2014 general election in UP, neither the issue of *vikas* (development) nor communal mobilization leading to the Muzaffarnagar riots of 2013 played a fundamental role. Moreover, the old mode of dominant intermediary and politically assertive castes such as Yadavs and Jatavs emerging as the core anchor of political power no longer worked. The confluence of weaker castes among the OBCs as well as Dalits and upper castes signifies a new shift in the interplay of caste, issues and election. In 2019, the BJP performed well despite the poor performance of the UP government evident in the lack of development, deteriorating law and order, poor health care and education, joblessness and farm distress. Similarly, the Central government under Narendra Modi, who played a key role in the UP campaign, in its first term experienced falling growth rates, lower investment and manufacturing, agrarian crisis and a badly implemented GST. However, instead of anti-incumbency, which affected elections earlier, we witnessed a pro-incumbency wave.

The 2019 national election is clearly different from earlier elections. Neither the theories of *political economy* nor *rational choice*, traditionally used to explain voter's choice, are useful in explaining the outcome. The voter did not vote along the lines of his/her economic self-interests but was swayed by issues of nationalism and national security. Thus, there is a need to focus on the *psychology of the voter* and, most importantly, the *war of perception*—personal and digital—used by the BJP to 'manufacture' voter consent.[1] Also, building on the earlier figure of Modi as a *chai wallah* risen from a humble background, a brand image was sought to be created of him as a strong leader/provider of good governance and welfare.

Using this theoretical backdrop, our chapter analyses the reasons underlying the victory of the BJP in UP. More immediately, despite an aggressive campaign, the SP–BSP–RLD *Mahagathbandhan* did not succeed in stopping the BJP; though the constituents received votes from a section of their core constituencies, these were not translated into seats, particularly in the case of the SP. The reluctance of the alliance to include the Congress meant that the index of opposition unity, despite the desire to defeat the BJP, remained low in UP.

The collapse of the Congress party in UP is most evident in the defeat of Rahul Gandhi in Amethi. Despite a spirited campaign, the Congress lost as it had not been able to revitalize its organization, find fresh young candidates or spread its alternative message of Nyuntam Aay Yojana (NYAY) or minimum income guarantee scheme. In many places, candidates put up by the Congress cut into the vote share of the alliance and the introduction of Priyanka Gandhi came too late to make an impact. There was not a clear message whether Rahul and Priyanka were fighting to win in 2019 or for long-term revival of the party.

However, the foremost reason for the victory of the BJP in UP has been the strong and populist leadership of Narendra Modi. While 2014 was described as 'not so much a BJP as a Modi victory'[2] due to his emphasis on development, the 2019 victory has been due to a highly personalized and plebiscitary electoral campaign by Modi that helped build his image as a doer. Rather than BJP leaders in UP, it was Modi's speeches at numerous rallies in the state that created a direct emotional connect with the voters and brought the party success.

ANALYSING THE RESULTS

Defeat of the *Mahagathbandhan:* Possibilities and Limitations

The key to understanding the electoral results in UP lies in analysing the possibilities and limitations that the SP–BSP–RLD alliance faced. The alliance was based on the strategy that the three parties would unite Yadavs, Jatavs and Muslims, who together add up to around 40 per cent of the state's population, thereby limiting the number of seats the Modi-led BJP could win. A number of factors encouraged this prospect: First, the combined vote share of the SP and the BSP in the 2014 elections (42.98%) was slightly more than that of the BJP (42.3%). Second, a template existed; the two parties had managed this experiment in the Gorakhpur, Phulpur and Kairana by-elections.[3] Third, it was felt that both parties could ensure transfer of their votes to each other in their corresponding seats; more than demographic arithmetic, it was felt that there would be positive chemistry between the workers of the three parties.

However, though the expected transfer of core votes took place, the alliance failed in appealing to the much larger non-core, that is, non-Yadav, non-Jatav and non-Muslim voters who were swayed by the BJP. As Table 7.1 shows, the SP–BSP–RLD alliance won barely 15 seats, despite getting 38.92 per cent vote share in 2019, while that of the BJP increased from 42.63 per cent to 49.55 per cent. On the

Table 7.1 *Seats and Percentage of Votes Won by Parties in 2014 and 2019 Lok Sabha Elections in UP*

Party	Seats Won in 2014	Percentage	Seats Won in 2019	Percentage
Bharatiya Janata Party	71	42.3	62	49.40
Indian National Congress	2	7.5	1	6.31
Samajwadi Party	5	22.0	5	17.96
Bahujan Samaj Party	0	19.6	10	19.26
Apna Dal	1	1.0	2	1.01
Total	80	100.0	80	100.00

Source: Compiled from the reports of the Election Commission of India.

other hand, the BJP had an advantage due to the presence of a sizeable number of upper castes, lower backwards and smaller Dalit groups across the state.[4]

Failed Caste Calculations

An important reason for the poor performance of the alliance was failure in its caste calculation. Table 7.2 shows that barring the Jats, the consolidation of the core constituencies of the alliance partners did happen.

- Only 7 per cent of the Jats voted for the alliance, whereas 91 per cent preferred the BJP.
- SP's core voters, the Yadavs, fully supported the alliance: three-fifths of them voted for the alliance, lower than in the 2017 assembly election, but higher than in 2014 when without an alliance the SP had obtained 53 per cent votes.
- The BSP fared better obtaining 75 per cent or three-fourths of the Jatav votes which is higher than 68 per cent in 2014. But in the case of the other SCs, it gained the support of 42 per cent, whereas 48 per cent preferred the BJP as in 2014.

Table 7.2 *How Castes and Communities Voted in the 2019 Lok Sabha Election in UP*

	Party Voted for Lok Sabha 2019 in Uttar Pradesh			
	Congress (%)	BJP+(%)	MGB (%)	Others (%)
Brahmin	6	82	6	6
Rajput	5	89	7	–
Vaishya	13	70	4	13
Jat	2	91	7	0
Other upper caste	5	84	10	1
Yadav	5	23	60	12
Kurmi and Koeri	5	80	14	1
Other OBCs	5	72	18	5
Jatav	1	17	75	7
Other SCs	7	48	42	3
Muslims	14	8	73	5
Others	1	50	35	14

Source: CSDS-Lokniti Post-Poll Survey, *The Hindu*, 26 May 2019, available at https://www.thehindu.com/elections/lok-sabha–2019/post-poll-survey-why-uttar-pradeshs-mahagathbandhan-failed/article27249310.ece?homepage=true (accessed on 24 September 2019).

Note: Figures may not add up to 100 due to rounding.

- Finally, three-fourths of the Muslim votes went to the alliance in 2019, but 14 per cent supported the Congress, particularly in seats contested by the SP, which may be a reason for the fairly large number of defeats of SP candidates compared to BSP candidates. In 2014, the SP alone had gained 58 per cent of the Muslim votes.

The disappointing performance of the alliance can be understood by placing it within the political discourse and power struggles among social groups in the post-Mandal period in UP. Throughout the 1990s, the SP failed to weld the backwards into a cohesive political community. While class-based changes due to education, urbanization, vernacular newspapers, satellite TV and so on acerbated already existing divisions, when in power, the SP undoubtedly favoured the Yadavs. It led to the emergence of the most backward classes (MBCs), who feel they are the most neglected and have in recent years become very demanding; a section that the BJP has been able to tap. Similarly, the BSP since the mid-1990s, with its preoccupation with power, has not been a democratizing force as earlier when it moved downwards to mobilize the smaller, poorer Dalit groups, who therefore view it as a purely Jatav party. It is this new voting bloc of the non-Yadav and non-Jatav Dalits who constitute a substantial section of the electorate and have been profitably mobilized by the BJP, first in 2014 and now in larger numbers in 2019. The 2000s have also witnessed within this category an upwardly mobile, aspirational class, strongly attracted by Modi in 2014 and continuing into 2019.[5]

Equally important, in 2019, the formation of the alliance created a division between Yadavs and Jatavs versus the lower OBCs and smaller SCs. The ambitious slogan '*ek bhi vote na ghatne paye, ek bhi vote na batne paye*' (not a single vote should go waste, not a single vote should be split) put forward on 7 April at the first rally of the BSP–SP–RLD was a call for the mutual transfer of votes between their core support bases, but was also seen as a 'veiled suggestion' to other communities that they were not needed in this alliance.[6] This created a counter-mobilization of lower backwards and smaller Dalits, who unwilling to return to erstwhile Yadav–Jatav dominance, moved towards the BJP in even greater numbers than in 2014. In fact, anti-Yadav sentiment was a major fulcrum in UP on which support for Modi and the BJP rested.

As a consequence, as Table 7.2 shows, over four-fifths of upper castes, four-fifths of Kurmis and Koeris and three-fourths of lower OBCs voted for the BJP. Along with non-Jatav Dalits, the three constitute around half of UP's population. Until 2012, many of these groups had voted for the SP and the BSP.

Competing Campaign Narratives

More than traditional caste calculations, two competing narratives used in the campaign divided the electorate and shaped voters' choices. On the one hand, agrarian-cum-economic issues such as lack of decent minimum support price for farm crops, non-payment/delayed payment by sugar mills, rise in cost of farming, stray cattle and lack of jobs. On the other hand, nationalism and the government's strong army action against Pakistan. The former set of issues was important for the Jats, Yadavs and other landowning communities. On the question of nationalism, these dominant intermediary castes argued that the Indian Army has always made the country proud, cheerleading Modi and the BJP as the sole custodian of nationalism and national security is unwarranted. For instance, during fieldwork,[7] a Yadav respondent in the Etawah constituency opined that the rank and file of the Indian Army are sons of farmers whom the Modi government is trying to crush. Together with Jatavs, they seemed to project the Modi-led BJP as a story of failures and unfulfilled promises; Muslims echoed the sentiment.[8]

On the other hand, the upper castes and non-Yadav OBCs and non-Jatav Dalits were strongly attracted by the issues of nationalism and army action against Pakistan, which Modi and other BJP leaders skilfully used in their speeches. While many were affected by the agrarian and economic problems outlined above—particularly the poorer OBCs—these issues did not merit attention in their political choice. In our field study,[9] the state government's performance was not rated well—83 per cent of the respondents reported stray cattle menace to be a serious issue, over half blamed the state government for it. But respondents held that Modi deserved 'ek chance aur'[10] to complete the good work he had begun, though most could not tell what this good work was. In the Braj region, while potato farmers were angry with the BJP for not helping them, they argued that potatoes can be stored in cold storage until prices improved. Rather, they pointed out that their OBC community had decided, as in 2014, to vote for the BJP.[11]

Thus, for an overwhelming majority of upper castes, non-Yadav OBCs and non-Jatav Dalits, Modi signified a bold and decisive leader. None of the respondents in these groups were willing to link their precarious economic situation with voting preferences; mention of welfare schemes such as PM Awas Yojana and Ujjwala Yojana was like a tactical, post-facto exercise to rationalize their pro-BJP stance.[12] Thus, it is the social profile of the electorates that seemed to have determined the pertinence of a set of issues, rather than issues that determined their voting behaviour. The narratives employed in the campaign divided the electorate into Modi detractors and Modi supporters; the latter proved to be more in number.[13]

Deepening Congress Crisis

Despite a spirited and sustained campaign by the Congress party to highlight the failures of the BJP government, it gained only one seat in UP, Raebareli held by Sonia Gandhi. As Table 7.2 shows, the party obtained little support from the upper castes, except for the Vaishya (13%) or from Jatavs and other SCs, both groups which had been its supporters prior to its decline in the 1990s. Also, just 2 per cent from the Jats, 5 per cent from the Yadavs and various OBC groups each, though it obtained 14 per cent support from the Muslims.

A major reason for the collapse of the Congress in UP is the failure of the party leadership to revive its organization and social base. In a state where identity remains important, the party does not have a single lower backward or Dalit leader, or young upper caste leaders to match those in the BJP. Rahul Gandhi's decision to contest from a second seat—Wayanad in Kerala—has helped him enter parliament, but the BJP projected him as running away from UP, where the party is weak.

Rahul Gandhi as the main campaigner for the Congress party addressed a total of 125 rallies.[14] In UP, he addressed 18 rallies for 80 seats; hardly any other senior Congress leader, including Jyotiraditya Scindia, appointed general secretary for western UP, campaigned vigorously in the state. The party had hoped that the appointment of Priyanka Gandhi as general secretary in charge of eastern UP would motivate workers, attract dissatisfied youth, rural and urban voters, Muslims, Dalits and backwards that had drifted towards the BJP, but the strategy proved unsuccessful. Nor did Priyanka's statement during the campaign that the Congress had put up 'weak' candidates in some seats to 'cut into the BJP vote bank' help the alliance.[15] Her apparent last minute withdrawal of candidature from Varanasi against Modi, which would have posed a challenge to the BJP, also worked against the Congress.

Congress Campaign

Three narratives were used by the Congress, as the main opposition party, to challenge the BJP. First, it tried to negotiate an alliance with the SP and BSP in UP, but failed as the former parties felt that the Congress had little to offer. This created uncertainty as the Congress kept trying to seal an alliance, and it increasingly seemed as though there was a tacit understanding and the Congress was lending an indirect helping hand to Mayawati and Akhilesh to defeat the BJP.[16] Mayawati attacked the Congress at several rallies and even threatened to reconsider support to the Kamal Nath-led Congress government in Madhya Pradesh. Akhilesh Yadav refrained from criticizing the Congress, but held that its main aim was not to defeat the BJP, but to form the state government in UP in 2022. Yet the alliance did not field candidates from the two Congress bastions of Amethi and Raebareli. The Congress, too, avoided making any direct attacks on the alliance and the doors still seemed open for a post-poll alliance.

Second, Rahul Gandhi attacked Modi, using the slogan '*chowkidar chor hai*' at rallies to allege financial irregularities in the Rafale deal. While initially it seemed to be an ingenious method of attack, Modi describing it as a personal attack turned around the slogan, launching a '*main bhi chowkidar*' programme in which all senior leaders of the party and many supporters, prefixed 'chowkidar' to their names on social media platforms, removing its value. More important, the slogan backfired as Modi projected himself as a victim, a 'clean leader' attacked by the Congress.[17] The BJP got a further advantage when Gandhi was pulled up by the Supreme Court for his slogan and had to apologize. Some Congress leaders later blamed the 'excessive negative campaign' against Modi, which did not go down well with electors, for the party's humiliating defeat.[18]

Third, the Congress party announced NYAY as part of its manifesto on 25 March 2019.[19] It was an attempt to counter BJP's narrative of nationalism, refocus the election on economic issues and project the Congress party as pro-poor. However, Lokniti surveys found that despite popularizing the scheme through advertisements, hoardings and speeches, it came too late and was not communicated effectively to the targeted beneficiaries. The post-poll survey found that while the number of those aware of the scheme had increased since the pre-poll survey, the increase was a marginal two percentage points among those who stood to benefit (those belonging to households earning only up to ₹3,000 a month). Rather, awareness about the NYAY scheme was greatest among the higher income groups, traditionally core supporters of the BJP, who are not beneficiaries of the scheme.[20]

The survey also found that the Modi government's PM Kisan Yojana (transfer of ₹2,000 to bank accounts of farmers every four months) might have ended up overshadowing and blunting the effect of NYAY. Three out of five farmers, who had received the money in the past one month, favoured giving the government another chance. This pro-government sentiment among such farmers did not wane even with the knowledge of NYAY, as they were determined to support the Modi government.[21]

BJP VICTORY: CREATION OF BRAND MODI

In 2019, as Table 7.1 shows, the BJP won 62 seats in UP, 9 less than in 2014, but increased its vote share to 49.4 per cent. As Table 7.2 shows, the BJP gained a high level of support from all caste groups: above 80 per cent from upper caste communities and 70 per cent from the Vaishya community, 91 per cent of the Jat, 80 per cent of the Kurmi and Koeri, 72 per cent of the other OBCs and almost half the votes of the other SCs. It even managed to gain the support of 8 per cent of the Muslims who constitute 19.26 per cent of the population in UP.

In caste terms, the seamless alliance of the upper castes with the lower caste non-Yadav OBCs and non-Jatav Dalits was due to BJP's intra-Hindu, caste-based, social engineering. While there is much focus on 'othering' of Muslims, little attention has been paid to the 'silent othering' of the traditionally dominant Yadavs by the BJP.[22] While the alliance fielded 10 Yadav candidates, the BJP fielded only one, in Azamgarh against Akhilesh Yadav. A similar strategy was adopted for the Jatavs too. This sent a strong message to the non-Yadav OBCs and non-Jatav Dalits combine, which provided the BJP almost 50 per cent of the votes in UP.

Viewed from the vantage point of UP, the key reason for BJP's excellent performance was a highly personalized campaign, constructed almost solely around Modi's image although there was no Modi wave.[23] Rather than state-level BJP leaders, it was Modi who was the kingpin of the campaign. Barring Varanasi, in most of the remaining seats, despite the poor quality of BJP candidates, their supporters endorsed them. There were even protests by workers and supporters in some constituencies,[24] but the party won all these constituencies with resounding margins.

Four narratives, constantly used by Modi in his speeches and reiterated in social media, moved the discourse away from the economy to nationalism and impacted the psychology of the voter. Through them, Modi was able to manage the anger among the party's supporters with government policies and gain the support of a large section of the electorate.[25] First, the propagation of an intense nationalist discourse or *desh bhakti* by top BJP leaders much before the 'actual' election which served to mark out and counter critics of the party ranging from students, activists and political leaders. This was reinforced during the campaign, by constant reference to Pulwama and the 'surgical strike' against Pakistan, in UP, a state which is a major recruiting ground for the army. The Balakot strike, despite loss of soldier lives, strengthened the already existing BJP support.[26] It pushed opposition and regional parties to build a national narrative, set aside their entrenched differences and form anti-Modi coalitions; the best example being former rivals SP and BSP in UP, which Modi denigrated as 'maha-milawat' or mixture with little ideological commonality.[27]

Second, the Modi government ably marketed the populist image of a massive welfare state just before the election. Beginning in 2014, the government introduced beneficiary schemes such as PM Ujjwala Yojana and PM Awas Yojana, distributed through a huge personal and digital outreach, which connected it to, as claimed by Amit Shah, almost 22 crore beneficiaries.[28] Importantly, this economic intervention was undertaken by the government through a more flexible 'deprived category' index developed with the help of the Socio Economic and Caste Census, instead of the old below poverty line (BPL) concept. The use of Aadhaar to pinpoint individuals within this category and transfer benefits electronically allowed the government to create a class of beneficiaries that may come from different caste groups but have a similar economic profile. While this did not remove caste affiliations, it gave value to the economic identity of smaller caste groups, which until now were hoping to corner benefits showing caste solidarity with dominant groups such as Yadavs and Jatavs in UP. Thus, the Modi government created new, workable, credible options to old caste alliances by creating a new paradigm for accessing state resources.[29]

The work of data collection began soon after the 2014 victory through call centres contacting beneficiaries. The constituencies which saw the most beneficiary outreach were 19 in UP and 4 in Maharashtra, amounting to 8 lakh beneficiaries. In February 2019, under Mera Parivar BJP Parivar programme, workers/sympathizers visited the beneficiaries with the soft message, 'Modi has given schemes to this many families in only five years. Give him another five and you can make that number even more'. This roused aspiration of many families in the selected areas who supported the BJP irrespective of how many persons had actually benefitted from the schemes.[30]

Third, employing the TINA (there is no alternative) factor helped voters set aside the criticism by opposition parties of BJP's failures on the developmental front. This tactic was strategically accompanied by an attack in Modi's speeches on the Congress 'dynasty' as a family enterprise headed by a *naamdar* (privileged) Rahul Gandhi who could not perform, in contrast to the *kaamdar* (worker) heading the BJP. This strategy particularly appealed to young voters who have not seen the Congress party during its period of dominance in UP.

Fourth, during the campaign, BJP leaders, most particularly Modi, used divisive communal discourse to consolidate his Hindu vote bank despite his slogan '*sab ka saath, sab ka vikas*' (togetherness of all, development for all).[31] Throughout the campaign, Modi attacked those who questioned government action after the Pulwama–Balakot incidents, describing them as 'soft' on Pakistan-sponsored terror. When Rahul

Gandhi decided to contest from a second seat, Modi derided him for choosing a seat where Hindus were in a minority. When during his nomination Muslim League supporters turned out in large numbers, BJP leaders asked if they were in Pakistan. Modi also ignored the nearly 50 constituencies where Muslim voters account for more than 30 per cent of the total electorate.[32] The Congress with little counter-strategy, apart from criticizing Modi, found it difficult to oppose these narratives and fell into the trap of reducing the 2019 election to a contest between Modi and Rahul Gandhi.

The CSDS survey indicates that if Modi had not been the preferred popular prime ministerial candidate of 47 per cent of the respondents, the BJP may not have been able to win the number of seats that it did in UP. Also that about 25 per cent of BJP's voters would not have voted for the party had Modi not been its prime ministerial candidate. Put simply, in the absence of Modi, the BJP may have got around 12 per cent less votes than it actually did. Moreover, in response to another question about what would had mattered to them more while voting—the party or the candidate— one-fourth of BJP voters in the state chose neither of the two options and instead spontaneously said Mr Modi.[33]

Finally, an important reason for BJP's victory is its highly organized electoral machinery, its well-trained cadres, which under the leadership of Amit Shah became active at least one year earlier. The senior workers of the party and committees dedicated to each constituency began working at least six months ahead of the campaign launch.[34] The division of the election into seven phases helped plan Modi's highly successful campaign in UP.[35] The digital reach of the party was enormous: it set up 161 call centres across India and sent out 9.38 crore text messages. While 2014 was the first digital election in which technology was used by the BJP to contact voters, by 2019 with Jio's ultra-cheap data almost doubling internet users, the IT cell undertook data collection to map potential voters. Local-level workers were then used to spread messages on non-affiliated WhatsApp groups in their neighbourhood. The number of digital and personal workers far outnumbered those of the Congress and other parties. The party also used paid advertising, spending ₹21 crore on Facebook and Google, compared to ₹4.5 crore spent by the Congress.[36]

CONCLUSION

Our analysis shows that the 2019 general election in the country and in the key state of UP marks a departure from earlier elections in outcome, campaign style and magnitude of defeat of opposition parties, especially the decimation of the Congress party. The BJP managed to gain a significant victory in UP, maintaining its hold and increasing its vote share, despite the formation of a seemingly strong opposition alliance against it. Significant economic concerns such as slowing of growth, lack of jobs or the looming agrarian crisis did not lead the electorate to punish the BJP government for non-performance. The electoral campaign, rather than promises to the electorate and criticism of the opposition as in the past, was a *battle of perceptions and opinions* fought on social media and through strident, rousing campaign speeches by Modi to sway the electorate and gain their support. There was no Modi *wave*; rather, it was Modi's personality, the highly organized and effective BJP machinery, and the weakness of opposition parties that underlay BJP's victory in UP.

The defeat of the SP–BSP–RLD *Mahagathbandhan* was because it did not attempt to move beyond its own core constituency and mobilize the non-Yadav, non-Jatav and non-Muslims. It failed to understand that Modi had managed to mobilize, using development and *Hindutva*, the lower backwards and smaller Dalits in 2014, and during his tenure using the promise of welfare schemes. Consequently, as the alliance had little to offer to these groups, they continued to support the BJP in larger numbers in 2019. In fact, its aggressive campaign using the plank of the dominant Yadavs, Jatavs and the Muslims created the ambience for a counter-mobilization of the rest in favour of the BJP. More than numbers, the chemistry between the allies did not work, leading to shrinking of seat and vote share, lower margins of victory and loss of regional strongholds. The social justice parties had in the 2000s lost legitimacy due to their lack of an economic vision for UP, and the RLD due to the constant shift of its leader Ajit Singh to different political parties. The alliance had only arithmetic in its favour, the electorate's emotional sentiment was with Narendra Modi.

The Congress, the oldest party in the country, is facing a crisis of great magnitude as it gained just one seat in UP, Rahul Gandhi was defeated from Amethi, and subsequently resigned as president of the party on 25 May 2019. In UP, the party lacks strong organization, effective leadership or workers. Priyanka Gandhi's induction into the party earlier might have given her a chance to build the party. Rebuilding the Congress in UP will be a Herculean task prior to the next assembly elections. Also, without an alternative vision to offer until late in the campaign when it unveiled NYAY and Rahul Gandhi's strategy of attacking Modi personally contributed to the presidentialization of the election. Clearly, the Congress has not stepped out of the existential crisis that enveloped it in 2014, at least in UP. There is now no strong national opposition party in the parliament, making the BJP a hegemonic ruling party, which is a great danger for our democracy.

For the BJP, UP is a key state to capture power at the centre. Aware of the poor governmental performance of the party in the state and lack of support to its non-performing sitting MLAs, a highly personalized and plebiscitary-like electoral campaign was organized around Modi to build his brand image as an effective national leader and performer. A charismatic personality, he was able to strike an emotional chord with the UP electorate and use three highly effective strategies: a divisive communal campaign to consolidate the Hindu vote by attracting the lower backwards and smaller Dalits into the saffron fold; the use of nationalism by constant reference to the Balakot strike against Pakistan and able marketing of schemes such as the PM Ujjwala Yojana, PM Awas Yojana and Swachh Bharat through a huge personal cum digital outreach programme. The BJP by attracting large numbers of almost all sections of the electorate has become the new single-dominant party in UP, similar to the erstwhile Congress party in the post-Independence period.

In sum, the 2019 elections illustrate that Indian politics has undergone a tremendous change. Caste calculations alone cannot ensure success as in the past; the sweeping victory of the BJP lies in its ability to recognize and cater to the rising social and economic aspirations of the poorer sections. In contrast, the *Mahagathbandhan* remained anchored in the Mandal discourse of the past; the ideology of social justice has lost resonance. Dynasty cannot help the Congress in the absence of strong and credible leadership and organization on the ground. However, most important has been the marketing of a strong, magnetic leader. While UP is undoubtedly plagued by joblessness, farm distress, sugar crisis and poverty, Modi's almost iconic figure and message that he can fix these problems if given one more chance seems to have resonated among the electorate, particularly the younger generation.

NOTES

1. Edward S. Herman and Noam Chomsky, *Manufacturing Consent: The Political Economy of the Mass Media* (New York, NY: Pantheon Books, 1988).
2. Sudha Pai and Avinash Kumar, 'Understanding the BJP's Victory in Uttar Pradesh', in *India's 2014 Election: A Modi-led BJP Sweep*, ed. Paul Wallace (New Delhi: SAGE Publications, 2015), 119–138.
3. Sudha Pai, 'Changing Political Preferences among Dalits in Uttar Pradesh in the 2000s: Shift from Social Justice to Aspiration', *Journal of Social Inclusion Studies* 5, no.1 (July 2019). Available at https://journals.sagepub.com/doi/full/10.1177/2394481119852190 (accessed on 24 September 24, 2019).
4. The RLD did not win a seat in its stronghold of western UP, and the BSP and SP won three each; in eastern UP, the BSP won seven seats and the SP gained only one. In Rohilkhand, the alliance had expected a number of seats due to the demographic preponderance of Yadavs and Muslims in combination with Jatav Dalits, but the SP gained only one seat.
5. Sudha Pai, 'Other Aspirational Class', *The Economic Times*, New Delhi, 24 May 2019.
6. Ravish Tiwari, 'BSP's Heartland Surge Flattens Identity Politics in UP, Bihar', *The Indian Express*, 24 May 2019. Available at https://indianexpress.com/article/explained/lok-sabah-elections-results-bjps-heartland-surge-flattens-identity-politics-in-up-bihar-5745501/ (accessed on 24 September 2019).
7. The fieldwork was conducted on 12 April 2019, part of a three-series longitudinal fieldwork in Uttar Pradesh covering all the 80 Lok Sabha constituencies. The study was supported by Peoples Pulse, a Hyderabad-based research institution and Asiaville Media outlet.
8. Sudha Pai and Sajjan Kumar, 'Election 2019: As Uttar Pradesh Votes, Will Modi Be a Factor?' *The Wire,* 11 April 2019. Available at https://thewire.in/politics/elections-2019-uttar-pradesh-modi-factor (accessed on 24 September 2019).
9. As noted above, the field study was supported by Peoples Pulse, a Hyderabad-based research institution and Asiaville Media outlet.
10. Literally—One more chance.
11. Sudha Pai and Sajjan Kumar, 'Phase-2 Not Easy Turf for the Mahagathbandhan in Uttar Pradesh', *The Wire*, 18 April 2019. Available at https://thewire.in/politics/elections-2019-uttar-pradesh-phase-2 (accessed on 24 September 2019).
12. An overwhelming majority of non-Yadav, non-Jatav, non-Muslim respondents in our field study, selected on the basis of purposive sampling in every Lok Sabha constituency, shared the perception that a Modi-led BJP was the need of

the hour on account of his bold and decisive leadership image, which helped BJP overcome its poor developmental record.

13. Ibid.
14. Sanket Upadhyay, 'Elections 2019: Breaking Down Election Campaigns of PM Modi and Rahul Gandhi in Numbers', *NDTV*, 18 May 2019. Available at https://www.ndtv.com/india-news/elections-2019-breaking-down-election-campaigns-of-pm-modi-and-rahul-gandhi-in-numbers-2039438 (accessed on 24 September 2019).
15. Ibid.
16. Sanchari Chatterjee, 'Congress Trying to Cut into BJP Vote Bank in UP and Help Mahagathbandhan?' *India Today*, 1 May 2019. Available at https://www.indiatoday.in/elections/lok-sabha-2019/story/congress-bjp-vote-bank-mahagathbandhan-1514306–2019–05-01 (accessed on 24 September 2019).
17. Rakesh Mohan Chaturvedi and Kumar Anshuman, 'Chowkidar Beats Chorhai: Modi Uses Insults to His Advantage', *Economic Times*, 24 May 2019. Available at https://m.economictimes.com/news/elections/lok-sabha/india/chowkidar-beats-chor-hai-modi-uses-insults-to-his-advantage/articleshow/69474044.cms (accessed on 24 September 2019).
18. *News18*, 'Negative Campaign Against Modi, "Chowkidar Chor Hai" Slogan Backfired, Says Congress Leader', *News18*, 24 May 2019. Available at https://www.news18.com/news/politics/negative-campaign-against-modi-chowkidar-chor-hai-slogan-backfired-says-anil-shastri-2157633.html (accessed on 24 September 2019).
19. NYAY aimed to provide direct cash transfer of ₹6,000/month or ₹72,000/year to the bank account of 5 crore of India's poorest families, preferably to a female member. At an average family size of 5, this translates to 25 crore people or 20 per cent of India's population. The estimated cost of NYAY at ₹3.6 lakh crore would be about 1.8 per cent of today's GDP. By the time NYAY is fully rolled out, this cost would likely drop well below 1.5 per cent of GDP; M. V. Rajeev Gowda and Salman Anees Soz, 'Why NYAY Can't Wait: Here Is What Congress Will Do to Mount a Final Assault on Poverty', *The Times of India*, 17 April 2019. Available at https://timesofindia.indiatimes.com/blogs/toi-edit-page/why-nyay-cant-wait-here-is-what-congress-will-do-to-mount-a-final-assault-on-poverty/ (accessed on 24 September 2019).
20. The Lokniti Team, 'Did NYAY Help the Congress Make a Leap?' *The Hindu*, 20 May 2019. Available at https://www.thehindu.com/elections/lok-sabha-2019/did-nyay-help-the-congress-make-a-leap/article27180048.ece (accessed on 24 September 2019).
21. Ibid.
22. In fact, socio-politically dominant caste groups in many states were neglected by the BJP: Marathas in Maharashtra, Patidars in Gujarat, Jats in Haryana, Yadavs in Uttar Pradesh and Bihar, Ahom in Assam, Tribals in Jharkhand, and Dalits, tribal and OBCs against politically entrenched Bhadraloks in West Bengal.

23. The 2019 elections in many ways are similar to elections during the Nehruvian period. It was the personal charisma of Nehru and the electoral machinery of the Congress that led to massive support for the Congress in UP and elsewhere, rather than a *wave* in favour of the party's performance.
24. The protests were centred in constituencies such as Gautam Buddha Nagar, Meerut, Shamli, Mathura and Aligarh in western Uttar Pradesh, Sitapur and Kanpur in Central UP, Banda in Bundelkhand and Faizabad, Basti and even Gorakhpur in Purvanchal region of the state; based on fieldwork report.
25. Fieldwork during the campaign showed that upper castes, non-Yadav OBCs such as Kashyap/Dhimar, Saini, Badhai Lodh Kurmi and a section of non-Jatav Dalits such as Khatiks, Valmikis, Pasis and Dhanuks rallied behind the BJP quite enthusiastically, citing the Modi factor as the most influential criterion and overriding consideration behind their decision to support the party.
26. Many observers have argued that initially economic issues were stridently put forward by the opposition during the campaign. It was the Pulwama incident and the Balakot strikes into Pakistan that swayed the electorate towards Modi. However, our field narratives indicate that nationalism had been made a central issue long before; Pulwama and Balakot merely provided a boost to BJP supporters and served to deepen the popularity of Modi.
27. Pranab Dhal Samanta, 'View: Fundamental Shifts in India's Electoral Politics Witnessed in the 2019 Poll Battle', *The Economic Times,* 21 May 2019. Available at https://economictimes.indiatimes.com/news/elections/lok-sabha/india/view-fundamental-shifts-in-indias-electoral-politics-witnessed-in-the-2019-poll-battle/articleshow/69417681.cms (accessed on 24 September 2019).
28. Karishma Mehrotra, 'How BJP Marketed to a New Voting Bloc: The 22 Crore Beneficiaries', *The Indian Express* 23 May 2019. Available at https://indianexpress.com/article/india/how-bjp-marketed-to-a-new-voting-bloc-the-22-crore-beneficiaries-5745514/ (accessed on 24 September 2019).
29. Ibid.
30. Ibid.
31. Nilanjan Mukhopadhyay, 'View: PM Modi's 2019 Campaign Is Bereft of His Doctrine of "Inclusiveness"', *The Economic Times*, 10 May 2019. Available at https://economictimes.indiatimes.com/news/elections/lok-sabha/india/view-how-pm-modis-2019-campaign-is-not-in-consonance-with-his-sabka-saath-sabka-vikas-doctrine/articleshow/69257803.cms (accessed on 24 September 2019).
32. Ibid.
33. The Lokniti Team, 'Did NYAY Help'.
34. At least 11 kinds of programmes—such as booth-level conferences and bike rallies—were launched before Modi began his rallies in the states. The party ran 14 different campaigns, such as '*Modi hai to mumkin hai*' (with Modi, it is possible), '*main bhi chowkidar hoon* (I too am a watchman)' and '*phir ek baar, Modi sarkar*' (Modi government once again).

35. Modi held an average of three rallies in every phase; between phases four and five, he held seven rallies trying to reach almost all regions/constituencies. In the fifth and sixth phases, he addressed seven rallies across Purvanchal. Kumar Anshuman, 'PM Modi Averages 3 Rallies in UP, 2 in West Bengal in Each Phase', *The Economic Times*, 13 May 2019. Available at https://economictimes.indiatimes.com/news/elections/lok-sabha/india/pm-modi-averages-3-rallies-in-up-2-in-west-bengal-in-each-phase/articleshow/69300294.cms?from=mdr (accessed on 24 September 2019).
36. Karishma Mehrotra, 'After 2014 Digital Debut, 2019 Push Came from BJP Cadre', *The Indian Express*, 24 May 2019. Available at https://indianexpress.com/elections/lok-sabha-elections-2019-results-after-2014-digital-debut-2019-push-came-from-bjp-cadre-5745537/ (accessed on 24 September 2019).

Chapter 8

Claims of Alternative Politics of AAP

Whither? Why? Punjab and the 2019 Elections

Pramod Kumar

Parliamentary elections in 2014 witnessed a distinct trend in Punjab compared to the rest of India. In 2014, the Aam Aadmi Party (AAP) sprung a surprise by winning seats. And, surprisingly, Bhartiya Janata Party's (BJP) stalwart Arun Jaitley was defeated from Amritsar constituency by Captain Amarinder Singh of the Congress party (Indian National Congress, INC). In the 2017 assembly elections, while the Congress party was routed in other parts of India, it won with a thumping majority in Punjab. In the 2019 parliamentary elections, the Modi wave bypassed Punjab, the AAP became history and Punjab limped back to bipolar politics. Are Punjab polls swinging like a pendulum creating waves of different parties within a short span? Has the political culture and terrain of Punjab become an ideological freak or, more likely, rudderless?

POLITICAL CULTURE, ALLIANCES AND REPRESENTATIONS

The history and culture of Punjab does not support such generalizations. Punjab politics can be located in three evolved axes. One is a stunted identity assertion ranging from religious, communal and secular Punjabi identities. Second is the majoritarian arrogance and minority persecution complex in the main communities, that is, the Hindus and Sikhs. Sikhs are in a majority in Punjab, while otherwise a minority in India, while Hindus are a majority in India and a minority in Punjab. The third axis is the intermeshed religio-caste categories as caste is not a category in itself for electoral mobilizations in Punjab.[1]

These axes lay down broad boundary conditions for politics to function. Within this background, electoral alliances and coalitions have formed between even diametrically opposed political parties. The Congress and the Akalis merged in 1937, 1948 and 1956.[2] Most of the Akalis joining the Congress did not return to the Akali fold. Prominent among them were Partap Singh Kairon, Swaran Singh, Baldev Singh, Bhai Mohan Singh, Darshan Singh Pheruman and now Captain Amarinder Singh. The political culture of Punjab is, no doubt, competitive, but not conflictual. In the post-Operation Blue Star and the Sikh carnage following 1984, the Congress party faced opposition, but it regained power in the 2002 assembly elections. In the 2017 assembly polls, the Congress and the BJP entered into an understanding to defeat the AAP endorsed by both the BJP and the Congress central leadership.[3]

The logical inference that can be drawn is that the voters do not see political parties as antagonistic, but competitive. Many people keep both the blue turban (symbol of the Akalis) and white turban (symbol of the Congress) readily available with them per the need. To hinge a whole campaign on the premise that both the Congress and the Akali seem to be inter-mixed and then expect that the people will vote for a third party may not bring corresponding results.

Political parties have not only merged with each other, but have also formed coalitions. In the reorganized Punjab, between 1967 and 1980, four post-election coalitions were formed between the Akalis and the Bharatiya Jana Sangh. In the post-terrorism phase, the Akalis and the BJP have formed three pre-election coalitions in view of the lessons learned from the decade of terrorism. The Congress apologized for Operation Blue Star and the brutal riots of 1984, and the competing political parties gave representation to all the existing fault lines of religion and caste rather than representing exclusive communal interests.

For instance, the Shiromani Akali Dal (SAD) party, which has mainly been a party of Jat Sikh peasants, gave representation to the Punjabi Hindus with 11 out of 94 SAD candidates for the 2012 assembly elections. The BJP, which largely represents urban Hindu traders, gave representation to Sikhs. Similarly, the Congress made inroads into the SAD support base of rural Jat Sikhs by fielding an equal number of rural Jat Sikhs with the SAD. The Dalits, who constitute around 32 per cent of the population, have been represented in all the political formations. Of the 585 Members of the Legislative Assembly (MLA) in Punjab from 1997 to 2017, Dalits constituted 26.8 per cent, OBCs 7.7 per cent and the urban traders (primarily Khatris) 22.7 per cent. But a majority of the MLAs, that is, 42.7 per cent came from the rural Jat peasantry.

With the 'uncertain religious allegiance'[4] of the Dalits and in the absence of caste as a defining parameter for social position, the Dalits found representation in all the political parties. Even the Jat-dominated SAD have had a higher representation of the Dalits in four of the five assembly elections (1997–2017) and, in the remaining one, the Congress had a higher number of Dalit legislators. Dalit legislators also have representation within the Bahujan Samaj Party (BSP) and Communist parties. Thus, Punjab's electoral politics has shown the signs of blurring religious and caste fault lines. To mobilize people into exclusive categories like Hindu Banias or Scheduled Castes may not be sufficiently explanatory.

CROWDING OF THE ELECTORAL SPACE: FROM MANIFESTOS TO MENU-FESTOS

Historically, Punjab elections have been a bipartisan affair. The main opposition was supposed to be the major beneficiary of the anti-incumbency vote. However, in the 2017 assembly and 2019 parliamentary elections, there was also a third party, the AAP, and a third front consisting of AAP dissenters, wayward Akalis, religious fundamentalists and do-gooder politicians. These elections were also different as all the three political formations had high stakes. The Congress party's resurgence at the national level largely depended on Punjab. For the AAP, victory in Punjab would have provided the much-needed fodder to Kejriwal's (supreme leader of the AAP) ambition to launch himself as a prime ministerial choice. For the Akalis, these elections were a fight for their survival and to save their alliance with the BJP.

Unlike the Akalis and the Congress, the new incumbent AAP did not have any historical baggage nor any historical advantage either. And unlike Delhi, Punjab did not have a large footloose population—as the people of the state had their culture and history.[5] Both the Congress and the Akalis have regional flavour to their advantage, while the AAP was yet to evolve a regional identity of its own. The only advantage that it had was their anti-drug and anti-corruption political stance.

Further, the judgment that quashed the 2004 Water Termination Act passed by the Punjab Legislature denying the neighbouring state of Haryana its share of water led by Capt. Amarinder Singh, then Congress chief minister of Punjab, had added another dimension to the political theatrics. The AAP could not take a forceful position as the states of Delhi and Haryana were also stakeholders in this conflict. However, it is also a fact that the termination of all agreements including that of 1981 by the Punjab assembly in 2004 did not make the Congress party lose elections in Haryana in 2004, and it won elections in Punjab in 2007. It appears that after 50 years of the water sharing dispute, people seem to have become indifferent to the political rhetoric, judicial and administrative diversions on this issue.

This election also witnessed blatant promises made by the political parties. In its election campaign, the Congress promised to send the competing leadership to jail for their alleged misdeeds rather than activizing the justice delivery system, empty or false promises like a farmers' debt waiver, one government job for each family, and eradicating the drug crisis within a month. SAD promised to dole out *aata-dal*, sugar, utensils including pressure cookers, gas, stoves, *shagun* at the time of marriage, bicycles for the girls, pension to the farmers, incentives for the suicide victims of the farmers' families and houses for the homeless.

The AAP, in continuation with the 2014 parliament elections and 2015 Delhi assembly elections, used its own cocktail of doles and promises. They issued 'menu-festo' rather than manifesto.[6] There was a menu card for the farmers, traders, students, Dalits, industrialists, women, etc., to cater to everyone's taste replacing the manifesto which is by definition a declaration of the principles, policies, intention and, of course, ideological commitment. It was reinforcement of the thought that the voters' perception constitutes the reality. It does not matter who was the leader and what he believed in. The focus was to market that image of a leader which the voters wanted the most.

EMERGING FAULT LINES IN ELECTORAL POLITICS

The accumulated anti-incumbency of the 10-years rule of the Akali-BJP manifested through various protests like ad hoc and contractual workers demanding permanent government jobs, the peasantry agitating for adequate support prices for their crops, the followers of Sikhism protesting the revoking of the pardon granted to the Dera Sacha Sauda chief by the Sikh clergy and the subsequent violation of the Sikh scriptures culminated into holding of the Sarbat Khalsa[7] (congregation of the Sikhs) in 2015. The desecration of the religious scriptures and revoking of the pardon to the Dera Sacha Sauda chief, accused of blasphemy, provided teeth to the political discourse in the elections.

In 2007, the Dera Sacha Sauda chief, Gurmeet Ram Rahim Singh, had appeared in an advertisement dressed up as Guru Gobind Singh, the 10th Sikh Guru. This led to widespread clashes between the Dera followers and the Sikhs. An organization called Ek Noor Khalsa Fauj was constituted by Jathedar Balwant Singh Nandgarh of Takht Sri Damdama Sahib to oppose and stop the congregation of the Dera followers. The Akal Takht (supreme temporal authority of Sikhs) issued the directive in May 2007 for social boycott of the Dera chief.[8] In a flip-flop move, on 24 September 2015, the Akal Takht exonerated the Dera chief in the 2007 blasphemy case. This led to widespread protests. The followers of the Sikh Panth and the radicals launched a movement against the Jathedars, 'and accused that the pardon was granted at the behest of the SAD, which is eyeing Dera votes in 2017 assembly polls'.[9]

CONFLICT BETWEEN INSTITUTIONALIZED SIKH RELIGION AND DERAS

This context led to the articulation of the conflict between the institutionalized Sikh religion and the followers of the Dera who mainly come from the lower castes. Deras are the product of a liberal cultural tradition and have been the symbols of plurality and diversification of the religious spectrum. Historically, their evolution has been intermeshed with the drive to consolidate the Sikh religion. The prominent Deras which evolved as a reaction to the consolidation of the Sikh religion were Nanakpanthis, Sewapanthis, Nirmalas and Udasis. The contemporary Deras are not the offshoot of Sikhism. These are the congregations of followers transcending religious, caste and class divisions through reverence for the living Guru.

These Deras have not only represented marginalized social sections but have also questioned the monolithic articulations of Sikhism leading to discrimination against the lower castes. It has led to conflict with the institutionalized religion. There have been incidents of violence involving various Dera followers with sections of Sikhs such as Dera Nirankari in 1978, Dera Bhaniarwala in 2001, Dera Sacha Sauda in 2008–2009, Dera Nurmahal in 2002 and Dera Sachkhand Ballan in 2009–2010.[10] The causes for these conflicts are rooted in the various practices and rituals of the Deras such as the notion of the living Guru which is strictly opposed in institutionalized Sikhism and imitation of the imagery of Sikh Gurus by the Dera heads.

There are six major Deras in Punjab, including Radha Soami, Namdhari, Dera Sacha Sauda, Nurmahal, Nirankari and Dera Sachkhand Balan. They draw their discourses from multiple traditions such as, Islam, Sufism, Kabir Panth, Christianity and Sikhism and couch them in regional dialects, myths and symbols. Dera 'babas' (self-appointed Godmen) excessively rely on oral discourses. In this region, oral tradition is dominant and text reading is not very popular. Therefore, these 'babas' become the sole mediators between God and the devotees for imparting holistic knowledge and guidance in politics.

Together, these Deras have influence in around 56 constituencies. The Radha Soami in 19, Dera Sacha Sauda in 27, Dera Nurmahal in

8, Dera Nirankari in 4, Dera Ballan in 8 and Dera Namdhari in 2 constituencies. Not all the deras are actively engaged in politics. However, Dera Sacha Sauda came into prominence in the 2007 elections when it openly supported the Congress. As a consequence, the Akalis suffered a loss in around 21 assembly constituencies. Unlike the past, the Akali Dal did not make any emotional appeal like danger to the Sikh Panth or exhibiting any frenzy against the followers of the competing Deras. On the contrary, they were accused of patronizing these deras, particularly Dera Sacha Sauda, by managing a pardon for the Dera chief who angered Sikhs by imitating their Guru.

DESECRATION OF RELIGIOUS SECTS

Along with this, a number of incidents of Guru Granth Sahib's desecration were reported in 2015 mainly from the districts of Muktsar, Bathinda, Faridkot and Moga. On 12 October, the first incident of desecration was reported from Bargari, Faridkot district. In this incident, 110 torn *Angs* (pages) of the Sikh holy book were found.[11]

Between 13 and 16 October 2015, a number of Sikh organizations held protest marches. On 14 October 2015, around 6,000 protesters clashed with the police and two died in the police firing, while more than 50 people were injured, including 24 policemen at Behbal Kalan. The Government of Punjab appointed a Judicial Commission headed by a retired judge of the Punjab and Haryana High Court to investigate the incidents. The protests also spread to different districts of Punjab. The radical organizations and AAP members launched a morcha in Bargari. Their main demands were: (a) punishment to the culprits of sacrilege of Guru Granth Sahib, (b) action against the police involved in Behbal Kalan firing and (c) release of the Sikh prisoners who had completed their jail terms.[12] These protests adversely affected the SAD performance in the elections.

RADICALIZATION OF RELIGIOUS AGENDA LEADING TO ALIENATION OF THE URBAN HINDUS

The widespread protest against securing a pardon for the sacrilege committed by Dera Sacha Sauda Baba Ram Rahim from the Sikh clergy, stealing of the holy Guru Granth Sahib from a Sikh temple and its denigration, and the police firing leading to the killing of protesters made the SAD vulnerable in its own support base. These protests culminated into the organization of the Sarbat Khalsa on 9 November 2015 on the outskirts of Amritsar, with an aim of strengthening Sikh religious institutions and traditions.

The organization of the Sarbat Khalsa by the protagonists of a separate Sikh State with alleged support of the Congress and the AAP led to the alienation of not only of Dera followers but also urban Hindus and liberal Sikhs.[13] No doubt, it gave the Congress party and the AAP an advantage in the traditional Akali support base in a particular region of Punjab.[14] The political battle was being fought in the religious domain (Panthic) rather than on economic and social development, the agrarian crisis and governance deficits.

After winning the 2017 elections, the Congress party continued to operate in the religious domain. The Punjab Assembly on 28 August 2018, adopted an amendment to the Indian Penal Code (IPC) that imposes a life sentence upon those convicted of desecrating the Guru Granth Sahib, Bhagavad Gita, Quran and Bible, with the intention of hurting the religious feelings of people. Earlier, Section 295A of the IPC already provided for imprisonment up to three years for deliberate and malicious acts intended to outrage religious feelings. The amendment has been described as 'bad in law' and 'politically expedient'. Thirty-four former civil servants reminded the Chief Minister Captain Amarinder Singh of Congress' chequered history of fishing in the communal waters for short-term political ends.[15]

The Congress position generated fear among the Hindu minority in Punjab as well as among the Dalits. The Congress was explicit in competing to capture Sikh religious institutions and conciliation with the radical Sikhs. This might help the Congress to win elections, but it is bound to produce tragedies by polarizing identity politics. The struggle to capture Sikh religious institutions, such as the Shiromani Gurdwara Parbandhak Committee (SGPC) and Akal Takht, by the Congress targeting Akali Dal's control of these institutions is bound to boomerang as had happened earlier. The protests by the radicals supported by the Congress have also very carefully appropriated the absence of the counter narrative to 'Khalistan'.[16] The state, on the one hand, allowed the coming together of fundamentalist groups in order to appropriate the religious (Panthic) constituency and, on the other, its inept handling of the violation of the sanctity of the Sikh religious scriptures provided enough fodder to the fringe groups to articulate their divisive agenda in the mainstream politics.

The voting pattern in elections reflected this polarization. In the 2017 assembly elections, the vote share of the main political parties decreased as compared to the 2012 assembly elections. The Congress party's vote share decreased by 1 per cent with 77 seats, that of the SAD by 10 per cent with an all-time low 15 seats and the BJP by 2 per cent with 3 seats. The vote share of the AAP remained the same with 24 per cent as compared to the 2014 parliament elections. In terms of the seat share, it registered a decline from 33 assembly segments in 2014 to 20 assembly seats in 2017 elections. This was a watershed election for the SAD and the AAP (see Table 8.1).

An unusual understanding between the Punjab Congress and the BJP to defeat the AAP changed the electoral dynamics in Punjab. The AAP was seen as a formidable challenge by the Congress. It was also seen as supporting the agenda of Sikh radicals much to the dislike of BJP urban supporters.[17] The Congress and the BJP entered into a pact that the BJP will support the Congress candidate in all constituencies other than 23 constituencies contested by the BJP. The BJP will not extend support to its alliance partner the SAD in the remaining 96 constituencies. This can be easily discerned from the shift in the urban vote share as it constitutes the traditional vote bank of the BJP. The urban vote share of the Congress went up from 43.5 per cent in 2012 to 49 per cent in 2017, while the urban vote share of the BJP declined from 28 per cent in 2012 to 19 per cent in 2017. It can be safely concluded that the understanding advantaged the Congress.

In the 2019 elections, there was no pact between the Congress and the BJP. The urban vote share of the BJP increased from 19 per cent in 2017 to 27 per cent in 2019. And the Congress party's urban vote share declined from 49 per cent in 2017 to 45 per cent in the 2019 election (see Table 8.2).

Table 8.1 *Punjab Elections 2012–2019*

	Parliament				Assembly			
Year	Party	Contested	Won	Vote %	Party	Contested	Won	Vote %
2012					BJP	23	12	7.18
					SAD	94	56	34.73
					CPI	14	–	0.82
					CPM	9	–	0.16
					BSP	117	–	4.29
					INC	117	46	40.09
					PPOP	92	–	5.16
					Others	612	3	7.56
2014	BJP	3	2	8.77				
	SAD	10	4	26.37				
	CPI	5	0	0.4				
	CPM	3	0	0.13				
	INC	13	3	33.19				
	BSP	13	0	1.91				
	AAP	13	4	24.47				
	Others	75	0	1.15				
	IND	118	0	3.61				

(Continued)

Table 8.1 *(Continued)*

Year	Parliament				Assembly			
	Party	Contested	Won	Vote %	Party	Contested	Won	Vote %
2017					BJP	23	3	5.43
					CPI	23	0	0.22
					CPM	12	0	0.07
					INC	117	77	38.77
					SAD	94	15	25.42
					AAP	112	20	23.88
					LIP	6	2	1.23
					BSP	111	0	1.53
					Others	647	0	3.43
2019	BJP	3	2	9.74				
	SAD	10	2	27.76				
	INC	13	8	40.58				
	AAP	13	1	7.46				
	CPI	2	0	0.31				
	CPM	1	0	0.08				
	BSP	3	0	3.53				
	Others	233	0	10.54				

Source: Election Commission of India Reports (2012, 2014, 2017 and 2019).

Table 8.2 *Location-Wise, Party-Wise Seats Contested and Won, and Votes Polled in 2012, 2014, 2017 and 2019*

	INC				BJP				SAD				AAP			
	2012	2014	2017	2019	2012	2014	2017	2019	2012	2014	2017	2019	2012	2014	2017	2019
Rural	61	61	61	61	5	5	5	5	56	56	56	56	–	61	60	61
Won	**19**	**11**	**37**	**37**	**3**	**5**	**1**	**5**	**38**	**28**	**11**	**13**	**–**	**17**	**12**	**2**
%	**39.4**	**32.5**	**36.9**	**40.8**	**3.4**	**3.6**	**2.5**	**5.0**	**41.1**	**34.9**	**30.4**	**32.2**	**–**	**22.3**	**24.3**	**6.1**
Urban	15	15	15	15	10	10	10	10	5	5	5	5	–	15	12	15
Won	**6**	**13**	**14**	**11**	**5**	**–**	**0**	**2**	**3**	**–**	**0**	**1**	**–**	**1**	**0**	**0**
%	**43.5**	**43.6**	**49.1**	**44.6**	**27.9**	**18.6**	**18.6**	**26.6**	**12.7**	**8.1**	**7.2**	**11.9**	**–**	**17.9**	**15.7**	**2.3**
Semi-urban	41	41	41	41	8	8	8	8	33	33	33	33	–	41	40	41
Won	**21**	**13**	**26**	**21**	**4**	**3**	**2**	**7**	**15**	**9**	**4**	**7**	**–**	**15**	**8**	**5**
%	**40.1**	**30.7**	**38.4**	**39.0**	**6.5**	**7.3**	**5.8**	**10.0**	**31.8**	**25.8**	**23.6**	**27.5**	**–**	**29.9**	**25.8**	**11.0**
Total	117	117	117	117	23	23	23	23	94	94	94	94	–	117	112	117
Won	**46**	**37**	**77**	**69**	**12**	**8**	**3**	**14**	**56**	**37**	**15**	**21**	**–**	**33**	**20**	**7**
%	**40.1**	**33.2**	**38.3**	**40.6**	**7.2**	**6.7**	**5.4**	**9.2**	**34.7**	**28.4**	**25.4**	**28.2**	**–**	**24.5**	**23.9**	**7.4**

Source: Calculated from Constituency-wise Electoral Rolls and Election Commission of India Reports (2012, 2014, 2017 and 2019).

The electoral outcomes in the 2019 parliamentary elections were in conformity with the 2014 elections in which the voters were no longer bound to a political party and functioned as footloose voters. The only difference was that it worked to the disadvantage of the AAP and the SAD. Comparing the 2014 parliament elections to the 2019 elections, the percentage vote share of the political parties, that is, the Congress (40.5) with eight seats, the BJP (9.7) with two seats, the SAD (27.7) with two seats increased and the only party with decreased vote share was the AAP (7.4) with one seat (see Table 8.1).

In this election, the AAP was reduced to a position of mega spoiler. It made the Congress party lose in 11 and the SAD–BJP alliance in 30 assembly constituencies. The Lok Insaaf Party made the BJP–SAD alliance lose in three constituencies.

This was also reflected in terms of electoral competition. The 2019 parliamentary elections were less volatile as compared to the 2014 elections. In this election, as compared to 2014, the effective number of the parties by votes decreased from 3.7 to 2.3 and the effective number of the parties by seats decreased from 4.02 to 3.8 (see Table 8.3).[18] This clearly indicated that Punjab returned to its traditional bipartisan election mode.

In terms of electoral volatility,[19] it continued to be high, but was not as high as in 2014. Between 2009 and 2014, it was 25 and was

Table 8.3 *Taagepera and Shugart Index for Parliamentary Elections in Punjab 2004–2019*

Election Year	Effective Number of Parties by Votes	Effective Number of Parties by Seats
2004	2.19	3.93
2009	2.09	3.00
2014	3.76	4.02
2019	2.32	3.85

Source: Calculated from Election Commission of India Reports Punjab (2004, 2009, 2014 and 2019).

reduced to 17.1 between 2014 and 2019. It was 11 between 2004 and 2009 (see Table 8.4). This shift worked to the disadvantage of the AAP.

The BJP and the Congress could garner maximum advantage at the expense of both the SAD and the AAP. The BJP and the Congress won more seats for each percentage of votes polled in the 2019 parliamentary elections; the BJP with a multiplier of 1.5 and the Congress with a multiplier of 1.5 as compared to the SAD with a multiplier of 0.5 and the AAP with a multiplier of 1.03[20] (see Table 8.5). Thus, the BJP and the Congress in the 2019 election showed a greater capacity to translate vote share into seats as compared to the SAD and the AAP.

The outcome of 2019 parliamentary elections can be understood in the context of political developments from 2014 onwards. These developments scripted the withering away of the AAP from Punjab's electoral scene.

WHY PUNJAB WENT THE MODI WAY?

Punjab could stand out as Amarinder played Modi in Punjab. He remained grounded refusing to be trapped and refrained from blindly following the Congress Party's plank, that is, Modi bashing. He appropriated and extended Prime Minister Modi's narrative on national security and at the same time nurtured Punjab-specific identity politics.

AMARINDER PLAYED MODI IN PUNJAB

After the Pulwama attack, he echoed Prime Minister Modi's assertion, but with significant additions. He asserted that, 'Pakistan killed 41, we should kill 82', calling for 'tit for tat'. He further added that, 'Pakistan can't hold India to ransom just because they are a nuclear nation, even we are'. He cautioned Pakistan on terror and at the same time endorsed the building of the Kartarpur Corridor as a promotion of the people-to-people contact enabling Sikhs to more easily visit their religious shrines in Pakistan. He endorsed Prime Minister Modi's stand unlike other Congressmen, to act on a mix of military, diplomatic and economic measures against Pakistan.

Table 8.4 *Pedersen Index of Electoral Volatility*

Election Years	BJP	AAP	SAD(B)	SAD(M)	CPI	CPM	INC	BSP	LIP	SAD(T)	Others	Total Net Change (TNC)	Pedersen Index of Electoral Volatility
2004–2009	0.42	0	0.43	3.43	2.22	1.67	11.06	1.92	–	–	0.99	22.14	11.07
2009–2014	1.29	24.47	7.48	0.1	0.07	0.01	12.04	3.84	–	–	0.23	49.53	24.77
2014–2019	0.97	17.01	1.39	0.12	0.09	0.05	7.39	1.62	3.45	0.08	2.13	34.29	17.15

Source: Calculated from Election Commission of India Reports Punjab (2004, 2009, 2014 and 2019).

Table 8.5 *Seat-Vote Multiplier for Different Parties in Previous Parliament Elections*

Election Years	BJP	AAP	SAD (B)	INC
2004	2.20	–	1.80	0.45
2009	0.76	–	0.91	1.36
2014	1.75	1.26	1.17	0.70
2019	1.58	1.03	0.55	1.52

Source: Calculated from Election Commission of India Reports Punjab (2004, 2009, 2014 and 2019).

He also disagreed with the Congress Party's position of questioning the reliability and effectiveness of the army strikes against Pakistan. He refused to comment on the veracity of the number of terrorists killed in the strikes, 'whether it was one or 100, the message had gone loud and clear that the nation will not let the killing of its innocent soldiers and citizens go unpunished'.[21] This appealed to 'patriotic and nationalist Punjabis' irrespective of religious and caste affiliations.

BLENDED NATIONALISM WITH IDENTITY POLITICS

Not only this, the Congress Chief Minister blended nationalism with identity politics as has been done by the BJP in other states. At the national level, alleged violations against cows led to violent reactions from Hindu fundamentalists. Similarly, in Punjab, alleged desecration of religious books led to extreme reactions. Religious sentiments were invoked and, in turn, it provided fodder to the radical elements. Amarinder Singh in a statement to the electronic media accused Pakistan's ISI of trying to destabilize Punjab by desecration of religious books, including the Guru Granth Sahib, the Gita and the Bible. He distinguished between desecration and the police action in Bargari. Whereas the 'Bargari brigade' led by the Congress ministers targeted the rival political party, the Akali Dal which engaged in a counter campaign. It became a toxic mix of nationalism and religious identity that was nurtured in India and Punjab.

DECIMATION OF THE AAP

Another major factor in the decimation of the AAP in Punjab is back to bipolar politics. The vote share of the AAP declined from 24 per cent in 2014 to 7 per cent in the 2019 elections. In all the constituencies except Bathinda, Sangrur and Khadoor Sahib, the vote shares of both the losing and the winning parties, that is, the Congress and the Akali Dal have increased at the expense of the AAP.

This election also provided resurgence to the Akali–BJP alliance. The vote share of the Akali Dal increased by 2 per cent as compared to the 2014 parliament elections and the vote share of the BJP increased by 1 per cent from 2014 to 2019 elections. And, as compared to 2017 assembly elections, the combined vote share of both the BJP and the SAD increased by 7 per cent in the 2019 parliament elections.

The SAD–BJP alliance doubled their seat share and the Congress party's share declined by 14 per cent as compared to the 2017 elections. Significantly, the Congress could maintain its rural constituencies, whereas its support in the semi-urban and urban constituencies has declined. The Akali Dal could not increase their seat share in rural Punjab. Their major gains are in the semi-urban and urban constituencies.

TAKEAWAYS

So, what are the takeaways of the elections in Punjab? First, anti-incumbency campaigns devoid of any ideological persuasion without a regional and positive agenda may not be appealing. For instance, in Punjab the SAD did not even bring out its own manifesto and announced a Common Minimum Programme along with the BJP. These parties did not even raise their traditional demands such as transfer of Chandigarh and Punjabi-speaking areas to Punjab, sharing of the river waters and formal consultation forums for the regional parties in decision-making at the national level. Other issues such as petroleum prices, fertilizer subsidies, doubling the farmers' income and employment generation policies also received little attention.

Another lesson is that the regional parties should develop their own vision and thoughts on national security. These include building people-to-people connections in South Asia, opening of trade with Pakistan to the benefit of Punjab farmers and overcoming agrarian distress rather than succumbing to a particular kind of discourse on national security or stand in negation.

The regionalization of the political and economic agenda is needed to reinforce diversity sensitivity and to promote a region-specific development paradigm.

NOTES

1. Pramod Kumar, 'Coalition Politics in Punjab: From Communal Polarisation to Catchall Parties?' In *Coalition Politics in India: Selected Issues at the Centre and the States*, ed. E. Sridharan (New Delhi: Academic Foundation, 2014), 221–223.
2. Ibid, 255.
3. Interviews with the senior Congress and the BJP leaders from 17 December 2016 to 27 December 2016 in Chandigarh.
4. A thoroughgoing polarization of Punjab politics has been prevented partly by the presence of a large SC population, of uncertain religious allegiance, to whom all parties must appeal. Second, the leading secular parties in Punjab, particularly Congress and CPI, have successfully appealed to both Hindus and Sikhs in the past. Here too the parties have not been simply reflecting social tendencies, but they have been actively promoting an ideology of secularism and inter-communal political cooperation. The dynamic of the entire system and its dualism has consisted in the drives of the communal parties, particularly the Akali Dal, to monopolise support from one community, and the contrary efforts of the Congress to build inter-communal support. See Paul R., Brass, *Language, Religion and Politics in India* (London: Cambridge University Press, 1974), 399.
5. Pramod Kumar, 'An Election of Many Firsts: Can Punjab's Politicians Get Their Act Together in Time and Reconnect with the Average Voter?', *The Hindu* (14 November 2016).
6. Ibid.
7. Sikhs following the 10th and the last Guru started the tradition of deciding matters concerning the community at the biennial meetings which took place at Amritsar on the first of Baisakhi and on Diwali. These assemblies came to be known as the Sarbat Khalsa and a resolution passed by it became a *Gurmata* (decree of the Guru). The Sarbat Khalsa appointed *jathedars* (group leaders), chose agents and entrusted them with powers to negotiate on behalf of the Sikhs. The first event occurred in 1733. See Khushwant Singh, *A History of*

the Sikhs. Volume 1: 1469–1838, 2nd edition (New Delhi: Oxford University Press, 1999), 116–119.

The Five Member Panthic Committee (FMPC) declared the formation of Khalistan on 29 April 1986, spelling out 'social structure of Khalistan' whose main objective was the 'welfare of humanity (*sarbat da bhala*) and service to society' following Gurbani: 'Condemned are those hand and feet that do not serve others, since all else is futile activity' (1986, 26). Its policy intends to promote cultural life, encourage unity of humankind and feeling of cooperation. The humanity (sic) would not be allowed to be divided on bases of caste, untouchability, social inequality, rural-urban, black and white and such other arbitrary divisions. These would be abolished with state power (FMPC 1986). Gurmata adopted on 26 January 1986 makes it clear: 'This august assembly of Sarbat Khalsa clarifies that Sikhs are slaves in India and freedom is their fundamental right'. See Birinder Pal Singh, 'Sikh Militants' Terms of Discourse: Religion, Khalistan/Nation and Violence', *Sikh Formations* 12, no. 2–3 (2016): 191–206.

8. Kamaldeep Singh Brar, 'Punjab Withdraws Security of Takht Damdama Sahib', *Hindustan Times* (18 December 2014).
9. Harkirat Singh, 'Akal Takht Revokes Pardon to Dera Head Gurmeet Ram Rahim', *Hindustan Times* (17 October 2015).
10. Pramod Kumar, 'Punjab Polls: Doles, Deras and Drugs', *The Tribune* (28 January 2017).
11. In 2015, between the 13th and 16th of October, several incidents were reported regarding desecration from various places in Punjab. For instance, the *Angs* of the Guru Granth Sahib were found torn, 35 *Angs* in Mishriwala village of Ferozepur district, 39 *Angs* in Bath village of Tarn Taran and a 3-inch cut was reported in 745 *Angs* in Kohrian village of Faridkot. Along with the Guru Granth Sahib, incidents were also reported of torn *Angs* from the Panj Granth (a smaller text of selected verses from the Guru Granth Sahib). Several other incidents were also reported such as in Nawanshahr three saroops were burnt and in Muktsar (Kotli Ablu) a Gurudwara caught fire along with its Bir (burnt to ashes).
12. Surjit Singh, 'We Support Cause of Bargari Morcha, Linking It with ISI Unfair, Says Former Cabinet Minister Sewa Singh Sekhwan', *Hindustan Times* (18 October 2015).
13. The event was opposed by the SAD. It alleged that the Congress and the AAP are behind the anti-national and secessionist forces who want to stoke the fires of communalism in the state. *The Economic Times*, 'Congress, Foreign Forces behind Sarbat Khalsa: Sukhbir Singh Badal' (13 November 2015).
14. Pramod Kumar, 'Back to the State. A Lesson from Punjab: High Command Politics Is Past Its Sell-by Date', *The Indian Express* (13 March 2017).
15. *The Tribune*, 'Withdraw Anti-sacrilege Bills: Ex-bureaucrats to Amarinder. Say Blasphemy Laws Prone to Misuse Against Minorities' (4 September 2018). Similar views were also expressed by a senior political analyst: 'this is corrosive

pattern of competitive communalism that pushed Punjab into tragedy of terrorism in the past, as that again threatens to intensify religious radicalism in the state'. Ajai Sahni, 'Another Weapon to the Bigoted', *The Tribune* (2018, September 1). Making religious sentiments the basis for law is a recipe for competitive mobilisation and conflict not at peace. Pratap Bhanu Mehta, 'A Blasphemous Law', *The Indian Express* (25 August 2018).

16. The consensus in the country to ensure justice for the Sikhs butchered in 1984 anti-Sikh riots was extended to rehabilitate the terrorists. This provided claim to a section instigating revenge for the hurt Sikh psyche and a separate Sikh state. This was further reinforced by eventually conceding the twice denied appeal of the Dal Khalsa for conferment of martyrdom on the leaders of Khalistan by the Akal Takht. These organizations, after having acquired legitimacy, raised their claim to control the SGPC and the Akal Takht and 'liberate' these from the SAD. Pramod Kumar, 'Rising Tide of Anger in Punjab', *Deccan Herald* (22 November 2015).
17. Punjab has a history of political contestants who can be labelled as spoilers. Spoilers are those who have a capacity to make others lose rather than their own win. These spoilers become relevant in constituencies where the difference between the winner and the runner up is small. Between 1997 and 2017 elections, the effective number of parties sharing votes was higher as compared to their share in seats. Parties such as BSP, SAD (Tohra) and People's Party of Punjab (PPP) and even the AAP act as a major spoiler in these elections without winning even a single seat. In 1997, the BSP polled 8 per cent of the votes without winning a seat led to the defeat of nine Congress, five Akalis and three BJP candidates. In 2002 elections, the vote share of BSP was polled around 6 per cent votes and it led to the defeat of 10 Congress, 15 Akalis and 2 BJP candidates. In these elections, Akali Dal (Tohra) got around 5 per cent votes that led to the defeat of seven Akali candidates. In 2007 elections, BSP emerged as the main spoiler with only 4 per cent votes which led to the defeat of 18 Congress and 14 Akali candidates. However, in 2012, there were two main spoilers, that is, BSP and PPP. BSP and PPP led to the defeat of 22 Congress and 29 SAD candidates. These political groups acted as spoilers for main political parties. The BSP and the PPP acted as wild cards, whereas Akali Dal (Tohra) group spoiled the chances of the Akali Dal (Badal). Pramod Kumar, 'Punjab Elections: Game of Spoilers', *Times of India* (9 January 2017).
18. *Taagepera and Shugart Index:* The effective number of parties, in terms of percentage of votes and seats secured by parties in elections to the directly elected chamber of parliament, is calculated for all the general elections using the Taagepera and Shugart procedure ($N=1/\sum Pi^2$ where Pi is the fractional share of i-th party and $\sum$ stand for the summation of overall components).
19. *Pedersen Index of Electoral Volatility:* It is computed by adding the absolute value of change in percentage of votes gained and lost by each party from one election to the next, then dividing the sum by 2. Thus, in a party system with 'n' parties, electoral volatility is=TNC/2, where TNC is total net change in

party support. The electoral volatility thus has a range of '0' (perfect stability of electoral support to parties, where no party gained or lost votes) to 100 (perfect instability, where there is total shift of voters from one party to the other).

20. *Seat-Vote Multiplier:* It is a ratio of the proportion of seats won by a party to the proportion of votes won by it. It is expression of the relationship between percentage of votes a party secures in an election and the seats it secures in the legislature. It is given by: 1/([vote share of a party/100]/[numbers of seats secured by the party/total number of seats in the legislature]).
21. *Punjab Today*, 'Pak Won't Hesitate to Nuke India If Faced with Defeat, Warns Capt Amarinder', Amritsar (4 March 2017).

Chapter 9

Madhya Pradesh

A Potemkin Village of the New India under Modi 2.0

Avinash Kumar and Pooja Rani

No pollster had predicted that the BJP in Madhya Pradesh was going to get a whopping nearly two-thirds of the total polled votes in the 2019 Lok Sabha Elections. The Congress was reduced to just one seat with only a little over 38 per cent vote share. BJP's candidate from Bhopal, Pragya Singh Thakur, an accused in the 2008 Malegaon bomb blasts, defeated Digvijay Singh, a senior Congress leader and two-time former chief minister of the state. The result of the 2019 Lok Sabha Elections was a shocker in several states, but what happened in Madhya Pradesh was truly mind boggling.

Madhya Pradesh along with Rajasthan and Chhattisgarh in the Hindi heartland are three states where the electoral verdict against the BJP in December 2018 forced people to start believing in the rise of new politics at the national level. The Congress party had suffered its worst defeat in independent India in the 2014 parliamentary elections. It was written off until as late as the Uttar Pradesh assembly elections in November 2017 when suddenly it bounced back with gusto. The Congress party under its new leadership was being recognized as a game changer that had smashed the aura of invincibility built around Prime Minister Narendra Modi and the BJP President, Amit Shah.

What led to this change in the voting pattern and behaviour of the people in just five months? This chapter makes an attempt to decode the 2019 victory of the BJP in Madhya Pradesh. The chapter is divided in two parts. The first part attempts to explain what happened in the state assembly election in 2018 and the second part attempts to understand the factors that shaped the outcome of the Lok Sabha election in May 2019.

HARD-FOUGHT VICTORY OF THE CONGRESS IN 2018

A careful examination of the result of the assembly election reveals that the victory was not emphatic. The Congress formed its first government in the reorganized Madhya Pradesh after three successive defeats since 2003. The party had suffered a crippling blow by the BJP in 2003 which won 173 out of 230 seats and 42.5 per cent votes as against the Congress' 38 seats and 31.6 per cent votes. In the subsequent assembly elections, the insignificant gains made by the Congress were primarily because of the anti-incumbency factor of the ruling BJP. In 2018, it was expected that the Congress party riding on the wave of farmers' anger would be able to trounce the BJP. But the Congress once again failed to reach the majority mark. It ended up being just behind the magic figure of 116 seats with 114. It needed to ally with the Bahujan Samaj Party (BSP), the Samajwadi Party (SP) and a few independent MLAs to form the government. BJP bagged 109 seats, only 56 less than its 2013 tally, and equal percentage of votes as that of the Congress.

It is particularly notable that this victory of the Congress party in the state assembly happened at a time when there was a BJP-led NDA government at the Centre. So it was seen more as a vote against the Modi government than the anti-incumbency of Shivraj Singh Chouhan's state government. Chouhan was successful in retaining his image as a popular leader by winning his own assembly seat of Budhni by a comfortable margin of nearly 59,000 votes. The Congress increased its tally from 9 seats in 2013 to 35 out of the 66 assembly constituencies in the farm belt of Malwa–Nimar. It also registered significant victories in the tribal-dominated districts of Dhar, Jhabua, Alirajpur and Khargone as well as Mahakoshal, winning 24 out of 38 seats in the region. Congress swept the Gwalior–Chambal region by winning 21 out of the 27 seats. The only region in which the Congress did very badly was Vindhya Pradesh, bagging only 6 out of 30 seats, mainly due to the BSP factor.

Figure 9.1 shows the change in seats won by political parties in the assembly election in 2018 over the assembly election in 2013.

Of the total 230 seats, the BJP and the Congress were able to hold 110 seats; Congress on 31 out of its 58 seats and BJP on 79 out of 165 seats won in 2013. Congress gained 83 seats from the BJP and the BJP gained 30 seats from Congress. Among the other seven seats, the BSP gained two, both from the BJP; and independent candidates gained five seats, four from the BJP and one from Congress (see Figure 9.1).

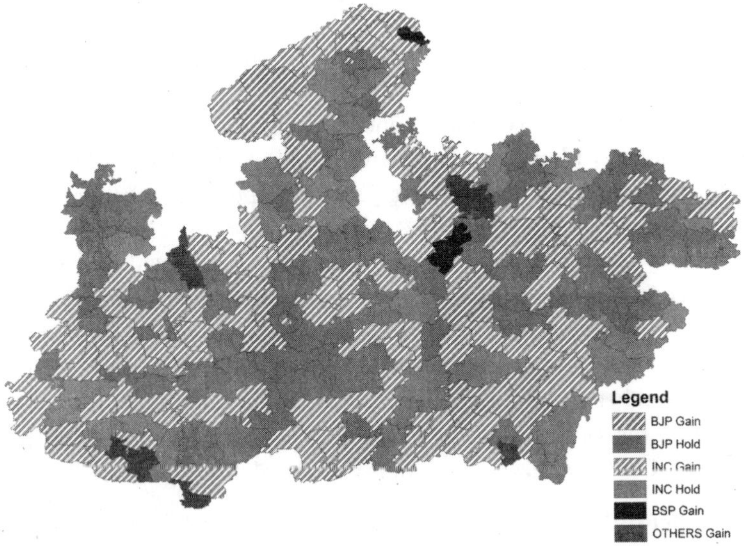

Figure 9.1 *Constituency-Wise Change in 2018 Assembly Election over 2013*

Source: https://www.ndtv.com/elections/madhya-pradesh/all-phases (accessed on 26 September 2019).

Note: This figure is not to scale. It does not represent any authentic national or international boundaries and is used for illustrative purposes only.

That the Modi–Shah duo lacked a magic wand was expressed not just by independent observers but also within the BJP and Rashtriya Sayamsevak Sangh (RSS). The BJP's formal statements kept asserting the anti-incumbency and local factors, but many insiders were reported to have accepted that the party's defeat was because of the Central government's policies, particularly the shift from developmental promises made in 2014 to issues such as the Ram temple and name change of towns and districts.[1] Many within the BJP were reported to have emphasized the agrarian crisis marked by the falling price of agricultural commodities resulting in farmer suicides. The Congress had started making inroads into the minds of people especially after the Mandsaur police firing in which six farmers, participating in a protest demanding loan waivers and a minimum support price for their produce, were killed in June 2017. According to state government reports, more than 18,000 farmers committed suicide due to farm debt in the past 15 years.[2]

A year after the police firing in 2018, the Congress president marking the first anniversary of protesting farmers went to Mandsaur again as part of his Kisan Samriddhi Sankalp Rally. He promised to waive farmer loans within 10 days if voted to power in Madhya Pradesh. Congress reiterated this promise as its core agenda item when it began its poll campaign in September 2018 from Bhopal in its Sankalp Yatra roadshow. In the wake of this promise, it was reported that many farmers did not sell their paddy produce so as to reap the benefit of the promised loan waiver. The State Cooperative Marketing Federation procured just 67,148 metric ton (MT) of paddy from farmers between 15 November and 8 December 2018 as compared to 4.30 lakh MT between the same periods in 2017. The procurement carried out by the MP Civil Supplies Corporation was also almost negligible.[3]

Other issues were the persisting negative effect of demonetization on a large section of the population and that of the hurriedly imposed GST, particularly on the trading community. According to the CSDS pre-poll survey held between 18 and 25 October 2018, unemployment and price rise were reported as the two biggest election issues. The survey also reported that although the Congress was doing well among rural voters, it was not mainly on account of distress in the farming sector. About 43 per cent of farmers were reported to have said that they would vote for the BJP as opposed to 40 per cent of non-farmers who said so. In other words, farmers, except the agricultural labourers, were reported in the survey to still be with the BJP.[4]

When the results were announced on 11 December 2018, the Congress lost seven out of the eight assembly seats in the Mandsaur parliamentary constituency, but it surprised many by its impact on not just the farmers but a large section of the state's population. The Malwa region, with its 66 assembly seats (nearly 30% of the assembly total) has always been the key to electoral success in the state. It actually saw the highest jump in its voting percentage as compared to the previous election.[5] The Congress gained 26 seats more than its tally in 2013 (from 9 to 35) in this region. The high turnout in the farmer-dominated districts, including those in the Bundelkhand region, clearly indicated that the CSDS pre-poll survey had failed in capturing the rural voters' anger against the government. What the CSDS pre-poll survey reported significantly was that very few respondents spontaneously identified emotive issues such as the Ayodhya dispute, cow protection, reservation, triple talaq and so on as important election issues. It also pointed out that among those voters who considered these issues to be very important in the election, Congress was favoured over BJP by a fairly large proportion.

Thus, while the victory of Congress did not guarantee it with a smooth ride in power, what emerged as a serious concern for BJP after the election was that its communal agenda of exploiting the religious sentiments of Hindus was no longer a viable electoral strategy for ensuring electoral victory not just in Madhya Pradesh but also in other Hindi heartland states.

POST-ASSEMBLY

Unexpectedly, the Congress legislature party chose Kamal Nath instead of the young leader Jyotiraditya Scindia as the leader of the legislative party as the chief minister of Madhya Pradesh. Soon after the swearing-in ceremony in December 2018, the state government announced its decision to waive off the farm loan of up to ₹2 lakhs. It claimed that more than 34 lakh farmers would benefit. In February 2019, the government also quashed the BJP's flagship scheme, the Bhavantar Bhugtan Scheme, that is, paying farmers the difference between minimum support price (MSP) and marketing prices, launched in 2017 after the Mandsaur farmers' protest. It maintained that the BJP scheme led to only benefiting the *banias* (businessmen).[6]

The BJP countered by alleging that the government's loan waiver was nothing but a political gimmick, warning of a state-wide protest against the government's decision to discontinue its Bhavantar Bhugtan Scheme. The real game, however, started with the beginning of the Model Code of Conduct in early March 2019 for the parliamentary elections due in April-May 2019. The state government claimed that until then farm loans of only 25 lakh farmers were waived off, and the remaining approvals would happen after the Model Code of Conduct gets removed. This gave an opportunity to the BJP and it started alleging that the Congress government never intended to waive off loans of the farmers in the first place. The party mobilized those farmers whose loans waiver applications were pending.

Screenshots of messages sent to the farmers were uploaded on social media sites where the government stated that the pleas would be approved only after the Lok Sabha polls.[7] But the BJP knew that its tactics wouldn't counter the increased vote base of the Congress and it needed other strategies to repeat its 2014 performance. RSS provided the key.

STRATEGIZING FOR THE 2019 LOK SABHA ELECTIONS

While the state was witnessing competitive politics, the country witnessed the killing of 40 jawans of the Central Reserve Police Force (CRPF) in a terror attack in Jammu and Kashmir's Pulwama district on 14 February 2019. With Lok Sabha elections two months away, this obviously was going to dominate the political discourse. But what followed was much more than the expected.

BJP confronting the growing nation-wide economic crisis, particularly after the defeat in the three assembly elections in the Hindi heartland, saw it as an opportune moment to weave its ideology of

Hindutva into the politics of muscular nationalism. It carefully scripted the national security debate post-Pulwama attack, including the February 26 Balakot air strike across the Pakistan border by the Indian Air Force, projecting Modi as the only protector of the country. By the time the Election Commission announced the 17th General Election on March 10, this package of nationalism coated with Hindutva had become a commanding narrative consuming all parts of the country, especially the Hindi heartland.

This became quite evident in all of Modi's election campaigns post-Pulwama. He spoke almost nothing about his five years of achievement or his much-hyped policies such as demonetization and GST. His election speeches were a display of Hindutva nationalism projecting himself and his party as the only saviours of the country. He went to the extent of suggesting that the opposition's rise to power would only help Pakistan. In an election rally in Jammu as early as on 28 March, Modi claimed, 'Pakistan is praying that the 'chowkidar' should somehow lose the elections....'[8] Referring to the Balakot air strikes a day later in his election rally in Koraput, Odisha, Modi said, 'Pak is counting dead bodies, but opposition seeks proof.'[9]

On 1 April while launching the BJP–Shiv Sena alliance's campaign in Wardha, commenting on Congress President Rahul Gandhi's decision to contest from Wayanad in Kerala (apart from his traditional constituency of Amethi in Uttar Pradesh), Modi said:

> The Congress insulted Hindus. People have decided to punish it in the election. Leaders of that party are now scared of contesting from constituencies dominated by majority (Hindu) population. That is why they are forced to take refuge in places where the majority is in a minority.[10]

At another public meeting in Badayun, Uttar Pradesh, on 13 April, Amit Shah, the BJP president, said:

> Rahul baba if your party wants to do 'Ilu' (an expression used in a 1990s Hindi song referring to romantic sweet talk) with terrorists you can do that. But our intention is clear, if a shot is fired, we will reply with a bomb.[11]

The complaint against all these communal remarks by the prime minister and his party men to the Election Commission by the opposition remained either unaddressed or they were given clean chits.[12]

With this narrative by the prime minister himself, the BJP successfully transformed Hindutva nationalism into a uniform national narrative. On the other hand, the RSS concentrated more on the careful organizational manoeuvres by looking at the caste and regional forces to accommodate them, even if it needed dropping of sitting MPs and seat adjustments.

DRAWING THE BATTLE LINES

Lok Sabha elections (seven phases in the country, beginning 11 April and ending on 19 May 19) in Madhya Pradesh were divided into four phases—on 29 April, 6 May, 12 May and 19 May (see Figure 9.2).

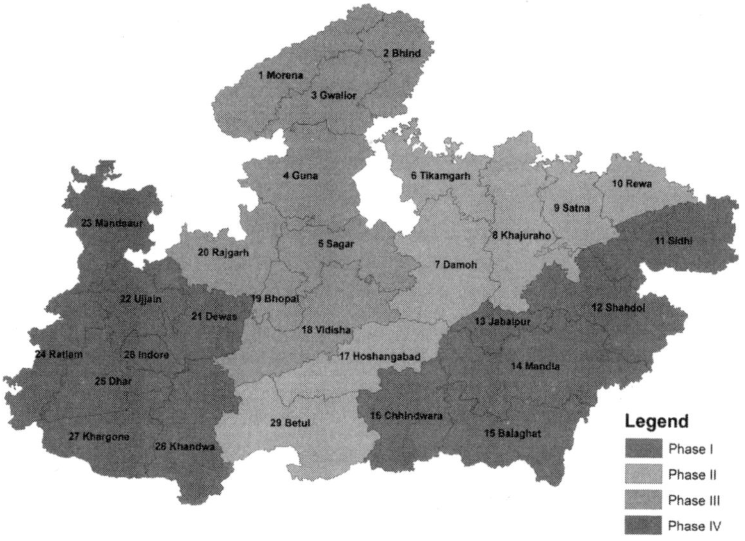

Figure 9.2 *Phase-Wise Lok Sabha Election in Madhya Pradesh*

Source: Arya, Rakesh, Map Library, CSRD, SSS, JNU.

Note: This figure is not to scale. It does not represent any authentic national or international boundaries and is used for illustrative purposes only.

Fearing the anti-incumbency factor, the BJP gave tickets to its sitting MPs in only 11 seats (Sidhi, Jabalpur, Mandla in the first phase; Tikamgarh, Damoh, Satna, Hoshangabad and Rewa in second phase; Rajgarh in third phase; and Mandsaur and Khandwa in fourth phase) out of its 26 constituencies. Of the total 10 MPs from the reserved seats for SCs and STs in 2014, only 2 (one SC and one ST) were repeated. Even the Gwalior MP, Narendra Singh Tomar, who had been a union minister in the Modi cabinet (2014–2019) was made to change his seat and contest from Morena. New candidates were fielded in the remainder 14.

For the Congress, the battle was tough as usual. While in one seat it repeated its popular candidate Jyotiraditya M. Scindia from Guna, on the other seat Nakul Nath replaced his father (Kamal Nath), who had become the chief minister of the state. In addition to that only 5 candidates who were the runner ups in the 2014 Lok Sabha Elections were fielded once again. The party's major focus with these new faces was issues that had given it an edge in the recently concluded assembly elections. However, in addition to the promises made earlier, it had hoped that Rahul Gandhi's latest pro-poor poll blitzkrieg (announced on 25 March 2019) the Nyuntam Aay Yojana (NYAY—an Indian version of the Universal Basic Income—UBI), which promised to credit ₹72,000 annually to the poorest people of the country, would help them consolidate the poor and the marginalized groups further into its fold.

Congress was also aware that it would be very difficult to bring back the SCs, STs and the OBCs who over time had gravitated towards the BJP. Attempting to address this situation, the Congress government passed an ordinance on 9 March 2019 that the reservation quota for OBCs would be raised from 14 to 27 per cent. OBC candidates were given party tickets in several regions rather than the *savarnas* (upper castes) who were still reluctant to openly support the Congress.[13] As regards the SCs and STs, the Congress had supported the movement of teachers on the issue of 200-point roster for the application of reservation in teaching positions for SCs and STs following a country-wide protest on the same.

In addition, it had also made a dent in BSP base by fielding Devashish Jarariya, a young and popular face of the BSP, for an SC reserved seat. On 28 March, after the Congress released its manifesto, simultaneous press conferences and workers' meets were held in all the state's 52 districts. District campaign committees were instructed to deploy 10 cadres per booth to promote NYAY to voters. But the Congress was weak organizationally resulting from internal factionalism that became visible during the Lok Sabha election. It was also short of adequate funds as expressed by many within the party.

Soon after NYAY was announced, BJP president Amit Shah directed the state's senior BJP leaders and MPs to increasingly attack the Congress party over national security. A BJP MP from the Vindhya region who admitted that the Modi government's failure to create jobs was hurting the party's prospects, reportedly said:

> He [Amit Shah] has asked us to portray the Congress' pledge to reduce the Army's presence in Kashmir and revoke the sedition law as an unpardonable compromise with terrorist forces. We have been asked to run a whisper campaign that the Congress is in collusion with the enemy [Pakistan/terrorists].[14]

Thus, it was quite clear from the beginning that the BJP would rely on Hindutva nationalism to take the focus off social and economic issues during the elections. The clear and distinct message of Hindutva nationalism being their core agenda became quite clear on 17 April, when the BJP announced that the Malegaon blast accused Pragya Singh Thakur as its candidate in Bhopal against the former chief minister Digvijay Singh. BJP wanted Thakur challenging Singh from Bhopal to be an open battle between the two ideas of India, that of secular nationalism versus Hindutva nationalism!

Thakur was released from jail in April 2017 after nearly seven years on medical grounds and was still being tried under the Unlawful Activities (Prevention) Act. The defence and justification for this move came from none other than Amit Shah who was reported to have said, 'Sadhvi Pragya will challenge the man who coined the term (saffron) terror, Digvijay Singh.'[15] He added that it was the Congress who after the Samjhauta Express blast in 2007 had pushed 'sadhus and sadhvis' into jail.[16] Thakur claimed that her fight was about giving justice to saffron and saints. Referring to Digvijay, she said:

> He has sown the seeds of defamation of our Sanatana Dharma and the saffron. He termed the saffron and Hindutva as terrorism.... I will ensure that the saffron gets its due respect.[17]

Pragya Singh Thakur was a clear indication to the committed RSS and BJP workers that there was no looking back from the Hindutva nationalism. Thakur continued this path with narrating stories of her torture for holding up the bhagwa flag, her curses and her deification of Nathuram Godse, and statements like, 'I am proud of the Babri demolition and was on the dome that day.'[18] She wore the symbolic notices sent by the Election Commission as the badges of honour! The message was strongly reinforced by the RSS, which independent of the BJP's campaign, concentrated all its energies on those seats (Dhar, Ratlam, Khargone, Dewas, Balaghat, Khajuraho and others) where the party seemed to be weak.[19]

RSS MADE THE DIFFERENCE

Dividends of this divisive agenda started paying off quickly. Several newspapers soon started reporting that issues such as falling crop prices, unemployment and inflation, water crisis, and GST which were important just six months before and had cost the BJP dearly in the assembly elections were fading from the political discourse. Anand Bhakto, while reporting for *Frontline* from Rewa observed:

> At an eatery at Chorhata, Rewa, Ramsharan Shukla and his friend were interrupted contemptuously when they voiced their disillusionment with the Modi government. 'See, here's someone who is cursing Modi *ji*. What hasn't he done for this country?' asked the visibly offended owner of the eatery. 'What has he done?' Ramcharan countered. 'Did he bring back black money? No, he allowed the loan defaulters to flee.' 'There is no alternative to Modi', announced one Chandrabhan. The others nodded. The sentiment was echoed everywhere. 'We vote

> whichever way the wind is blowing', said Lavkush Baiga, a tribal person from Gandhigram village, 10 km from Sidhi. 'He has worked for the poor; we are getting medicine at subsidised rates.' His friend, Bijay Kumar Baiga, said: 'Every child in our village knows Modi.' Rajaram Sen, a barber from Danga village, concurred....[20]

Reporting about Gwalior, Bhakto further added:

> People described their vote as a token of allegiance to Prime Minister Narendra Modi, who, in their assessment, is a strong leader. 'The country is under threat; we had this Pulwama terror strike. We need a headstrong leader like Modi. In any case, who is the alternative?' asked Arvind Mittal, a physician in Deen Dayal Nagar....[21]

Similarly, Tabassum Barnagarwala, reporting for the *Indian Express* from Bina, about 160 km from Bhopal, observed:

> Bina mushroomed on the industrial map with the Bharat Oman Refineries Ltd in 2011. A barbed-wire wall away, Guddi Bai Banjara (35) glances at the glass-and-steel facade from her hut in Agasode village, points to the reddish water in the local borewell. 'They took away our land, our source of income, and left us here to die', she fumes. Seven kilometres away, Bhakrai village awaits a water tanker every afternoon. The local well water has turned oily. Central government data shows the refinery acquired land from 12 villages in Bina. Residents there say prices have escalated since then. In 2016, the 'International Journal of Environmental Sciences' published the results of a geochemical study in Agasode, which found that chemicals linked to crude oil were contaminating the soil and water. And yet, all of this has never been a poll issue in Bina—not in 2014, not now. In Elections 2019, the talk here is all about 'Hindutva' and nationalism....[22]

The report further argued that:

> In town, Chandan Ahirwar's paan stall bears no BJP flags. But from 8 am till 10.30 pm, the RSS worker tells customers about the Balakot attack, the return of IAF pilot Abhinandan Varthaman, and the surgical strike of 2016.... There are several RSS workers who campaign in Bina as they go about their daily jobs, says Ahirwar.... When India struck in

> Pakistan's Balakot in February, about 1,500 km away in Dehri village, farmer Santosh Thakur says he was glued to television for two days. 'Has any other Indian Prime Minister had such guts. What did India do to Pakistan after the 2008 Mumbai attacks?' he asks. Thakur is part of a group sitting outside a temple nearby. 'Only BJP can secure this nation, build a Ram mandir', he says. 'Bina never saw progress, nor will it see. But it is time we vote for national security', says Raghuraj Singh, Thakur's neighbour.... 'The BJP would have never given her a ticket if she did not get a clean chit', Singh says. 'A woman cannot be part of terrorism'.... A short walk away, at the town square, is the tea stall of Santosh Verma. 'I voted for the Congress in the Assembly election. But in the Centre, there is no alternative to Modi,' he says. 'People at the stall discuss the Kashmir issue, and how Modi is the only man who can resolve it. I want Modi in the Centre...' he says....[23]

It was quite clear that even when the Congress workers were discussing local issues and the NYAY scheme, the voters only wanted to discuss national security and Hindutva. Soon the Congress fell into this trap and that became quite visible in one of the most keenly watched battles for Bhopal. Winning the Bhopal seat for Congress, which it hadn't won since 1984, would not have been an easy task for Digvijay Singh. But once Thakur entered the fray, Singh started to make mistakes which had repercussions across the state. Writing for *The Wire* Neeraj Mishra commented:

> He went about proving his Hindu credentials by organising *sadhu* roadshows and *yagnas*. He painted the town more saffron than BJP itself. The messaging was garbled.... The only strategy that would have worked was attacking Shivraj and his 13-year government savagely for the corruption under their watch—the many Dumper, recruitment, Vyapam and e-tender scams. If he had fought on the streets with the thousands who lost their jobs, medical seats and lives under Shivraj; for the many thousand farmers around Bhopal whose land has been captured by MNCs for wheat and Basmati farming—that may have worked. But he didn't say a word about them. His friendly attitude towards BJP leaders alienated his followers, who have toiled for 15 years with no rewards. The baba-sadhu show impressed nobody; the other party had the copyright over it.[24]

Singh's open critique of the Kamal Nath government's decision to remove security from the RSS office in Bhopal and the demand to reinstate it immediately also confused many voters.[25] Once the Congress was into its trap, the task for the RSS became easy. The RSS had started campaigning in the state soon after the defeat of BJP in the assembly elections. Its chief Mohan Bhagwat had camped in Indore from 19 to 22 February meeting senior workers and motivating them to expand their reach for elections.[26] Soon after Thakur's name was announced, the RSS workers went canvassing door to door for her.[27] Names of most of the new candidates who were replacing the sitting MPs were being cleared by the RSS. The RSS was strictly speaking about nationalism, national security and asking 'people to vote judiciously for the party they think will stand for the country and countrymen functionary.'[28]

The role of the RSS became more evident when several leaders soon after their victory on 23 May were reported to have thanked the RSS. V. D. Sharma, a little-known BJP leader in Bundelkhand, who had made a belated entry in the electoral fray, and whose candidature was opposed widely in Khajuraho, after winning the election with a margin of nearly 5 lakh votes said, 'I am thankful to the RSS and Modi ji and, of course, the people of the constituency for their blessings.'[29]

At the end of the counting on 23 May 2019 the BJP virtually obliterated the Congress in the Lok Sabha election by winning 28 out of 29 seats. The only seat that the Congress won was Chhindwara where Chief Minister Kamal Nath's son Nakul Nath won by a small margin of 37,536 votes.[30] Jyotiraditya Scindia lost the traditional Guna seat to BJP by more than 125,000 votes.[31] Digvijay Singh lost the Bhopal seat to Pragya Singh Thakur by a margin of over 360,000 votes. On the contrary, an RSS worker Shankar Lalwani, despite facing protest of the local BJP workers making his Lok Sabha poll debut, won the Indore seat against Congress by a margin of nearly 5.5 lakh votes.[32] By garnering 17 per cent higher vote share than what it had secured in the 2018 assembly election, the BJP proved that the electorate which had deserted it during the assembly election had returned to the party's fold on the agenda of Hindutva nationalism in the state. A comparison of the community-wide vote share per the Lokniti-CSDS Post Poll Surveys

Table 9.1 *Lokniti-CSDS Post-poll Surveys: 2018 Assembly and 2019 Lok Sabha Elections*

	Voted for Congress (%)		Voted for BJP (%)		Voted for Others (%)	
	2018 VS	2019 LS	2018 VS	2019 LS	2018 VS	2019 LS
Overall	40	35	41	58	19	7
Upper Castes	33	25	58	75	9	–
OBCs	41	27	48	66	11	7
Dalits	49	50	33	38	18	1
Adivasis	40	38	30	54	30	8
Muslims	52	67	15	33	33	–
Others	37	47	48	26	15	26

Source: https://www.thehindu.com/elections/lok-sabha–2019/post-poll-survey-kamal-nath-government-falls-in-popularity-charts/article27249419.ece (accessed on 26 September 19).

during the 2018 assembly and 2019 Lok Sabha elections indicates that most communities except for Dalits and Muslims had deserted the Congress (see Table 9.1). The shift among the OBC voters particularly was very significant.

Thus, Madhya Pradesh provided the BJP with a test case for paving the way to use the shell of democracy to undermine democratic aspirations. In other words, it used the methodology of democracy to undermine democracy, and made Madhya Pradesh a Potemkin village of the new India under Modi 2.0!

NOTES

1. V. Sridhar, 'Writing on the Wall', *Frontline*, 4 January 2019, 7. Available at https://frontline.thehindu.com/cover-story/article25035588.ece?homepage=true (accessed on 24 September 2019).
2. Kashif Kakvi, 'Congress' Farm Loan Waiver in MP, A Reality Check', *Newsclick*, 19 December 2019(a). Available at https://www.newsclick.in/congress-farm-loan-waiver-mp-reality-check (accessed on 24 September 2019).

3. Available at http://timesofindia.indiatimes.com/articleshow/67063764.cms?utm_source=contentofinterest&utm_medium=text&utm_campaign=cppst (accessed on 24 September 2019).
4. Available at https://www.lokniti.org/media/upload_files/Lokniti-CSDS-ABP%20News%20Pre%20Poll%202018%20Report.pdf
5. Neemuch district, which is adjacent to Mandsaur, recorded the highest gain with 4.2 per cent followed by Sehore with 4 per cent, see https://www.firstpost.com/politics/madhya-pradesh-elections-high-turnout-in-malwa-farmers-anger-may-mean-bad-news-for-bjp-say-political-experts-5648891.html (accessed on 24 September 2019).
6. Available at https://www.news18.com/news/politics/kamal-nath-govt-scraps-shivraj-chouhans-flagship-scheme-for-farmers-ex-cm-warns-of-protests-2010303.html (accessed on 24 September 2019).
7. Available at https://www.news18.com/news/politics/bjp-slams-congress-as-kamal-nath-govt-says-farm-loan-waivers-only-after-lok-sabha-polls-2063713.html (accessed on 24 September 2019).
8. Available at https://www.business-standard.com/article/news-ians/pakistan-wants-chowkidar-to-be-defeated-says-modi-119032800968 _1.html (accessed on 24 September 2019).
9. Available at https://www.youtube.com/watch?v=lJWYggZSp78
10. Available at https://www.ndtv.com/india-news/lok-sabha-elections-2019-pm-narendra-modi-jabs-rahul-gandhi-over-wayanad-says-leaders-scared-of-cont-2015909 (accessed on 24 September 2019).
11. Available at https://www.business-standard.com/article/news-ani/rahul-can-do-ilu-ilu-with-terrorists-but-bjp-government-will-give-a-befitting-reply-to-them-says-shah-119041000014_1.html (accessed on 24 September 2019).
12. Available at https://www.deccanherald.com/lok-sabha-election-2019/ec-gives-clean-chit-to-pm-in-sixth-case-732193.html (accessed on 24 September 2019).
13. Anand Bhakto, 'Battles Line Redrawn', *Frontline, 24* May 2019, available at https://frontline.thehindu.com/cover-story/article27057583.ece (accessed on 24 September 2019).
14. Anand Bhakto, 'Dividends of Division', *Frontline*, 10 May 2019, available at https://frontline.thehindu.com/cover-story/article26919695.ece (accessed on 24 September 2019).
15. Available at https://thewire.in/politics/pollvault-bhim-army-chief-makes-u-turn-modi-keeps-up-attack-on-congress (accessed on 24 September 2019).
16. Available at https://thewire.in/politics/sadhvi-pragya-malegaon-blast-bjp-bhopal-elections-2019
17. Available at https://www.financialexpress.com/elections/sadhvi-pragya-on-bhopal-battle-uma-bharti-forced-digvijaya-singh-into-10-year-exile-now-comes-retirement/1552063/ (accessed on 24 September 2019).
18. Neeraj Mishra, 'Pragya Thakur Aside, Why Digvijaya Could Have Never Won the Seminal Seat of Bhopal', *The Wire*, 25 May 2019, available at https://

thewire.in/politics/pragya-thakur-digvijaya-singh-bjp-congress-bhopal-election (accessed on 24 September 2019).

19. Kashif Kakvi, 'How RSS Turned the Wind in Favour of BJP Four Months After Losing MP Assembly Polls', *The Wire*, 25 May 2019, available at https://thewire.in/politics/rss-bjp-madhya-pradesh-win (accessed on 24 September 2019).
20. Bhakto, 'Dividends of Division'.
21. Bhakto, 'Battles Line Redrawn'.
22. Tabassum Barnagarwala, 'In Bina, Dirty Water, Wait for Jobs—and Hindutva on Ground', *The Indian Express*, 8 May 2019, available at https://indianexpress.com/elections/in-bina-dirty-water-wait-for-jobs-and-hindutva-on-ground-lok-sabha-elections-5715895/ (accessed on 24 September 2019).
23. Ibid.
24. Mishra, 'Pragya Thakur Aside'; also see https://thewire.in/politics/saffronisation-bhopal-elections-digvijaya-singh-pragya-singh (accessed on 24 September 2019); https://indianexpress.com/elections/madhya-pradesh-digvijaya-campaign-gets-computer-baba-push-lok-sbaha-elections-5715926/ (accessed on 24 September 2019).
25. Available at https://www.indiatoday.in/elections/story/digvijay-kamal-nath-madhya-pradesh-rss-bhopal-headquarter-1491858–2019–04-02 (accessed on 24 September 2019).
26. Kakvi, 'How RSS Turned the Wind'.
27. Ibid.
28. Ibid.
29. Ibid.
30. The Congress has lost Chhindwara seat only once to BJP in the 1997 by-election since 1957.
31. Scindia had defeated the BJP on this seat by a margin of 120,792 in the 2014 Lok Sabha Election.
32. Kashif Kakvi, 2019(b). Op. cit. Earlier Indore was represented by the former Lok Sabha Speaker Sumitra Mahajan who had opted out of the 2019 General Election.

B. Kashmir and Western Cluster

Chapter 10

Jammu and Kashmir Elections

A Precursor to 'No More Two Flags, Two Constitutions'

Reeta Chowdhari Tremblay and Husnain Iqbal

On 5 August 2019, the Bharatiya Janata Party (BJP) fulfilled its long-standing promise to constitutionally fully integrate Jammu and Kashmir (J&K) with India, revoking the state's special status, downgrading its administrative and political status by splitting it into two union territories. With its phenomenal success in the general elections and the formation of a majority government, the BJP has replaced the historical constitutional entente between the people of Kashmir and the Indian state (recognizing distinct Kashmiri political and cultural identity) with ethnic majoritarianism.

Using the rationale of protecting India from both external and internal security threats, Indian Home Minister Amit Shah presented to the Rajya Sabha a Presidential Order removing Article 35A which grants special citizenship (property and employment) rights to J&K. It also brought about a change to the process of amending the special status, making it possible for Shah to introduce two resolutions—the first recommending to the President that he issue another order to revoke completely Article 370 and the second bifurcating the state into two union territories, Jammu and Kashmir (with a legislature) and Ladakh (without a legislature). Following the Presidential notification, these resolutions were duly passed in the shortest period of time by the parliament with a substantial majority and with a large number of opposition parties supporting the government. The implications of all these three measures are obvious: no restrictions for non-permanent Kashmiri residents to buy property and seek employment in the state, enhanced powers for the central government with regard to control over land and law and order and converting an asymmetrical federalism provision into a symmetrical one—no longer, as Shah tweeted, *do nishan, do samvidhan* (two flags, two Constitutions).

Since the formation of the new government after the 2019 elections, the BJP had been carefully putting all its ducks in a row to prepare for this historic move. On 2 August in the Lok Sabha, Home Minister Shah blamed Jawaharlal Nehru for his historical blunders (taking the Kashmir issue to the UN and promising a plebiscite) and the previous governments for appeasing the secessionist and hardline religious groups like the Jamaat-e-Islami. Sticking to its ideological agenda of the state's full integration with India (repealing Articles 370 and 35A), Shah proposed to look at the Kashmir issue with *naya nzariya aur nayi soch* (a different eye and a different mindset). In order to get some of the regional parties on board, BJP's first set of actions was to introduce a significant piece of legislation to give reservation in educational institutions and government jobs to socially and educationally backward classes as well to people living along the Line of Actual Control (LAC) within 10 km of the international border.

Also, President's rule was extended for a further six months, a move which at the time gave no indication of the extreme scenario which was to follow. In the event, however, it would allow the central government to bypass the regional legislative assembly (which remains suspended), legally to bring forward the revocation of Articles 370 and 35A and the state's conversion into union territories. In the expectation of a strong reaction from the Muslim Valley and its mainstream leaders, more than 35,000 additional central forces personnel were deployed in the Valley in order to strengthen the security forces' counter-insurgency operations and law-and-order duties. For the first time ever, the Amarnath Yatra was cancelled. Pilgrims, tourists and non-Kashmiri students of professional educational institutions were asked to leave the state and return home. All educational institutions were closed and all major political leaders (including Omar Abdullah and Mehbooba Mufti) were either put under house arrest or detained in government jails. The Valley, under curfew, with no internet connectivity and a complete lock-down, is silent while there is jubilation in Hindu-majority Jammu.

While it is understandable that the BJP was eager to realize its long-standing promise of making J&K an integral part of India with no special status, one might ask the question: why this urgency? Our analysis below shows that since 2014, the BJP has been eager to form a majority government in the state without any coalition partners but found it impossible to realize this goal with the present structures of assembly seats (37 in Jammu versus 46 in the Valley). In 2014, its mission 44+ (seeking 44 assembly seats out of 87) was not realized. And it is highly unlikely that the BJP could have formed a majority government in the state at this juncture. We point out below that the 2019 elections did not radically alter the political landscape (the religious and regional polarization) as the BJP and the National Conference (NC) split J&K's six seats both in number and geography. Under these circumstances, the most the BJP could have expected was to participate in a coalition government. And, based on its experience in the Peoples Democratic Party (PDP)-BJP coalition government (2014–2018), it would have found challenging to pursue counter-insurgency, with zero tolerance for home-grown militancy, in the Valley. In addition, by bringing the state under direct central control, it can now easily continue to respond to the demands of Jammu's Hindus to be equal political partners to the Valley's Muslims.

SETTING THE CONTEXT FOR THE 2019 PARLIAMENTARY ELECTIONS: PERSISTENT REGIONAL FRACTURED MANDATES

J&K which has six Lok Sabha constituencies—three in Kashmir Valley (Baramulla, Srinagar and Anantnag), two in Jammu region (Udhampur and Jammu) and one in Ladakh—continued to be a battleground state both internally and externally. Local groups were to continue periodically to confront Indian security forces, while brief violence erupted between regular Indian and Pakistani forces a few months before the 2019 parliamentary elections. The 2019 elections in the state took place during the President's rule imposed on 20 December 2018. In June 2018, the BJP walked out of the unpopular PDP-BJP coalition government, leaving Mehbooba Mufti's party a minority in the Legislative Assembly which was then suspended. Quitting the coalition government opened the path for the BJP to reframe and reclaim its national narrative. And within that narrative, J&K was to figure prominently. The BJP openly suggested that the coalition government was tying its hands in protecting the larger interest of India's integrity and in bringing the deteriorating situation in the state under control. It was now free to pursue an aggressive Kashmir policy where security forces would hunt down militants, where separatists parties and leaders would be banned and where the National Investigation Agency (NIA) would have a free hand, without interference from its former coalition partner—the soft separatists—to pursue cases against those separatists allegedly linked to diverting funds from Pakistan to terrorists.

Despite an appeal by all regional political parties to the Election Commission (EC) to hold simultaneous elections for both Lok Sabha and the Assembly, the latter elections were postponed for security reasons. The EC cited the constraint of limited availability of central forces and other logistics for the security of candidates in the wake of recent violence, including the Pulwama attack. It was the first time since 1996 that assembly elections in the state have not been held on time. In preparation for the Lok Sabha elections, there was a massive deployment of additional security forces. Although the BJP takes credit for holding peaceful elections in the state with negligible violence, the Valley looked more like a war zone than a vibrant civic space.

J&K recorded the lowest voter turnout in the country (44.9% versus the 67.5% all-India average); in particular, the Valley's three constituencies recorded a mere 19.2 per cent—the lowest since the activation of the electoral process in 1996. The NC won the three seats in the Valley which is overwhelmingly Muslim (96.4% Muslim, 2.5% Hindus). Repeating its 2014 performance, the BJP won two seats in the Jammu region, with its complex demographics. This region has a majority Hindu population (62.6%) but a substantial Muslim minority (33.5%), is divided

Table 10.1 *Lok Sabha Per Cent Voter Turnout*

	1996	1998	1999	2004	2009	2014	2019
Kashmir	42.6	31.5	16.2	22.7	31.2	31.2	19.2
Ladakh	80.9	73.4	81.9	73.5	71.9	70.8	64.0
Jammu	48.2	52.6	43.2	44.7	47.2	69.3	71.3
J&K State	46.6	43.0	31.2	35.2	39.7	49.7	44.9
India	57.9	62.0	60.0	58.1	57.0	66.4	67.5

Source: The Election Commission of India.

on linguistic lines (Kashmiri, Dogri and Pahari) and has a significant tribal minority, the Gujjars including the pastoral nomadic Bakkerwal community (between 18% and 20% of the state's population). Finally, as in 2014, the BJP won the Ladakh seat which is 48.4 per cent Muslim, 39.6 per cent Buddhist and 12.0 per cent Hindu (see Table 10.1).

The biggest winner of these elections was the BJP which had campaigned for a zero tolerance of terrorism and the abrogation of Articles 370 and 35A.[1] In the Hindu-dominated Jammu region, it increased its voter share by over 11 percentage points with a voter turnout of 71.3 per cent. Even though all three major political parties—the NC, the Congress and the PDP—decided to fight the BJP and its Hindutva agenda in the Jammu region, presenting themselves as a secular alternative and not competing against each other, the BJP candidates received overwhelming support in Jammu's two constituencies (see Table 10.2).

As expected, given the unpopularity of the PDP-BJP coalition government, the biggest loser in the Valley was the PDP. The NC replaced the PDP and won the Valley's three seats albeit with negligible voter participation. Another loser in this contest was Sajjad Lone's party, the People's Conference (PC), to which several influential PDP legislators had defected after the collapse of the PDP-BJP coalition.[2] The PC had tried to present itself as a viable alternative to the NC and the PDP by openly critiquing them for their poor governance record.[3] Its informal alignment with the BJP in 2014 and thereafter did not fare well with the voters, despite its siding with the other Valley-based parties to

Table 10.2 *Lok Sabha Per Cent Voter Share for Udhampur (Udh) and Jammu (Jam)*

	NC		Congress		PDP		BJP		Other	
	Udh	Jam	Udh	Jam	Udh	Jam	Udh	Jam	Udh	Jam
1996	–	–	21.7	34.2	–	–	37.6	26.0	40.7	39.8
1998	32.9	26.8	7.1	18.1	–	–	48.7	43.3	11.3	11.8
1999	19.2	22.1	19.1	19.0	–	–	49.0	43.5	12.7	15.4
2004	11.5	14.7	39.6	38.9	–	–	31.9	36.8	17.0	9.6
2009	–	–	37.9	45.3	5.0	5.5	35.7	30.9	21.4	18.3
2014	–	–	40.9	19.6	2.1	9.1	46.8	49.3	10.3	21.9
2019	–	–	31.1	37.5	–	–	61.4	58.0	7.5	4.4

Source: The Election Commission of India.

protect the special status of the state. Although it came in the second place in Baramulla (22.65% of votes polled), in Srinagar it managed to get 15.4 per cent votes, coming in third after the NC and the PDP. In Anantnag, it secured only 1.32 per cent votes (see Table 10.3).

All mainstream parties of the Valley unanimously vowed to fight for maintaining J&K's special status within India. Countering the BJP's promise to revoke Article 370, NC leader Farooq Abdullah suggested that India reopens the issue of accession and deliver on the promise of plebiscite. Similarly, Omar Abdullah asserted that the state would continue to strive for the restoration of autonomy, reversing all integrative measures adopted between 1955 and 1977, while PDP leader, Mehbooba Mufti, said the relationship between India and J&K would have to be renegotiated if Article 370 were scrapped. However, all parties faced hardened voters in the Valley: campaign rallies were small and in certain parts of South Kashmir, the home base of the PDP, Mehbooba was not even allowed to enter the town.

DECONSTRUCTING THE RESULTS

The 2019 Lok Sabha results confirm the hardening of the religious/regional polarization in its two major parts—Kashmir Valley and

Table 10.3 *Lok Sabha Per Cent Voter Share for Baramulla (Bar), Srinagar (Sri) and Anantnag (An)*

	NC			Congress			PDP			BJP			Other		
	Bar	Sri	An	Bar	Sri	An	Bar	Sri	An	Bar	Sri	An	Bar	Sri	An
1996	–	–	–	36.1	18.6	16.5	–	–	–	–	12.1	11.2	63.9	69.3	72.3
1998	43.2	59.7	31.8	3.9	30.5	55.9	–	–	–	1.4	4.6	3.2	51.6	5.3	9.1
1999	43.9	57.3	37.7	–	19.0	9.1	–	–	–	1.4	2.2	1.0	54.7	21.5	52.3
2004	38.1	50.3	23.6	18.6	–	–	35.2	38.5	49.6	2.7	1.6	3.2	5.4	9.6	23.6
2009	46.0	52.0	–	–	–	46.5	31.3	41.3	44.9	–	0.2	0.3	22.7	6.5	8.2
2014	31.3	37.0	36.0	–	–	–	37.6	50.6	53.4	1.4	0.4	0.4	29.6	12.0	10.3
2019	29.3	57.1	32.2	7.6	–	26.8	–	19.6	24.4	1.7	2.5	8.2	61.4	20.7	35.2

Source: The Election Commission of India.

Jammu—each with its divergent electoral responses. Competing regional political narratives—the nationalist/secessionist/irredentist in the Valley and the pro-integration/Hindu in Jammu—translate into contrasting electoral trends. The decision criteria of the citizens of each region emerge as the product of their respective unique perceptions and experiences relating to their collective identity issues, regional/religious/nationalism dynamics and satisfaction or dissatisfaction with governance.

The seeds of polarization were sown during the 1983 assembly elections as the Congress party actively mobilized Jammu's Hindus to counter the autonomy politics of Sheikh Abdullah's NC.[4]

But it is the 1996 elections which made the BJP a viable contender and major player in J&K. The Indian State initiated an electoral process in order to reactivate civil society after six years of President's rule, imposed in response to the breakdown of law and order in the wake of a mass-supported secessionist movement accompanied by political insurgency. That is when the Hindu-dominated constituency began its shift towards the BJP.[5] In 1996, the BJP won one out of two Jammu Lok Sabha seats with a 31.1 per cent vote share; a solid 17.8 per cent point increase from the 1989 elections. It won 8 out of 37 Jammu Assembly seats with a 21 per cent vote share, while in Hindu-majority Jammu it doubled its share of votes from 22 to 40.5 per cent.

A major consequence of the religious/regional polarization has been the rise of coalition politics and the emergence of Jammu region as an equal partner to Kashmir Valley in the governance of the state. In the 1996 assembly elections, the NC emerged as the largest party in each region with 40 out of 46 seats with a 48.15 per cent vote share in the Valley, 14 out of 37 seats with 23.7 per cent vote share in Jammu and 3 out of 4 seats with a 46.6 per cent vote share in Ladakh. Nevertheless, it was soon to lose that hegemonic position. Persistent regional fractured mandates led to an uninterrupted sequence of coalition governments in the state: the PDP-Congress (2002–2008); NC-Congress (2009–2014) and PDP-BJP (2015–2018). Jammu, which has felt marginalized since the state's accession to India, now feels its

Table 10.4 *J&K Assembly Elections—Per Cent Voter Share*

	1996	2002	2008	2014
BJP				
Jammu	21.1	12.3	22.0	40.5
Kashmir	1.0	1.6	1.0	2.2
Ladhak	5.8	–	0.7	22.1
J&K State	12.1	8.6	12.6	23.0
Congress				
Jammu	20.0	29.8	23.0	20.8
Kashmir	18.8	14.4	10.5	18.0
Ladhak	39.0	5.6	27.3	50.0
J&K State	20.0	21.4	17.7	18.0
National Conference				
Jammu	23.7	23.9	14.3	14.4
Kashmir	48.2	35.7	27.5	29.1
Ladhak	46.6	44.6	28.4	8.1
J&K State	34.8	28.2	23.1	20.8
PDP				
Jammu	–	1.8	6.9	11.0
Kashmir	–	24.5	27.4	37.3
Ladhak	–	–	0.5	11.8
J&K State	–	9.0	15.4	22.7

Source: The Election Commission of India.

demands for equal participation are being met and has emerged as an important factor in the religious/regional polarization and divergent, conflictual electoral paths. Jammu gave a huge mandate to the BJP in 2014 (Lok Sabha and Assembly), shutting out Congress and both mainstream Valley-based parties (see Table 10.4). And given the Valley's persistent demands for autonomy and *azadi*, it is unlikely that regional polarization, fractured electoral mandates and coalition politics will disappear anytime soon.[6]

DIVERGENT PATHS: VOTER TURNOUT

As Table 10.2 indicates, the voter turnout in the 2019 Lok Sabha elections was 72.2 per cent in the Jammu region, much higher than the Valley's meagre 19.1 per cent, reflecting BJP's successful mobilization of Jammu's Hindu population. The voting patterns of Jammu region in this election represent a conflation of two historical responses. Since 1952, a minority Hindu community has remained committed to the Hindu nationalist symbols and to BJP's backing the cause of the state's complete accession to India via the revocation of Article 370. The much wider general Hindu population for its part has sought political and administrative parity with the Valley and had traditionally voted for the Congress or other smaller parties for their secular symbolism but since 1996 began a gradual shift to the BJP.

Modi's muscular policy against terrorism including surgical strikes against terrorist camps in Pakistan-administered Kashmir took place after the Uri attacks. On 26 February prior to the 2019 elections, air strikes targeted the Jaish-e-Mohammed camp in Balakot, Pakistan, in reprisal for the Pulwama attack in J&K by the *jihadi* group that killed 46 Indian paramilitary soldiers. These events have galvanized nationalist feelings among Jammu's Hindus.

During the PDP-BJP coalition government, Jammu's Hindus were generally dissatisfied with BJP's unfulfilled promise of equal development including the so-called beef politics and the handling of the Kathua rape and murder of an eight-year-old nomadic girl. Right-wing Hindu groups demanded the release of the rapist/murderer, but Hindus have nevertheless continued to support Modi and his vision of Indian nationalism. The Valley has consistently voted in lower numbers as compared to Ladakh and Jammu, both in parliamentary and assembly elections (see Table 10.5).

Unlike the situation in Jammu, the story of voter turnout in the Valley is much more complex as it has taken different trajectories in each of its three parts—North, Central and South Kashmir. When it comes to Lok Sabha elections, Kashmiri Muslims have voted in low numbers, given their limited interest in national issues, unless they connect with their identity-based demands. Limited participation has shown a steady decline since 1996 suggesting their further removal from

Table 10.5 *Assembly (A) versus Lok Sabha (LS) Elections Per Cent Voter Turnout—Comparable Periods*

	1996	1996	1998	1999	2002	2004	2008	2009	2014	2014	2019	2019
	A	LS	LS	LS	A	LS	A	LS	A	LS	A	LS
Kashmir	**45.4**	42.6	31.5	16.2	**29.7**	22.7	**51.6**	31.2	**56.5**	31.2	–	19.2
Ladakh	**68.8**	80.9	73.4	81.9	**75.9**	73.5	**68.6**	71.9	**71.9**	70.8	–	64.0
Jammu	**60.4**	48.2	54.7	46.8	**55.8**	44.5	**71.6**	49.0	**75.9**	68.0	–	72.2
J&K State	**53.2**	46.6	43.0	31.2	**43.7**	35.2	**61.4**	39.7	**65.9**	49.7	–	44.9

Source: The Election Commission of India.

national politics. But assembly elections present a different picture and voter turnout has experienced an upward surge in the last two elections.

Elections are a tricky business in the Valley. The electoral arena has come to be occupied by two mainstream regional parties—the NC and the PDP. Each has carved out its own political space within their distinct agendas of governance, autonomy and the India–Pakistan equation with regard to the Kashmir issue. The electoral and democratic politics in the Valley, however, remains limited and is circumscribed by the serious concerns of a larger alienated citizenry (e.g., human rights violations, excesses by security forces, civilian killings) who continue to be mobilized in favour of *azadi* by the nationalist/secessionist groups. The electoral success of either party largely depends upon the broader context of issues permeating the Valley generating protest politics and state government response.

The 2008 elections took place after the protracted Amarnath land row.[7] The 2014 elections were held against the backdrop of a politically charged atmosphere in the Valley, starting with the Shopian incident of 2009, followed by the discovery of 2,700 unmarked mass graves containing almost 3,000 bodies, a four-month-long series of protests in June 2010 against the killing of three young men in a fake encounter and ending with the 2013 Afzal Guru hanging.[8] The PDP, with its 'healing touch', soft nationalism and anti-incumbency campaign, was to get the vote out in its favour. But the 2019 elections were held in a changed environment: an increasing home-grown militancy, the 2016 Burhan Wani and Post-Wani killings and a dysfunctional PDP–BJP coalition.[9] While the PDP–BJP coalition government was to remain unpopular in the Valley, both the NC and the PDP were to lose credibility, becoming effectively discredited.

In disaggregating the voter turnout by its geographical location (see Table 10.6), it is interesting to note that most of Central Kashmir consistently stays away from the electoral process. Poll boycott calls have had consistently greater resonance in urban areas like Srinagar and areas contiguous to it where there is a strong support base for the separatist leaders and militant groups. Neighbourhoods in and surrounding Srinagar such as Amirakadal, Hazartbal, Idgah, Khanyar, Batmaloo and home bases of leaders such as Mirwaiz Farooq and Shabir Shah have witnessed a much lower voter participation in assembly elections.

Table 10.6 *Kashmir Valley Assembly Elections Per Cent Voter Turnout by Region*

		1996	2002	2008	2014
Baramulla	(North)	50.4	44.3	56.6	65.4
Srinagar	(Central)	37.2	21.8	40.4	49.4
Anantnag	(South)	49.4	23.9	57.6	54.9
J&K State		53.2	43.7	61.4	65.9

Source: The Election Commission of India.

Most of North Kashmir, some of which borders on the Line of Control, vote consistently in high numbers. The two exceptions are the urban towns of Baramulla and Sopore. Sopore, Jamaat's stronghold as well as Hurriyat leader Geelani's home turf and Afzal Guru's native place, has remained embroiled, on and off, in militancy-related violence. In 1993, Indian security forces opened fire on locals in Sopore, burned down the bazaar (250 shops and 50 homes), killing at least 57 civilians.

In South Kashmir, voter turnout has fluctuated up and down. Higher voter participation in 2008 was largely to support the PDP. The PDP was founded in 1999 in South Kashmir under the leadership of Mufti Sayeed, and his daughter, Mehbooba, incorporating into the party's campaign manifesto issues with which it felt the common people could identify. For instance, the PDP promised a corruption-free government, unconditional dialogue with militants and the disbanding of the Special Operations Group while providing a 'healing touch' to those affected by the militancy. However, the 8.8 per cent voter turnout in the 2019 elections is directly related to the killing of Burhan Wani and other young militants from South Kashmir and acute disappointment with the PDP. Contrary to BJP's claims that militancy is confined to a very small number of towns/villages in South Kashmir, the disaggregated numbers show that a lack of support for the electoral process remains spread out in all three geographical regions of the Valley with some urban constituencies having consistently opted out of the electoral process (see Table 10.7).

Table 10.7 *Kashmir Assembly Elections per Cent Voter Turnout in Constituencies with Less than 40 Per Cent*

North Kashmir (Baramulla: 15 Constituencies, 1–15)				
	1996	2002	2008	2014
Sopore	38.2	8.1	19.9	30.8
Baramulla	37.4	24.2	33.3	39.7
Central Kashmir (Srinagar: 15 Constituencies, 16–30)				
	1996	2002	2008	2014
Hazratbal	23.6	7.1	28.9	29.5
Zadibal	12.7	4.8	17.3	23.9
Eidgah	20.0	4.8	22.0	27.8
Khanyar	12.7	4.2	17.4	26.2
Habba Kadal	5.4	3.2	11.6	21.3
Amira Kadal	11.5	3.1	14.9	24.8
Batmaloo	19.4	4.0	19.9	24.5
South Kashmir (Anantnag: 16 Constituencies, 31–46)				
	1996	2002	2008	2014
Tral	–	11.6	–	38.2
Pampore	–	19.2	–	–
Pulwama	–	18.1	–	38.1
Rajpora	–	36.7	–	–
Wachi	–	28.3	–	–
Shopian	–	26.9	–	–
Noorabad	–	23.4	–	–
Kulgam	–	24.4	–	–
Hom Shali Bugh	–	22.9	–	37.6
Anantnag	34.2	7.2	–	39.7
Devsar	–	35.6	–	–
Dooru	–		–	–

South Kashmir (Anantnag: 16 Constituencies, 31–46)				
	1996	2002	2008	2014
Kokernag	39.0	15.3	–	–
Shangus	–	25.4	–	–
Bijbehara	36.3	16.7	–	–
Pahalgam	–	33	–	–

Source: The Election Commission of India.

BJP'S INCREASING HEGEMONY IN HINDU JAMMU AND THE VULNERABILITY OF JAMMU'S MUSLIMS

BJP's share of votes has increased significantly since the period of militancy. Jammu exhibits the most visible divide between the Hindu-dominated districts and the peripheral and backward Muslim-dominated districts. One witnesses two different elections here. The secular political space has fundamentally come to be confined to the Muslim-dominated areas, albeit shrinking as Hindu minorities opt for the BJP. In Hindu-dominated Jammu, the Hindu vote has followed the national trend giving an overwhelming support to the BJP. The BJP has come to acquire a hegemonic status, pushing aside all minor parties and reducing the support for the Congress party.

Table 10.4 shows the massive support which the BJP received in Jammu's two Parliamentary constituencies—Udhampur and Jammu. In Udhampur, its vote share was 61.4 per cent, up from 49.8 per cent in 2014 and 35.7 per cent in 2009. Similarly, in Jammu, its vote share rose from 49.3 per cent in 2014 to 58 per cent in 2019. This was accompanied by wiping out smaller opposition parties like the Panther's Party and encroaching upon Congress's vote. A similar trend is evident in BJP's performance in the 2014 assembly elections (see Table 10.8). In 25 Hindu-dominated constituencies (Assembly), the BJP increased its vote share from 27.4 per cent in 2008 to 48.1 per cent and doubled its seat count from 11 to 22. Again, the electoral space has shrunk for minor political parties as well as for the NC and the Congress.

Table 10.8 *Assembly Elections Jammu District: 25 Hindu-Dominated Constituencies (55, 58, 60–81, 84)*

Number of Seats Won by Party and Per Cent Vote Received										
Year	NC		Congress		PDP		BJP		Other	
1996	*5*	16.1	*4*	21.8	–	–	*8*	23.9	*8*	38.3
2002	*3*	20.3	*13*	30.0	*0*	1.2	*1*	14.2	*8*	34.3
2008	*3*	15.7	*6*	21.3	*0*	2.8	*11*	27.4	*5*	32.9
2014	*2*	11.4	*0*	17.6	*0*	6.3	*22*	48.1	*1*	16.6

Source: The Election Commission of India.

Table 10.9 *Assembly Elections Jammu District: 12 Muslim-Dominated Constituencies (51–54, 56–57, 59, 82–83, 85–87)*

Number of Seats Won by Party and Per Cent Vote Received										
Year	NC		Congress		PDP		BJP		Other	
1996	*9*	39.2	*0*	15.6	–	–	*0*	14.4	*3*	30.8
2002	*6*	33.7	*2*	27.0	*0*	3.4	*0*	6.1	*4*	29.8
2008	*3*	27.1	*7*	26.6	*0*	14.8	*0*	10.4	*2*	21.2
2014	*1*	20.9	*5*	28.0	*3*	21.3	*3*	22.7	*0*	7.1

Source: The Election Commission of India.

There are 12 Muslim-dominated Jammu Assembly constituencies. Among them, Poonch is predominately Muslim (90.4%), Ramban, Reasi and Rajouri are, respectively, 70.7 per cent, 62.7 per cent and 57.7 per cent Muslim. Other constituencies are either almost evenly split between Hindus and Muslims or have a sizeable Hindu community. The last 2014 assembly election results show that votes in these constituencies have been generally shared by the NC, the Congress and the PDP, whereas the BJP has consolidated its vote among the Hindu minorities. It increased its share of votes from 14.4 per cent in 1996 to 22.7 per cent, capturing three seats, in 2014. Except for the two constituencies of Poonch and Haveli, where Muslims are 90.4 per cent of the population, BJP candidates received between 16 per cent and 45.4 per cent of the vote in the 2014 assembly elections (see Table 10.9).

Although still visible, the secular space is shrinking in these constituencies. BJP's success has been possible by its consolidating the Hindu vote and mobilizing the Gujjar (tribal) voters (a major portion of the Muslim population). In an effort to woo the Gujjars, Modi declared in one of his rallies in 2013, referring to them as 'my own people': 'Shouldn't all you Gujjar families get benefits as tribals?' He asked: 'Should you get your rights or not?' and he projected a wider developmental agenda in their favour. In the 2019 elections, the BJP specifically courted them. With the three-decade-old ongoing secessionist movement in the Kashmir Valley, this economically vulnerable and politically underrepresented nomadic community has inadvertently become entangled between the militants in the Valley and the security forces, and also caught between competing Hindu and Muslim nationalist narratives. Many Bakkerwals have been coerced by militants into providing them shelter and food and keeping them hidden from the security forces, who therefore view the community as informants, sympathetic to the Islamic jihadists.

Meanwhile, Hindus of various Jammu districts which the Bakkerwal community visit or where they maintain temporary settlements see these Muslim nomads as contributing to changing the region's religious demography. For the BJP, one of the toughest tasks was to distance itself from the Hindu right-wing nationalists in the 2018 brutal rape and murder of an eight-year-old girl in Kathua.[10] In responding to the national and international outrage, Modi promised that 'no culprit will be spared and complete justice will be done'. The union cabinet passed an ordinance making the rape of a girl under 12 punishable by death and increasing the minimum punishment for female rape from seven years to 10 years, extendable to life imprisonment. It remains to be seen how the BJP combines its Hindutva agenda with the development promise for the vulnerable tribal-Muslim community.

LOOKING AHEAD

BJP's bold move to scrap special status of J&K and turning the state into two union territories has indeed ensured that the Jammu region will effectively be an equal partner to Kashmir Valley in the governance of its affairs. It has also satisfied Ladakh's persistent demands to be separated from the Valley-dominated administration and be brought under the direct central control. With regard to Jammu region, the BJP government is now in the position to redraw the electoral map by changing the size and boundaries of existing constituencies. At present, compared to 46 Valley constituencies, the Jammu region has 37 which, over the years, has given rise to the claims of Jammu's political discrimination. Jammu would also receive attention from the BJP government to ensure that its Hindu identity remains protected by ridding the region of Muslim Rohingya refugees (about 5,700 in number) and settling on the pending citizenship issue of West Pakistani Hindu refugees, who arrived in the Jammu region after the partition of India. However, BJP's revocation of the special status along with its aggressive, muscular policies and an open war against terrorism is most likely not going to play out well in the Valley. BJP's action of converting the state into a union territory (which will have no control over land) will be interpreted as the Hindu majoritarian state pushing forward a settler colonial project. Once things settle down, home-grown terrorism and everyday resistance are likely to grow in intensity. As our analysis above of the voter turnout, particularly, in the Central and South Kashmir, has shown, Kashmiri Muslims are extremely proactive concerning their special status and their collective identity. The consequences of all this cannot be anything but, at a minimum, the increasing alienation of the Valley's Muslims and their deepening distrust in the Indian democracy, further reinforcing Hindu/Muslim fault lines and Kashmiri demand for *azadi*.

NOTES

1. Article 35A was effectively enshrined as Section 6 of the state's constitution which grants the state legislature the right to define special rights and privileges with regard to employment and acquisition of property in the state as well as the grant of scholarship to its state subjects. The BJP has defended its position of doing away with Article 35A by providing three reasons. First, that it was erroneously included by a Presidential Notification and it was neither approved by India's Constituent Assembly nor was it part of any constitutional amendment. Second, that it discriminates against the citizens of India. Third, that this provision has economically hurt the people of J&K due to their inability to attract Indian/private investment for the state's development agenda.
2. In 2014, Hasseb Drabu, the most prominent of the PDP leader (former finance minister and co-author of the PDP–BJP coalition government's Agenda of

Alliance) resigned from the party. This was to start the trend of defections. Some of these defections in 2018 and 2019 include: Basharat Bukhari joined the NC; Peer Mohammad Hussain, former Wakf Board chairman also joined the NC; Javed Mustafa Mir joined the new party led by the former IAS officer Shah Fasel, J&K People's Movement; Imran Ansari (former minister in the PDP-BJP coalition government) joined People's Conference; Abid Ansari, a top Shia leader also joined the People's Conference.

3. The J&K People's Conference was founded by the separatist leader Abdul Ghani Lone and Molvi Iftikhar Hussain Ansari in 1978. In 2002, it contested through proxy candidates for the legislative assembly and two of them succeeded in getting elected. In 2014, it again won two seats.
4. The Congress, identifying itself with the regional politics of Jammu (its political and administrative discrimination by the so-called Valley-centric Kashmir government) won 26 out 37 seats in Jammu region. Indeed, from 1977 onwards, Kashmir's distinctness and its autonomy within the Indian federation were to emerge as the major thematic framework of the government of Sheikh Abdullah (who had come into power as a result of the 1975 Indira-Abdullah accord), thus formally putting autonomy on the Valley's political agenda. After the liberation of Bangladesh, Abdullah felt that this was the best Kashmir could hope for. A sustained rhetoric of autonomy, calling for the pre-1953 status, and the reversal of the integrative measures which had diluted Article 370, helped Abdullah to maintain a strong popular base in the Valley. This put Jammu's Hindus more on the defensive, pushing for representational and administrative equity with the Valley.
5. During the 1990s, BJP's increasing influence in the Jammu region was also a response to militant attacks in Jammu. In 1995, there was an explosion during the Republic Day parade in Jammu's Bakshi Stadium. In 2002, there were two fidayeen attacks (one in March and one in November) in Jammu's Ragunath Mandir. In 2001 and 2004, Jammu's railway station was also subject to fidayeen attacks.
6. Rekha Chowdhary provides a detailed picture of State elections in her recent book *Jammu and Kashmir: 1990 and Beyond Competitive Politics in the Shadow of Separatism* (New Delhi: SAGE Publications, 2019).
7. See Reeta Chowdahri Tremblay, 'Kashmir's Secessionist Movement Resurfaces: Ethnic Identity, Community Competition, and the State', *Asian Survey* 49, no. 6 (2009): 924–950.
8. In May 2009 in Shopian, the rape and murder of two women was mishandled initially by Omar's administration, even he scolded journalists for using the word 'rape' and not 'alleged rape'. Angry residents of Shopian resorted to large-scale protests against the administration. For several months, Shopian virtually remained a no-entry zone for the government. In 2010, during four-months of stone pelting protests, 112 young men were killed.
9. Examples of this dysfunctionality include the PDP and the BJP at loggerheads over the violence that followed the Wani killing; the PDP disapproval of BJP's

stand commending Major Leetul Gogoi for tying a Kashmiri civilian to his jeep as a human shield to escape stone-pelters during by-elections; differences over holding dialogue with Pakistan and the separatist leadership in the Valley.

10. Her abduction and rape was meant to frighten the nomadic Muslim community and drive them away from lands which local Hindus believe have been undergoing a demographic transformation by the nomadic settlements. The Kathua xepisode exposed the existing deep fault lines between Hindu-majority Jammu and the predominately Muslim Kashmir Valley in the sharply divided state. The Kashmir Valley united to demand justice, while Jammu was dominated by a vocal minority with a militant Hindu nationalist agenda. This minority formed a new group, Hindu Ekta March, backed by two BJP ministers of the state's PDP-BJP coalition government, which staged protests claiming the police had made wrongful arrests. The J&K Bar Association's Jammu wing joined them in demanding that the investigation be shifted from the J&K Crime Branch to the Central Bureau of Investigation.

Chapter 11

Gujarati Voters' Faith and Pride

The 2019 Elections

Ghanshyam Shah

The outcome of the 2019 elections in Gujarat had a sense of déjà vu. The outcome was similar to those of 2009 and 2014 elections. It witnessed similar modus operandi for election engineering crafted by its former Chief Minister Narendra Modi and BJP President Amit Shah. As argued earlier, election marketing has reduced voters to consumers whose choices are manufactured by manipulating their perception and priorities. Chanakya rajniti (statecraft) coupled with Goebbel's propaganda take a toll on citizens' autonomy.[1] Despite the better performance of the Congress-led UPA as perceived by two-third Gujarati voters in 2009, the BJP secured more votes and seats.[2] And now, notwithstanding mounting distress in everyday socio-economic life, Modi–Shah duo with meticulous planning and strategy has once again captured a vast majority of the voters across socio-economic strata.

ELECTION OUTCOME

This time, Gujarat has surpassed its earlier record of 63.77 per cent of 1967 in voting turnout with 64.11 per cent. The BJP broke its earlier record and secured 63 per cent votes, second highest, next to Himachal Pradesh among the Indian states. BJP's vote share has increased by 3 per cent over the 2014 elections. The gap over the Congress has widened from 4 per cent in 2004 to 31 per cent in 2019 (Figure 11.1).

However, within less than one and a half years of its sweeping victory in 2014, the BJP suffered reversal in rural local government elections in 2015 (Figure 11.2). Although it maintained its strength in municipal corporations, its seats declined from 79 per cent to 49 per cent in rural-urban municipalities as well as in District and Taluka Panchayats. Correspondingly, the Congress secured 48 per cent and 44 per cent seats in the District and Taluka Panchayats, respectively.

This trend is also reflected in the 2017 state assembly elections.[3] In 2014 parliament elections, the BJP won 169 out of 182 assembly segments. But in 2017, it secured 99 seats. The Congress improved its vote share in rural areas. Its assembly seats increased from 55 to 77. To arrest this trend before the 2019 polls, BJP won five District Panchayats out of 23 and 10 Taluka Panchayats out of 129 from the Congress in June 2018. The Congress blamed BJP's money and muscle power for the defection.[4] The grassroots level political manoeuvring helped the BJP in capturing 173 out of 182 assembly segments in 2019. The outcome has almost morally paralysed Gujarat Congress.

MODI CENTRIC

Like 2014, Narendra Modi almost converted the Westminster Parliament elections to the US Presidential elections. He and his acolytes repeatedly asked electorates in every constituency in Gujarat to vote for Modi rather than the candidate.[5] Since 2005 Modi has skilfully built his public stature and indispensability step by step within the party. When he became the chief minister of Gujarat, replacing Keshubhai Patel, he was not much known outside the RSS–BJP circles. He won the first elections from the BJP's safe constituency in 2001 with barely 1,400 votes. With Godhra episode and communal carnage in 2002, he emerged as the saviour of Hindus. By launching 'Gaurav Yatra' (holy procession celebrating pride) on the eve of assembly elections 2002, he invoked Gujarati and Hindu pride, ridiculed average Muslims,

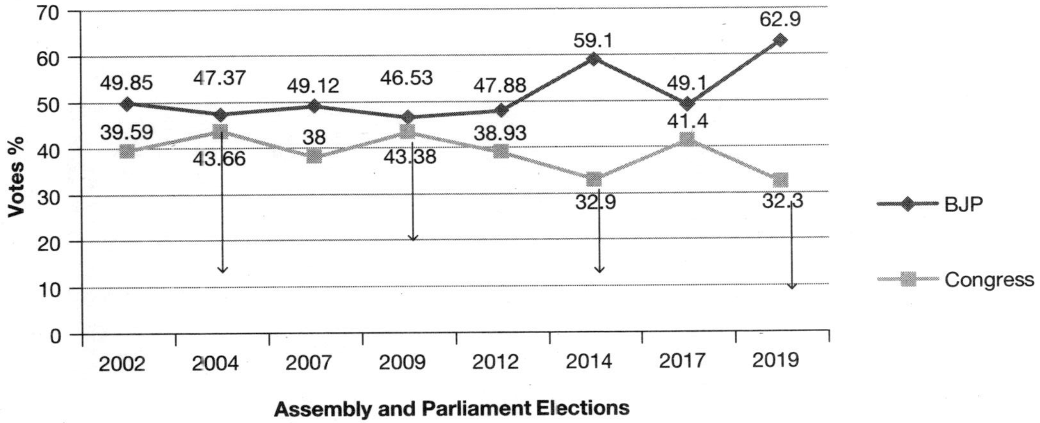

Figure 11.1 *Vote Shared by BJP and Congress in State Assembly and Parliament Elections*

Source: Election Commission of India (Reports for different elections).

Note: Arrows indicates parliament election.

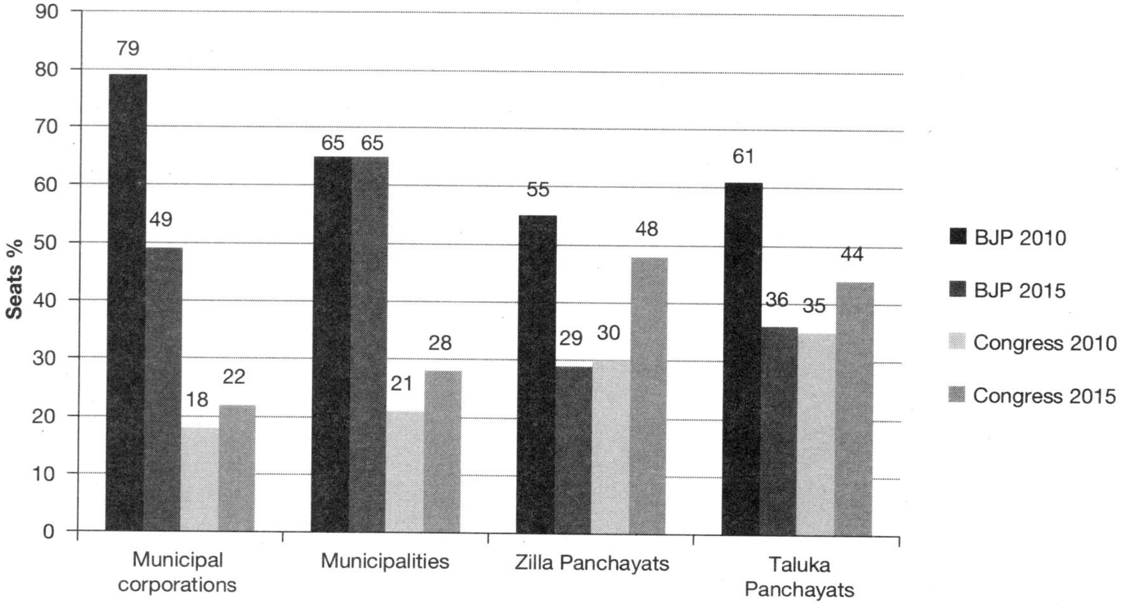

Figure 11.2 *Local Governments' Elections 2010 and 2015*

Source: Based on election results. Available at http://www.electionresultsnews.in/gujarat-district-taluka-panchayat-election-results–2015/ (accessed on 14 January 2017).

invoked fear of Muslim hooligans and challenged Pakistan's ruler Miya Musharraf.[6] His coterie projected him as the saviour of *dharma* (religion) born to destroy evils.

After 2002 elections, having realized limitations of sustainability of emotions, he first carved out his image as an honest person having no personal and family interests, as well as a *vikas purush* (personification of development), a master merchant selling dreams.[7] To legitimatize this image, he successfully crafted a strategy to win over the dominant strata of civil society.[8] Litterateurs, self-styled 'non-political' liberals had begun praising his determination and strong mind. Later, they lauded him as the country's representative to the world in the global context. During the world economic crisis of 2008–2009, he projected Gujarat model of India's economic 'development' and 'good governance'. Business tycoons called him CEO of India. Simultaneously, he meticulously built his image as the only saviour of India's economic growth. That paved a way for his victory in 2014 elections.[9]

The process of reinforcing this image building of the strong political leader accelerated on a wide-scale with him becoming prime minister (PM). Along with the PM's tweet, Mann Ki Baat (radio programme), WhatsApp and media advertisements, his team used various forms of social media in English and regional colloquial languages to strengthen his image of a strong, determinant and dedicated leader. In mid-2016, fake news went viral in social media and there was a tweet that he had been declared the best prime minister in the world by UNESCO. Later, following demonetization in November 2016, to buttress his image as a workaholic and dedicated person aiming for the bright future of the country, a message as 'true story' by a senior civil servant, projecting himself as non-partisan, did the rounds that the PM was routinely working 18–20 hours a day and sometimes for 36 hours without sleep (!), at the cost of his health. The PM had reached a state of self-actualization above his criticism. He was always concerned with only one thing, 'What more can we do to make India better…it is clear of one thing; in these 5 years he will leave a lasting legacy….'[10] The same message was repeated in early 2019 with an added sentence: 'Do we support this (legacy)?' His social media campaign emphasized that Modi took tough decisions such as demonetization and Goods and Services Tax (GST) for long-term interests of the country. He was 'very well aware of what he is doing! He doesn't need to be on back foot. Winning elections must never be the sole aim of any leader who is determined to clean the country of its corruption....' His promoters pleaded on social media that 'Those who make uproar with a marginal rise in prices of onion and potato, why we are not proud of shining India's prestige in the world?'

Ever since the defeat of NDA in 2004, Modi invented a story regarding 'injustice to Gujarat' by the Congress, that is, the Nehru–Gandhi family. Sardar Patel and Morarji Desai were its victims. During 2014 polls, Modi was projected as 'Gujarat pride: our Gujarati prime minister'. People were hammered that 'Gujarat will get justice...when a Gujarati becomes a prime minister'.[11] And, it has been repeated in 2019. In election meetings, Modi reiterated that:

> I am your man in Delhi.... Before 2014, visitors from Gujarat to Delhi could have only a glimpse of PM' house. Now 'they have tea with me.... Will such an opportunity ever come again?.... I have the right to seek 26 lotuses (seats) from people of Gujarat.[12]

He called upon people of Gujarat to strengthen his position.

Though a section of media and Congress called Modi as 'feku' (boastful), it couldn't counter the vigorous campaign for Modi as 'a strong' man. On the other hand, the Congress could not project Rahul Gandhi as a strong leader. During 2014 and 2019 election campaigns, Modi frequently mocked Rahul Gandhi on social media and in face-to-face informal chats calling him *pappu* (spoiled child, childish, dumb kid). The Congress had no one in Gujarat who could compete with Modi's image to arouse Gujarati pride. The party did not engage in counter-propaganda related to 'injustice to Gujarat' by the earlier Congress regime.

ORGANIZATION

Though both parties have an organizational structure from polling booth to the state, organizationally the BJP is far superior to Congress in mass contact, a line of command and dedicated *karykarta*, that is, workers. Since the early 1980s, the organizational structure of the Congress has been gradually dismantled and functioning on an ad hoc basis. No serious efforts have been made in Gujarat to rejuvenate it from the grassroots level. On the other hand, the BJP has scrupulously built its structure brick by brick over the years. Political power has strengthened its patronage network by distributing tangible and non-tangible benefits as well as legitimizing its idea of India. BJP outfits and footloose soldiers have been actively engaged in between elections as well harping on Hinduness, community pride and nationalism, often applauding macho Modi's image.

Amit Shah, president of the party, has managed Gujarat elections since 2007. A devotee of Chanakya and Savarkar, he believes, 'Elections have to be fought with a great degree of precision and ruthlessness.'[13] As a part of his micro-planning for the election process in 2012, he divided polling booths into three categories—A, B and C—on the basis of BJP's votes, 60, 40–60 and less than 40 per cent votes in the respective booths in the preceding elections. Concentrated efforts were made on the C booths to improve the party's votes. Besides preparing social demographic information of the voters, each booth consisted of a committee, booth president and also heads of each page (around a hundred voters) of the electoral list. The party had evolved different strategies from constituency to constituency and booth to booth for improving/consolidating its position.

Rahul Gandhi, though respected by cadre, does not enjoy a comparable aura and command over the party's rank and file. The Congress also formed booth level units and volunteers called 'janmitra' (people's friends). Except for a few places, these units remained on paper. Though Gandhi used to frequently say that the Congress' battle with the BJP was ideological, neither he nor any Congress leader from Gujarat spelt out specifically the differences between Congress and BJP's ideology. In practice, a line between Congress' so-called soft Hinduness and BJP's Hindutva is thin as most of the Congress ranks and files in Gujarat share anti-Muslim prejudices with the average BJP worker. The difference is in its nature and extent of fanaticism. Training programmes and the manual for janmitra provide information about the work that the Congress had done since Independence for building India in various sectors, Modi government programmes and failures in creating jobs, harassment of people by GST and demonetization, injustice to tribal and women and atrocities against Dalit. But it shied away from highlighting insecurity faced by minorities and increasing incidents of mob lynching, the terror of cow vigilante and so on. An average grassroots Congress worker with a middle-class mindset is an average Indian with no ideological orientation. S/he is mainly interested in the patronage system to procure and distribute favours. Party loyalty of the workers is fragile. The party launched a mobile app called Shakti (power) platform in 2018 to get feedback from janmitra and Congress workers at different levels to 'break walls between leaders and workers.' It, however, failed in translating its objective as several fake persons registered and virtually sabotaged the programme.[14] A senior Congress leader told me that Rahul Gandhi was surrounded by liberal academicians and technocrats who had no roots with people. Hence, according to him, inconvenient feedback from ground level were not attended by the high command.

Feeble party loyalty is evident in the defection of several elected Congress leaders who were with the party for several years. As mentioned above, within two years of its victory in many local governments, the party could not stop the defection of District and Taluka Panchayat members to the BJP. Similarly, more than five Congress MLAs and a few prominent senior party functionaries crossed over and joined the ruling party in 2018. The BJP immediately made two of them ministers and promised similar rewards for others. The media reported that the BJP had battalion parachutes to penetrate in the Congress and hijack their members. Such defections on the eve of the elections demoralized party workers. Besides, few BJP leaders publicly said that CCTV cameras watched them. If they did not vote for the BJP, they would not get government benefits, and 'would be taken to task'.[15]

ECONOMIC ISSUES AND NATIONAL PRIDE

According to a survey carried out in the last quarter of 2018, a majority of the voters were unsatisfied with government's economic performance.[16] For them, employment and agriculture-related issues like water were the top priority. Since 2015, Gujarat witnessed agitations by youths around these issues reflected in the 2017 state Assembly elections. The Congress pledged to create more jobs in private and public sectors, write off bank loans of farmers, and the Nyuntam Aay Yojana (NYAY) promised to provide ₹72,000 annually to the poorest 20 per cent of households.

On the other hand, to appease farmers, the BJP increased its minimum support price of 22 crops in July 2018. It also soon announced PM Kisan Samman Nidhi Scheme (PM-Kisan) in December 2018 providing ₹6000 per annum to small and marginal farmers. Following the union government, in February 2019, in its interim budget, the Gujarat government increased its allocation to welfare programme, and also it gave the first instalment to poor farmers under the PM-Kisan scheme.[17]

POST-PULWAMA\BALAKOT NARRATIVE AND PATRIOTISM

Congress' plea of 'Chowkidar Chor' alleging corruption involving Modi remained a non-starter in the middle class. The BJP countered it with 'Main Bhi Chowkidar', asserting the sturdiness of the watchman (Modi). The party organized demonstrations and meetings of watch guards working in government and private sectors. The allegation did not shake Gujarati middle class' faith in Modi, though a few were willing to believe that Modi might have favoured Ambani[18] for funding the party and not for personal gain. On the other hand, Gujarat BJP president accused Rahul for naming Ambani because he is a Gujarati.[19]

However, with Pulwama's incident in which 40+ CRPF personnel were killed by terrorists on 14 February 2019, the BJP changed the narrative of the election campaign. On that night, semi-spontaneous functions were organized in cities paying homage to the paramilitary martyrs. The BJP skilfully used these emotions arousing patriotism, nationalism and anti-Pakistan phobia; a threat to the country's security. On 26 February, the Union Government conducted the Balakot airstrike inside Pakistan's border and allegedly destroyed the terrorists' camp. When a Congress man commented that people have the right 'to know the facts of the Air Force operation', he was accused by the BJP to be pro-Pakistani and branded as 'anti-national' and terrorist. With a view to creating a public image of the Congress being 'pro-Pakistani', the Chief Minister of Gujarat Vijay Rupani said: 'Pakistan wants Congress to win and BJP to lose this election.' He also said that the BJP government might have faulted in 'development', but the party is:

> working towards making the country secure with zero tolerance. This election is a national election and based on national issues. And the major national issue is, in whose hand will the country remain safe?...at present, none else but PM Modi can provide safety to the country.[20]

Amit Shah while filing his nomination papers organized a road show with the slogan 'Kashmir Humara Hai'. High-pitch nationalism coupled with jingoism created a feeling that the country's security was in danger and Modi was the only strong leader to protect the country. This had a hurricane effect even on those voters who were on the fence and also a small section of pro-Congress voters across caste and class lines for shifting their vote in favour of the BJP.

ECONOMIC DISTRESS, CASTE AGITATIONS AND VOTING

Though Modi won all 26 parliament seats from Gujarat in 2014, the state had witnessed several agitations against BJP's economic policies and projects, particularly in rural areas. A few were successful grassroots collective actions forcing the government/investors to withdraw their projects. These agitations were issue-based, independent of each other with non-political party character and indifferent to a macro-political economy.[21] Moreover, soon after the 2014 elections, the ruling party faced protests, mostly localized, from different sections on the issues of unemployment, agrarian distress, fee hike in private schools and GST. A few of the agitations with caste-based formations spread across the state.

Agitation by youths from the Patidar caste, a dominant middle caste, led by Hardik Patel, former Vishva Hindu Parishad (VHP) activist, demanded reservations for the community. The agitation launched in 2015, continued intermittently until the 2017 assembly elections. The government used many repressive tactics to diffuse and suppress the agitation including police actions and sedition charges against leading activists. It also created divisions among the activists persuading community elites to stay away from the agitations.

Simultaneously, to pacify the agitators, the government issued an ordinance offering a package in September 2015 for upper-caste 'poor' students, providing subsidies in college fees, scholarships and also reservation in jobs and educational institutions to 10 per cent for upper castes. Gujarat's High Court struck down the decision. Then, the government constituted the Gujarat Unreserved Education and Economic Development Corporation (GUEEDC) in September 2017 to provide various benefits to the students of 'unreserved' communities.

Moreover, business and industrial interests representing the community undertook the responsibility of providing economic help and the creation of 10,000 jobs, hostels, education institutions and coaching classes for Patidar youths. In January 2019, the Modi government amended the Constitution and introduced 10 per cent reservation to economically poor non-reserved communities, virtually for upper castes. This decision, according to the PM would 'enhance the confidence of "New India"'. Patidar and other upper caste organizations publicly congratulated Modi for providing reservations to them. Over and above, during the campaign, more than a thousand Patidar NRI (non-resident Indians) from various countries, landed in Gujarat canvassing for Modi. The construction of Sardar Patel's statue—the tallest of the world—also boosted Gujarati pride in general, and of the Patidars in particular.

Though Patidars constitute less than 12 per cent of Gujarat's population, both parties fielded more than one-fourth Patidar candidates. The Congress depended more on Hardik Patel than its own long-time leaders from the community. Amit Shah crafted 'mission Patidar' to appease office-bearers of various Patidar organizations. Modi, Rupani (CM) and Shah frequently praised Patidars for their hard work and social services. During the campaign, Modi attended community functions celebrating their lineage goddess and praised their caste spirit and nationalism.

Various upper castes supported the initial phase of the Patidar agitation. Some however opined that there are many other subtle ways to get their things done rather than agitations. The formation of GUEEDC by Gujarat government and 10 per cent reservation announced by the Modi government reassured them that the BJP was their government which looks after their interests. This coupled with a plea for national security was reflected in the election outcome. Two-thirds of the upper caste voters voted for the BJP, 65 per cent of Patidars and 81 per cent of other upper castes voted for BJP[22] (Figures 11.3 and 11.4).

OTHER BACKWARD CLASSES/CASTES

Other Backward Classes/Castes (OBCs), divided into 146 castes in Gujarat is not a cohesive social category. Of them, 11 social groups are Muslim. The OBCs include poor peasant castes such as Kolis, Kshatriyas called Thakors, nomadic tribes, pastorals as well as artisan-trading castes such as Ganchi (oil presser), Suthar (carpenter), Kumbhar (potter), Valand (barber) and so on who are now urbanized and have relatively improved their economic status with the growth of the market economy. Among OBCs, numerically largest caste-clusters, around 24 per cent of the population, are Kshatriyas of the central and north Gujarat; and Kolis of Coastal region of Saurashtra and south Gujarat. Since the early 1990s, the BJP has the strong and consistent support of Kolis. Kshatriyas vacillate between the BJP and Congress from election to election.

Following the Patidar agitation, Alpesh Thakor of the Kshatriya-Thakor Sena (KTS) launched an agitation of the OBCs, though virtually only of Thakors raising issues of employment and stringent implementation of the prohibition law. The government immediately met the demand related to prohibition. Though Kshatriyas are already beneficiaries of reservations in government jobs under the OBC category, the problem of unemployment remains unresolved. KTS demanded strict implementation of the 1995 announced policy for industries to provide 85 per cent employment to 'local' people in industries. Later, Alpesh joined the Congress party, contested and won in the assembly elections.[23]

In mid-2018, he launched an agitation for the implementation of 85 per cent reservation for local in industries. It was alleged that he instigated local against migrant north-Indian labourers. That backfired.

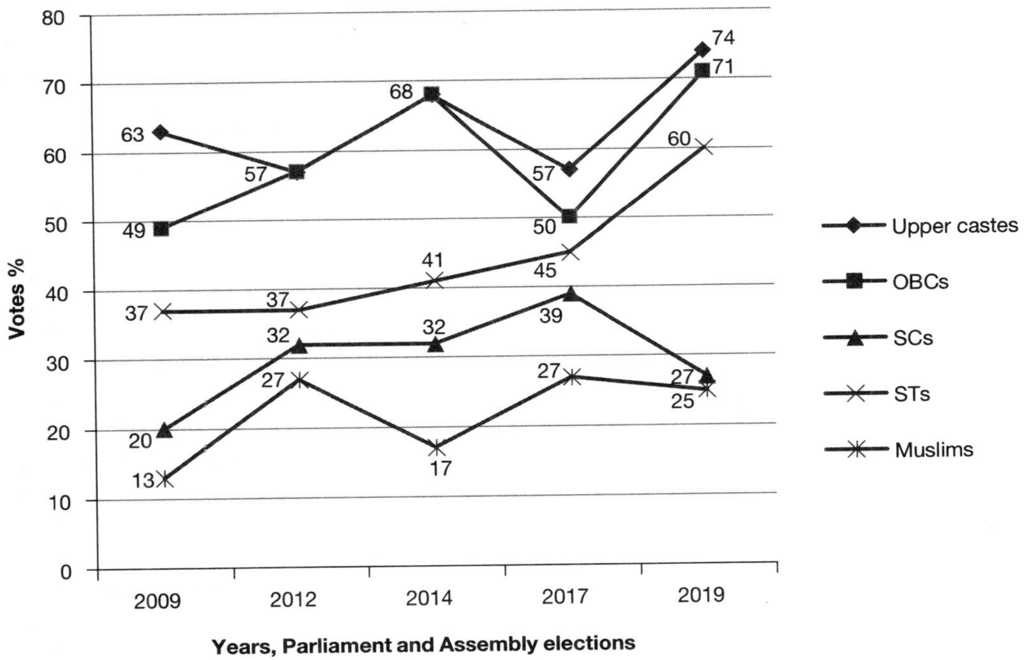

Figure 11.3 *BJP Voters in Different Assembly and Parliament Elections by Castes/Communities*

Source: National Election Survey—Lokniti (CSDS).

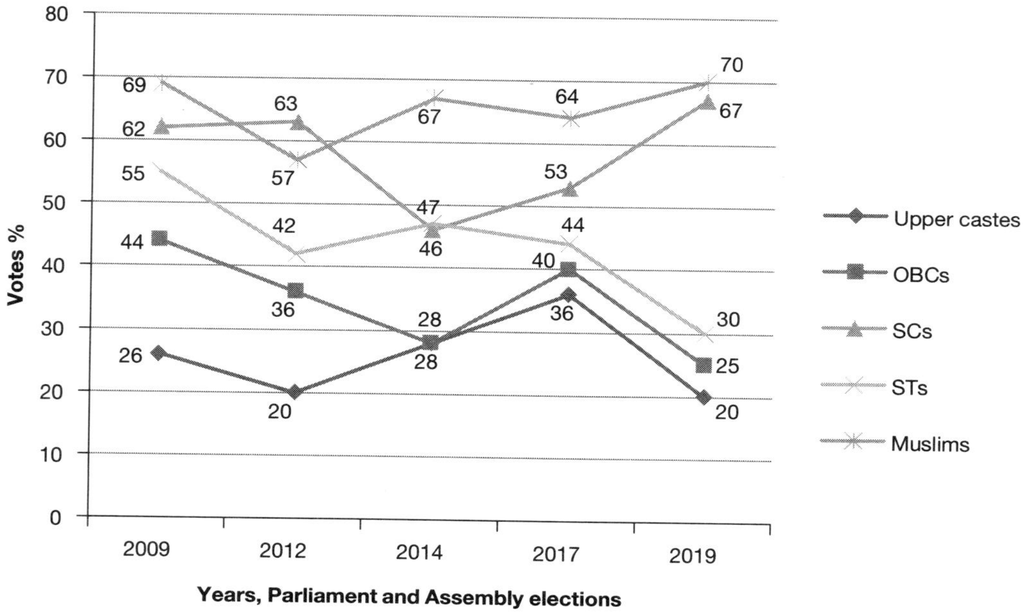

Figure 11.4 *Congress Voters in Parliament and Assembly Elections by Castes/Communities*

Source: National Election Survey—Lokniti (CSDS).

He was advised by Congress leaders to refrain from an anti-migrant agitation which was damaging the party's image in other states. By end of 2018, Alpesh accused Congress leaders of ignoring him. The BJP wooed him and on the eve of the 2019 Lok Sabha elections, he resigned from his various party positions. It is widely believed that he worked for the BJP. For Kshatriyas who had been susceptible to militant Hinduism since the 1950s,[24] post-Pulwama high pitched nationalism worked as a catalytic in their support for the BJP.

Kolis have been BJP's stronghold since the late 1990s. Gradually, the party has also won over leaders of different small OBCs particularly pastoral and artisan castes. With multifarious strategies for winning over different OBC castes, the BJP captured their 71 per cent votes, so far the highest (Figures 11.3 and 11.4). The Congress lost its Kshatriya strong base Anand constituency where it secured five out of seven assembly seats in 2017.

SCHEDULED CASTES

Scheduled castes constitute only 7.55 of Gujarat's population. The practice of untouchability and atrocities against them, particularly in rural Gujarat, continue unabated. The incident of fogging four Dalits by *gau-rakashaks* (cow-vigilantes) in 2016 led to widespread agitation of Dalit youths against government's inaction. Their struggle demanding justice continued intermittently for over a year.[25] Jignesh Mewani emerged as a Dalit leader who contested the 2017 assembly election as an independent. The Congress supported him and he won.

Though the Congress as in the past got more votes from SCs than the BJP, it did not get overwhelming support. One-fifth of the SC votes went to BSP, NOTA (none of the above) and independent candidates. Incidents of atrocities against Dalits have not declined in the last five years. The government frequently announced its determination against the accused, but the anti-Dalit situation in the state has remained unchanged. Even those Dalits who were actively supporting the BJP for the last three decades have felt that the BJP has become an upper caste party. BJP votes of SC declined further from 39 per cent in 2017 to 27 per cent in 2019. In the absence of BSP and an alternative party, the Congress got 67 per cent SC votes in 2019 (Figures 11.3 and 11.4).

SCHEDULED TRIBES

Scheduled Tribes (STs) constitute nearly 14 per cent of the state with three reserved seats in parliament and 27 seats in the state assembly. They are the poorest among the poor and continue to be the most backward on all social indicators such as education, infant and mother mortality rate, and poverty. Tribal have always resisted and also confronted the state in different ways against 'injustice' and the imposition of the mainstream culture on them. A section of them have recently revived their demand for a separate state called Bhilistan and have formed Bharatiya Tribal Party which had an alliance with the Congress in the 2017 assembly elections.

The Congress which already has a relatively strong institutional network in tribal areas secured 17 out of 26 seats assembly seats in 2017. But in 2019, with meticulous micro-planning and concentrated efforts of Amit Shah, the BJP won all the three tribal reserved seats, securing a majority of votes from 19 out of 26 assembly segments. It captured 60 per cent ST votes, highest in the last six decades. Congress vote share of tribal had been reduced to merely 30 per cent—lowest in its history. At the same time, however, more than half assembly segments from where the Congress got a majority were tribal constituencies.

MUSLIMS

Muslims constitute 11 per cent of Gujarat's population. Since the early 1980s, they have been marginalized in electoral politics. Like in the past, messages circulate in everyday life through face-to-face chit-chats and gossips. Now on social media, prejudices against Muslims among the majority community are reinforced. They are frequently accused of anti-national, anti-social and aggressive behaviour. Fears spread that if the Congress gets power, Muslims would be pampered and would create riots. This time a message, particularly in middle-class networks, was viral that the UPA government planned to pass a

Sachar Committee[26] bill giving reservation and many other benefits to Muslims. That would have made Hindus vulnerable. In Gujarat, Muslims have already been marginalized. The Congress neither in past nor this time made any effort to win over the confidence of Muslims. Despite this, a majority of them voted for the Congress as they do not find other alternatives.

ECONOMIC STRATA AND VOTING

The BJP has been the preferred party of upper and middle-income strata across social groups over the Congress in Gujarat since the early 1990s. Nevertheless, the proportion of their support to the party was reduced from 28 per cent and 17 per cent respectively in the 2017 assembly election. It was because of demonetization, GST and a rising rate of unemployment. The BJP regained its position, particularly among the middle-class from 48 per cent in 2017 to 70 per cent in 2019[27] (Figure 11.5). I have come across middle-class youths who were critical of Modi until the Pulwama incident. Rise of jingoism around the anti-Pakistan/terrorist attacks restored their faith in Modi.

More striking is that the BJP has penetrated significantly among lower and poor strata with securing the majority of their votes (Figure 11.5). Following Rahul Gandhi's jibe on Modi's government as 'suit boot ki sarkar', Amit Shah declared that the party would observe Deendayal Upadhyay's birth centenary year (2016–2017) as the *Garib Kalyan* (welfare of the poor). The party karyakartas were mobilized in the implementation of the government's welfare programmes. On the other hand, in between the elections, the Congress failed to highlight the government's sluggishness in implantation of 'right'-based programmes such as rural employment, food security, education and so on that it formulated. No efforts were made to mobilize have-nots demanding their rights. And, its promise for 'minimum income guarantee' on the eve of elections did not influence the imagination of the poor. It has lost its pro-poor image. On the other hand, BJP's programmes providing tangible benefits of the direct bank transfer with Jan Dhan Yojana, Ujjawala with LPG cylinder, Swachh Bharat with toilet, the release of the first instalment of ₹2000 under PMKSY on

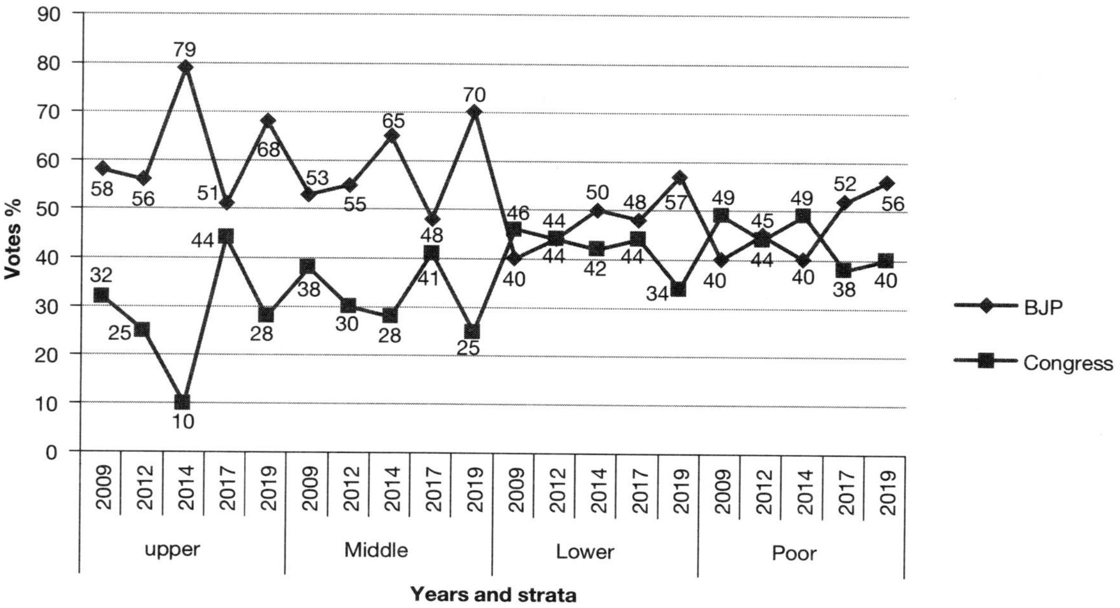

Figure 11.5 *Economic Status and Party Voted in Assembly and Parliament Elections*

Source: National Election Survey—Lokniti (CSDS).

the eve of elections as well as the call for national security helped the BJP to harness votes of the poor.

OVERVIEW

During its five years in power, the Modi government has not met the expectations of a majority of people, specifically on the economic front. There is widespread distress among farmers regarding youth unemployment and agricultural development, though not translated into anger. Modi has skilfully sidetracked these issues and the opposition party in Gujarat has failed in bringing these issues effectively into the election campaign. Instead, the BJP emphasized Modi's charisma embedded with the image of a strong, dedicated and determined leader. The Gujarati middle class has started believing that 'he can do no wrong'. In order to build such a mindset, the Amit Shah and Modi duo have built an efficient organization with a battalion of karyakartas and footloose soldiers. They have mastered election engineering with detailed micro-planning and dynamic approach varying from time to time, constituency to constituency and community to community. Except for the religious minority community and Dalits, the BJP has captured a majority of votes across society irrespective of caste and economic status.

On the other hand, the organizational structure of Gujarat Congress is worn out. Ideologically it is spineless. And, its electoral promises of creating more jobs have failed in catching the imagination of people. It has lost its pro-poor image. Though a majority of Dalits and Muslims voted for the Congress, they were not positive votes for the party as the party has not stood firmly with them.

NOTES

1. Ghanshyam Shah, 'Gujarat: Goebbel's Propaganda and Governance—The 2009 Lok Sabha Elections in Gujarat', in *India's 2009 Elections*, eds. Paul Wallace and Ramashray Roy (New Delhi: SAGE Publications, 2011) 167–191; Ghanshyam Shah, 'Mega Marketing and Management: Gujarat 2014 Elections', in *India's 2014 Elections*, ed. Paul Wallace (New Delhi: SAGE Publications, 2015) 258–283.

2. Shah, 'Goebbels Propaganda'.
3. Ghanshyam Shah, 'BJP's Sixth Victory in Gujarat: A Puzzle', *Economic and Political Weekly* 53, no. 2 (13 January 2018): 20–25.
4. Available at https://rightlog.in/2018/06/bjp-congress-panchayats-gujarat-01/ (accessed on 21 June 2018).
5. For instance, Nirmala Sitharaman, then defence minister asked voters in Vadodara, 'Vote for Prime Minister vote for Prime Minister Narendra Modi by choosing the "lotus", and not the candidate fielded by the party from the seat'. Available at https://indianexpress.com/elections/vote-for-pm-modi-not-bjp-candidate-nirmala-sitharaman-to-voters-lok-sabha-5662966/ (accessed on 7 April 2019).
6. Ghanshyam Shah, 'Gujarat After Godhara' in *India's 2004 Elections*, eds. Ramashray Roy and Paul Wallace (New Delhi: SAGE Publications, 2007), 151–179.
7. Ajay Umat, 'Swapanonasodagar', *Divya Bhaskar*, 18 December 2005.
8. Shah, 'Goebbels Propaganda'.
9. Shah, 'Mega Marketing'.
10. Pratik Sinha, 'Busted: "True" Story by Manish Malhotra, about Modi Working 18–20 Hours a Day'. Available at https://www.altnews.in/busted-true-story-manish-malhotra-modi-working-18–20-hours-day/ (accessed on 26 January 2018).
11. Shah, 'Mega Marketing'.
12. Available at https://www.tribuneindia.com/news/nation/i-m-your-man-in-delhi-modi-tells-gujaratis/760503.html (accessed on 19 April 2019).
13. Aniban Ganguly and Shawanand Dwivedi, *Amit Shah and the March of BJP* (New Delhi: Bloomsbury 2019), 131.
14. Betwa Sharma, 'How Project "Shakti" Misled Rahul and Deepened Congress's Lok Sabha Rout', Huffpost, 29 May 2019. Available at https://www.huffingtonpost.in/entry/bogus-app-rahul-gandhi-congresss-lok-sabha-rout_in_5cee2e83e4b0793c23476816 (accessed on 26 September 2019).
15. Available at https://www.news18.com/news/politics/modi-is-watching-gujarat-mla-threatens-voters-with-less-funds-if-they-dont-for-bjp-2104711.html (accessed on 16 April 2019).
16. Available at https://adrindia.org/content/adrs-survey-governance-issues-and-voting-behaviour-2018 (accessed on 26 September 2019). See also https://bestmediainfo.com/2018/01/abp-news-lokniti-csds-mood-of-the-nation-survey-2018/ (accessed on 26 September 2019).
17. Available at https://accommodationtimes.com/salient-feature-of-gujarat-interim-budget-2019–20/ (accessed on 20 February 2019).
18. It is believed that Anil Ambani of Reliance company was a major beneficiary of Rafale deal. See https://www.newsclick.in/anil-ambani-emerges-shadows-modis-rafale-deal (acessed on 30 November 2017).
19. *The Times of India* (Ahmedabad) 27 March 2019.

20. Available at https://www.ndtv.com/india-news/gujarat-chief-minister-vijay-rupani-says-congress-victory-will-see-pakistan-celebrate-diwali-2012227 (accessed on 26 March 2019).
21. Ghanshyam Shah, *Democracy, Civil Society and Governance* (New Delhi: SAGE Publications, 2019).
22. I thank Lokniti CSDS for providing and permitting me to use data collected for National Election Study.
23. Shah, 'BJP's Sixth Victory'.
24. Ghanshyam Shah, *Caste Association and Political Process in Gujarat: A Study of Gujarat Kshatriya Sabha* (Bombay: Popular Prakashan, 1975).
25. Ghanshyam Shah, 'Neo-liberal Political Economy and Social Tensions: Simmering Dalit Unrest and Competing Castes in Gujarat', *Economic and Political Weekly* 52, no 35 (2 September 2017): 62–70.
26. In 2005, UPA government appointed a committee headed by Justice (Retired) Sachar to examine social, economic and educational condition of Muslim Community in India. The Committee submitted it report in 2006, highlighting condition of Muslim and suggested measures how to remove impediments those preventing Indian Muslims from fully participating in the economic, political, and social mainstream of Indian life.
27. Computed combing family's monthly income and assets, for methodology see Lokniti Team, 'National Election Study 2009: A Methodological Note', *Economic and Political Weekly* 44, no.39 (September 2009), 196–202.

Chapter 12

Onward March of BJP in Maharashtra

Suhas Palshikar and Nitin Birmal

If one were to accurately describe the nature of electoral competition in Maharashtra since 2014, the state would qualify for a tag of 'no contest' state. In both 2014 and 2019, Maharashtra produced an extremely one-sided outcome to bring it on a par with many states of North and Central India such as Madhya Pradesh, Rajasthan and Gujarat. What makes the case of Maharashtra rather interesting, however, is the fact that Maharashtra's route to shaping of BJP's dominance has been different from that of Gujarat or other states of Central–North India.

- First, the party is still not able to carve out a durable base for itself in the state. Its victories in 2014 and 2019 have come riding on the back of uncertain social equations.
- Second, competitiveness—though not reflected in the outcome—has not completely disappeared in Maharashtra. That is why the BJP chose to make peace with its warring ally Shiv Sena on the eve of elections. It is another matter that the state BJP may have subsequently rued that decision because contesting alone, it may have bagged quite a few more seats for itself.
- Third, in Maharashtra, the Congress was in power for 15 long years between 1999 and 2014. BJP gained power only in 2014 at the

state level and within five years from then managed to repeat its impressive electoral performance. Yet the societal dominance that BJP enjoys in Gujarat is somewhat elusive in Maharashtra in 2019.

- Finally, above all, in Maharashtra, BJP's emergence is more due to failures of its rivals—the Congress and Nationalist Congress Party (NCP). They have not only exported their many district-level leaders to the BJP but these two parties have also ceded ground to the BJP among their long-time social base, the Maratha community.

But, of course, these details pale into insignificance when one examines the outcomes of the parliamentary elections of 2019 as well as 2014. This chapter aims at discussing the magnitude of the victory gained by the BJP with its Shiv Sena ally and explore the possible reasons behind that victory.

THE RESULT

Almost as an exact repetition of 2014, the BJP and Shiv Sena won 41 seats out of 48 from the state. The seat tally of the two parties was also the same as in 2014–23 and 18 respectively. This left only seven seats for the entire opposition. This can give an idea of the one-sidedness of the electoral outcome. Against its two seats in 2014, the Congress was reduced to only one in 2019. Its coalition partner NCP won four seats, same as in 2014, and the remaining two seats went respectively to the All India Majlis-e-Ittehad-ul Muslimeen (AIMIM), which was allied to Vanchit Bahujan Aghadi (VBA; literally, front of the deprived majority) for the Aurangabad seat, and an Independent from Amaravati. Table 12.1 gives the details of the electoral outcome of 2019, in terms of both seats and votes.

When the election outcome is so one-sided, there is also a flatness to it, which is seen in the regional details. Congress's lone seat came from Vidarbha. Ironically, that seat was won by an ex-Shiv Sena person who was given a Congress ticket. Of the four seats won by the NCP, three came from western Maharashtra—Satara, Baramati and Shirur—while the fourth one came from Raigad (Konkan region). An Independent supported by Congress and NCP, Navnit Kaur Rana, won

Table 12.1 *Maharashtra Lok Sabha 2019 Result*

Parties	Contested	Seats Won	Change from 2014	Vote (%)	Change from 2014
NDA	48	41	**0**	50.88	**2.93**
BJP	25	23	**0**	27.59	**0.27**
SHS	23	18	**0**	23.29	**2.66**
UPA	47	5	**–2**	34.24	**–2.73**
INC	25	1	**–1**	16.27	**–1.86**
NCP	19	4	**0**	15.52	**–0.45**
SWP	2	0	**–1**	1.54	**–0.73**
BVA	1	0	**0**	0.91	**0.31**
AIMIM	1	1	**1**	0.72	**0.72**
VBA	47	0	**0**	6.93	**6.93**
Other parties	724	1	**1**	6.33	**–7.86**
NOTA	48	0	**0**	0.90	**0.01**
Overall	**915**	**48**		**100.00**	

Source: CSDS Data Unit.

Notes: Alliances based on Lok Sabha 2019; turn out: 60.79 per cent; change from 2014: 0.47 per cent.

the Amaravati seat from Vidarbha. In the case of the Shiv Sena and BJP alliance, they split the seats between them in the regions of Mumbai-Thane, Western Maharashtra and Marathwada more or less equally. The BJP won handsomely in North Maharashtra and adjoining western Vidarbha, while the Shiv Sena's seats came from all regions of the state.

Table 12.2 shows the vote share of different parties in each region. While BJP polled more than 46 per cent in North Maharashtra, Shiv Sena polled more than 49 per cent votes in Konkan region. Together, the BJP and Shiv Sena polled handsomely in all regions. A measure of their success can be seen from the fact that in the Congress–NCP bastion of western Maharashtra, BJP and Shiv Sena polled almost 49 per cent votes. Despite much hype, AIMIM and VBA were not

Table 12.2 *Maharashtra Lok Sabha 2019 Result by Regions*

		Congress		NCP		UPA		BJP		Shiv Sena		NDA		AIMIM		Other Parties	
Regions	Total Seats	Won	Vote (%)	Won	Vote (%)	Won	Vote (%)	Won	Vote (%)	Won	Vote (%)	Won	Vote (%)	Won	Vote (%)	Won	Vote (%)
North Maharashtra	6	0	18.32	0	13.84	0	32.17	5	46.86	1	8.28	6	55.14	0	5.28	0	7.41
East Vidarbha	4	0	14.99	0	8.59	0	23.58	1	12.25	2	33.98	3	46.23	0	13.50	1	16.69
Marathwada	8	0	16.37	0	15.24	0	31.61	4	26.08	3	21.76	7	47.84	1	13.01	0	7.54
Mumbai-Thane	10	0	19.46	0	8.66	0	33.24	4	23.22	6	34.32	10	57.55	0	4.30	0	4.91
Western Maharashtra	11	0	7.98	3	25.31	3	39.67	5	26.72	3	21.84	8	48.56	0	7.59	0	4.18
Konkan	3	0	1.92	1	30.09	1	32.01	0	0.00	2	49.59	2	49.59	0	3.94	0	14.46
West Vidarbha	6	1	32.59	0	6.39	1	38.98	4	41.28	1	8.43	5	49.72	0	5.20	0	6.10
Overall	**48**	**1**	**16.27**	**4**	**15.52**	**5**	**34.24**	**23**	**27.59**	**18**	**23.29**	**41**	**50.88**	**1**	**7.65**	**1**	**7.23**

Source: CSDS Data Unit.

very effective in terms of vote share: Only in Marathwada and eastern Vidarbha they were able to attract over 10 per cent votes. With an impressive difference of more than 16 per cent votes between United Progressive Alliance (UPA) and National Democratic Alliance (NDA), the outcome clearly indicated the demise of Congress and emergence of BJP along with Shiv Sena as its replacement.

Caste and community composition of candidates of major parties provides an interesting pattern. While the two major alliances continued to focus more on the Maratha–Kunbi community, VBA primarily fielded OBC candidates as seen from Table 12.3. Together, the BJP and Shiv Sena appeared to have an understanding about the social composition of their candidates. Shiv Sena ensured that enough tickets were given to Maratha community, while the BJP gave more tickets to the OBCs. While Congress fielded one Muslim candidate (from Akola), Sena–BJP alliance did not field any Muslim candidate. In the case of the Congress–NCP alliance, OBC candidates were found more in the case of NCP. Overall, Shiv Sena emerged as the main vehicle of the Marathas along with the NCP, while BJP functioned as the vehicle of the OBCs, though NCP actually managed to combine both Maratha

Table 12.3 *Caste and Community Background of Candidates of Main Parties*

Caste/Community	BJP	Shiv Sena	Congress	NCP	VBA
Maratha	07	15	03	10	00
Kunbi	03	01	06	01	01
Upper Caste	03	02	04	01	01
Non-maharashtrian	02	00	02	00	01
OBC	05	01	02	06	24
SC	02	03	05	00	13
ST	03	01	02	01	04
Muslim	00	00	01	00	04

Source: Compiled by authors from information collected through newspapers and party sources.

and OBC constituencies more effectively. Both Shiv Sena and NCP avoided giving candidature to any non-Maharashtrian candidate. So the non-Maharashtrians got tickets mainly from Congress and BJP. Although caste and community alone cannot be the factors in shaping voter choices, this mapping of social composition of candidates gives us an idea about how parties perceive their social constituencies and how these are cultivated by giving tickets.

NCP gave a ticket to popular television star Amol Kolhe, who was then playing the role of Chhatrapati Sambhaji, the protagonist of the Marathi serial on the life of Sambhaji Raje. Kolhe defected from the Shiv Sena and joined the NCP on the eve of the elections. Another 'star' attraction was presented by the Congress from Mumbai (North), Urmila Matondkar known for her Hindi movie presence. Kolhe won his, but Matondkar lost her election. While Prakash Ambedkar chose to contest from two constituencies (losing both), Akola in Vidarbha and Solapur, his candidature from Solapur meant a division of Congress's Dalit votes there. In Solapur, BJP fielded the Lingayat Swami (Mahaswamiji, Dr Jaisiddeshwar Shivacharya) in a constituency having a sizable Lingayat population—both these factors resulted in the defeat of Congress candidate Sushilkumar Shinde.

POLITICAL CONFIGURATIONS

Electoral politics in Maharashtra has been marked by bipolarity since the 1990s. It was in 1989 that the BJP and Shiv Sena first came together and since then have managed to firm up their alliance for over two decades despite many problems, natural to such coalition making. Pramod Mahajan was supposed to be the architect of this long-time understanding between the two parties, though the BJP was tempted to seriously consider the possibility of going it alone because an alliance meant limits on its expansion in the state. 'Shat pratishat Bhajapa' (cent per cent BJP, i.e., BJP to contest on its own and win), was the slogan of the party at one stage after its 1999 victory at the centre.[1] But its leadership had to finally agree on continuing with the alliance in order to defeat Congress. Ironically, the Shiv Sena–BJP alliance also ensured that the two congress parties—NCP and Congress—were forced to keep their alliance too. They were first forced to join hands immediately after the formation of the NCP in 1999. That was a post-election coalition which allowed them to form the government in the state after a hung assembly was elected. They remained together consistently since then.

Politics suddenly changed following the 2014 Lok Sabha elections. Victory was the undoing of the Shiv Sena–BJP alliance, whereas defeat caused the break-up of the Congress–NCP coalition! Following the BJP's electoral ascendance in 2014, though the Shiv Sena joined the Union Government, it continued to sulk. Finally, on the eve of the assembly election of 2014, Shiv Sena decided to part company with the BJP and contest independently—for the first time since its rise in 1990. The two congress parties, which too had a relationship of suspicion and distrust, followed suit and dissolved their coalition. Thus, the bipolarity of electoral politics was breached and resulted in another hung assembly in 2014—the BJP missing majority by a bare 20 seats. Although the NCP momentarily thought of extending support to the BJP, Shiv Sena decided to re-align with BJP. The new alliance was fraught with deep bitterness and continuous one-upmanship, and was overshadowed by the brinkmanship of the Shiv Sena which played the role of 'opposition' all through 2014–2019.[2]

In fact, it was only the political management skills of Chief Minister Devendra Fadnavis and the patience of the BJP leadership that ensured the survival of the awkward coalition. Not so curiously, the Shiv Sena leadership could never arrive at a firm decision to sever its ties with the BJP in spite of being a bitter critic of the BJP during this period. Therefore, it was also not a surprise that the two parties decided to form an alliance yet again on the eve of the Lok Sabha elections of 2019. With Amit Shah's visit to Sena chief Uddhav Thackeray,[3] the alliance was forged and the two parties went into the polls as a united political force. Notwithstanding minor hiccups, the campaign of the Shiv Sena and BJP was reasonably effective and in one voice.

The re-union of Shiv Sena and BJP left the Congress and NCP with no choice but to come together, and in any case, there was already a continuous effort for them to join hands. With Sharad Pawar being active in forging an alliance of non-BJP forces nationally, the coalition at the state level was a forgone conclusion. The Shiv Sena–BJP alliance also speeded up the opposition alliance. NCP tried to broaden the non-BJP coalition at the state level by persuading the Congress to include the Maharashtra Navnirman Sena (MNS), but Congress declined and MNS decided not to contest Lok Sabha polls altogether. The Congress–NCP alliance did accommodate the Raju Shetti faction of Swabhiman Paksh but failed to take along the forces led by Prakash Ambedkar.

Ambedkar had already charted a separate path by entering into an understanding with AIMIM—the party that had made an impact in Marathwada region in 2014. This was seen as an experiment in bringing together two key social forces—Dalits and Muslims. Furthermore, Ambedkar formed VBA, thus enticing the OBCs to also come on board. While the core base of this coalition was always seen as non-BJP voters, and therefore would hurt the Congress–NCP, the expectation was also that OBC votes could be diverted away from BJP. Amidst allegations that Ambedkar made unviable or exaggerated demands from Congress and NCP, talks between him and Congress failed. As already mentioned, Ambedkar himself filed his candidature from Solapur, where Congress's Sushilkumar Shinde was contesting. Such tactics were also seen as efforts to endanger anti-BJP forces in the state.

In short, while the Shiv Sena and BJP were able to smoothly forge a coalition, the Congress and NCP were not able to broaden their coalition beyond inclusion of Raju Shetti.

On the contrary, as elections approached, some key Congress and NCP leaders shifted their political allegiances to BJP. Notable among these was the decision of the Vikhe Patil family from Ahmednagar district to defect from the Congress party. Sujay Vikhe Patil, son of Leader of Opposition Radhakrishna Vikhe Patil, not only joined the BJP[4] but was also given candidature from Ahmednagar constituency. Similarly, a strong family from Solapur district, the Mohite-Patils of the NCP (seen as Pawar loyalists at one time) also joined the BJP.[5] These are only two instances of desertions which in a sense represent a repeat trend from 2014, when the two Congress parties lost many of its stalwarts to the opposition.

Thus, a complex reconfiguration took shape on the eve of the election: Re-union of Shiv Sena and BJP on the one hand, and further shrinking of the social base of Congress and NCP in different regions of the state on the other hand. This reconfiguration suggested that right at the beginning of the electoral race, the BJP and Shiv Sena were in a position of advantage despite a public picture created in the media that they were going to face a tough challenge. The fact that they had an advantage was also corroborated by the pre-poll survey conducted by Lokniti at the end of March 2019, just before voting was to commence.[6]

THE CAMPAIGN

Although the BJP garnered votes in Modi's name, the actual campaign did have a strong state-specific flavour. While Fadnavis and Uddhav Thackeray were the key campaigners for the BJP and Shiv Sena (Fadnavis even campaigned vigorously for Shiv Sena candidates), Sharad Pawar was the most energetic campaigner for his NCP as well as the Congress. The state Congress did not have any popular leaders to campaign. Ashok Chavan, state Congress chief was focused on his own constituency where he lost. Sushilkumar Shinde, ex-chief minister and senior leader, was similarly busy in a triangular contest in Solapur where Prakash Ambedkar was also a candidate. While Shinde too lost, he was mostly non-available for campaigning outside his home constituency.

The campaign was taking place in the backdrop of an impending drought and water scarcity in the state. So the BJP and Shiv Sena had to underplay the ambitious project of 'Jalyukt Shivar'[7] for which their government had spent huge resources. Sharad Pawar, on the other hand, often raised the issues of agriculture, drought and prices of agricultural commodities. Just as BJP and Shiv Sena were reticent about the agriculture issue, the Congress and NCP did not bring in corruption or Rafale deal (controversy involving the purchase of fighter aircrafts from a French company).

Curiously, all parties were silent on the question of Maratha reservation—an issue that had dominated state politics over the previous several years. The BJP–Sena government had pacified the Maratha activists engaged in pro-reservation agitation by passing a law and assuring competent legal defence in the ongoing case challenging

Maratha reservation law in the Mumbai High Court. They hoped to benefit from it, but probably in view of the case pending in the court, all parties avoided much discussion on this issue. However, there was also no discussion at all about the alleged plight of the Marathas and the various decisions the state government had taken to address them.

A lacklustre campaign by the Congress meant that the ambitious NYAY scheme (Nyuntam Aay Yojana; a proposed scheme of cash transfers to poor households ensuring a minimum income for them) of the party was not adequately popularized through the campaign. In contrast, the BJP emphasized both the Kisan Samman Yojana and the Fasal Bima Yojana. Thus, while the BJP and Shiv Sena had an advantage among urban middle class voters, their campaign made it a point to address the rural voters and cut into Congress and NCP votes. Congress and NCP did not have a counterstrategy in response nor did they have the network of workers to campaign effectively.

The most crucial driver for the BJP and Shiv Sena campaign was the state assembly elections scheduled for six months after the Lok Sabha elections. The two ruling parties made it very clear to the sitting MLAs that in distributing tickets for assembly, performance of party candidates in their respective assembly segments would be taken into account. This ensured vigorous local campaigning by most sitting MLAs of the two parties.

EXPLAINING THE OUTCOME

Huge victories are simultaneously easy and hard to explain. They are easy to explain on the one hand because most social sections contribute to such victories—such as different caste groups, and also the rural and urban voters belonging to different classes. Such victories emerge through the shaping of large umbrella coalitions of social sections. They are also shaped by a combination of leadership, policy and the failures of the opponents. Large-scale victories are hard to explain on the other hand because there will always be objective facts that defy the politics behind such victories. Thus, suffering through demonetization or difficulties caused by GST could be very potent reasons for voters to not vote for BJP and Shiv Sena, but evidently, NDA was able to neutralize those adverse sentiments. There is also an additional difficulty of pinpointing what exactly may have 'caused' and what may have 'contributed' to such victories. The victory of BJP and Shiv Sena in the 2019 parliamentary elections fits into this paradox.

As previously presented, the victory of BJP and Shiv Sena was large scale because the alliance lost only seven seats; polling 50 per cent of the total votes that spanned the entire state. Moreover, this victory came in the backdrop of 'double incumbency'—the BJP (and Shiv Sena) exercised power at the Centre and also in the state in the preceding five years. This meant that they needed to beat the anti-incumbency at both levels. The victory also becomes more significant as there appeared to be a strong alternative coalition challenging the BJP and Shiv Sena.

Both the BJP and Shiv Sena won handsomely and the latter even improved its vote share. We noted that a survey conducted just a week and a half before voting began indicated a good lead for the BJP and Shiv Sena. That trend only consolidated during the campaign. Over 43 per cent voters seemed to have made up their minds before the campaign began.[8] Among them, 58 per cent voted for the BJP–Shiv Sena alliance.[9] This gives us an idea about the scale of advantage the BJP and Shiv Sena had in this election. This was probably because almost two persons in every three (63%) were satisfied with the performance of the state government and similarly two out of three (65%) were satisfied with the Central government.[10] Just as Modi was popular, it must also be noted that public opinion in the state was not against the state government either. Thus, the divergence of public opinion over an all-India choice and the choice at the state level did not obtain in Maharashtra.[11]

At the state level Devendra Fadnavis was the main campaigner for the BJP and for Shiv Sena it was Sena chief Uddhav Thackeray. The fact that Modi was a popular leader made a difference—22 per cent of NDA voters might have voted for some other party, but voted NDA because of Modi. This proportion was greater among BJP voters—28 per cent.[12] This follows an earlier pattern and also is consistent with the all-India level. Thus, a reasonable level of satisfaction with the state government, astute alliance with Shiv Sena, and Modi's image and popularity ensured victory for the BJP and its Shiv Sena ally. The fact thatthe Congress campaign was dispirited and Rahul Gandhi's popularity failed to match that of Modi were additional factors in favour of the BJP. Finally, the leadership of state government also mattered in this outcome—handling of the Shiv Sena and also neutralizing intra-party factions, Fadnavis not only emerged as the key leader at state level but also became BJP's only face at the state level in his capacity as chief minister.

SIGNIFICANCE OF MAHARASHTRA'S OUTCOME

Maharashtra is second only to Uttar Pradesh in terms of number of MPs it sends to the Lok Sabha. In 2019, it sent 41 MPs belonging to NDA. Maharashtra, a large and developed state with large investments and an expanding service sector is thus important to any ruling party in New Delhi both in terms of numbers, and in terms of the resources it controls and marshals. Besides, if one looks at the Lok Sabha outcomes in terms of leads in assembly segments, then the BJP and Shiv Sena were leading in more than 200 assembly segments (233 out of 288). This indicates that the Lok Sabha outcome places the BJP and Shiv Sena in a very strong position for the assembly elections scheduled for October 2019.

The 2019 outcome indeed was primarily part of the all-India trend, nevertheless the significance of Fadnavis' leadership and ability to ensure a balance among various social sections cannot be ignored. When the BJP came to power, it inherited a tricky issue in the form of Maratha demand for reservations as a backward class. After the High Court struck down the ordinance a previous government had promulgated, the state government was confronted with huge and continuous protests mobilized by the Maratha community. The state government successfully managed to pacify the agitating Maratha youth and their many organizations. It also swiftly legislated for Maratha reservations and in addition provided special scholarships and other facilities to youth from the Maratha community. These measures ensured that the anger of the Marathas was neutralized, if not turned into affection. The issue of Maratha reservations is sensitive not only because of the vociferous demand in favour, but because of simmering opposition from the other

OBCs. But the state government ensured that this opposition would not come out into the open or snowball into an anti-government platform. In this it was aided by the Congress and the NCP. Both these parties traditionally depend on Maratha support and as such they could not capitalize on OBC disappointments in this regard. Having lost that opportunity to corner the BJP, the Congress and NCP went on to lose Maratha votes in the Lok Sabha elections and thus again faced debilitating defeat.

This has the possibility of changing the history and character of the state's politics. Already, 2014 Lok Sabha and assembly elections changed it considerably.[13] As we argued earlier, defeat of the Congress and NCP in 2014 brought forward the critical issues of how the Congress space would be appropriated, what the response of Maratha elite would be to the changing power equations and the role to be played by OBCs in the future.[14] Though as Sarthak Bagchi has subsequently argued,[15] the Maratha networks are resilient enough to survive such setbacks and flexible enough to shift political allegiance in order to ensure their share in power, the Maratha leadership now has to depend on BJP and Shiv Sena to insulate itself from an OBC backlash.

Thus, a new political equation is developing. This new equation in the case of the BJP means the combined power of urban middle classes and OBCs; it has four MPs from an OBC background elected in 2019. In the case of the Shiv Sena, the new equation that Maratha leadership has to rely on is made up of urban non-agrarian Maratha interests enjoying greater clout than the rural Marathas. These urban Marathas are necessarily dependent on factors that have less to do with the broader rural interests of the Maratha community. This was evident in the course of the pro-reservation agitation. Youth from small towns were in the forefront and the appeal was more firmly rooted in caste identity and symbolism than ever before.

In this sense, the second convincing victory of the BJP–Shiv Sena alliance has brought Maharashtra onto the threshold of not only a new stage of limited competitiveness in which Congress and NCP would be marginalized but also a new social equilibrium that pushes the Marathas further away from the centre of power in the state.

NOTES

1. Priyanka Kakodkar, 'Taming the Tiger', *The Hindu*, Comment, 12 September 2014. Available at https://www.thehindu.com/opinion/op-ed/comment-taming-the-tiger-in-maharashtra/article6401844.ece (accessed on 16 July 2019).
2. Suhas Palshikar, 'Shiv Senecha Double Role (Marathi)', *BBC Marathi*, News Portal, 23 January 2018. Available at https://www.bbc.com/marathi/india-41475978 (accessed on 10 July 2019).
3. Ketaki Ghoge, 'BJP, Shiv Sena Seal Deal to Contest Lok Sabha, Maharashtra Polls Together', *Hindustan Times*, 19 February 2019. Available at https://www.hindustantimes.com/mumbai-news/bjp-shiv-sena-seal-deal-to-contest-lok-sabha-maharashtra-polls-together/story-88BLHU151Z2CGZsJhcUl4H.html (accessed on 7 July 2019).
4. *Indian Express*, 'Sujay Vikhe Patil Joins BJP, Leaves Congress, NCP Red Faced', *Indian Express*, 13 March 2019. Available at https://indianexpress.com/elections/sujay-vikhe-patil-joins-bjp-leaves-congress-ncp-red-faced-5623456/ (accessed on 25 September 2019.
5. Parthasarathi Biswas, 'Ranjitsinh Mohite Patil to Join BJP, Father Vijaysinh Expected to Follow Suit', *Indian Express*, 20 March 2019. Available at https://indianexpress.com/elections/ranjitsinh-mohite-patil-to-join-bjp-father-vijaysinh-expected-to-follow-suit-lok-sabha-elections-2019–5634744/ (accessed on 7 July 2019).
6. For methodology of the pre-poll survey and actual vote share projection for Maharashtra, from pre-poll survey, see https://www.lokniti.org/media/upload_files/Compiled%20Report%20Day%204.pdf (accessed on 10 July 2019).
7. It is a scheme initiated by the BJP–Shiv Sena government since 2014. Under this scheme, farmers are given financial support to build a small water reservoir in their farm in order to protect themselves from vagaries of monsoon. For a critical assessment of the scheme, see Neha Bhadbhade, Sarita Bhagat, K. J. Joy, Abraham Samuel, Kiran Lohakare, Raju Adagale, 'Can Jalyukt Shivar Abhiyan prevent Drought in Maharashtra?', Economic and Political Weekly 54, no. 25 (22 June 2019): 12–14.
8. Nitin Birmal and Rajeshwari Deshpande, 'Replicating 2014, but with a Higher Vote Share', *The Hindu*, 29 May 2019. Available at https://www.thehindu.com/elections/lok-sabha-2019/replicating-2014-but-with-a-higher-vote-share/article27277460.ece (accessed on 7 July 2019).
9. NES 2019, Maharashtra Post poll, CSDS Data Unit.
10. Birmal and Deshpande, 'Replicating 2014'.
11. Sandeep Shastri, 'Leadership Sweepstakes and the Modi Factor', *The Hindu*, 20 May 2019. Available at https://www.thehindu.com/elections/lok-sabha-2019/leadership-sweepstakes-and-the-modi-factor/article27189676.ece (accessed on 7 July 2019).

12. NES 2019, Maharashtra Pot Poll, CSDS Data Unit.
13. Suhas Palshikar, 'Maharashtra Assembly Elections: Farewell to Maratha Politics?' *Economic and Political Weekly* 49, no. 43–44 (1 November 2014): 10–13.
14. Suhas Palshikar and Nitin Birmal, 'Maharashtra: Congress' Dramatic Decline', in *India's 2014 Elections: A Modi-led BJP Sweep,* ed. Paul Wallace (New Delhi: SAGE Publication, 2014), 284–301.
15. Bagchi Sarthak, 'Re-evaluating Maratha Politics in Maharashtra: 2014 Assembly Elections and After', in *How India Votes: A State-by-State Look*, eds. Ashutosh Kumar and Yatindra Singh Sisodia (Hyderabad: Orient BlackSwan, 2019), 270–287.

C. Eastern and Southern Cluster

Chapter 13

West Bengal 2019

The Summer of Our Discontent

Sriroop Chaudhuri

INTRODUCTION

The 2019 Lok Sabha elections marked a paradigm shift in the political dynamics of Bengal as Pratim Ranjan Bose curtly summarized:

> For nearly 40 years, since 1980, the state remained isolated from national politics. The local narrative was ruled by Leftist ideologies, which survived on the politics of confrontation with the Centre. Trinamool Congress (TMC), which was a product of this trend, now stands broken. It's a new post-ideological Bengal which is not afraid to change its loyalty, and BJP is not a political untouchable, which means the State is no more a preserve of regional parties.[1]

Premonitions of a major mood swing underpinned by a saffron surge were apparent in the exit poll surveys (Table 13.1). Most surveys indicated that 'Didi' (Mamata Banerjee), the AITC supremo and chief minister of West Bengal, would continue to rule, but Prime Minister Narendra Modi would make significant inroads.[2]

And for once they were right! In 18 of 42 constituencies, the BJP steamrollered the AITC, claiming 40.22 per cent of the popular vote,

Table 13.1 *Party-Wise Probable Seat Counts of Exit Poll Surveys Conducted by Various Agencies for the 2019 Lok Sabha Elections in West Bengal*

Party	AITC	BJP
News18–IPSOS	36–38	3–5
India Today–Axis May India	19–23	19–22
Times Now–VMR	28	11
Republic–CVoter	29	13
Republic–Jan Ki Baat	18–26	13–21
NDTV	26–34	1
ABP News–Nielsen	31	8

Source: Author's own compilation from various sources.

22 per cent more than the 2014 Lok Sabha elections. For the first time, the BJP stands as the prime opposition in the state, establishing its claim for the assembly polls due in 2021. It gives the saffron brigade a clear edge in at least 126 of 294 assembly seats. What adds to the AITC's alarm is that the BJP is gaining momentum at their 'expense'. Three Gram Panchayats (GPs), one Zila Parishad and four municipal boards swung from the AITC to BJP soon after the parliamentary results, with more swings anticipated. Moreover, during June–July, five AITC MLAs (Member of Legislative Assembly) switched to the BJP.

But how did the BJP, with little organizational imprint and despised by the liberal intelligentsia for its hard right-wing Hindutva agenda, carve a notch in a state known for its secularist stand since Independence?

It is more baffling given the plethora of social welfare programmes implemented by Banerjee since assuming power in 2011 (Table 13.2). Her programmes garnered wide appreciation both nationally and globally. It included the United Nation's prestigious Public Service Award in 2017 for her flagship programme, the Kanyashree Prakalpa (girls' education scheme), which outshone 552 projects from 62 nations worldwide.[3] The BJP government itself acknowledged the work done towards the Mahatma Gandhi National Rural Employment Guarantee

Table 13.2 *Selected Social Welfare Schemes Initiated by the AITC in West Bengal since 2011*

Scheme	Launch Date	Salient Features
Gitanjali	2011	Housing scheme for economically weaker sections (EWS); grant of ₹70,000 provided in the plains, while ₹75,000 in the hills region, the Sundarbans and Jangalmahal; nearly 3 lakh beneficiaries till 2017.
Sabala	2011	Improving the nutritional status of adolescent girls, equip them with life skills, and training and knowledge on family welfare, health and hygiene; 12.74 lakh beneficiaries till date.
Kanyashree Prakalpa	2013	Empowering girl child, supporting education and, thus, preventing early marriage; benefitted over 48 lakh adolescents across 16,600 institutions.
Shishu Sathi	2013	Providing free-of-cost operations for children up to the age of 18 years, covering the treatment of congenital cardiac diseases, cleft lip/palate and club foot, available at all state-run facilities; 12,000 children benefitted.
Yuvashree	2013	Providing financial assistance of ₹1,500 per month to 1 lakh of the job seekers registered in the employment bank portal.
Sikshashree	2014	Providing fellowships for scheduled caste (SC) category students of grades V–VIII; transferred directly into the bank accounts; about 38 lakh students benefitted in 2014–2017.
Gatidhara	2014	Providing loans of up to ₹10 lakh on easy instalment basis to enable people to buy cars, small trucks, etc., for commercial use, with a subsidy of 30% or up to ₹1 lakh over the sanctioned loan while repaying the loan. Families with a monthly income of ₹25,000; 13,393 beneficiaries till 2017 with ₹125 crore disbursed.

(Continued)

Table 13.2 *(Contiuned)*

Scheme	Launch Date	Salient Features
Sabooj Sathi	2015	Gifting bicycles to students of grades IX–XII, for easier commute to school; 70 lakh beneficiaries till date.
Khadya Sathi	2016	Offering 5 kilogram (kg) of food grains per family member per month at ₹2/kg; 8.66 crore beneficiaries (90.6% of state population).
Sabujshree	2016	Correlating concepts of environmental protection with a sense of gender equity; mother of a newborn girl child is handed over saplings—so the tree grows up under her care like her girl; 15 lakh seedlings distributed till date.
Swasthya Sathi	2016	Cashless group health insurance scheme (i.e., including families) for all those employed by the state government's departments, both permanently and part-time; 35 lakh beneficiaries till 2017.

Source: Official website of AITC.
Note: (1 USD=68.5 ₹)

Act (MGNREGA) under her rule, besides judging Bengal among the top three states implementing the rural housing scheme.[4] Another winning programme is the Krishi Karman (agricultural excellence), awarded by the Central government for five consecutive years of record grain production.[5]

However, indications of saffron surge were apparent with the 2014 Lok Sabha elections only. Although the BJP managed to win only two seats (Asansol and Darjeeling), it secured runner-up spots in three others (Maldaha South, and Kolkata North and South) grabbing 16.8 per cent of vote share, far better than 2009 tally (6.10%). In 14 constituencies, BJP's vote share amounted over 20 per cent (Figure 13.1). Considering the Indian National Congress (INC) won only four seats (Maldaha North and South, Baharampur, Jangipur) with 9.69 per cent of vote share and the LF (Left Front) just two (Raiganj and Murshidabad) with 25.32 per cent, the BJP did exceedingly well. Moreover, its vote share swelled by 13 per cent from that in the 2011 assembly elections.

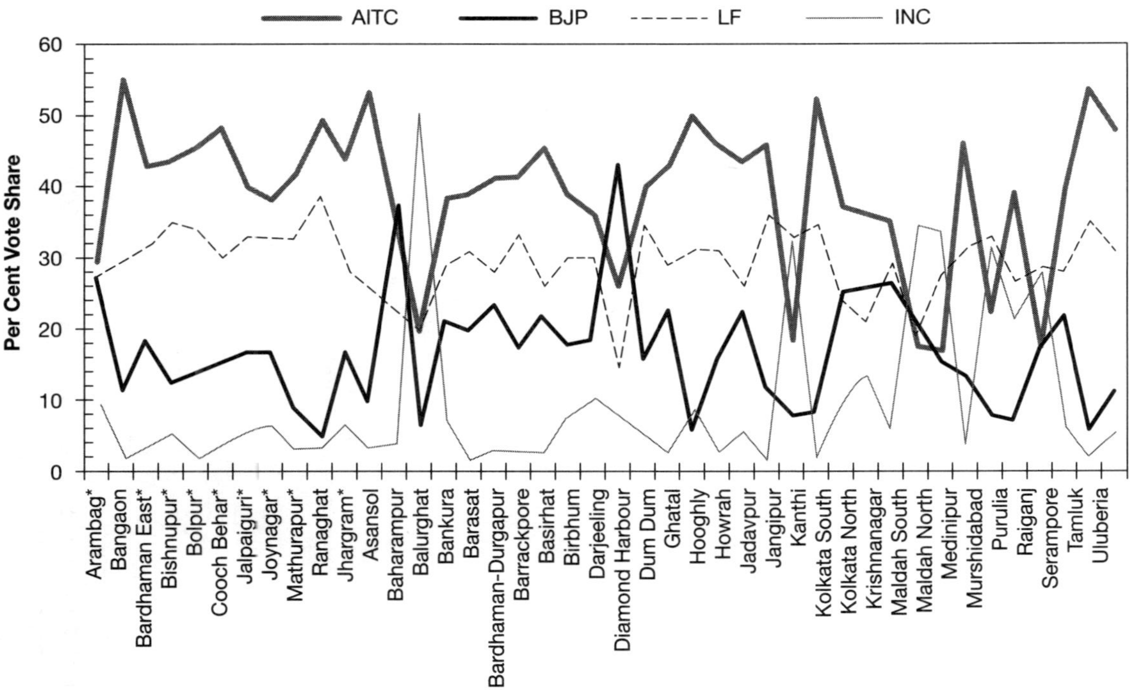

Figure 13.1 *Constituency-Wise Per Cent Vote Share for BJP in 2014 Lok Sabha Elections in West Bengal*

Source: Election Commission of India.

2019 LOK SABHA ELECTIONS

Although the AITC managed to expand its support base—from 39.79 per cent (2014) to 43.29 per cent (2019) vote share—it lost seven out of eight constituencies in North Bengal to the BJP, besides substantial grounds in the west (Figure 13.2).

It retained most of the southern and central districts from 2014. But the BJP emerged as runner-up in all, outsmarting both the LF and INC

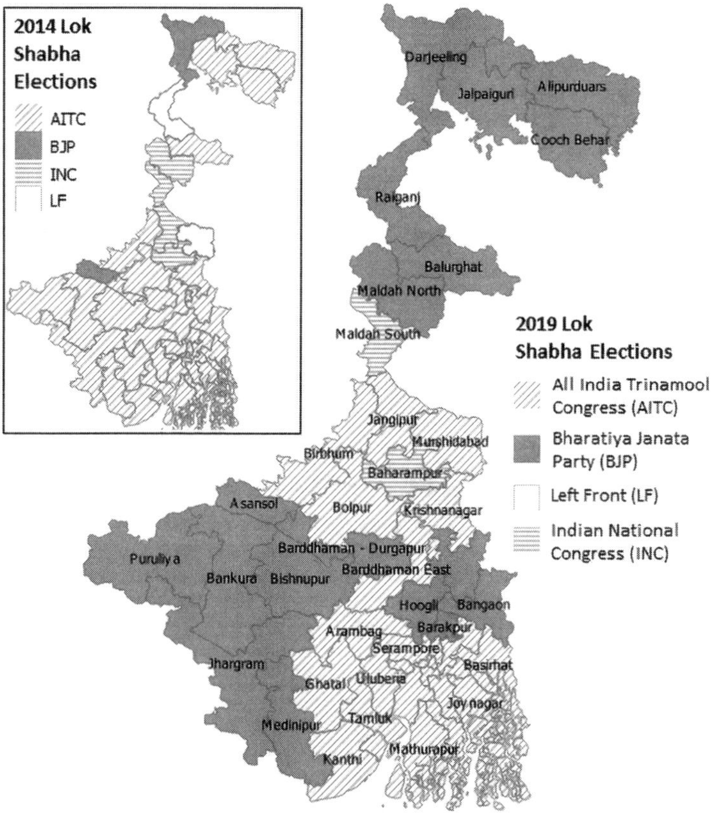

Figure 13.2 *Constituency-Wise Winning Party in 2014 and 2019 Lok Sabha Elections in West Bengal*

Source: Election Commission of India.

Note: This figure is not to scale. It does not represent any authentic national or international boundaries and is used for illustrative purposes only.

(Figure 13.3). What adds to saffron glory was that, known primarily as an urban party, it bagged 7 of 12 reserved constituencies, indicating their growing acceptance among marginal populations. It included the tribal belts of Jangal Mahals–Bankura (with 49.23% vote share versus 36.52% for AITC), Purulia (49.3% versus 34.19%), Jhargram (44.56% versus 43.73%), and Medinipur (48.62% versus 42.31%). All these have been long-time bastions of the AITC, and tipped the balance in their favour in the 2011 assembly elections, terminating the record 34-year dominance by the LF government.

Fact to the matter is that since 2014, it has been steady ascent for the BJP (Figure 13.4). In 12 constituencies, its vote share has jumped by over 30 per cent, including constituencies previously won by the AITC (e.g., Ghatal, Tamluk, Kanthi, Arambag and Mathurapur). By contrast, the AITC suffered losses in 13 constituencies, including few reserved constituencies (e.g., Arambag, Bangaon, Jhargram, Bishnupur and Bolpur). In reserved constituencies, the BJP has upped their tally by a third of total vote share on average. Overall, the AITC has dropped down to 22 seats from 34 in the 2014 elections (Table 13.3).

Interestingly, although the AITC outscored the BJP in terms of the 'absolute' account of the vote share (43.25% versus 40.22%), in-depth analyses (using analysis of variance [ANOVA]) revealed that the margin is 'not statistically' significant (at a probability level of 0.05; Table 13.4). In other words, there is no room for complacency for the AITC vote managers—only a vanishing edge goes between the two.

What adds to the worry of the AITC is that both the INC and LF have been relegated to fringes. In other words, possibility of vote division has become obscure—a situation likely to favour the BJP in coming elections. In fact, both the LF and INC have been on downward spirals since the 2009 Lok Sabha elections, with vote shares steadily plummeting (Table 13.3). For the INC, it is only Baharampur (45.47% vote share) and Maldaha South (34.73%) constituencies this time. But even in the latter, it is marginal with the BJP pooling 34.09 per cent votes at the runner-up spot. The LF is almost eliminated with their vote share dropping to single digit in 32 of 42 constituencies (Figure 13.4). Worse, all their candidates, except Bikash Ranjan Bhattacharya (Jadavpur constituency), forfeited their security deposits.[6]

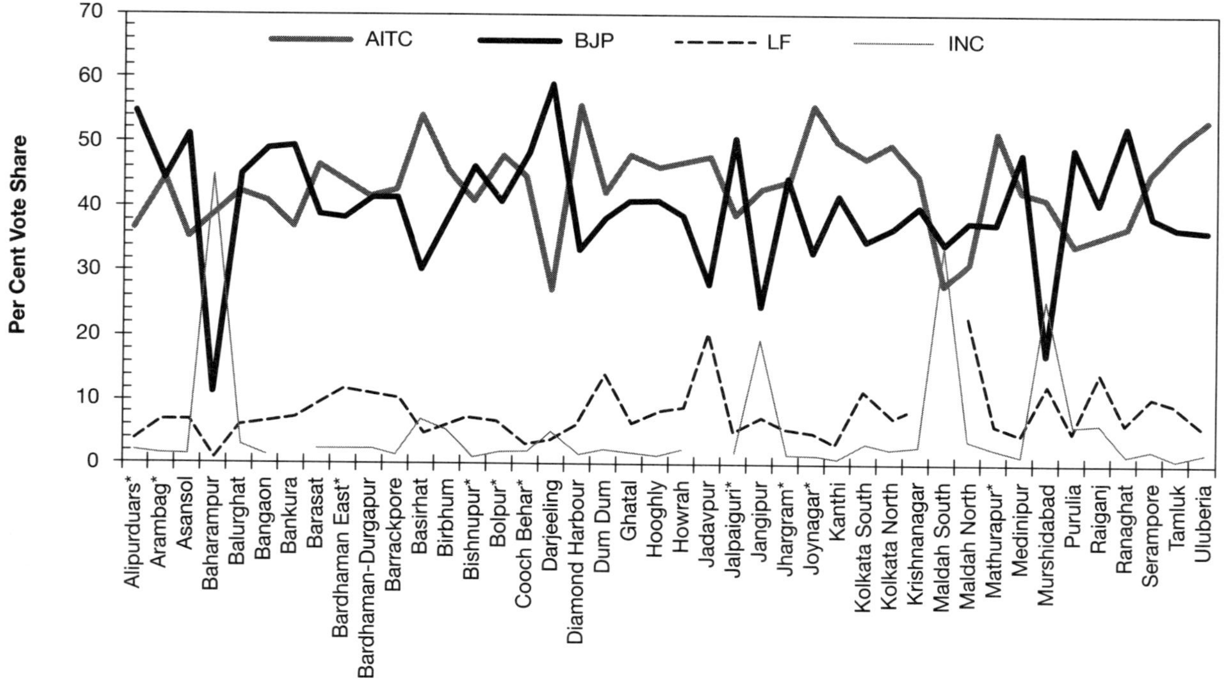

Figure 13.3 *Constituency-Wise Per Cent Vote Share for Major Parties in 2019 Lok Sabha Election in West Bengal*

Source: Election Commission of India.

Note: '*' denotes reserved constituency.

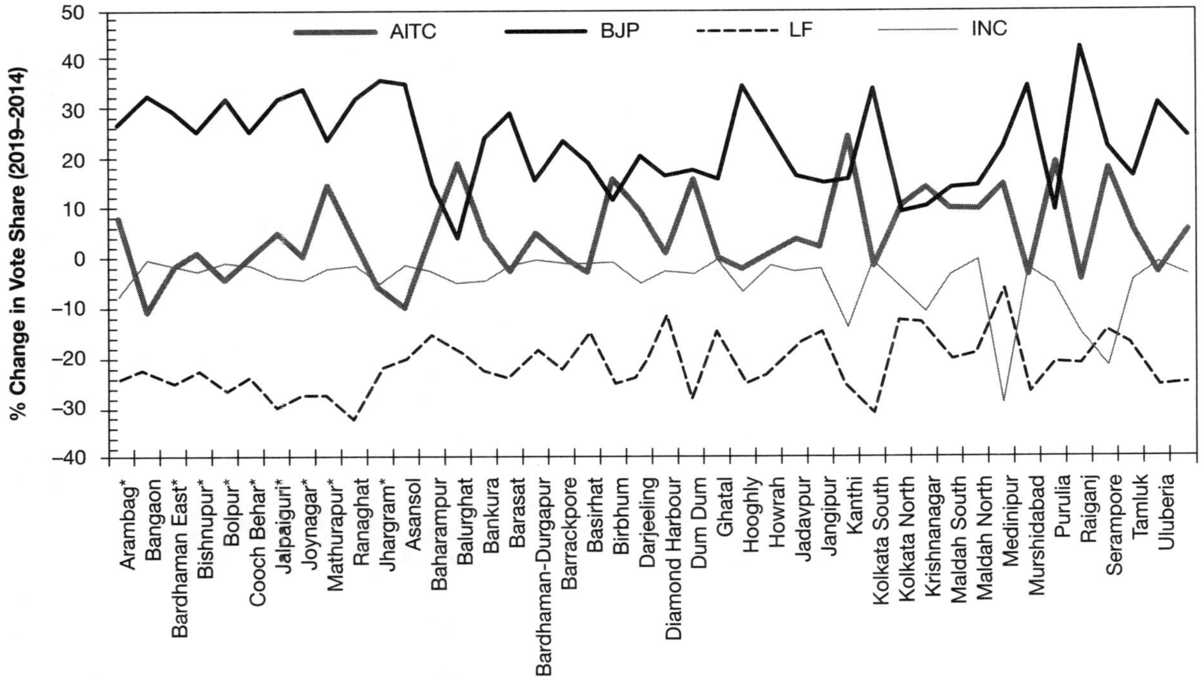

Figure 13.4 *Constituency-Wise Changes in Per Cent Vote Share for Major Parties between 2014 and 2019 Lok Sabha Election in West Bengal*

Source: Election Commission of India.

Note: (–)ve values indicate drop in vote share in 2019; '*' denotes reserved constituency.

Table 13.3 *Number of Constituencies Won by the Major Players Year Wise in Different Lok Sabha Elections in West Bengal*

Party	2004	2009	2014	2019
AITC	1 (21.0%)	19 (31.18%)	34 (39.05%)	22 (43.29%)
BJP	0 (8.1%)	1 (6.14%)	2 (17.20%)	18 (40.22%)
LF	35 (50.7%)	15 (43.30%)	2 (25.32%)	0 (5.64%)
INC	6 (14.6%)	6 (13.45%)	4 (9.69%)	2 (7.10%)

Source: Election Commission of India.

Notes: Values in the parentheses indicate per cent vote share. AITC: All India Trinamool Congress; BJP: Bharatiya Janata Party; LF: Left Front; INC: Indian National Congress; IND: Independent; LF includes Communist Part India, Communist Party India (Marxist), All India Forward Block (AIFB) and Revolutionary Socialist Party (RSP). In 2004, the LF was termed as Third Front; the AITC and BJP combined forces as NDA (National Democratic Alliance), while the INC combined forces with Jharkhand Mukti Morcha, Party for Democratic Socialism and Independents to be termed as United Progressive Front (UPA).

Table 13.4 *Analysis Of Variance (1-Way ANOVA) Results, Computed Using Respective Parties Vote Share Percentages in Various Years*

Differences Between Parties	Computed Probability Value (P_{comp})	Critical Probability Value (P_{crit})	Computed F Value (F_{comp})	Critical F Value (F_{crit})
AITC 2019–BJP 2019	0.0600	0.05	3.47	3.96
LF 2019–INC 2019	0.1200	0.05	2.49	3.96
LF 2014–INC 2014	0.0001	0.01	101.71	3.95

Source: The Author.

Notes: AITC: All India Trinamool Congress; BJP: Bharatiya Janata Party; LF: Left Front; INC: Indian National Congress; conditions for statistical significance between parties: value for $P_{comp} < P_{crit}$ and value for $F_{comp} > F_{crit}$

Adding to ignominy, they have now begun 'resembling' the INC! It ensues from the observation that there is no 'statistically discernible difference' between the two parties in terms of vote share (at probability level of 0.05). This is embarrassing for the LF as this difference was significant in 2014 (at the probability level of 0.01; Table 13.4). In other words, the LF is soon going to face major identity crises in a state they ruled for more than three decades. The question is: Is it going to alter political equations in coming years, especially the 2021 assembly polls?

How did this come to be?

'Operation Bengal' was drafted by Modi and the national party president Amit Shah following the 2018 panchayat elections. Both leaders saw Bengal as the 'Gateway to East' and an opportunity to make up for their 'anticipated' losses, as suggested by many pre-poll surveys in the Hindi heartlands. Their emphasis on this plan is expressed in Modi addressing 17 public meetings in Bengal three months prior to the elections—unprecedented for a prime minister. Calling Banerjee, a 'speed breaker' to Bengal's development, Modi relentlessly chipped away at the hegemony of the AITC.[7] In addition, other central leaders, including Amit Shah, Yogi Adityanath (chief minister of Uttar Pradesh) and Smriti Irani made frequent trips to the state to rile up voters' discontent against the ruling party. Central allegations against Banerjee's eight-year rule included nepotism, bribery and corruption in public sectors, armed assaults on opposition workers, driving away opposition workers from villages besides framing them with false charges, proliferation of syndicate raj in urban centres, alleged involvement of several AITC core members in various chit fund scams, lack of commerce and industry, rising unemployment, shortfalls of dearness allowance (DA) for the state employees, unable to restructure the remuneration schemes following the 6th Pay Commission. Presently, the Central employees receive about 23 per cent more DA than their state counterparts. On top of all, there was Banerjee's alleged policy of 'Muslim appeasement' that irked the voters.

However, there was a long list of issues running counter to the BJP as well, which included the National Register for Citizen's (NRC), Citizenship Amendment Bill, communalism, demonetization, GST, the Rafale scam, rise in farmers' suicides, revitalization of the economy and a host of promises about new job creation. But here lay the dichotomy, as political processes in Bengal have always operated on regional concerns. And the issue at hand was 'change'—mimicking the political situation in 2011 when the AITC came to power riding an anti-incumbency tide against the LF. Issues against the BJP, no matter how grave, were largely national, which did little to tarnish Modi's 'visionary' image—globalization and development propelled by strong nationalist ideals. It got the new generation voters, in particular, at their sway. The issue of nationalism has been a game changer with the Balakot airstrike (February 2019). Political analysts widely agree that it significantly revived Modi's image as the 'protector' of the nation. The BJP leadership deftly used it to uphold Modi's integrity to fight terrorism and his stand to maintain India's sovereignty.

PANCHAYAT ELECTIONS 2018: CAT ON A HOT TIN ROOF?

Although the AITC held on to its command in rural areas by winning over 78 per cent of the Gram Panchayats, the BJP emerged as runner-up in 20 districts[8] (Table 13.5).

The most intriguing feature of this election, and what unambiguously validates the claim of growing anti-incumbency in the state, was rise of the Independents (IND) as the third largest party in the GPs, after the AITC and BJP, and ahead of both the LF and INC. The INDs bagged over 5 per cent GPs in Jhargram, North Dinajpur, East and West Medinipur and Purulia districts (Figure 13.5). Major part of the IND candidate pool actually comprised the disgruntled AITC workforce.[9] It weakened the AITC's command in many rural areas and set the stage for the 2019 elections. Providing rehabilitation to the surrendered Maoists, ahead of devoted party workers, was a major cause of discontent at grass roots. Commenting on the results, Churamani Mahato, a frontline AITC leader and state minister of the backward classes from Jhargram district, himself admitted, 'People did not take to our rural/tribal development story.'

The panchayat elections were a golden opportunity for the AITC to have an unbiased picture before the parliamentary battle in 2019. It

Table 13.5 *Number of Administrative Units Won by Major Parties in 2018 Panchayat Elections in West Bengal*

Party	Gram Panchayat	Panchayat Samiti	Zila Parishad
AITC	38,118 (78.4%)	8,062 (87.5%)	793 (96.2%)
BJP	5,779 (11.9%)	769 (8.3%)	22 (2.7%)
LF	1,713 (3.5%)	129 (1.3%)	1
INC	1,066 (2.2%)	133 (1.4%)	6 (0.7%)
IND	1,857 (3.8%)	112 (1.2%)	2 (0.2%)
Others	103 (0.2%)	9 (NA)	–
Total	48,636	9,214	824

Source: Election Commission of India.

Notes: Values in the parentheses indicate per cent vote share.

AITC: All India Trinamool Congress; BJP: Bharatiya Janata Party; LF: Left Front; INC: Indian National Congress; IND: Independent; LF includes Communist Part India, Communist Party India (Marxist), All India Forward Block (AIFB) and Revolutionary Socialist Party (RSP); NA: Not Available.

'squandered' it by wielding muscle power that kept over 42 per cent voters from exercising their fundamental democratic right, as accused by the oppositions.[10] This allegation is supported by the fact that out of total 58,692 seats, AITC won 20,076 (34.2%) uncontested![11] It included 16,814 of the total 48,650 GP seats, 3059 of the 9,217 Panchayat Samiti seats and 203 of the 825 Zila Parishad seats. Opposition candidates were intimidated, and on many occasions forced by AITC muscle men to withdraw nominations. Poll violence took alarming forms in South and North 24 Parganas, North Dinajpur, Nadia, Medinipur, Murshidabad, Birbhum, Bardhaman, and Cooch Behar districts.

Allegations against the ruling party ranged from rigging to booth capturing, stealing and vandalizing ballot boxes, intimidating voters, provoking opposition workers into conflicts and armed assaults on opposition workers.[12] Adding to the discontent, little action was taken by the state law enforcement agencies against the ruling party cadre, despite repeated opposition protests that included accusations of 'cordoning' entire villages to prevent the opposition from getting to the

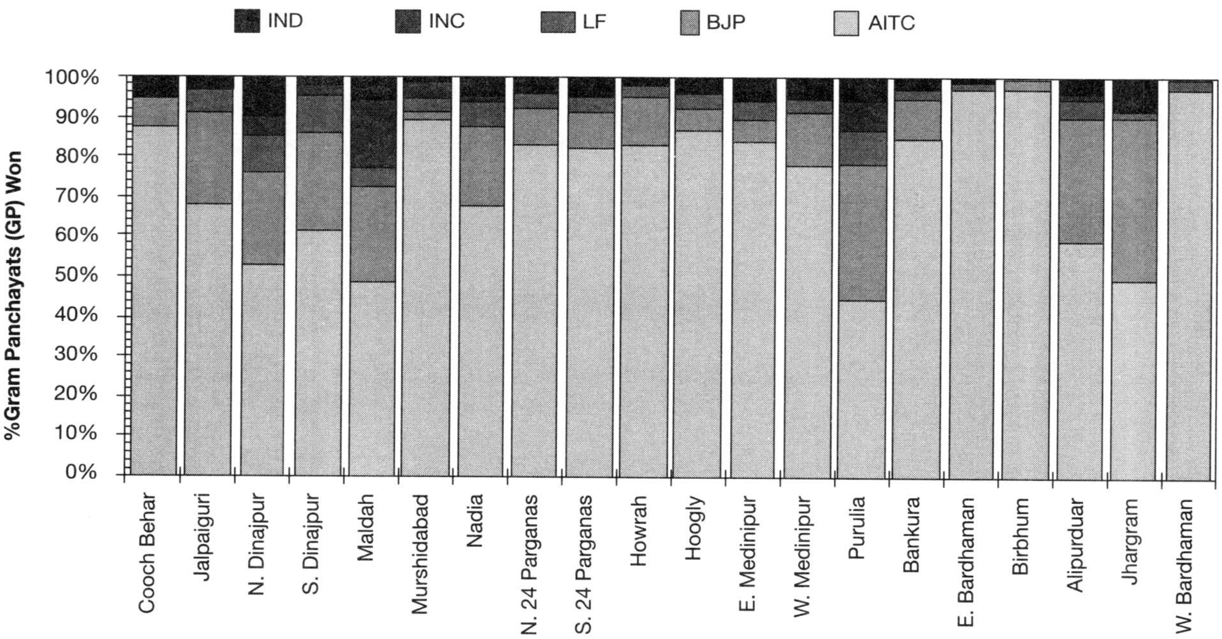

Figure 13.5 *District-Wise Per Cent Gram Panchayats (GPs) Won by Major Parties in 2018 Panchayat Elections in West Bengal*

Source: Election Commission of India.

ballot booths. The BJP claimed that 52 of its workers were slain in poll violence.[13] Condemning the violence, the Calcutta High Court halted the election process and ordered the State Election Commission to prepare detailed reports.[9] The BJP leadership deftly moulded it to their favour[14] and soon the catch line became 'Chup Chap Fule Chhap' (keep quiet and put it on the [BJP ballot] lotus). The 2019 elections came as a means of protest, particularly to those who couldn't (or were not allowed to) exercise their fundamental democratic rights in the Panchayat polls.

2019 BENGAL: A SAGA OF SOCIO-RELIGIOUS TRANSFORMATION

Under such circumstances, the BJP's rise is widely reckoned as an outcry for change, underpinned by stark socio-religious transformations. In this regard, the CSDS-Lokniti post-poll survey includes some startling facts (Table 13.6). Most notable is a shift in the minority vote. Since 2014, the BJP's support swelled by three-fold among the OBCs (Other Backward Classes) and Dalits, and five-fold among the Adivasis (tribal). On the other hand, AITC's support shrunk by 13–15 per cent on average.

These communities had been AITC's trusted vote banks for years while completely new turf for the BJP. But as political analysts argue,

Table 13.6 *Potential Apportionment of Vote among Different Communities in the 2019 Lok Sabha Elections in West Bengal*

	BJP		AITC		LF		INC	
Community	2014 (%)	2019 (%)	2014 (%)	2019 (%)	2014 (%)	2019 (%)	2014 (%)	2019 (%)
OBC	21	65	43	28	26	4	4	2
Dalit	20	61	40	27	29	6	8	4
Adivasi	11	58	40	28	41	12	5	2
Upper caste	24	57	38	31	27	9	5	3

Source: The CSDS-Lokniti Post-poll Survey.

Note: CSDS: Center for Studies for Developing Societies.

results of the 2019 Parliamentary Elections have been the outcome of a series of dynamic social transformations in Bengal, 'The social character of the Bengal BJP reveals an unexpected "subaltern" bias. If we assume there is a loose correlation between caste and class, it implies that the BJP has become the choice of poorer Hindus, particularly in the rural areas.'[15] It is in fact substantiated by scatterplot regression analysis, which revealed a strong linear relationship ($R^2=0.91$) between increases in BJP's vote percentage (2014–2019) among various socio-religious communities and corresponding drops for all other parties (AITC, LF and INC) (Figure 13.6). It implied that since 2014, most communities began viewing the BJP as the 'only' credible opponent to challenge the AITC's dominance. It raises the likelihood of a more bipolar battle in the 2021 assembly polls, rather than traditional multiparty contest with major vote swings in favour of the BJP.

MUSLIM APPEASEMENT

As the final showdown drew nearer, an intriguing debate that stirred the state polity was: 'Will the Muslims follow the earlier trend to vote for different parties or will they choose to vote for one party, in an election which is deeply polarized on communal lines?'[16] It is substantiated by the CSDS-Lokniti survey results, which showed that since 2014 the BJP has grown substantially in proportion among the upper caste voters (from 24% in 2014 to 57% in 2019), while the AITC lost substantial ground (Table 13.6).

In an unprecedented manner, both parties went full blast on religious lines in their election rallies.[17] The survey reflects a clear polarized religious direction. Muslims support for the AITC grew by about 30 per cent since 2014 elections, while Hindus support for the Lotus grew from 21 per cent in 2014 to 57 per cent in 2019 (Table 13.7). The AITC support by Hindus fell by about 8 per cent. Such religious division is believed to be consequences of Banerjee's 'relentless' effort to woo Muslim voters who account for 27–28 per cent of the state electorate.[15]

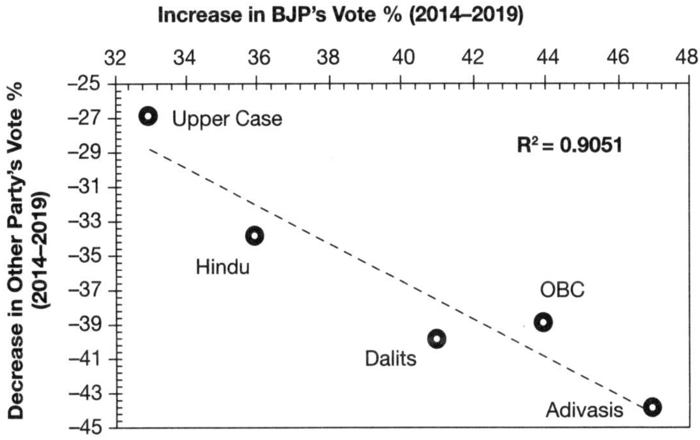

Figure 13.6 *Linear Regression Coefficient (R^2) Computed between Increase in BJP's Vote Per Cent (Positive Values along Top X-Axis) among Different Social Groups and Corresponding Drops (Negative Values on Y-Axis) for Other Parties in 2019 Lok Sabha Elections in West Bengal*

Source: The Author.

Notes: 'OBC' indicates Other Backward Classes; Equation used to estimate the regression line (dotted)– BJP increase in vote% = (BJP vote% 2019 – BJP's vote% 2014) + Σ [(AITC vote% change 2014–2019), (LF vote% change 2014–2019), (INC vote% change 2014–2019)].

Table 13.7 *Potential Apportionment of Vote among Hindus and Muslims in the 2019 Lok Sabha Elections in West Bengal*

	BJP		AITC		LF		INC	
	2014 (%)	2019 (%)	2014 (%)	2019 (%)	2014 (%)	2019 (%)	2014 (%)	2019 (%)
Hindu	21	57	40	32	29	6	6	3
Muslim	2	4	40	70	31	10	24	12

Source: The CSDS-Lokniti post poll survey.

Note: CSDS stands for Center for Studies for Developing Societies.

Since assuming office in 2011, she courted Muslims with measures that antagonized the Hindus who sought 'refuge' with the BJP. They ranged from setting up Haj Houses to sanctioning some 400 Madrasa hostels, financial assistance to Muslim students, new campus ground for Aliah University and so on. Immersions of Goddess Durga had to make way for Muharram, the day of mourning in Islam. This infuriated Hindus, lower and upper caste alike, triggering state-wide protests, and tilted the balance in BJP's favour. It was slammed by the Calcutta High Court as dividing communities on religious lines.[18] Questioning the motive as fundamental, the court admonished the government to insure that 'people should have equal rights to practice their activities irrespective of religious belonging.'[19]

The most controversial among her decisions took place in April 2012. It provided imams (clerics) and muezzins with state allowances of ₹2,500 and ₹1,500 respectively. It outraged the Hindu communities and substantiated the BJP's repeated claims about Banerjee's Muslim appeasement policy to win votes. It gained momentum as the Calcutta High Court struck it down as 'unconstitutional' and 'against public interest', following the plea of the then BJP State General Secretary Asim Sarkar. The Calcutta High Court order cited Articles 14 and 15/1 of the constitution: 'The state shall not discriminate against any citizen on grounds of religion, race, caste, sex, place of birth, or any of them.' The allowance immediately was ordered to be stopped immediately.[20] Similarly, the Calcutta High Court accused the state government of 'squandering public funds' under Article 166 of the Constitution by releasing them to the state-controlled Wakf Board that oversees Islamic religious endowments.[21]

The announcement aggravated the Muslim communities as well. Md. Quamruzzaman, the general secretary of the All India Minority Youth Federation (ABMYF), labelled it a cheap attempt to gain political mileage: 'We had high hopes from Mamata Banerjee but we are disappointed. She has betrayed us and used us only as a vote bank.'[22] Expounding on it, he maintained, 'The monthly honorarium of ₹1,000 to imams is of little value at current market prices. Instead, let governments update the Wakf estates. The Wakf can then take care of the imams and muezzins.'[23] The amounts announced were substantially lower than the ₹10,000 promised earlier.[24]

The Hindu drift towards the BJP was fuelled further by Banerjee's order to stall the Rath Yatra, a chariot rally organized by the BJP as part of their nationwide 'save democracy' campaign. Jibing the whole concept as BJP's 'danga yatra' (riot rally), she stated that Rath Yatra is not meant to cause communal violence and kill people.[25] A similar stance banned the BJP's armed rally during the Ram Navami.[26] Responding to it, the state BJP chief Dilip Ghosh retorted: 'Ram Navami rallies are a part of our tradition. We are carrying arms to protect ourselves. It has nothing to do with elections. If TMC has a problem with armed rallies then they should change their thought process.'[27]

Moreover, Banerjee's recital of Islamic verses and her patronization of various Islamic festivals, such as Eid, flared discontent among orthodox Hindus. Jishnu Basu, secretary to the RSS for the south Bengal chapter said: 'She is Bengal's biggest anti-Hindu leader. Since 2011, there have been riots, deaths and infiltration from Bangladesh. The damage she has done in seven years (2011–2018) cannot be rectified in decades.'[28]

LF SWING: THE X FACTOR

The panchayat polls made the LF a fringe operator in the state polity. A growing hypothesis amongst the political analysts was that in 2019, the LF would incline to the BJP for retribution. Although former LF Chief Minister Buddhadev Bhattacharjee objected it, by calling it a 'jump from frying pan to fireplace', as Judgment Day drew nearer, a move towards the BJP seemed increasingly likely. Scatterplot regression analysis reveals that there might well be some substance to it. The shifting trend is substantiated by a strong positive correlation (R_2=0.35) between the BJP's 'observed' vote share in 2019 and that 'predicted' by considering LF vote transfer from 2014 (Figure 13.7a).

The latter is determined by adding the difference of the LF's vote percentage between 2014 and 2019 with BJP's 2014 vote percentage.

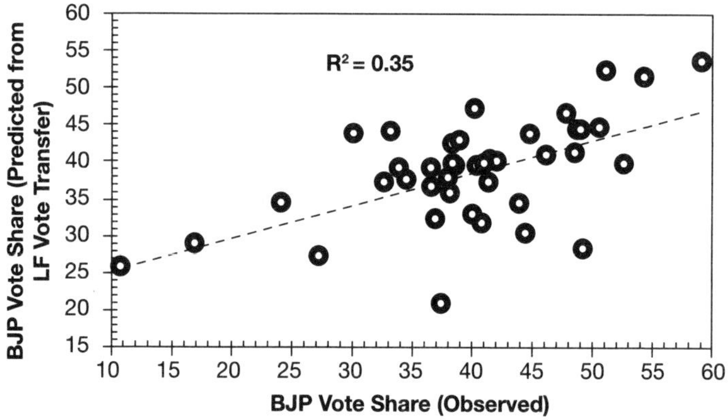

Figure 13.7a *Linear Regression Coefficient (R^2) Computed between BJP's Per Cent Vote Share (Observed) and That Predicted (Y-Axis) from Possible LF Vote Transfer, Considering All 42 Constituencies in 2019 Lok Sabha Elections in West Bengal*

Source: The Author.

Note: Equation used to estimate the regression line (dotted): BJP's vote share predicted=BJP vote share 2014+(LF vote share 2014 – LF vote share 2019).

However, considering only 18 constituencies that the BJP won, hinted at a much stronger influence (R^2=0.51) of LF vote swing on BJP's recent performance (Figure 13.7b).

Even in 15 other seats where the AITC grabbed 40 per cent of popular vote, there were close ties between BJP's observed and 'predicted' share, considering possible LF transfer. Interestingly, this bunch included some of the most prestigious and strategically important seats for the ruling party, such as Dum Dum, Jadavpur, Kolkata North, Kanthi, Howrah and so on (Figure 13.8). It included some of the reserved constituencies as well. Over all, in 30–32 of total 42 seats, the LF vote turned out as the X factor for the BJP, as much as their arch rivals.

The possibility was made clear in the CSDS-Lokniti post-poll survey with a 39 per cent swing of the LF and 32 per cent of INC to BJP (Table 13.8). Even the AITC's own pre-poll survey concluded: 'We hope to win over 30 seats but if the Left loses more than 10 per cent of its share, we may even go down to 25', admitted a frontline AITC leader.[29] The BJP knew

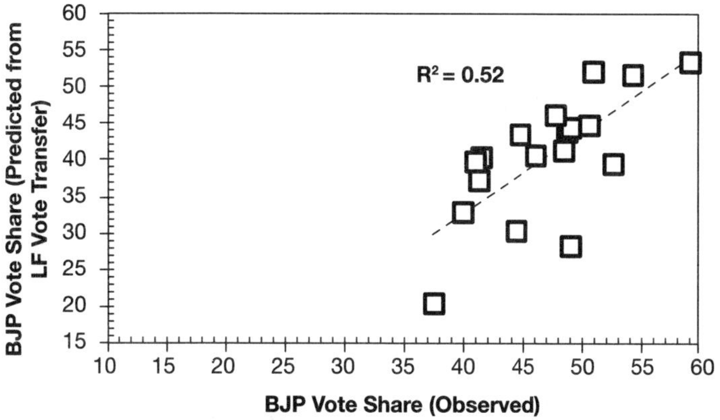

Figure 13.7b *Linear Regression Coefficient (R^2) Computed between BJP's Observed Vote Share (X-Axis) and That Predicted (Y-Axis) from Hypothesized LF Vote Transfer Considering 18 Constituencies Won by BJP in 2019 Lok Sabha Elections in West Bengal*

Source: The Author.

Note: Equation used to compute the regression line (dotted): BJP's vote share predicted=BJP vote share 2014+(LF vote share 2014 – LF vote share 2019).

it already and was set to bank on it, as Assam minister Himanta Biswa Sarma reflected: 'The right-thinking people [who] belong to LF, belong to INC, and even belong to AITC... are voting for BJP... In a political sense, you can say that CPM votes are being transferred to the BJP.'

The bonhomie was already apparent in Medinipur (east), Maldaha and Nadia (north) districts as workers of both parties combined to form boards in the 2018 panchayat elections.[30] LF leadership admitted it as well: 'it was not party policy; but as the villagers wanted one-to-one fight against AITC, it had to be respected.'[31] The BJP state president Dilip Ghosh maintained, 'Our key aim is to keep AITC out of gram panchayat boards and we will not hesitate in joining forces with any Opposition party including the CPI (M) for the purpose.'

This seems to be an ideological paradox as BJP's right-wing Hindutva agenda contrasts with the LF atheist ideology.[32] However, it was an act of survival in face of annihilation, owing to burgeoning AITC terror.[33] The belligerence is not surprising. The LF received the

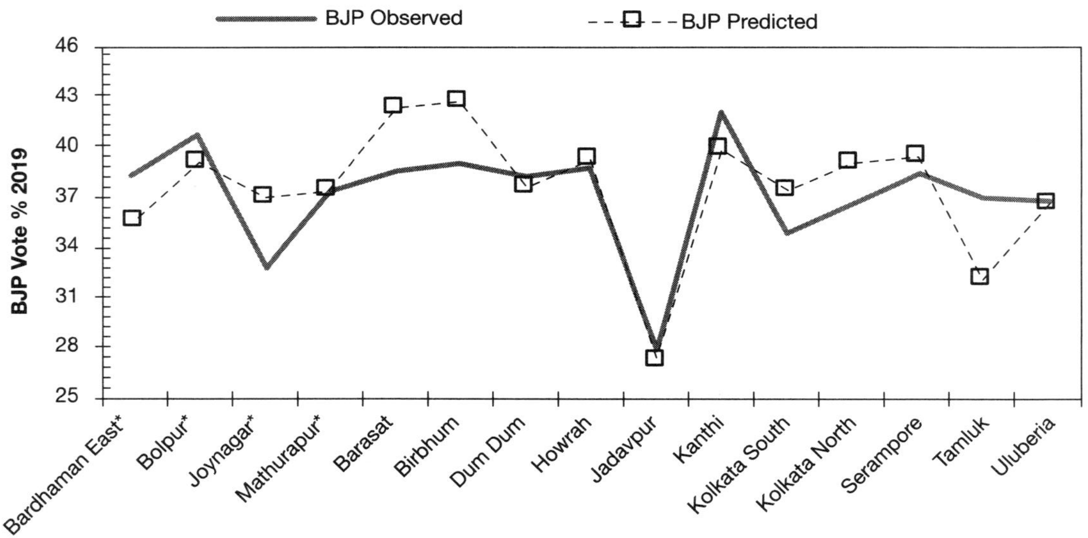

Figure 13.8 *Trends between BJP's Vote Share in Constituencies Won by the AITC by Claiming over 40 Per Cent of Total Vote Share in 2019 Lok Sabha Elections in West Bengal*

Source: The Author.

Notes: The grey solid line represents BJP's vote share observed in 2019. Equation used to compute BJP's predicted vote share 2019 (dotted line)=BJP's observed vote share 2014+(LF vote share 2014 – LF vote share 2019); '*' indicates reserved constituencies.

Table 13.8 *Probable Vote Switches From LF and INC in 2019 Lok Sabha Elections*

Voter Type	BJP (%)	AITC (%)	LF (%)	INC (%)
Traditional LF voters	39	31	30	–
Traditional INC voters	32	20	4	32

Source: CSDS-Lokniti Post-Poll Survey 2019.
Note: CSDS: Center for Studies for Developing Societies.

worst of poll violence during the 2018 panchayat elections. But even before that, since 2011, LF workers had been suffering violence in all areas of their lives by the AITC muscle power. For major parts of the state, LF party offices were shut down immediately after the 2011 polls. Arguably, of about 3,000 party offices over half stopped functioning after 2011.[34] The legendary LF organization crumbled as the AITC wielded its muscle power across rural Bengal, systematically decimating the LF workforce to make Bengal an opposition-free state.

Faced with existential crises, they sought refuge with the BJP, as Sarthak Roychowdhury, professor of economics and political commentator concluded: 'CPI (M) workers relentlessly asked for support from the leadership in the districts and villages but were left in a void. They were desperate to save existence and exercise their minimum rights. They got that from BJP.'[35] Sitaram Yechury, the general secretary of the CPI (M) maintained: 'This (voting for BJP) was the natural tendency among those for whom the priority was relief from terror and repression by AITC'. However, he maintained that, 'This was the result of an extreme polarisation between BJP and AITC…squeezing out the democratic space for other parties.'[36]

The shift was most apparent among the marginal population: 'In terms of social profile, the BJP increasingly resembles the Left, minus any Muslim support. This is why there is a direct correlation between BJP advance and Left decline'[15]. Ironically, these were the people that hurled the AITC to the forefront of state politics between 2006 and 2011. The Bangaon constituency, a long-time AITC stronghold, presents a classic scenario where the 'Matuas', consisting of Bangladeshi settlers, dominate the electorate (65%). During his campaigns, Modi made visits to the constituency to meet the voters in person and assure them of a fair and 'inclusive' government to look after Matua interests. Surprisingly, BJP's Santanu Thakur won with an overwhelming majority to which his aunt, AITC candidate and sitting MP, Mamatabala Thakur exclaimed: 'The entire Left vote went to BJP, which led to my defeat.'

UNEXPECTED EDGES

Political analysts believe that 'defectors' have been critical for the BJP. At least 12 of 42 candidates the BJP fielded in 2019 came from other parties. They include some sitting MPs/MLAs—Arjun Singh (Barrackpore; sitting MLA, AITC), Saumitra Khan (Bishnupur; sitting MP, AITC), Anupam Hazra (Jadavpur, sitting MP, AITC), Nishith Pramanik (Cooch Bihar; sitting MP, AITC) and Khagen Murmu (Maldaha North, sitting MLA, LF). They brought in a readymade support base that gave the BJP an unexpected edge.[37] Except for Hazra, all the rest won from their respective constituencies. Even Hazra came second in the Jadavpur constituency ahead of Bikas Ranjan Bhattacharya, a frontline LF leader and former mayor of the Calcutta Municipal Corporation.

The BJP also gained from AITC's policy of abuse during the campaigns, spearheaded by Banerjee herself. The final months saw a war of words—allegations, counter allegations, mutual debasement—between the AITC and BJP. Banerjee skewered Modi calling him 'king of thieves' in her rallies.[35] On multiple occasions she addressed Modi as 'liar', 'Hitler's grandfather' and 'expiry babu'. Even personal remarks weren't spared: 'A man who cannot take care of his wife, will not be able to take care of the country either' (referring to Modi's election affidavit over marriage).[38] It did not ring right with the voters: 'after all he is our Prime Minister. How can a CM use such abusive language?' In a way it created the same impact as INC President Rahul Gandhi's 'Chowkidar Chor Hai' (the watchman is the thief). Many political analysts ascribe INC's humiliating defeat to such subversive propaganda.

Moreover, on several occasions, the state government denied the BJP permissions of their chosen venue to hold rallies, including that of Yogi Adityanath (Balurghat, South Dinajpur district)[39], Amit Shah (Jadavpur, in Kolkata)[40] and even Modi himself (in Kawakhali, Darjeeling district).[41] Yogi was finally forced to conduct his rally via telephone! It boomeranged. State BJP leadership instantly swung it in their favour saying: 'Didi (Banerjee) has already lost it to Modi'. They kept hammering it in every public meetings, calling it Didi's dirty political ploy to throttle democracy.

NOTES

1. Pratim Ranjan Bose, 'Election Results 2019: Bengal Votes for the BJP, Breaks Many Stereotypes', *Business Line*, 23 May 2019, 201. Available at https://www.thehindubusinessline.com/news/elections/election-results-2019-bengal-votes-for-the-bjpbreaks-many-stereotypes/article27216896.ece (accessed on 15 June 2019).
2. Jyotiprasad Chatterjee and Supriyo Basu, 'Post-poll Survey: When the Left Moved Right in West Bengal', *The Hindu*, 28 May 2019. Available at https://www.thehindu.com/elections/Lok Sabjha-sabha-2019/when-the-left-moved-right/article27266690.ece (accessed on 27 June 2019).
3. Indrajit Kundu, 'UN Honours Mamata Banerjee with Highest Public Service Award for Girl Child Project Kanyashree', *India Today*, 23 June 2017. Available at https://www.indiatoday.in/india/story/mamata-banerjee-un-public-service-award-kanyashree-netherlands-984439-2017-06-23 (accessed on 2 July 2019).
4. Aman Sharma and Madhuparna Das, 'Mamata Banerjee Didn't Fail to Implement Key Rural Schemes in Bengal', *The Economic Times*, 13 September 2018. Available at https://economictimes.indiatimes.com/news/politics-and-nation/bengal-shows-mamata-Ms. Banerjee-for-key-schemes-of-central-govt/articleshow/65791376.cms?from=mdr (accessed on 25 June 2019).
5. Madhuparna Das, 'Mamata Banerjee Tells Her Cabinet to Plan and Sell "Better Versions" of Modi's Schemes', *The Economic Times*, 6 July 2018. Available at https://economictimes.indiatimes.com/news/politics-and-nation/mamata-Ms. Banerjee-tells-her-cabinet-to-plan-and-sell-better-versions-of-modis-schemes/articleshow/64878032.cms?from=mdr (accessed on 22 June 2019).
6. Press Trust of India, 'All but One Left Front Candidate Loses Security Deposit in West Bengal', *The Economic Times*, 24 May 2019. Available at https://economictimes.indiatimes.com/news/elections/Lok Sabha-sabha/west-bengal/all-but-one-left-front-candidates-lose-security-deposit-in-west-bengal/articleshow/69481742.cms (accessed on 23 June 2019).
7. Chaterjee and Basu, 'Post-poll Survey'.
8. Meghdeep Bhattacharyya and Sandip Chowdhury, 'BJP Tightens Grip on Runner-up Position', *The Telegraph*, 05 May 2018. Available at https://

www.telegraphindia.com/states/west-bengal/bjp-tightens-grip-on-runner-up-position/cid/1456625 (accessed on 16 June 2019).

9. Arkamoy Dutta Majumder, 'Calcutta High Court Stalls West Bengal Panchayat Election Process till 16 May', *Live Mint*, 13 April 2018. Available at https://www.livemint.com/Politics/skQy7cDDWTnTT35Y4IbffO/Calcutta-high-court-stalls-West-Bengal-panchayat-election-pr.html (accessed on 27 June 2019).
10. Gyan Verma, 'Elections 2019: In Bengal, the BJP Charts a New Course', *Live Mint*, 30 April 2019. Available at https://www.livemint.com/elections/Lok Sabjha-sabha-elections/elections-2019-in-bengal-the-bjp-charts-a-new-course-1556211612673.html (accessed on 28 June 2019).
11. Indo-Asian News Service, 'West Bengal Panchayat Election 2018: Six Killed as Violence Mars Rural Polls; over 41% Voting Recorded till 1 pm', *Firstpost,* 16 May 2018. Available at https://www.firstpost.com/politics/west-bengal-panchayat-election-2018-six-killed-as-violence-mars-rural-polls-over-41-voting-recorded-till-1-pm-4468541.html (accessed on 28 June 2019).
12. *Business Standard*, 'West Bengal Panchayat Polls: 72% Turnout; Violence Claims 12 Lives; Updates', *Business Standard,* 14 May 2018. Available athttps://www.business-standard.com/article/elections/clashes-mar-west-bengal-rural-poll-bjp-candidate-among-21-injured-updates-118051400255_1.html (accessed on 24 June 2019).
13. Prabhash Dutta, 'In Mamata Banerjee vs Narendra Modi Fight, Why BJP Is So Combative in Bengal This Lok Sabha Election', *India Today,* 16 May 2019. Available at https://www.indiatoday.in/elections/Lok Sabjha-sabha-2019/story/mamata-Ms. Banerjee-narendra-modi-bengal-Lok Sabjha-sabha-election-1526442–2019–05-16 (accessed on 19 June 2019).
14. Daniyal Shoaib, 'West Bengal: Will Anger at Rigging in Last Year's Panchayat Polls Singe Trinamool—and Help BJP?' *Scroll.in* 26 April 2019. Available at https://scroll.in/article/921179/west-bengal-will-anger-at-rigging-in-last-years-panchayat-polls-singe-trinamool-and-help-bjp (accessed on 28 June 2019).
15. Swapan Dasgupta, 'A Profound Transformation in Bengal', *The Telegraph*, 5 May 2019. Available at https://www.telegraphindia.com/opinion/post-election-data-indicates-a-transformation-in-west-bengal-with-regard-to-the-bjp-and-hindutva/cid/1691461 (accessed on 28 June 2019).
16. Suvojit Bagchi, 'Who Gets West Bengal's Muslim Vote?' *The Hindu*, 17 May 2019. Available at https://www.thehindu.com/elections/Lok Sabjha-sabha-2019/who-gets-west-bengals-muslim-vote/article27165507.ece (accessed on 25 June 2019).
17. Jyotindra Dubey, 'Hindu Uprising in West Bengal Brings BJP at the Forefront', *India Today*, 22 May 2019. Available at https://www.indiatoday.in/elections/lok-sabha-2019/story/hindu-uprising-in-west-bengal-brings-bjp-at-the-forefront-1532311-2019-05-22 (accessed on 26 June 2019).
18. The Wire, 'High Court Cancels Mamata Banerjee's Order on Durga Puja Idol Immersion', *The Wire*, 21 September 2017. Available at https://thewire.

in/communalism/calcutta-high-court-cancels-mamata-banerjees-order-on-durga-puja-idol-immersion (accessed on 24 June 2019).

19. Debashish Konar, 'Calcutta HC Flays Bengal Govt over Immersion Ban on Muharram', *The Times of India*, 21 September 2017. Available at https://timesofindia.indiatimes.com/city/kolkata/calcutta-hc-flays-bengal-govt-over-immersion-ban-on-muharram/articleshow/60766331.cms (accessed on 25 June 2019).
20. Press Trust of India, 'Mamata's Allowance for Imams, Muezzins Unconstitutional: High Court', *The Hindu*, 2 September 2013. Available at https://www.thehindu.com/news/national/other-states/mamatas-allowance-for-imams-muezzins-unconstitutional-high-court/article5085896.ece (accessed on 25 June 2019).
21. Times News Network, 'Setback for Mamata as HC Rejects Dole to Imams and Muezzins', *Times of India*, 3 September 2013. Available at https://timesofindia.indiatimes.com/city/kolkata/Setback-for-Mamata-as-HC-rejects-dole-to-imams-and-muezzins/articleshow/22243165.cms (accessed on 19 June 2019).
22. Indrajit Kundu, 'After Mamata's Durga Puja Sop, Muslim Clerics Demand Hike in Imam Stipends', *India Today*, 4 October 2018. Available at https://www.indiatoday.in/india/story/after-mamata-s-durga-puja-sop-muslim-clerics-demand-hike-in-imam-stipends-1355572–2018–10-04 (accessed on 27 June 2019).
23. *The Times of India*, 'Bengal Imams Oppose "SOPS"', 17 January 2018. Available at https://timesofindia.indiatimes.com/city/kolkata/bengal-imams-oppose-sops/articleshow/62531484.cms (accessed on 21 June 2019).
24. Romita Datta, 'West Bengal Imams Reject State Govt Allowance', *Live Mint*, 1 January 2013. Available at https://www.livemint.com/Politics/9lmX0Wu6BXLp3PTHh747gI/West-Bengal-imams-reject-state-govt-allowance.html (accessed on 28 June 2019).
25. Indrajit Kundu, 'Rath Yatra Is Not Meant to Kill People, Mamata Takes a Jibe at BJP', *India Today*, 28 December 2019. Available athttps://www.indiatoday.in/politics/story/west-bengal-mamata-Ms.Banerjee-bjp-rath-yatra-1418953-2018-12-28 (accessed on 26 June 2019).
26. Debjani Chatterjee, 'Bengal BJP Plans Ram Navami Arms March, Mamata Ms. Banerjee Serves Warning', NDTV, 25 March 2018. Available at https://www.ndtv.com/india-news/ram-navmi-bjps-big-plans-in-bengal-mamata-Ms. Banerjee-asks-cops-to-stay-alert-1828311 (accessed on 26 June 2019).
27. Press Trust of India, 'Mamata Criticises Ram Navami Rallies in Bengal', *Business Standard*, 13 April 2019. Available at https://www.business-standard.com/article/pti-stories/mamata-criticises-ram-navami-rallies-in-bengal-119041300426_1.html (accessed on 29 June 2019).
28. Tanmay Chatterjee, 'Mamata Quotes Hindu, Islamic Scripts at Every Rally; Won't Help, Says BJP', *Hindustan Times*, 18 May 2019. Available at https://www.hindustantimes.com/india-news/mamata-recites-hindu-islamic-scripts-at-every-rally-won-t-help-says-bjp/story-qiSqQH7QNArKZ3EfhFE2HN.html (accessed on 28 June 2019).

29. Saubhadra Chatterji, 'Trinamool's Internal Analysis Indicates Left Vote May Shift to BJP in Bengal', *Hindustan Times*, 16 May 2019. Available at https://www.hindustantimes.com/Lok Sabjha-sabha-elections/tmc-s-worry-will-left-voters-shift-to-the-bjp/story-s7VBH08sHWd8r4BxzZo16M.html (accessed on 26 June 2019).
30. *The Hindu*, 'CPI(M), BJP Workers Jointly form Panchayat Boards in Bengal', *The Hindu*, 1 September 2018. Available at https://www.thehindu.com/news/national/other-states/cpim-bjp-workers-jointly-form-panchayat-boards-in-bengal/article24836540.ece (accessed on 1 July 2019).
31. Press Trust of India, 'West Bengal Panchayat Polls: CPI(M)–BJP Join Hands to Fight TMC', *Business Line,* 8 May 2018. Available at https://www.thehindubusinessline.com/news/national/west-bengal-panchayat-elections-cpim-bjp-join-hands-at-grassroot-level-to-fight-tmc/article23813489.ece (accessed on 1 July 2019).
32. Sreemoy Talukdar, How Narendra Modi Won West Bengal: Collapse of Left Front Vote, Mamata's Tactical Errors, PM's Brand Delivered Victory', *Firstpost*, 24 May 2019. Available at https://www.firstpost.com/politics/how-narendra-modi-won-west-bengal-collapse-of-left-front-vote-mamatas-tactical-errors-pms-brand-delivered-victory-6695581.html (accessed on 28 June 2019).
33. Shaoib Daniyal, 'Strange Shift: Bengal's Left Front Is Melting Away— into the BJP', Scroll.in, 17 May 2019. Available at https://scroll.in/article/923128/strange-shift-bengals-left-front-is-melting-away-into-the-bjp (accessed on 26 June 2019).
34. Tanmay Chatterjee, 'Amid TMC-BJP Tussle, Left Looks to Regain Bengal Ground', *Hindustan Times*, 2 June 2019. Available at https://www.hindustantimes.com/india-news/as-tmc-bjp-faceoff-continues-cpi-m-eyes-regaining-lost-ground-in-bengal/story-r7mbKsYvc2m9VuCzUrr1SP.html (accessed on 27 June 2019).
35. Tanmay Chatterjee, 'From Marx to Modi: How Left Voters Ensured BJP's Bengal Victory', *Hindustan Times*, 25 May 2019. Available at https://www.hindustantimes.com/lok-sabha-elections/from-marx-to-modi-how-left-voters-ensured-bjp-s-bengal-victory/story-JRkvW9zyEpUfXFKTkEgb0J.html (accessed on 2 July 2019).
36. Hindustan Times, 'Left Supporters Voted for BJP in Bengal, Admits Sitaram Yechury; Voters Found BJP a Credible Force, Says Congress MP', *Hindustan Times*, 4 June 2019. Available athttps://www.hindustantimes.com/india-news/left-supporters-voted-for-bjp-in-bengal-admits-sitaram-yechury-voters-found-bjp-a-credible-force-says-congress-mp/story-PHiYFh6NkXCewiSoen0B0M.html (accessed on 28 June 2019).
37. Madhuparna Das, 'Decline in Left Front's Vote Share Benefits BJP', *The Economic Times*, 24 May 2019. Available at https://economictimes.indiatimes.com/news/elections/Lok Sabjha-sabha/west-bengal/decline-in-left-fronts-vote-share-benefits-bjp/articleshow/69473464.cms (accessed on 27 June 2019).

38. Abhishek Law, 'Mamata–Modi War of Words Takes a Turn for the Worse', *Business Line*, 8 May 2019. Available at https://www.thehindubusinessline.com/news/national/mamata-modi-war-of-words-takes-a-turn-for-the-worse/article27061115.ece (accessed on 2 July 2019).
39. *Hindustan Times*, 'Yogi Adityanath's Bengal Rally Denied Permission by Mamata Govt', 3 February 2019. Available at https://www.hindustantimes.com/india-news/yogi-adityanath-s-rally-denied-permission-by-bengal-govt/story-Om68RruW5jCN7D9ZXMglwN.html (accessed on 1 July 2019).
40. Press Trust of India, 'Amit Shah Denied Permission to Hold Rally in Bengal, BJP Cries Mamata's Dictatorship', *India Today*, 13 May 2019. Available at https://www.indiatoday.in/elections/lok-sabha-2019/story/bjp-announces-protests-over-denial-of-permission-to-shah-s-rally-in-bengal-1523534–2019–05-13 (accessed on 2 July 2019).
41. Asian News International, 'BJP Accuses Mamata Govt. of Denying Permission of Venue of PM's Rally', ANI, 30 March 2019. Available at https://www.aninews.in/news/national/politics/bjp-accuses-mamata-govt-of-denying-permission-for-venue-of-pms-rally20190330185547/ (accessed on 1 July 2019).

Chapter 14

Biju Janata Dal's Fifth Term in Odisha

Pradeep Nayak

A historic landslide in the 2019 assembly elections as well as success in the simultaneous parliamentary elections mark the continuing dominance of the Biju Janata Dal (BJD) regional party. It continues to rule for a fifth term in an economically backward but developing state and consecutively for 25 years. Naveen Patnaik's leadership and persona as a popular CM continues to be a primary factor for the party's success. The BJD was formed in December 1997 in the name of the legendary political leader of Odisha. To cash in on Biju Patnaik's popularity and personal appeal, the regional party was then named the Biju Janata Dal.

Naveen's critics, rivals and supporters emphasize his personality traits when expressing their comments on the performance of his government.[1] This chapter discusses the historic win of a regional political party in a state under the singular leadership of Naveen Patnaik, especially going against nationwide trends of voting based on majoritarianism and Hindu consolidation. It examines the political strategies of the BJD and other parties, issues involved in the Lok Sabha and Vidhan Sabha elections in 2019, and how split voting occurred in some Lok Sabha seats proving the importance of the Modi factor.

The politics of Odisha takes place within a state whose population is 90 per cent scheduled castes and tribes, and other backward castes.

Upper castes' hold over politics still continues, though there have been effective challenges to their hegemony from the numerically superior intermediate peasant castes.[2] The state's progress in Human Development Index since the last two decades shows some perceptible improvements. Yet in terms of poverty, per capita income of people, migration, malnutrition and health indicators, the state continues to lag behind other states. These data are giving rise to the continuing demand by the state's political elites for a special category state status so that Odisha can receive increased Central government funding.

THE CONTEXT OF GENERAL ELECTIONS IN ODISHA

The political context of the national elections held in April–May 2019 involves BJP's expectations following its electoral losses in Hindi-speaking northern states in February 2019. It seemed to be clear that the ruling BJP party with its National Democratic Alliance (NDA) partners would face a formidable challenge from opposition parties in the upcoming Lok Sabha elections. Agrarian distress, nationwide rallies by farmers, and sluggish economic and unemployment data compounded the problems for the Narendra Modi-led government. At the national level, the BJP focused on making alliances with regional and caste-based alliances projecting the leadership of Narendra Modi as prime minister. The BJP through its well-organized and disciplined cadres continued consolidating pro-Hindu bases based on exaggerated national security concerns and fear of Islamic terrorism sponsored by Pakistan, especially in the context of the Pulwama suicidal terror attack.

BJP's second term in May 2019 is historic as the alliance arithmetic by political parties were less effective than the aggressive presidential style of campaigns by the BJP under the leadership of Modi, harping on the fear of national security concerns. The economic concerns of common people were pushed into the background. Various studies have pointed out that BJP's victory was a success of pro-Modi Hindu consolidation and BJP's smart social engineering by aligning and co-opting the castes and communities excluded by opposition parties. The massive media campaign centring around Modi's image as an effective and strong leader who can provide leadership and take decisive action such as the Balakot air strike in the wake of the terror strike in

Pulwama, failure of the opposition to present a unified front under the leadership of Congress, a deepening religious divide and massive use of money had given a clear upper hand for the BJP to sweep the general elections. Interestingly, the consolidation of Hindu votes in BJP's favour in the 2014 general elections were 22 per cent, which rose to 40 per cent in Odisha run by Naveen Patnaik's BJD since 2000.[3]

The general elections were held in a staggered manner for 542 seats from 11 April 2019 to 19 May 2019, which pulled around 67 per cent of votes. Many exit polls had predicted a comfortable victory for BJP-led NDA under Modi's leadership that had an assortment of caste-, region- and ethnic-based parties. The general elections were fought in a presidential-style campaign, posing a challenge to the opposition about their leadership in running the country.

Modi in his campaigns in Odisha attacked the United Progressive Alliance (UPA), especially the Congress and some personality-based regional parties for promoting dynastic rule and blaming them for the country's woes. Polarization of votes, primarily a Hindu–Muslim divide, played a critical role in the sweeping victory of the BJP in the Hindi or cow belt of India. The Hindutva narrative of national security, terrorism and political stability at the Centre under the leadership of Modi had its positive impact in Karnataka, Odisha, West Bengal and Maharashtra. In the states where the BJP was defeated in the Vidhan Sabha polls such as Madhya Pradesh, Chhattisgarh and Rajasthan a few months earlier, the BJP swept almost all of the Lok Sabha seats emphasizing so-called nationalism issues.[4]

The BJP flushed with funds had tried to lure away many disgruntled leaders from the opposition through co-option and nationalist appeals. The issues poised by the BJP were its commitment to hyper nationalism, Hindutva and welfare policies, and whether PM Modi is to be given a second chance to lead the country. This simple question had obfuscated other burning economic issues before the voters across the states.[5]

The general election results reveal that many regional parties like TDP in Andhra Pradesh and regionalist parties like RLD and SP in Uttar Pradesh were humbled by the landslide mandate in favour of Modi. Even the TMC in West Bengal, the TRS in Telengana and the BJD in Odisha were deeply impacted by the personality-driven electoral victory of the BJP harping on fear, insecurity, desire for a strong leader and majoritarianism. In south Indian states like Tamil Nadu, the so-called Modi magic or Modi wave did not work. The voters in Kerala, Tamil Nadu and Andhra Pradesh turned away from BJP's narrative of nationalism. In Telengana, where there is a substantial Muslim population, the BJP secured 4 Lok Sabha seats owing to polarization.[6]

In 2019, the BJP sought to increase its Lok Sabha seats in eastern regions such as Odisha and West Bengal fearing that it might lose some seats in the northern Hindi belt. Frequent visits by Narendra Modi and BJP President Amit Shah to Odisha worried Naveen Patnaik as he also feared that the anti-incumbency factor might harm the BJD. The BJP was upbeat after its performance in the three-tier Panchayati Raj elections where it replaced the Congress in second place in 2017.

The Lok Sabha elections were held in the state in the context of the Modi wave and brand Naveen in the aftermath of his successful organization of the World Men's Hockey cup in November 2018. State and national elections were conducted as a battle between two personalities. Naveen Patnaik sought to confine the election campaign to state-specific issues such as his demand for a special category state and central neglect of Odisha in various fronts of development. On the other hand, Modi and Amit Shah sought to highlight the failures of the state in implementing central schemes and its continuing backwardness despite two decades of BJD rule under Naveen Patnaik.[7] The simultaneous elections were fought bitterly by the BJD and BJP. Naveen Patnaik concentrated his attack on BJP leaders in the state for their failures to protect the interest of the state in Mahanadi, Polavaram, and railways and mining issues. Patnaik avoided raising any national level issues such as the terror attack in Pulwama and air strike by the Indian air force in Pakistan territory. The national and regional level issues were often blurred.

POLL STRATEGY BY POLITICAL PARTIES

Naveen Patnaik shortly before the assembly elections declared that he would reserve 30 per cent of Lok Sabha seats only for women, not for

Vidhan Sabha seats. It was a clever strategy to corner the opposition on their commitment to empower women in giving gendered representation. The Mission Shakti project of Odisha government was started in 2001 for empowering women and raising their socio-economic well-being through formation of self-help groups (SHGs) had acted as a bulwark against an anti-incumbency wave in rural areas. More than 6 lakh SHGs had been formed covering 70 lakh women. These SHGs were given liberal financial assistance and loans in liberal terms for carrying out various micro-level livelihood and income generating activities.[8] Naveen Patnaik adopted a shrewd strategy of beating an anti-incumbency factor by managing women empowerment policies successfully. He astutely declared his Lok Sabha reservation quota for women and decided to put a SHG leader to contest Aska Lok Sabha seat in south Odisha. This surprised many political observers. The declaration posed a dilemma for the Congress and BJP state units as they were not able to support or oppose it as it would involve other parties in India.

Patnaik's government launched a number of massive welfare programmes and construction of public amenities works throughout the state in the backdrop of former ally BJP's resurgence. He showed his firm grip in the party by denying tickets to over 35 sitting MLAs, changed party candidates in 80 assembly seats and 6 sitting MPs were not re-nominated in order to beat any anti-incumbency trend. In three assembly seats, the sons of senior MLAs were given party tickets. The BJD managed to win at least 34 of 49 Vidhan Sabha seats where it had fielded new candidates. In important Vidhan Sabha constituencies, Naveen co-opted leaders from opposition parties. In the process, he decimated the intra-party feud, asserted his supremacy and led the party to fight an anti-incumbency factor.[9]

Naveen Patnaik chose to contest from the Bijepur Vidhan Sabha constituency in western Odisha as well as from Hinjli assembly seat in coastal south Odisha so to assist his party's prospects in the face of aggressive media and mobilization efforts by the BJP. He won both the seats with handsome margins.[10] Matching the aggressive campaigns by PM Narendra Modi and BJP President Amit Shah, Naveen Patnaik matched the places where the duo had visited by organizing mammoth meetings and road shows. These benefited BJD workers' morale and sent a message that his popularity was not on the wane.[11]

These campaigns did not focus on national issues. Patnaik harped on his so-called 'double engine' formula of politics; empowering women at the community level such as SHGs and Panchayati Raj institutions. It differed from the so-called double engine model of the state BJP unit, which advocated voting BJP for both the Vidhan Sabha and Lok Sabha polls. This was indeed a shrewd political response to deflect and blunt BJP's double engine strategy of combining both elections so as to propel growth.[12] Naveen Patnaik never lost an opportunity to point out the absence of a BJP chief ministerial candidate.

The BJP accused the BJD of raising scams and corruption in chit funds, mining, land, bribe by grass-roots level officers, and the safety and security of women. But these accusations were not very effective. The BJP also aggressively campaigned through the media by projecting itself as an alternative to the ruling BJD especially after its stunning success in Zila Parishad elections in 2018. BJP's Amit Shah had declared that his party would win 120 seats in the assembly elections in 2019 in his visits to Odisha prior to elections. It relied on Narendra Modi's leadership as it attacked the BJD. The BJP was routed earlier in the 2014 Lok Sabha elections as it had won only 1 out of 21 Lok Sabha seats and 10 seats out of 147 Vidhan Sabha seats. It counted on improving its 2019 electoral results in the areas in which it had won Zila Parishad seats the previous year.

The Congress Party was in disarray as it had been out of power in Odisha since 1999. The faction-ridden state leadership could not muster funds and even candidates for some Vidhan Sabha seats. Many veteran Congress leaders refused party tickets fearful of being defeated by the BJP or BJD. Congress had been reduced to third position in the Lok Sabha and Vidhan Sabha, and Congress national leaders showed little interest. State Congress leaders fought the elections on their own strength and could not match the ruling BJD and BJP in terms of mobilization of voters and money power.[13] It has lost its appeal especially among young voters and the energy and motivation of its workers and leaders were at a low ebb.

ANALYSIS OF VOTES IN LOK SABHA AND VIDHAN SABHA POLLS

In the 2019 Assembly elections, BJD candidates were elected in one-sided contests in 45 seats. In 65 seats, there were direct contests between the BJD and BJP, and the Congress and BJD candidates. In 2019 Lok Sabha elections, the BJP swept all five Lok Sabha seats in western Odisha whereas in the Vidhan Sabha elections, the BJD retained more seats in the Vidhan Sabha segments of western Odisha. In the Bargarh and Bhubaneswar Lok Sabha constituencies, the BJP could not win a single Vidhan Sabha seat, yet its candidates won Lok Sabha seats. The BJP's vote shares in Lok Sabha elections has shown a steady rise from 22 to 38.4 per cent. The Congress's vote share in parliamentary elections was almost halved, from 26.4 per cent in 2014 Lok Sabha elections to 13.8 per cent in 2019. It is clear that Congress support has been transferred to the BJP.[14] Other parties including independents polled 5 per cent in Lok Sabha and 6.2 per cent in Vidhan Sabha elections.

The BJD's votes in Lok Sabha and Vidhan Sabha elections revealed that the BJD had polled less in the Lok Sabha elections (42.77%) than in the Vidhan Sabha elections (44.72%) (for detail analysis see Table 14.1 and Table 14.2). It can be safely argued that the vote share increase for the BJP in both general and Vidhan Sabha elections have been at the cost of the Congress.[15] A post-poll survey conducted by CSDS found a trend of voting preference for Naveen as chief minister (68%) and

Table 14.1 *BJD's Performance in Vidhan Sabha Elections 2000–2019*

Year	Seats Contested	Seats Won	% Vote Polled
2000	84	68	29.40
2004	84	61	27.36
2009	129	103	38.86
2014	147	117	43.35
2019	146	112	44.70

Sources: Election Commission of India, *The Statistical Report on General Election from 2000 to 2014 to Legislative Vidhan Sabha of Odisha* (New Delhi: Election Commission of India); 'Modi Again, Naveen', *The Samaj*, 26 May 2019.

Table 14.2 *Percentage of Votes Polled in Vidhan Sabha Elections 2000–2019*

Year vs Elections	BJP	BJD	Congress	Left	Others	Polling %
2000	38	84	26	2	5	59.10
2004	32	61	38	2	4	66.05
2009	6	103	27	1	4	65.30
2014	10	117	16	1	3	73.65
2019	23	112	9	–	2	73.08

Sources: Election Commission of India, *The Statistical Report on General Elections from 2000 to 2014 to Legislative Vidhan Sabha of Odisha* (New Delhi: Election Commission of India); 'Modi Again, Naveen',*The Samaj* 26 May 2019.

Table 14.3 *Performance of Major Parties in Lok Sabha Elections 2014 and 2019*

Party	2014 LS	Seats won	%Votes	2019 LS	Seats won	% Votes
BJD	21	20	44.10	21	12	42.80
BJP	21	1	21.50	21	8	38.14
Congress	21	0	26.00	21	1	13.18

Sources: Election Commission of India, *The Statistical Report on General Election from 2000 to 2014 to Legislative Vidhan Sabha of Odisha* (New Delhi: Election Commission of India); 'A Fractured Lok Sabha Mandate', *Dharitri*, 28 May 2019.

Modi (68%) as prime minster, but 87 per cent voted for Modi as PM and 57 per cent voted the BJD for Lok Sabha seats (see Table 14.3).[16]

THE NATIONAL AND REGIONAL: VIDHAN SABHA AND LOK SABHA ELECTION RESULTS

At the national level, the BJP secured 37.6 per cent of votes with 303 seats. Its support base came from the lower castes and OBCs, and rural populace across India. The BJP's victory has upturned the caste calculation of many political parties despite high discontent in various policies and dissatisfaction. Electoral majorities can be constructed overcoming mass resentments by resorting to non-economic issues such as hyper nationalism.[17]

The BJD received its drubbings in Lok Sabha elections in western and northern Odisha but in the Vidhan Sabha elections, it re-established its dominant positions there. The divided mandate to Lok Sabha and Vidhan Sabha polls in 2019 in these regions are described by observers as the voters' preference for Modi in Lok Sabha elections and Naveen Patnaik in Vidhan Sabha polls. But the political reality is that cadre-based party like the BJP had in fact consolidated its winning position in these regions where it had trounced BJD candidates in Zila Parishad seats elections held in February 2017. The BJD in its manifesto claimed that the party would continue to strive for its populist programmes and fight for Odia *swabhiman* (dignity and pride). It cited its efforts in making Odia language listed as the classic language and setting up an Odia university as a case of the party's commitment for Odia identity. Its campaign focused on 'Naveen Odisha: Empowered Odisha' and 'Naveen is part of my family' which sought to evoke a sentimental connection of Naveen with Odiyas.

On the other hand, there is no alternative (TINA) to the Modi factor had created a driving force for the BJP's Lok Sabha victory. Identity-based issues also led to a vitriolic campaign by the BJP against Muslims and for Hindu consolidation. These included preferential treatment for Muharram over Durga Puja in West Bengal, giving a Lok Sabha ticket to terror accused Pragya Thakur in Madhya Pradesh, defending a series of orchestrated lynching of cow traders and other hate crimes, communal polarization in West Bengal and accusing Rahul Gandhi of filing for a Lok Sabha seat in a constituency dominated by minorities in Kerala. Not a single Muslim MP was elected on a BJP ticket supporting the critics' apprehension of communal polarization and majoritarian consolidation.[18] The landslide mandate for the BJP in the Lok Sabha elections results once again legitimized Narendra Modi's leadership and the politics of Hinduness or Hindutva as the core of Indian politics and culture.

Naveen Patnaik could counter Modi wave due to his clean image, harping on the politics of regional and Odiya identity, a strong organization, welfare measures and absence of a credible state opposition individual to his leadership. Similar factors also worked in favour of Modi at the national level. On the divided or split voting in the Lok Sabha and Vidhan Sabha elections, it can be seen that the BJP increased its Lok Sabha tally from one seat in 2014 to eight seats in the 2019 elections, whereas BJD's seat share fell from 20 seats it won in the 2014 elections to just 12 seats in the 2019 elections. Though many analysts have concluded that Naveen Patnaik countered the Modi wave in Odisha, the fact is that the BJP achieved a nearly 73 per cent increase in its vote percentage winning 8 Lok Sabha seats and 23 MLA seats. BJP's results clearly reveal the importance of the Modi factor. The BJP has replaced the Congress and has emerged as the main opposition party.[19]

The Vidhan Sabha elections were a mandate for the status quo in the state and as related to the centre. BJD's victory was significant in the sense that despite a massive wave of support generated for Modi through a media blitzkrieg, and in the wake of hyper nationalism and internal security concerns, the voters preferred Naveen Patnaik's leadership in the state government. The consolidation of his leadership also has seen the declining position of the Congress and rise of the right-wing majoritarian BJP.[20]

BJD's electoral victory must be primarily focused on the party's leader as assisted by his coterie who helped shape the party's political strategy. Naveen Patnaik's historic fifth term victory must take into account his leadership as he personifies the party. Hardly any second rung leader has been allowed to emerge out of his shadows.

A similarity in the state and parliamentary elections in Odisha in 2019 was that none of the parties raised the agenda of development, environmental pollution, sustainable development and agrarian crisis. Rather, the votes were against change and for strong leaders to secure their country in this uncivil and nasty world against the unknown.[21] Another similarity in Narendra Modi and Naveen Patnaik's victory is the voting participation role of women which continue to show a rising trend in Odisha as well as across India. Women-centric populist schemes launched by both leaders created a favourable predisposition of women towards these leaders.[22]

CONCLUSION

The landslide victory of the BJP is attributed to the organizational prowess of the BJP and its Sangh Parivar working under the leadership of Narendra Modi and his domineering media campaign. It highlighted his populist schemes such as direct cash transfer through Jan Dhan, subsidized cooking gas and electricity connections, construction of toilets, loans for the self-employed and the media imagery of Modi as incorruptible and a strong leader free from dynastic links. Similar taglines are attributed to Naveen Patnaik as a pro-poor leader having successfully launched schemes from womb to tomb for all sections of society, and his proven image as a strong, incorruptible and simple living leader. The BJD also has formidable organizational networks like the BJP in the villages and cities across the state.

Lok Sabha elections highlighted states in India's federation going to the polls with each having micro- and macro-levels of political issues and narratives. The issues across the states and within the state are different due to caste, class, religious, ethnic factors and other secular factors such as rural and urban, and peasants and non-farm populace divides. The political strategies of a regional party entrenched in power and a national party seeking to remove it would be different. Therefore, it is logical to say that the spectacular victory of Naveen Patnaik in the Vidhan Sabha polls and a creditable performance of the BJP in the Lok Sabha and Vidhan Sabha elections reflect a complex mix of split voting, regional and majoritarian identity politics.

At the all-India level, the ascendancy of the BJP was marked with the rise of divisive majoritarian politics based on hyper nationalism. In Odisha, it certainly had a serious impact, but the contests were more related to Naveen and Modi's personality and leadership styles and politics. The personality-driven campaign of the BJP at the national level revolving around Narendra Modi found its match in Odisha, where Naveen Patnaik faced a tough electoral battle in simultaneous elections due to BJP's resurgence after its spectacular victory in the previous panchayat elections.

The election results in 2019 have revealed two contradictory trends. In the Vidhan Sabha elections results, the BJD led by Naveen Patnaik has shown its dominant position in the state's politics. But Patnaik's attempt to defeat the polarizing and majoritarian politics of the BJP since his dissociation from the BJP-led NDA coalition over the deadly communal riots in Kandhamal in 2008 has not been successful. The politics of Hindutva in the state become increasingly legitimized with the decline of the Congress Party's inclusive secular ideology.

NOTES

1. Ruben Banerjee, *Naveen Patnaik* (New Delhi: Juggernaut, 2017); PTI, 'Political Layoff? Odisha CM Naveen Patnaik Dropped 44 Ministers in 17 Years', *The Financial Express*, 23 December 2017.
2. John Hariss, 'Comparing Political Regimes across the Indian States: A Preliminary Essay', *Economic and Political Weekly* 34, no. 48 (27 November 1999): 3367–3377; Jayant Sengupta, 'State, Market and Democracy in the 1990s: Liberalization and the Politics of Identity', in *Democratic Governance in India,* eds. Niraja Gopal Jayal and Sudha Pai (New Delhi: SAGE Publications, 2011).
3. Sandeep Shastri, Suhas Palshikar and Sanjay Kumar, 'Explaining the Modi Sweep Across Regions', *The Hindu,* 26 May 2019; Shreya Sardesai and Vibha Attri, 'The Verdict Is Manifestation of the Deepening Religious Divide in India', *The Hindu*, 30 May 2019.
4. *The Economic Times,* 'Election Results: BJP Set to Return to Power as Modi Wave Sweeps Most of India', *The Economic Times*, 23 May 2019. Available at https://economictimes.indiatimes.com/news/elections/lok-sabha/india/election-results-bjp-set-to-return-to-power-as-modi-wave-sweeps-most-of-india/articleshow/69458269.cms (accessed on 2 August 2019).
5. Sriram Ramkrishanan, '2+2 Is Not 4: How the Modi Wave Will Reshape National Politics', *The Economic Times,* 28 May 2019. Available at https://economictimes.indiatimes.com/news/politics-and-nation/2+2-is-not-4-how-tsunamo-2019-may-reshape-national-politics/articleshow/69530755.cms (accessed on 1 August 2019).
6. *The Deccan Herald*, 'Decoding Tamil Nadu's "Anti-Modi" Sentiment', *The Deccan Herald*, 16 April 2019. Available at https://www.deccanherald.com/opinion/in-perspective/decoding-tamil-nadus-anti-modi-sentiment-728784.html (accessed on 20 April 2019).
7. *The New Indian Express,* 'Amid BJP's Thumping Lok Sabha Win, Brand Naveen Rides against Modi Wave in Odisha', *The New Indian Express*, 25 May 2019.

8. Ashok Pradhan, 'Banking on Charisma, Naveen Looks to Beat Anti Incumbency', *Times of India*, 21 March 2019.
9. *The New Indian Express*, 'Campaign Goes Hi-tech, CM Naveen Patnaik on Top', *The New Indian Express*, 6 April 2019. Available at http://www.newindianexpress.com/states/odisha/2019/apr/06/campaign-goes-hi-tech-cm-on-top-1960943.html (accessed on 02 August 2019); *India Today*, 'From Partying with Mick Jagger to Being 5-Time CM: The Incredible Journey of Naveen Patnaik', 29 May 2019. Available at https://www.indiatoday.in/india/story/mr-clean-naveen-patnaik-wins-elections-odisha-chief-minister-1537626-2019-05-29 (accessed on 27 September 2019).
10. *The Hindu*, 'Naveen Files Nomination from Hinjili; to Contest from Bijepur Too', 21 March 2019. Available at https://www.thehindu.com/news/national/other-states/naveen-files-nomination-from-hinjili-to-contest-from-bijepur-too/article26594929.ece (accessed on 10 August 2019).
11. *The Times of India,* 'As BJP Looks East, Naveen Turns "Westward"', 18 March 2019.
12. *Business Standard*, 'Vote for Double-Engine BJP Govt to Usher in Development: PM in Odisha'. Available at https://www.business-standard.com/article/pti-stories/vote-for-double-engine-bjp-govt-to-usher-in-devp-pm-in-odisha-119032900786_1.html (accessed on 5 August 2019).
13. *The Times of India*, 'More Congress Leaders Return Party Ticket', 4 April 2019.
14. *Livemint*, 'How Split Voting in Odisha Helped BJP Win 8 Lok Sabha Seats,' 29 May 2019. Available at https://www.livemint.com/politics/news/split-voting-in-odisha-helps-bjp-snap-up-8-lok-sabha-seats-shows-data-1559067961302.html (accessed on 5 August 2019).
15. Sujit Bisoyi, 'Naveen's Talent for Picking Right Candidate Does the Trick', *The Times of India*, 25 May 2019.
16. Hilal Ahmed and Gyanaranjan Swain, 'Post-poll Survey: Naveen's Track Record Helps to Overcome BJP Blitz in Odisha', *The Hindu*, 28 May 2019. Available at https://www.thehindu.com/elections/lok-sabha-2019/naveens-track-record-helps-to-overcome-bjp-blitz/article27267792.ece (accessed on 1 August 2019).
17. Sanjay Kumar and Pranav Gupta, 'Where Did the BJP Get Its Votes from in 2019?' *Livemint*, 3 June 2019. Available at https://www.livemint.com/politics/news/where-did-the-bjp-get-its-votes-from-in-2019-1559547933995.html (accessed on 27 September 2019); *The Washington Post*, 'India's Modi Wins Resounding Election Victory with Potent Appeal to Nationalism', *The Washington Post*, 23 May 2019. Available at https://www.washingtonpost.com/world/asia_pacific/india-election-results-modi-remains-favored-to-win-as-counting-starts/2019/05/22/830b9f60-7cb4-11e9-b1f3-b233fe5811ef_story.html?noredirect= (accessed on 12 August 2019).
18. Venikitesh Ramkrishnan, 'Right on the Top', *The Frontline*, 3 June 2019.

19. *The Outlook,* 'Naveen Patnaik's BJD Warded Off a Saffron Storm but Odisha Did Ride a Modi Wave', *The Outlook*, 25 May 2019. Available at https://www.outlookindia.com/magazine/story/india-news-naveen-patnaiks-bjd-warded-off-a-saffron-storm-but-odisha-did-ride-a-modi-wave/301676 (accessed on 25 May 2019).
20. Prafulla Dass, 'Welfare State', *The Frontline*, 7 June 2019. Available at https://frontline.thehindu.com/dispatches/article28805876.ece (accessed on 2 August 2019).
21. Sunita Narain, 'Environmental Charter for the New Government', *Down to Earth*, 7 June 2019. Available at https://www.downtoearth.org.in/blog/general-elections-2019/secret-tales-of-polling-and-counting-booths-how-our-democracy-works-64786 (accessed on 15 June 2019).
22. Swati Pachauri, 'Verdict 2019: Why Did Women Vote for BJP?' *Down To Earth*, 12 June 2019. Available at https://www.downtoearth.org.in/blog/general-elections-2019/verdict-2019-why-did-women-vote-for-bjp—65030 (accessed on 12 August 2019).

Chapter 15

Populist Regimes, Electoral Dynamics and Contrasting Outcomes

Telangana and Andhra Pradesh in 2019

Karli Srinivasulu

INTRODUCTION

The context of the 2019 elections in the two states of Andhra Pradesh (AP) and Telangana is largely defined by the fact of their formation in 2014 following the bifurcation of the Telugu state of AP formed in 1956 on the basis of linguistic principle. This election happening after five years into the division obviously was centred around the problems related to the nature of state division. They also include issues springing up in the post-bifurcation scenario involving both the states and the centre as well. The electoral discourse, campaign strategy and popular mobilization by different parties were principally centred around the failures, limitations and inabilities of the ruling regimes in the respective states to address these issues, and the popular mandate was influenced by the perceptions, apprehensions and concerns thus related to it.

Unlike in 2014 when both states held assembly and Lok Sabha elections together, this time only AP had simultaneous elections.

Telangana held state elections earlier in December 2018. This accounts for a certain variation in the electoral agenda, campaign styles, issues and nature of competition, and popular perception of electoral issues in these states. The Lok Sabha election is especially significant for all the competing parties which have conspicuously been high on their populist agenda: The ruling party highlighting their success in keeping their promises and making new ones; the opposition parties offering to do more and better if voted to power. In spite of the immense populist thrust of these two state regimes, the electoral outcomes have been different. If the Telangana Rashtra Samithi (TRS) received an overwhelming majority in the assembly elections and put up a fairly good performance in the Lok Sabha elections, then the Telugu Desam Party (TDP) despite its track record of delivering its promises was trounced badly. This obviously calls for a deeper analysis.

The presentation here is made in four sections. Section one seeks to contextualize the 2019 elections in Telangana and AP by focusing on the post-bifurcation blues these states have witnessed. Section two examines the electoral performance of parties and their changing social support bases. Section three analyses the centrality of development and competitive welfare populism in the two states and why despite the similarity of their populist thrusts, the electoral outcomes have been different. In the last section we sum up the analysis.

THE CONTEXT OF 2019 ELECTIONS

The political developments following 2014 elections heralded two distinct tendencies in the respective state politics. These new states, which had almost six decades of common political history, after the division charted their own distinct political trajectories in terms of parties, policy regimes and style of governance. While in the undivided state the two dominant parties were the Congress and TDP, after the division the Congress has been on a decline in both states. It has almost been decimated in AP and absorbed by the Yuvajana Sramika Rythu Congress Party (YSRCP) which is an offshoot of the Congress like the Trinamool Congress Party in West Bengal emerging as a substitute to the Congress. Unable to find a leader comparable to the aggressive persona of Y. S. Jagan Mohan Reddy, son of the former Congress CM the late Y. S. Rajasekhara Reddy, the Congress gave up without much of a struggle. Jagan's rise and consolidation closely resembles that of Mamata Banerjee in West Bengal. The decline of the Congress in AP can be seen in the popular perception of the bifurcation to the detriment of the interests of coastal Andhra and Rayalaseema regions being the result of Congress action. In the 2019 elections we see its total eclipse by the YSRCP.

In Telangana, the TDP could be seen meeting a similar fate. The TDP which had a formidable and stable presence in Telangana region suffered from a credibility crisis during the Telangana movement as it has been seen as protective of Andhra interests. Despite its organizational strength and support base, especially among the OBCs in Telangana, the TDP found it difficult to resist the ideological offensive launched and sustained by the TRS with a view to usurp the social and political space occupied by the TDP. The TRS' social, political and symbolic conflict with the TDP saw a heightened expression leading to a determined effort to decimate the TDP in Telangana.[1]

In contrast, the Congress continues to be a major force in Telangana opposed to the ruling TRS. The core leadership of the Congress in both the states hails from the dominant Reddy community. If the Reddy leadership of the Congress in AP finding a leader in Jagan Mohan Reddy shifted to the YSRCP, in Telangana they continue to be in the Congress. It made them focus on strengthening of the Congress as the TRS led by a numerically minority landed caste of Velamas being in power has not been found acceptable to them. Because of absence of a strong and confident leadership for the Congress at the national and state level and the Congress' inability to rejuvenate itself, as it seems unlikely in the immediate context, and given the aggressiveness of the BJP to make its mark in Telangana there could be a mass exodus of the Reddy political elite to the BJP. This would be a similar process whereby a section of the prominent Kamma and Kapu political elite from the Congress swell up the ranks of the BJP, which has been witnessed in AP during the last few years. Despite its strong ideological self-image, the BJP has welcomed the new entrants into its fold to emerge as a major electoral force and the vulnerability of the Congress in Telangana and of the TDP in AP seem to come in handy.

ELECTORAL CONTESTATION AND ADVERSARIAL POLITICS

The TRS by disassociating the assembly elections from that of the Lok Sabha, as it transpired, confined the campaign almost entirely to the state with the national issues remaining marginal to the election and thus reaped rich dividends. The TRS went in for state elections in December 2018, four months early, improving its seat and vote share from that in 2014. In the house of 119, the TRS won 88 seats with 47 per cent votes recording a remarkable rise from its tally of 65 seats and 33.64 per cent vote share in 2014. The TRS' ally, All India Majlis-e-Ittehadul Muslimeen (AIMIM), won seven seats in the old city of Hyderabad reasserting its hold on its traditional bastion (see Table 15.1 for complete results).

The Congress forming a pre-election alliance Mahakutami (meaning grand alliance) with the TDP, CPI and Telangana Jana Samithi could not measure up to the strength of the TRS. The Congress despite a marginal improvement in its vote share lost a couple of seats to settle

Table 15.1 *Assembly Elections in Telangana (Total Seats 119)*

	2018 Elections		2014 Elections	
Party	Seats Won	Vote (%)	Seats Won	Vote (%)
TRS	88	46.9	65	33.64
INC	19	28.4	21	25.00
TDP	2	3.5	15	14.70
BJP	1	7.1	5	7.03
AIMIM	7	2.7	7	3.73
CPI(M)+CPI	0	0.8	2	2.70
Others	2	10.6	4	13.20

Source: Election Commission of India and Andhra Jyothi (Hyderabad Edition), 12 December 2018.

for 19. The most significant development is the decline of the TDP in its seat and vote share from 15 and 14.70 per cent in 2014 to 2 and 3.5 per cent in 2019. The BJP despite the bustling activity on its side with the top national leadership campaigning could not arrest its decline.

The presence of the TDP in the Mahakutami instead of being an advantage to the Congress turned out to be an embarrassment politically and disadvantage electorally. With the announcement of the alliance, the TRS which till then had campaigned highlighting its developmental and welfare policies made a strategic shift in its electoral game plan by focusing on the TDP, thus discrediting the alliance as inimical to Telangana's interests. The TDP has from the beginning been perceived as an Andhra party due to the fact that its main leadership and core support belongs to the Kamma caste, which is a dominant peasant and entrepreneurial caste of the Andhra region. During the protracted Telangana movement with the TDP opposed to the state bifurcation this image became further cemented. Naidu who was the CM of the undivided state for two terms sought to balance through his 'two eyes' proposition that both the regions are equally dear to him with not much result. The battle lines became clearly drawn; either one is for statehood for Telangana or against it.

Critical to the overwhelming victory of the TRS is the persona of Chandrababu Naidu. With the entry of Naidu as one of the chief campaigners for the Mahakutami, the focus of the TRS campaign took an aggressive and personalized adversarial posture. Banking on the image of Naidu as a hard-line opponent of the Telangana demand, his entry became projected as an effort at the return of Andhra dominance. His representations to the centre raising objections on various irrigation projects in Telangana and post-bifurcation imbroglios became highlighted effectively to ignite apprehensions and misgivings on the very nature of the Mahakutami: its potential undoing of the Telangana state due to the presence of the Naidu-led TDP.

The resultant party-political polarization was not accidental, but a deliberate strategy that the TRS banked on in its campaign and succeeded in tuning it to its victory. The Congress-led Mahakutami by focusing on the persona of K. Chandrashekar Rao (KCR) and his family rule could be seen as strengthening the TRS campaign, asserting

KCR's stature, reinvigorating the subdued Telangana identity and associated claims of pride and autonomy. The Congress could not extricate itself and in fact became an uncanny victim of KCR's high voltage adversarial politics. Adept as he is, KCR played it to the maximum and reaped electoral dividends.

With the trouncing of the Mahakutami in the assembly polls, the alliance parties went their own ways in the parliamentary elections. The TDP for the first time in its three and half decade history chose to abstain from the 2019 parliamentary elections in Telangana. The election to the national legislature necessitated a visible shift in the issues raised, and the voters' perceptions and preferences. This accounts for the variation between the assembly and the Lok Sabha results. The TRS sought to play a key role in national politics through its call for a 'federal front' of non-BJP and non-Congress parties. In contrast, the TDP tried to forge a non-BJP alliance in which the Congress would be a major player along with regional parties in different states.

The TRS was expected to repeat its assembly performance and emerge as a key player in national politics through its call for a 'federal front' and was understandably disappointed. It won 9 out of a total of 17 parliamentary seats with a vote share of 41.29 per cent. What accounts for the decline in the TRS' popular vote by 8.6 per cent since the assembly polls is attributed to the perceived arrogance of the supremo, his neglect of administration including undue delay in the cabinet formation and his efforts to attract opposition MLAs to the ruling party.[2] The Congress won three seats marginally increasing its vote share since the assembly polls.

BJP's Rise in Telangana

What is surprising is the significant performance of the BJP with four seats and a 19.45 per cent vote share, thus registering a quantum jump since the 2014 parliamentary elections and especially the 2018 assembly polls. It campaigned that Telangana would be important for the BJP march into the south after Karnataka. The results in this election have definitely elevated the spirits of the BJP rank and file (see Table 15.2 for Lok Sabha results).

Table 15.2 *Lok Sabha Elections in Telangana (Total Seats 17)*

	2019 Lok Sabha		2014 Lok Sabha	
Party	Seats Won	Vote (%)	Seats Won	Vote (%)
TRS	9	41.29	11	33.90
INC	3	29.48	2	20.50
BJP	4	19.45	1	8.50
TDP	–	–	1	3.10
YSRCP	–	–	1	2.90
AIMIM	1	2.78	1	1.40
Others	-	7	-	29.7

Source: Election Commission of India and Andhra Jyothi (Hyderabad Edition), 25 May 2019.

Telangana being part of the Nizam's state has historically witnessed tensions between Hindus and Muslims, especially during the reign of the last Nizam. With rise of the Congress-led nationalist movement and the communist peasant rebellion that extended well up to 1951, the Nizam and the private Muslim militia called the Razakars went on a communal rampage till the union government militarily integrated Hyderabad state through what is called the 'Police Action' in September 1948. This historical fact is highlighted on 17 September annually by the BJP as 'Liberation Day' emphasizing the Nizam as a Muslim ruler.[3]

With the rise of its electoral fortunes nationally since 2014, the BJP's focus has shifted to south India with Telangana as a principal target. The advance of the BJP which contested on its own is evident in its winning four MP seats, two having been represented by prominent TRS leaders including KCR's daughter in Nizamabad in the last Lok Sabha. BJP's performance is not accidental as it is reflective of a perceptible rise in the Hindu identity vote for the BJP since the last election from 10 to 22 per cent.[4] Critical to this development is TRS' pro-Muslim stance evident in KCR's open appreciation for the Nizam rule and policy support to Muslims. These include the promise of reservations, financial support to Muslim brides called Shadi Mubarak, support for the celebration of festivals like Eid and alliance with the AIMIM. BJP has been using these issues for the deepening of the communal divide abetted by the Sangh Parivar's long-standing grassroots work in the field of rural education resulting in critical electoral victories. BJP's performance in the 2019 elections has evidently enthused both leadership and cadre to announce Telangana as the new entry point for their prospective electoral expedition into the south.

DISCURSIVE SHIFT AND TDP'S DEFEAT IN ANDHRA PRADESH

The debacle of the TDP in Andhra Pradesh was unexpected (see Tables 15.3 and 15.4 for Andhra Assembly and Lok Sabha results). TDP became reduced in the state assembly from 102 to merely 23 and in the Lok Sabha from 15 in 2014 to just 3 seats in 2019. The YSRCP saw a phenomenal rise both in terms of seats and vote share from 67 to 151 seats and 44.12 to 49.9 per cent vote share. What contributed to the TDP debacle? This time the TDP with no electoral alliance went to polls on its own. In 2014 there was an alliance between the TDP, BJP and cine actor Pawan Kalyan's Jana Sena party. It brought together a broad social bloc consisting of the dominant castes of Kamma, Kapu (represented by Pawan Kalyan) and the OBCs. In contrast, the YSRCP could bank essentially on Reddy, SCs (scheduled castes) and minorities. With the absence of that alliance in 2019, the support bases of the parties obviously became fragmented both socially and spatially. What the electoral outcome demonstrates is a sharp polarization of voters between the two principal contenders, that is, the TDP and YSRCP. The poor performance of the BJP and Jana Sena also bears evidence of this fact.

It is an enigma of sorts that the TDP which put in place a formidable populist policy regime with detailed attention to different social segments could be trounced so decisively, which the party has yet to come to terms with. With all the contesting parties earnestly turning populist, a level playing field could be seen emerging in the state with people taking these policies for granted irrespective of who comes to power. The raison d'etre for the TDP's defeat has to be looked for elsewhere.

The TDP regime has been continuously under political and public watch for its shortcomings and mistakes. This is evident in the stories

Table 15.3 *Assembly Elections in Andhra Pradesh (Total Seats 175)*

Party	2019 Elections		2014 Elections	
	Seats Won	Vote (%)	Seats Won	Vote (%)
YSRCP	151	49.90	67	44.12
TDP	23	39.20	102	44.45
INC	0	1.18	0	2.94
BJP	0	0.84	4	2.18
CPI(M)+CPI	0	0.43	0	0.65
Others	1	8.45	2	5.66

Source: Election Commission of India and Eenadu (AP Edition) 24 May 2019.

Table 15.4 *Lok Sabha Elections in Andhra Pradesh (Total Seats 25)*

Party	2019 Lok Sabha		2014 Lok Sabha	
	Seats Won	Vote (%)	Seats Won	Vote (%)
TDP	3	39.59	15	28.10
YSRCP	22	49.15	8	28.90
BJP	–	0.96	2	8.50
Others	–	10.30	–	34.50

Source: Election Commission of India and Eenadu (AP Edition) 24 May 2019.

of imbroglio in the capital construction, corruption scandals involving the ruling party MLAs, sand and land mafia ruling the roost, and the pronounced display of Kamma arrogance and dominance. The Janmabhoomi Programme has been central to the developmental process under the TDP regime. The committees it constituted have allegedly become platforms for local party leaders to distribute benefits to their relatives and supporters. In spite of popular resentment, the re-fielding of most of the tarnished MLAs in 2019 is seen as a misstep. This has been one of the major factors for the erosion of the regime's credibility.[5] Naidu's failure to deliver on any of his major promises like building a world-class capital at Amaravati, constructing a new airport at Bhogapuram near Visakhapatnam or completing the Polavaram project was another factor. Inability to showcase any major achievements facilitated the opposition to further target him. Adding to this is the widespread perception of his loss of control as the supremo over the rank and file of the party. All this worked to the detriment of the TDP and diminished the image of its leader.

The major shift in the TDP's political strategy was to break its alliance with the BJP by coming out of the NDA government. The Naidu regime has been continuously under criticism by the YSRCP and other parties for its inability to get Special Category status for AP which was promised by the UPA at the time of bifurcation, and by the BJP as an ally of the TDP during the 2014 election campaign. Added to this was its failure to get the centre's support for the Polavaram Project and to address the revenue deficit of the new state. With its credibility impacted adversely, the TDP sought to shift the blame onto the BJP for its failure to keep up its promises. By making a dramatic exit from the NDA, the TDP focused its attack on the BJP both in the parliament and in the state. This strategy did not help the TDP but contributed to the dismal performance of the BJP in AP compared to 2014.

In contrast, the YSRCP leader, young and dynamic, has been popular through his ceaseless *padayatras* promising Rajanna Rajyam as his father Y. S. Rajasekhar Reddy's rule of undivided AP is fondly referred to. There is a popular buzz of giving 'one chance' to Jagan as a reward for his continual popular contact. The anti-TDP mood is due to the so-called 'excesses' of local TDP leaders and the supremo's inability to restrain them as well as the unsuitability of his son to lead the party. They occasion a sense of uncertainty about TDP's future providing an advantage to Jagan. Jagan exuded total control over the party organization and its social base while the TDP could not keep intact its support among the Kapus, OBCs and youth as they could be seen as distracted by other players in the electoral arena. OBCs who have traditionally been the strong support base of the TDP have nurtured disgruntlement against the TDP ever since it decided to include the dominant caste Kapus comprising 15 per cent of AP's population in the OBC category for the purpose of reservation in education and employment. It is clear from the Lokniti CSDS post-poll survey[6] that while just 8 per cent of farmer respondents have stated that the TDP government has been 'successful' and 48 per cent 'somewhat successful' in rendering support to the farmers, the remainder found it to be wanting. Naidu's regime clearly lagged behind in comparison with KCR's popularity among the farming community and young voters.

DEVELOPMENT AND POPULIST REGIMES IN TELANGANA AND ANDHRA PRADESH

Development has been high on the agenda of the regimes in both states though with different accents. In Telangana with its concern for backwardness, the priority issues identified for its development have been agriculture and irrigation. Historically the irrigation system has been built on the village tank system interconnected as a chain. During the Kakatiya era, the foundation was laid and continued in the subsequent periods. This system has been neglected after the formation of AP in 1956.[7] The Andhra region being part of the British governed Madras Presidency saw the development of major irrigation projects from the middle of the 19th century. The absence of a policy perspective and understanding along with the green revolution strategy in agriculture since the late 1960s led to the erosion of the traditional irrigation system and the social relations of agrarian production that sustained it. In recognition of the specificity and strength of Telangana's irrigation system, the TRS government launched Mission Kakatiya to revive this system by renovating the long-neglected village tanks.[8]

Given its priority to irrigation, a number of major and medium projects were also undertaken.[9] As a result, land acquisition has emerged as a major source of displacement leading to popular discontentment. The most militant protest against displacement for instance has come from the oustees as a consequence of the Mallanna Sagar reservoir being constructed as part of the Pranahita Chevella project in Medak district. In addition, a number of projects undertaken for infrastructural and industrial development have raised the issues of displacement, inadequacy of compensation and an absence of a proper rehabilitation policy. Most resistances given the extent, scope and scale of the projects have been scattered and localized. They are a result of the local initiatives of the victims with some support from local NGOs and other grassroots organizations. But no regime could ignore the fact of displacement, resultant popular disenchantment and its political costs especially in the electoral domain.

What had been high on the TDP regime agenda was the building of the capital city of Amaravati for the new state. The process was initiated with the acquisition of 33,000 acres of land through what is called 'land pooling' scheme, in which farmers were to participate 'as partners in development'.[10] This region being fertile and multi crop, the land pooling attracted huge resistance from farmers and opposition parties. The stories of government's use of coercive measures to acquire land and its disregard to the concerns of the landless labour, a majority of them belonging to the SCs, led to the unpopularity of the regime.

Land has been the most contentious issue in the so-called developmental process in both states. There have been protracted agitations against land acquisition for Special Economic zones (SEZs), power plants, irrigation projects and of course the new capital. In popular perception the 'eminent domain' power of the state has been used to acquire land for private corporate accumulation rather than for any substantial public purpose required by the law. The crisis that visited the popular classes as a result of the developmental projects was visible in the widespread dispossession, displacement and forced migration in search of employment. This experience has serious implications for the legitimacy of the regime and its electoral prospects. Populist welfarism has been expanded as a response to it.

Economic Reforms, Electoral Populism and Decline of Social Politics

It is instructive to examine the social basis of the populist turn with regard to electoral competition. There is a growing contradiction between the popular expectation for opportunities and the desire for a better livelihood, and the reality on the ground being in the other direction. The political economy of liberalization due to its resultant process of primitive accumulation has produced the conditions of dispossession, displacement and loss of livelihood of vast sections of popular classes as evident in the crisis of the farming, traditional occupational communities and small producers, and unorganized services and traders.[11] Political parties and regimes need to address the crisis in the socio-economic life of the popular classes to sustain their support and win elections.[12]

The TRS regime in Telangana is known for a wide range of populist schemes and policies that have contributed to its success. These include the subsidized rice scheme, Mid Day Meal Scheme in government schools, various Aasara Pension Scheme for the old aged, single women, widows and physically handicapped, Kalyana Lakshmi/ Shadi Mubarak for meeting the marriage expenditure of a girl belonging to a poor Hindu and minority community family, sheep and fish distribution schemes for OBC communities, and the two missions of Bhagiratha and Kakatiya. The TRS' record on the welfare front also has been quite remarkable. Moreover, the TRS government put in place a policy regime and instruments of governmentality for more effective governance and sustaining escalating costs.

It is surprising that the TRS neither in its long course of career as a 'movement' (*udyama*) party nor after coming in power in the new state paid sufficient attention to building the party organization. Its organizational mode has the MLA as the axis, seen as the supremo's man, who is bestowed with the party organizational, developmental and electoral responsibilities. The TRS returning to power in spite of the absence of a well-knit organizational structure is largely due to the charisma of its supremo and the track record of implementing basic schemes that addressed the mass of needy people. This helped its victory in spite of the lacklustre performance on the promise of two-bedroom houses, the non-implementation of three acres of land to the landless SC, ST families, deliberately neglecting education sector and being apathetic to universities.

Curiously on the front of social politics, which is crucial to understand the character of a party/regime, the TRS regime demonstrates social regression. Telangana experienced that the TDP played intense policy and social politics by accommodating and empowering the major OBC communities in institutional structures from Panchayati Raj up to the state assembly. The Telangana movement involved intense self-mobilization based on identities of caste, craft, community and gender, while TRS' electoral strategy gave almost negligible representation to the OBCs and women. Instead it sought to make use of the internal differences among the subaltern groups for its electoral gain. The Most Backward Castes (MBCs) consisting of semi-nomadic and satellite castes, smaller in number and existing on the margins of social structure have seen a rise in the assertion of their identity and solidarity. Separately from the OBCs, they have been demanding for their share in education, employment and political representation. TRS made attempts to patronize them so as to check the OBCs.

There is a strategic shift in the TRS' treatment of subaltern groups. Instead of emphasizing the political aspect, which empowers the elite of these castes, the TRS regime focuses on them as the target for occupation and caste-specific schemes. Thus, the schemes providing sheep to the Yadavas and fish to the Mutharasi, Besta and Gangaputras through their caste cooperatives as well as various forms of pension schemes for the beedi workers (majority of them are women), weavers, toddy tappers and other groups. Benefits for the farming community include the agricultural Rythu Bandhu[13] and Rythu Bima as patronage by the leader.

The TDP government in AP also followed a similar populist track with different nomenclature and variations in quantum. Along with the subsidized rice scheme, NTR Bharosa Pension scheme for the aged and the handicapped, Pasupu Kumkuma Scheme as support to the women self help groups (SHGs), unemployment allowance for youth, Chandranna Pelli Kanuka Scheme support to the marriage of poor girls, an insurance scheme called Chandranna Bima Yojana for Labourers and so on were put in place by the TDP as part of an elaborative welfare regime.[14] Despite these efforts, the TDP failed to reap electoral dividends largely due to the TDP regime having become led by self-interested leaders belonging to the dominant castes from the village to the assembly constituency level. Disadvantaged sections then turned towards the YSRCP. There is a general feeling that welfare measures have to be implemented by any party that comes to power as they have become the minimal condition of electoral acceptance. Jagan's promise to bring in Rajanna Rajyam by expanding welfare schemes and improving their implementation is seen as collaboration of this understanding.

Both Andhra and Telangana regions have been known for the vibrant presence of civil society associations and subaltern group activism. This is evident in the active social mobilization and dense discursive contestation in various social movements especially during the movement for separate statehood. But after bifurcation, the social forces which played a crucial role in the discursive domain have either largely been co-opted or rendered ineffective in both states. What transpired is the conspicuous prominence of the electoral-political domain leading to its usurpation of the social and cultural space. This is visible in the diminutive quality of public debate and social deficit in the electoral politics. The process of 'partyization' has significant impact on not only the quality of electoral discourse but also on the nature of representation. The preference by parties in both states for rich candidates has seen a conspicuous rise in their number and a massive increase in electoral expenditures.[15] AP over the last couple of decades has seen a phenomenal rise in the role of money and the 2019 elections have made it irreversible for the future. This will have a definite impact on the nature of the party system, the quality of democracy and popular representation.

CONCLUSION

The 2019 election happening five years after the state bifurcation continues to be centred around issues related to the division and the adversarial politics symbolized by the personas of Chandrababu Naidu and KCR. While KCR could successfully play on the Telangana sentiment by showing Naidu as the adversary of Telangana interests, the TDP could not succeed in doing the same to arouse the Andhra identity as an electoral issue. This was partly because of its electoral opponent YSRCP being another regional party. Electoral competition in AP was confined to the regional parties in spite of the efforts of national parties to make a mark. The weakening of the Congress in both the states for various reasons did open up space for the BJP to expand as indications from the Telangana's electoral outcome suggest.

There was an absence of any conspicuous anti-incumbency wave in both states, yet the polls threw up contrasting outcomes despite a high level of populist policy dispensation in them. This seems paradoxical in a context where there is a heightened flow of information through both the conventional and new social media. By all ethnographic evidence and media reportage this election has seen a phenomenal rise in the electoral expenditure with the ruling party obviously spending more by having access to more resources than the opposition. The rise of money power and un-inhibiting preference for wealthy candidates by political parties demonstrates this.

It is also important to note that the 2019 election has seen a visible impoverishment of politics in terms of agendas, thematics, narratives, policies and symbolics. AP and Telangana reflect the general trend in India today where politics is reduced to elections and parties have become electoral machines. The result of the obsession with the calculus of electoral gains and losses is the depreciation of substantive social politics as evident in the political discourse, legislative deliberations and electoral campaigns. This is also because of the decline of the civil society sphere in these states. The electoral campaign across the spectrum has seen a clear de-ideologization resulting in inter-personal allegations and scandalizing reaching a peak. The present electoral process and outcome amply demonstrates the blurring of ideological differences among political parties with an impact on their character and the quality of popular representation. This undoubtedly will have serious implications democratic politics in the long run.

NOTES

1. KCR's repeated political questioning: 'What is the need of an Andhra party in Telangana?' captures the intensity and urgency of the desire of the TRS to obliterate the TDP in Telangana. The bitterness with which the TRS continues to fight the TDP was partly a continuation of K Chandrasekhar Rao's (KCR) rivalry from his days in the TDP under N Chandrababu Naidu and a real or imaginary shared social base. This was projected as the opposition of Telangana *talli* (mother) the icon of Telangana identity to Telugu *talli*, the symbol of TDP's idea of Telugu identity.
2. Field notes, Hyderabad, April 2019.
3. The TRS government's refusal of the BJP's demand to officially celebrate 14 September as 'Liberation Day' led to a huge ideological controversy around the characterization of it as 'liberation' or 'integration'.
4. The CSDS Lokniti Post-Poll Surveys after the 2014 and 2019 elections bring this out. For details, see, *The Hindu* (Hyderabad Edition), 30 May 2019, p. 9.
5. Field notes, Vijayawada, March 2019. I am thankful to a number of academics, journalists and local political activists for helpful discussions.
6. *The Hindu* (Hyderabad Edition), 27 May 2019, p.10.
7. Gautam Pingle, 'Irrigation in Telangana: The Rise and Fall of Tanks', *Economic and Political Weekly* (Review of Agriculture) 46, no. 26/27 (25 June–8 July 2011): 123–130.
8. M. Dinesh Kumar, Nitin Bassi, K. Sivarama Kishan, Shourjomoy Chattopadhyay, Arijit Ganguly, 'Rejuvenating Tanks in Telangana', *Economic and Political Weekly* 51, no.34 (20 August 2016): 22–26.
9. The projects undertaken for construction are around 22 major and 9 medium irrigation projects. This is in addition to the 13 major and 37 medium projects. In spite of the high costs involved especially in the maintenance, lift irrigation is undertaken to suit to the topography of the region.
10. Dag Kolstø, 'Amaravati: The Making of a Disaster Capital in Andhra Pradesh?' *Economic and Political Weekly* 54, no. 20, (18 May 2019).
11. The case of SEZs demonstrates this. See, K Srinivasulu, 'Land Acquisition and Popular Resistance: Politics of Special Economic Zones in Andhra Pradesh' in *The Politics of Special Economic Zones in India*, eds. Rob Jenkins, Lorraine Kennedy, and Partha Mukhopadhyay (Delhi: Oxford University Press, 2014).
12. For an analysis of the paradox of Indian electoral democracy through the concept of political society as distinct from civil society, see Partha Chatterjee, 'Democracy and Economic Transformation in India', *Economic and Political Weekly* 43, no. 16 (19 April 2008. It is reproduced in Partha Chatterjee, *Lineages of Political Society* (Ranikhet: Permanent Black, 2011).

    For a critical discussion on Chatterjee's position see, K. Srinivasulu, 'Political Society, Caste Dominance and Subaltern Society: Reflecting on the Modes of Engagement with the Dalit Subalternity', in *Dalits, Subalternity and*

Social Change in India, eds. Ashok Pankaj and Ajit Pandey (London: Routledge, 2019.)

13. The Rythu Bandhu scheme has come under criticisms as it targets land owners rather than the actual tenant cultivator. There is a phenomenal increase in tenancy in the state with the traditional peasant owners moving out of agriculture to non-farm sectors and the backward castes leasing in these lands for cultivation. The Rythu Bandhu scheme does not take into account this change.
14. Field notes, Vijayawada, March 2019.
15. Available at https://timesofindia.indiatimes.com/city/hyderabad/andhra-pradesh-elections-2019-crorepatis-in-race-to-become-mps-mlas/articleshow/68521273.cms (accessed on 27 September 2019).

Chapter 16

Karnataka

BJP's Spectacular Victory over the Congress and JD(S)

Shivaputra S. Patagundi and Prakash Desai

Elections as the defining institutions of democracy have always been a major focus of attention for political theorists, analysts, journalists and practising politicians.[1] They are an important part of procedural democracy with implications for substantive issues in democratic politics. Election manifestos and electoral politics contribute to the articulation, interest and aspirations of people in public policy formulation and good governance.

The Congress Party and the Janata Dal (Secular) or JD(S) were rivals in Karnataka, especially in former old Mysore, but came together to form a hasty alliance following the results of the 2018 assembly election primarily for sharing power. Its performance was not satisfactory for various sections of the society, nor was the government stable during the entire period of the coalition in Karnataka and the overall development activities were not effective. Lack of clarity about its loan waver scheme disappointed a large number of farmers. These problems aggravated after Bharatiya Janata Party's (BJP) spectacular victory in the 2019 Lok Sabha election. Dissent in both the Congress and JD(S) began to grow. This resulted in the resignation of 17 MLAs, fall of the coalition government and replacement by the BJP government under the leadership of B. S.Yeddyurappa.

People have high expectations from the BJP government, but some ministerial aspirants complain about not being inducted into the ministry—reflecting some apprehensions about the BJP government's stability. The overarching influence of the strong BJP government at the centre, supplemented by an equally strong contingent of the state BJP MPs, is likely to overcome these apprehensions. With this brief background, it is important to analyse results of 2019 Lok Sabha election in Karnataka.

Surprises and unexpected electoral outcomes stimulate exploration of the causes and reasons for victory and defeat. Many political experts and politicians themselves belonging to the BJP were surprised about BJP's huge victory in winning 25 of 28 seats from Karnataka. Understanding the state level electoral base and related issues becomes pertinent and relevant due to diversities in terms of religion, caste, language and performance of parties from the viewpoint of development.

OUTCOME OF THE 2019 ELECTIONS

The BJP clearly dominated as the Congress and JD (S) managed to win one seat each and one seat was won by an independent candidate. The BJP swept to victory in Mumbai Karnataka, Hyderabad Karnataka, Central Karnataka and Coastal Karnataka regions. 'Modi's appeal has also cut across caste and creed lines since the party managed to win all the seven reserved constituencies—including five scheduled caste (SC) and two scheduled tribe (ST) seats, some of them considered to be the stronghold of the Congress.'[2] Former Prime Minister H. D. Deve Gowda, senior Congress leader Mallikarjun Kharge, former Chief Minister and former Union Minister Veerappa Moily and other prominent leaders suffered humiliating defeats. Overall, it was shocking for both the JD(S) and Congress.

BJP's victory was spectacular not only in the number of seats won but also in its high vote share[3]; it won 51.38 per cent of votes in the 2019 elections (see Table 16.1). 'In electoral terms, a vote share of this

Table 16.1 *Vote Share in Percentage*

Year	INC	BJP	JD(S)
1999	45.40	27.20	10.90
2004	36.80	34.80	20.40
2009	37.60	41.60	13.60
2014	40.80	43.01	10.97
2019	31.88	51.38	9.67

Source: Special Correspondent, 'Congress-JD (S) Coalition Decimated as BJP Sweeps Karnataka', The Hindu, 24 May 2019; Election Commission of India, 'General Election to Lok Sabha Trends and Result 2019'. Available at http://results.eci.gov.in/pc/en/partywise/partywiseresult-S10.htm?st=S10 (accessed on 30 September 2019).

magnitude has been unprecedented for any non-Congress party in Karnataka. The Congress managed such a spectacular win in 1984, in the election held following the assassination of Indira Gandhi.'[4] In the 2014 elections, both the Congress and JD(S) had managed moderate representation from the state,[5] but in this election they did not even retain the electoral success they had achieved. 'If the 2014 Lok Sabha elections were marked by anti-incumbency, pro-incumbency was the keynote of the 2019 elections as BJP decimated the opposition.'[6]

The politics of seat sharing between the Congress and the JD(S) substantially benefited the BJP in Karnataka as the result of the 2019 Lok Sabha elections demonstrated clearly that people at the grassroots level did not approve of the alliance. The Congress and JD(S) had been traditional rivals in the previous assembly and Lok Sabha elections of the former old Mysore region.[7] The arithmetic calculation of the coalition allies about transfer of votes did not succeed. According to the post poll survey:

> The belief that the alliance came together to merely deny the BJP a chance to come to power may well have caused sympathy among a segment of voters in favour of the BJP. Further, at the constituency level, the rivalry between the cadres of the Congress and the JD(S) led to a lacklustre campaign. Within both the Congress and the JD(S) there

> was unhappiness with the choice of candidates. All the infighting within these two parties could also explain their collective poor performance.[8]

The results in favour of the BJP in Muslim-dominated areas proved that the BJP is not an 'untouchable' party to a section of minorities.[9] Such support by a section of minorities also conveys the message that they are not affected by incidents such as attacks on Muslims elsewhere during the BJP regime from 2014 to 2019. The long-standing myth that 'the BJP would not be able to divide the larger social coalition of MOD (Muslims, Other Backward Classes and Dalits), which has always favoured the Congress, has been broken. At least a section of the MOD appears to have supported the BJP this time.'[10] These communities previously united in supporting the Congress as its regular vote bank. Changes in their voting behaviour were manifested in the 2019 elections.

It is true that 'the BJP's victory in Vokkaliga-dominated areas shows that it has managed to divide the votes of the dominant caste in Karnataka, which has traditionally aligned itself with the Janata Dal (Secular)',[11] but religion and caste became shelter for each other in these elections.

Another important factor that has played a major role in BJP'S spectacular victory is the organizational ability of the Rashtriya Swayamsevak Sangh (RSS) as well as the BJP. Their preparation for the election began much earlier and was very systematic. They made efforts to reach every section of the urban and rural areas in the state as a part of their electoral campaign. Large numbers of youth members of the party were actively involved in the campaign. The RSS and BJP's continuous interaction with youth in different public spheres appealed to them. This was not the case with both the Congress and JD(S). Senior leaders of the Congress and JD(S) concentrated on a few selected constituencies and their absence in others resulted in the inactivity of ordinary members. Overall, their organizational ability and performance was poor. Leaders of the Communist parties, especially youth leaders, made efforts to be an alternative to all parties in the state through their online and offline political activities. But their influence was confined to only a few areas where it had some political base.

Dynastic politics is another issue that became big news in Karnataka. A large number of people did not approve of the dynastic politics of Deve Gowda and his family's dominance in the party and in state politics. However, the family politics of the BJP leaders did not receive any negative response. The sons of B. S. Yeddyurappa and C. M. Udasi, another prominent BJP leader, were elected without any difficulties.[12]

Women's representation for the Lok Sabha is poor. Social indicators show that Karnataka is comparatively empowering women, but the same is not reflected in their political representation in representative institutions, especially in the Lok Sabha. There were 27 women candidates but only two won, one independent and another from the BJP. 'From Karnataka, the best representation of women in Parliament was in 1991 when three MPs were elected.'[13] The first time a woman candidate was elected to the Lok Sabha from Karnataka was in 1962.

With the defeat of many senior leaders 'the State's representation in the 17th Lok Sabha will be the youngest in at least two decades.'[14] It needs to be seen whether newly elected youth members of the Parliament from the state are going to make much of a difference or not, as far as discussion and debates on the issues of national importance and the issues important to the state are concerned. One of the long-standing facts about the political representatives from the state is that they have not been very articulate and assertive on the issues concerning the state. The average age of Karnataka MPs in the 14th, 15th and 16th Lok Sabha was 57.7, 57.9 and 61 years respectively, whereas, the average age of the state's MPs in the17th Lok Sabha is 56.7 years.[15] Table 16.2 provides information about MPs belonging to different age groups.

The electoral politics of Karnataka was influenced by many issues in 2019. The credible leadership of Narendra Modi and his distinct way of campaigning in Karnataka with seven rallies significantly influenced the electoral outcome of the 2019 elections. The leadership of Narendra Modi became more influential since there was no alternative leadership provided by the opposition, particularly the Congress party at the national level as well as the state leaders. The leadership of Narendra Modi became more acceptable than the leadership of any other political party. During the campaign, 'it was patently visible that the BJP

Table 16.2 *Age of the Members of Parliament from Karnataka*

Age Group of MPs	14th LS	15th LS	16th LS	17th LS
Below 30	0	0	0	2
30–40	2	0	0	0
40–50	7	7	2	3
50–60	8	8	12	10
60–70	5	7	8	10
Above 70	6	6	6	3

Source: Mohit M. Rao, 'Karnataka's Representation in 17th Lok Sabha Is the Youngest in Recent Years', *The Hindu*, 29 May 2019.

was taking every effort to make it a presidential style poll, with their candidates seeking votes in the name of the Prime Minister.'[16] Modi became more important than the party. More than half of the people who said that they had voted for the BJP were of the firm opinion that 'they would not have done so if Mr Modi were not the prime ministerial candidate.'[17]

The Centre for the Study of Developing Societies (CSDS)—Lokniti post-poll data indicated, 'The level of satisfaction with the central government was reasonably high.'[18] This was one of the reasons for the upsurge of the BJP in Karnataka. The Congress and the JD(S) did not effectively criticize the failure of the central government. 'The failure on the jobs front, the crisis caused by demonetization and the collapse of small businesses following the implementation of the goods and service tax regime hardly figured as a cohesive plot around which the opposition mounted an attack on the BJP for its failings.'[19] Security issues related to the Pulwama attack and the Balakot air strike too received great emphasis during the election campaign from both the BJP and the coalition allies.

Language related to personal attacks used by some political parties became controversial. The Election Commission advised political parties 'to refrain from using offensive and objectionable language against rivals and strictly follow the ECI guidelines in the interest of conducting free and fair elections.'[20] The Election Commission decided it had to intervene.[21]

The language and culture of the state were expected to become issues in the election, but they did not play any role in the voters' choice. The Karnataka government had taken a decision to have a separate state flag in the year 2018[22] and it was widely supported by intellectuals, activists as well as common people. Regarding the aspiration of the people on issues like having any cultural symbol, it was rightly observed that the non-Hindi-speaking regions of India would 'come up with creative ways of fighting for their cultural freedom.'[23] The election result indicated that voters did not give much importance to regional culture and related issues.

Caste identity was a more important factor for dominant communities such as Lingayats and Vokkaligas rather than ideology for getting more representation. Of the total 28 Lok Sabha seats, 9 are from elected members of the Lingayat community; all of them won by the BJP. Vokkaliga community's share in the victory is six seats; four from the BJP. 60 per cent of Vokkaligas and 87 per cent of Lingayats voted for the BJP (see Table 16.3). 'The post-poll data indicate that six out of every 10 Vokkaliga votes went this time to the BJP.'[24]

Table 16.3 *Castes and Communities Voting in Karnataka*

Caste/Community	Cong–JD(S) (%)	BJP (%)	Others (%)
Upper Caste	31	63	6
Vokkaliga	33	60	7
Lingayat	10	87	3
Other OBC	46	47	7
Dalit	49	42	9
Adivasi	36	54	10
Muslim	73	18	9
Others	36	55	9

Source: Veenadevi and Nagesh K. L., 'Post-poll Survey: Karnataka Heading towards Political Uncertainty', *The Hindu*, 27 May 2019.

These are the communities which were known for their progressive positions on socio-political issues. Lingayats, being a non-Vedic community, opposed social hierarchy and any kind of social domination over them by the others. Vokkaligas, being a community more within Hinduism, asserted freedom and equality in spiritual matters. In fact, it has its own cultural institutions like *maths*. In the politics of the state, it played a very significant role in changing the power structure of the state. Because of its stalwart leaders and community's willingness to remain united, it became one of the forward-looking communities of Karnataka in economic and political spheres.

The leaders of the Lingayat Dharma Mahasabha had warned that if the BJP government at the centre was not ready to meet its demand of separate religious status for the Lingayat community, it would have to face the consequences in the elections.[25] Although the BJP government did not respond to the demand of the Lingayats, the warning given by the organization did not materialise. A majority of Lingayat voters did not give any importance to the warnings.

It was expected that former Chief Minister and AHINDA[26] leader Siddaramaiah's presence in North Karnataka would help the JD (S)–Congress alliance because together with the Lingayat votes he would make it Li-Ahinda for the alliance.[27] The expectation of the Lingayats and AHINDA communities coming together did not come true despite the Congress governments' support for Lingayats' demand for a separate religious community in 2018. The community demanded a separate religious status and at the same time it 'is the largest established vote bank of the BJP.'[28] The call for a separate religious identity by intellectuals, some religious heads and activists did not work in favour of the Congress. Lingayats could have adopted a more convincing strategy but they did not and moreover there was no enthusiasm to do so. Their political beliefs 'are not in tandem with its cultural ideals'.[29]

The Congress and JD(S) believe in inclusive and secular democratic politics. They could have used better ways of expressing this to the people but failed in doing so. This failure is primarily responsible for the people moving towards the BJP. If secular and inclusive politics is to be alive in the future, the parties have to be more introspective about their mismanagement of political actions in the past. Factional politics of the coalition partners played a crucial role in determining the electoral outcome.

HIGH-PROFILE PARLIAMENTARY CONSTITUENCIES

Mandya constituency: This constituency covers the entire district of Mandya and a part of the Mysore district. It was regarded as a high voltage constituency because there was a clash between the independent candidate—actor turned politician, Sumalatha Ambareesh—and the JD(S) candidate Nikhil Kumaraswamy, son of the former Chief Minister of Karnataka H. D. Kumaraswamy. After the denial of the Congress party ticket, Sumalatha decided to contest from Mandya constituency as an independent candidate. Her husband Ambareesh, who recently passed away, was a politician and one of the prominent actors of the Kannada film industry. The BJP sensed that the public mood was in favour of Sumalatha and accordingly announced its support to her.

The support given by the members of Karnataka Rajya Raitha Sangha (KRRS), dissatisfied the local Congress and JD(S) leaders, party workers, women and youth, and enabled Sumalatha to win the Mandya Lok Sabha constituency. Sympathy support was also forthcoming on account of Ambareesh's death and the effective involvement of some actors from the Kannada film industry. Besides, Sumalatha's patience and politeness in responding to criticisms by the JD(S) must have also become a factor.

Gulbarga constituency: The most surprising result in this election was the defeat of Mallikarjun Kharge in Gulbarga by the BJP candidate Umesh Jadhav. According to some local reporters and social activists, even the section in the Lingayat community which was more vocal in demanding an independent religious identity for themselves was not so committed in the campaign for Kharge. Kharge's role in bringing several developmental projects to the Hyderabad Karnataka region and particularly the district did not appeal to the voters in the constituency. Some dissatisfied leaders belonging to the backward classes left the Congress and joined the BJP. All these leaders made a huge effort in wooing their community votes and defeating Kharge.

It was also revealed by some activists that leaders belonging to the backward classes did not like Kharge's growing credibility as a national leader because they were overshadowed by him. Some of these leaders had challenged Kharge's leadership when they were in Congress. The election gave them an opportunity to unite against him by actively involving themselves as leaders in the BJP district unit.

Kharge, being a leader with a progressive vision may not be liked by the conservative members of the Lingayat community and others. Jadhav, being an upcoming leader can be more easily managed by his opponents. In district power politics, Kharge has always been very vocal and progressive which made conservative elements of the Lingayat community uncomfortable.

Tumkur constituency: It was one of the prestigious constituencies in the elections since former Prime Minister H. D. Deve Gowda contested from it. Tumkur is a part of the old Mysore region in whichVokkaligas and Lingayats are the dominant communities. G. S. Basavaraj with the BJP ended up winning in this parliamentary constituency. Lack of unity between the coalition partners and the factional politics of the Congress and JD(S) may be important issues responsible for the defeat of Deve Gowda. Many of the Congress leaders in Tumkur were against the party's decision to give the seat to the JD(S) and some among these had even refused to campaign.[30] Most Lingayat and Vokkaliga votes consolidated for the BJP and the JD(S) respectively. Deve Gowda's introduction of the third generation of his family was not acceptable to a large number of voters. Some people did not like leaving his Hassan constituency to his grandson and contesting from Tumkur.

IMPLICATIONS OF THE 2019 ELECTION RESULTS FOR THE STATE POLITICS

The 2019 election has implications for state politics in terms of future political mobilization for social and political change. The present victory of the BJP and the strong presence of right-wing organizations in the state may encourage youth to support them. A large number of youths from the state preferred the BJP over the other parties in this election.[31] Such developments become a big challenge to the politics of the Congress and JD(S) in the state.

Karnataka witnessed the experience of fierce and strategic political mobilization of backward classes in the 1970s itself. It was Devaraj Urs who was the forefather of the idea of challenging the political domination of the dominant castes by mobilizing non-dominant castes.[32] This experiment was repeated and successfully deployed by Siddaramaiah who considers himself a follower of Urs. Looking at the 2019 election results, doubts arise with regard to the success of the strategy of mobilizing backward classes. In this election, the dominant castes strategically succeeded in dominating the political space. Majoritarian parties like the BJP succeeded in achieving greater electoral success even though leaders like Siddhramaiah were very much active in state politics.

The Tumkur constituency result has certain lessons for the Congress and JD(S). In every election, major political parties cannot deny the role and significance of alternative political forces. Both the Congress and JD(S) did not pay much attention to the presence of the Communist Party of India (CPI) candidate which resulted in the candidate getting more than 18,000 votes. Communist parties have a considerable presence in certain areas in Karnataka due to a strong network of trade unions and committed party workers.

Karnataka's governmental stability is a major casuality of the 2019 elections. 'The disaffection has led a large number of Congressmen to question the utility of the coalition on grounds of sectarian loyalties, personal interests, and future electoral prospects; some them with large interests at stake have decided to jump ship'.[33] 17 MLAs resigned from the assembly in July 2019 expressing their displeasure about the performance of the coalition government. The Congress and JD(S) attempted to retain these legislators by adopting various strategies but failed. Eventually, the H. D. Kumaraswamy-led coalition government fell on 23 July 2019. It was voted out of power after 14 months.

BJP formed the government under the leadership of B. S. Yeddyurappa on 29 July 2019. The speaker of the Karnataka Assembly disqualified 17 MLAs and tendered his resignation. According to the *Hindu* editorial:

> All in all, the goings on in Karnataka show that the Constitution can be twisted and misread to suit anyone's political interests. In an atmosphere in which political loyalties swing like a pendulum, constitutional functionaries appear to be inclined to give self serving interpretations to the founding law and let the web of confusion be disentangled by the judiciary.[34]

The disgruntled MLAs approached the Supreme Court of India against their disqualification. Karnataka Chief Minister B. S. Yeddyurappa's delayed expansion of the cabinet took place on 20 August 2019 after three weeks of forming the government. There is no representation from religious minorities and some districts in the ministry of B. S. Yeddyurappa. It appears that some objective parameters were adopted by the BJP high command for the expansion of the B. S. Yeddyurappa government. Many aspirants expressed their disappointment. It may provide scope for the growth of dissidence.

Formation of a ministry is becoming a more difficult task in recent times and is responsible for a growing number of dissatisfied legislators. As a result, the number of aspirants for ministerial posts has been increasing. Objective evaluation of the performance of legislators and ministers in terms of delivery of services to the people and party building needs to be considered while forming the ministry. Perhaps, an adoption of clearly and objectively defined parameters for appointing legislators as ministers is imperative. Perhaps, Narendra Modi's style of formation of a council of ministers can help to address these problems.

CONCLUSION

Many important issues confronting the state did not receive the required significance of both the political actors and the voters. Issues such as water disputes between Goa and Karnataka, farm loan waiver scheme, drought relief and other development issues could have received much more serious attention but that did not happen. Political parties could have used better ways of reaching the people through these issues, but failed in doing so. It may also be the case that people lost trust in the politics of welfare programmes of the Congress-JD(S) coalition government and were attracted to the political narrative of the BJP on Hindutva, nationalism, development and strong leadership. There was no genuine concern on the part of most people towards either developmental or cultural state issues.

The 2019 election results certainly show that the BJP electoral base has been strengthened statewide in Karnataka, winning the confidence of almost all sections of society. In the present politics, self-interests of political parties and individuals appear to have become more important than common good of the society. Such developments are not conducive for reinforcing the democratic political culture in Karnataka. However, balancing the self-interest and collective interest is imperative for strengthening democratic politics. The strengthening of intra party democracy also is necessary for promoting mutual respect.

NOTES

1. Ian Budge, 'Election Research', in *International Encyclopedia of Political Science*, vol. 3, eds. Bertrand Badie, Dirk Berg-Schlosser and Leonardo Morlino (London: SAGE Publications and IPSA, 2011), 725.
2. ManuAiyappa Kanthanada, 'Caste Takes a Back Seat to Narendra Modi's Appeal in Karnataka', *The Times of India*, 25 May 2019.
3. V., Sridhar, Rishikesh Bahadur Desai and Ravi Sharma, 'Karnataka: Ground Regained', *Frontline,* 7 June 2019. Available at https://frontline.thehindu.com/cover-story/article27324581.ece (accessed on 7 June 2019).
4. Ibid.
5. To know about the 2014 general elections in Karnataka, read S. S.Patagundi and Prakash Desai, 'Karnataka: Change and Continuity in 2014', in *India's 2014 Elections: A Modi-led BJP Sweep*, ed. Paul Wallace (New Delhi: SAGE Publications, 2015).
6. Editorial, 'TsuNamo again: BJP Landslide Indicates Some Deep Structural Shifts in Indian Politics', *The Times of India,* 24 May 2019. Available at https://timesofindia.indiatimes.com/blogs/toi-editorials/tsunamo-again-bjp-landslide-indicates-some-deep-structural-shifts-in-indian-politics/ (accessed on 7 July 2019).
7. Veenadevi and Nagesh K. L., 'Post-poll Survey: Karnataka Heading Towards Political Uncertainty'. *The Hindu*, 27 May 2019. Available at https://www.thehindu.com/elections/lok-sabha-2019/heading-towards-political-uncertainty/article27256076.ece (accessed on 12 June 2019).
8. Ibid.
9. Muzaffar Assadi, 'Existential Crisis', *Frontline*, 21 June 2019. Available at https://frontline.thehindu.com/politics/article27695352.ece (accessed on 25 June 2019).

10. Ibid.
11. Ibid.
12. Akram Mohammed, 'Political Dynasties Still Hold Sway in Karnataka', *Deccan Herald,* 24 May 2019. Available at https://www.deccanherald.com/lok-sabha-election-2019/political-dynasties-still-hold-sway-in-karnataka-735788.html (accessed on 22 June 2019).
13. Afshan Yasmeen, 'Two Women from State Heading to Lok Sabha This Time', *The Hindu*, 25 May 2019. Available at https://www.thehindu.com/news/national/karnataka/two-women-from-state-heading-to-lok-sabha-this-time/article27243939.ece (accessed on 22 June 2019).
14. Mohit M. Rao, 'Karnataka's Representation in 17th Lok Sabha Is the Youngest in Recent Years', *The Hindu*, 29 May 2019. Available at https://www.thehindu.com/news/national/karnataka/karnatakas-representation-in-17th-lok-sabha-is-the-youngest-in-recent-years/article27278991.ece (accessed on 19 June 2019).
15. Ibid.
16. Sandeep Shastri, 'Leadership Sweepstakes and the Modi Factor', *The Hindu*, 21 May 2019. Available at https://www.thehindu.com/elections/lok-sabha-2019/leadership-sweepstakes-and-the-modi-factor/article27189676.ece (accessed on 23 June 2019).
17. Ibid.
18. Veenadevi and Nagesh, 'Post-poll Survey'.
19. Sridhar, Desai and Sharma, 'Karnataka'.
20. Special Correspondent, 'EC Asks Political Parties to Refrain from Personal Attacks', *The Hindu*, 15 April 2019. Available at https://www.thehindu.com/news/national/karnataka/ec-asks-political-parties-to-refrain-from-personal-attacks/article26847877.ece (accessed on 2 July 2019).
21. Ibid.
22. Special Correspondent, 'Karnataka Takes Historic Decision to Have Separate State Flag', *The Hindu*, 8 March 2018. Available at https://www.thehindu.com/news/national/karnataka/karnataka-takes-historic-decision-to-have-separate-state-flag/article22980375.ece (accessed on 20 June 2019).
23. Chandan Gowda, 'The Kannada flag et cetera', *The Hindu*, 22 July 2017. Available at https://www.thehindu.com/opinion/lead/the-kannada-flag-et-cetera/article19326738.ece. (accessed on 20 June 2019).
24. Veenadevi and Nagesh, 'Post-poll Survey'.
25. Nolan Pinto, 'No Separate Religion Status, No Votes in 2019: Lingayat Outfit Warns BJP', *Indian Today*, 4 January 2019. Available at https://www.indiatoday.in/india/story/no-separate-religion-status-no-vote-2019-lingayat-outfit-warns-bjp-1423603–2019–01-04 (accessed on 12 June 2019).
26. AHINDA is an acronym constructed from a Kannada Phrase: Aplasankhyataru (Minorities, i.e., Muslims) Hindulidavaru (the Backward Classes), and Dalits (the Scheduled Castes).

27. Sandeep Moudgal, 'It is BJP's Lingayats vs Siddramaiah's Li-Ahinda', *The Times of India*, 21 April 2019. Available at https://timesofindia.indiatimes.com/elections/lok-sabha-elections-2019/karnataka/news/it-is-bjps-lingayats-vs-siddaramaiahs-li-ahinda/articleshow/68973266.cms (accessed on 15 June 2019).
28. The Wire Staff, 'Elections 2019: What Is Karnataka Voting For', *The Wire*, 18 April 2019. Available at https://thewire.in/politics/election-2019-karnataka-live-updates (accessed on 7 June 2019).
29. Prakash Desai, 'Quest for Egalitarian Socio-spiritual Order: Lingayats and Their Practices', *Journal of Human Values* 25, no.2 (2019): 97.
30. Akram Mohammed, 'Saffron Sweep in State: Cong, JD(S) Top Guns Fall', *Deccan Herald*, 24 May 2019. Available at https://www.deccanherald.com/lok-sabha-election-2019/saffron-sweep-in-state-cong-jds-top-guns-fall-735734.html (accessed on 22 June 2019).
31. Veenadevi and Nagesh, 'Post-poll Survey'.
32. To know more about the political experiment of Devaraj Urs, read: E. Raghavan and James Manor, *Broadening and Deepening Democracy: Political Innovation in Karnataka* (New Delhi: Routledge, 2009).
33. Velerian Rodrigues, 'Making Sense of Karnataka's Politics', *The Hindu*, 17 July 2019.
34. Editorial, 'BJP's Second Shot at Power in Karnataka Comes Amidst a Web of Confusion', *The Hindu*, 27 July 2019. Available at https://www.thehindu.com/opinion/editorial/bjps-second-shot-at-power-in-karnataka-comes-amidst-a-web-of-confusion/article28725814.ece (accessed on 21 August 2019).

Chapter 17

Tamil Nadu

Political Pluralism and Party System Changes

C. Manikandan and Andrew Wyatt

The events of early 2019 were of double significance in Tamil Nadu. Nationally fundamental questions were being asked of the quality of democracy,[1] and voters were given a choice on important development issues. Parties in Tamil Nadu joined these debates. At the same time, the state government was in a perilous position, with 22 assembly by-elections being held in April–May. If the outcome of by-elections had gone against the ruling All India Anna Dravida Munnetra Kazhagam (AIADMK), the government would have fallen and triggered a crisis in an already troubled party. The AIADMK suffered a massive loss in the Lok Sabha election, winning just 1 of 38 seats, but it did win 9 seats in the assembly by-elections and saved its state government.

The 2019 election was framed by the death of two major leaders in the space of two years. Chief Minister J. Jayalalithaa died on 5 December 2016. She had led the AIADMK for over 25 years in which time the party had contested eight national elections. In August 2018, the nonagenarian M. Karunanidhi died, having led the Dravida Munnetra Kazhagam (DMK) since 1969 and taken the party through 12 national elections. The passing of these leaders had two headline implications. First, in the leader-centred politics of the state, there was uncertainty about succession with the possibility that new personalities might be able to breakthrough with parties of their own. Second, the ruling AIADMK entered a prolonged crisis, including a party split, which drove them close to the Bharatiya Janata Party (BJP).

In short, further change in an already dynamic state party system looked likely. However, it is important not to focus only on leadership questions at the state level. National developments combined with grass-roots protests since 2017 have influenced politics in the state. The Tamil political elite have struggled to keep up with popular moods. The dramatic events since late 2016 created uncertainty which some described as a political vacuum (*araciyal veṟṟiṭam*) in the state.

THE POLITICAL CONTEXT

The high profile of regional issues in Tamil Nadu, even in national elections, is a legacy of the Dravidian movement, heavily influenced by E. V. Ramaswami Naicker, more commonly known as Periyar, who argued for a separate South India or 'Dravida Nadu'. The movement took an institutional form in the DMK (formed as a political party in 1949) who advocated maximum state autonomy as they came to power in 1967. The AIADMK split from the DMK in 1972 and took a softer approach to social activism, but Chief Minister Jayalalithaa, never shy of criticizing the governing party in New Delhi, strongly articulated concerns about regional autonomy, especially after returning as chief minister in 2011.

Central to Tamil Nadu's political culture is scepticism of centralized power in New Delhi along with enthusiasm for Tamil culture and state autonomy. Protecting the Tamil language resonates with public opinion. Federal ideas, with a preference for subsidiarity in cultural issues and decisions made at the state level to accommodate regional preferences, are seen to be common sense by voters and politicians. The Central government after 2014 did not connect with this sentiment. Attempts to promote Hindi and make certain policies nationally uniform caused unease in Tamil Nadu.

Other issues, not necessarily involving Centre–state relations, resulted in protests and confrontation with the authorities. In a series of events, it appeared that political parties were reacting to public sentiments rather than leading opinion. Resentments against the Central government increased after Jayalalithaa began treatment in hospital in late September 2016. The state government accepted the UDAY and food security schemes, even though it was well known that Jayalalithaa opposed these schemes. Jayalalithaa died in December 2016, sparking a struggle for succession in the AIADMK, and questions were raised about whether her successors were simply appeasing the Central government.

Shortly after Jayalalithaa died, the ban on *jallikattu* (bull chasing) inspired mass protests. The Supreme Court ruled in favour of a ban proposed by the Animal Welfare Board. Jallikattu is highly popular and the ban was cited as an example of official insensitivity to Tamil culture. Pro-jallikattu protests gained momentum in January 2017 at precisely the moment when the AIADMK was trying to settle the issue of leadership succession. The sight of crowds of protestors on Chennai's Marina Beach and in other parts of the state created a sense of urgency and the Central and state government moved to re-legalize jallikattu. This victory reinvigorated contentious politics in the state. It was widely thought that younger, non-partisan activists could resolve other major problems in Tamil Nadu which encouraged further protests.

The Neduvasal hydrocarbon extraction project became controversial with fears that wetland (farmland) would be turned into a desert. A group of farmers from Tamil Nadu spent more than 100 days protesting in New Delhi about farm distress. The move to standardize the entrance to medical degrees via the National Eligibility cum Entrance Test (NEET), as opposed to using marks from school exams, attracted widespread opposition in Tamil Nadu. In addition to these, the handling of cyclone Ockhi and the Kurangani forest fire led to strong criticism of the Central government. When the formation of the Kaveri water management board was delayed, black flags were shown to the prime minister during his visit to Tamil Nadu. The acquisition of farmland for the Green Express Highway was met with protests. Further criticism was raised against Modi in late 2018, when he did not visit the Delta after it was severely affected by the Gaja cyclone. Not all of the protests involved the Centre. Advocacy of prohibition, which was an issue in the 2016 assembly election, continued including local demonstrations against specific state-run liquor shops, and the bus strikes involved the state government. Further, a protest again Sterlite Copper Plant in May 2018 led to police firing in which 13 people died. These protests along with the internal crisis in the ruling AIADMK, demonetization fallout and GST set the context for the 2019 election.

FORMATION OF NEW PARTIES

The death of Jayalalithaa was followed by a complicated contest for control of the AIADMK party organization and the state government. The struggle was essentially between the family of Sasikala Natarajan and other senior members of the party. Sasikala was a close friend and aide of Jayalalithaa, who lived in Jayalalithaa's house in Poes Garden. It is reported that Sasikala wielded enormous power behind closed doors, including the selection of party candidates and ministers. When Sasikala was imprisoned in February 2017, following a corruption case, the leadership of her faction passed to her nephew T. T. V. Dinakaran.

The Sasikala family was opposed first by the interim chief minister, O. Panneerselvam (often known as OPS), and subsequently by Edappadi K. Palaniswami (EPS), who is the current chief minister. It is widely believed that the Central government influenced the succession process. After failing to take control of the AIADMK, Dinakaran formed an alternative called the Amma Makkal Munetra Kanzhagam (AMMK). The defection of MLAs threatened the AIADMK majority, as there was no guarantee that the party would win back enough seats in the by-elections to fill 18 vacant seats in the state assembly.

The DMK had a leadership transition too, as the health of the DMK President M. Karunanidhi declined. His son, M. K. Stalin, was appointed as the working president of the DMK in January 2017. After Karunanidhi died on 7 August 2018, Stalin was elected unopposed as party president by the DMK General Council. Questions remained about Stalin's competence, and the 2019 elections were a challenge for him to negotiate.

The absence of the two major leaders and subsequent political crisis in Tamil Nadu encouraged ambitious political entrepreneurs to explore opportunities. Two film stars, Rajinikanth and Kamal Haasan stepped forward. Haasan formed a party, Makkal Needhi Maiam (MNM), and claimed he could rid the state of corruption and solve the governance failures of established parties. Haasan also somewhat elaborated on his political views as he began building the MNM. In many ways he conformed to a populist style of politics familiar in Tamil Nadu. He claimed to favour the welfare of the Tamil people but suggested that the people should be critical and independent-minded. In other words, his approach overlapped with the tradition of the DMK's assertive populism.[2] Haasan showed some sympathy for national styles of politics, so distancing himself a little from the regionally oriented parties in the state. Rajinikanth equivocated and did not form a political party, to the disappointment of his many fans.

ALLIANCES

The DMK already had the core members of its alliance in place by late 2018. The Congress party and the Indian Union Muslim League (IUML) fought the 2016 assembly election with the DMK. The DMK took extra care to keep the Congress and the IUML satisfied because even if the DMK won all the by-election seats, Congress (eight MLAs) and the IUML (one MLA) would be needed to form a new government. Furthermore, the DMK would make other gains if the Congress participated in a new government at the Centre. Formalizing the DMK alliance went smoothly, apart from some tension when the DMK considered bringing the Pattali Makkal Katchi (PMK), a party that cultivates Vanniyar caste identity, into the alliance. The Viduthalai Chiruthaigal Katchi (VCK) considered this unacceptable, given conflict with Dalits over issues such as inter-caste marriage. In terms of caste politics, the DMK tried to drive a wedge between the PMK and the Vanniyar caste group, hoping it would be perceived as 'anti-PMK and pro-Vanniyar'.

Even before making a formal alliance, the EPS–OPS-headed AIADMK forged a close relationship with the BJP. The improving chances of joining a BJP coalition government at the Centre brought the PMK into the AIADMK-led alliance at the last moment. The BJP connection also helped the AIADMK form alliances with other small parties, including the Desiya Murpokku Dravida Kazhagam (DMDK) and the Puthiya Thamizhagam (PT). In 2018, the AIADMK, divided between two factions, looked in total disarray. However, the AIADMK attracted enough allies to become competitive and restore some credibility.

In keeping with Kamal Haasan's 'new' approach to politics, the MNM did not join either of the two main alliances, but it allotted one Lok Sabha seat and three assembly seats to the Republican Party of India. He campaigned for a corruption-free Tamil Nadu. The allocation of seats among the two main alliances reflected the federal context of party politics in India.[3] The main Dravidian parties gave priority to their state ambitions when allocating seats among their allies.[4] The key objective for both the DMK and AIADMK was a victory in the by-elections to enable them to control the state government. Thus, the two main Dravidian parties did not allocate any state assembly seats to their allies and demanded strongest possible effort from their allies in these campaigns. In return, the Dravidian parties claimed far fewer Lok Sabha seats in 2019 compared to 2014. The DMK only contested 20 out of 39 seats versus 34 in 2014, and the AIADMK contested the same number as opposed to 39 in 2014.

THE CAMPAIGN

The campaign began well before the polling dates were announced. Since 2015, the DMK has projected Stalin as an approachable, strong and dignified leader, ready to take on further responsibilities. This theme was communicated in a DMK programme of Gram Sabha meetings that began on 9 January 2019 that aimed to connect with the electorate. These continued over six weeks with the aim to hold a meeting in every Village Panchayat of the state, with senior leaders in attendance where possible. Stalin was reported and pictured taking questions and hearing grievances from ordinary voters, a format very different from the elaborately staged mass rallies that parties use during formal campaigning.

During the January 2019 Pongal festival, the AIADMK government gave a ₹1,000 gift to all families in Tamil Nadu. A little later, the AIADMK announced ₹2,000 for families who live below the poverty line (BPL). Since the model code of conduct prohibits the implementation of new policies (that might include inducements to voters), the government could not make the BPL payments. However, the AIADMK leaders promised the ₹2,000 after the election. Making direct cash transfers to families prior to elections is new to Tamil Nadu.

The prime minister made several high-profile visits to the state before polling dates were announced. On 27 January 2019, he visited Madurai, laid the foundation stone for the AIIMS hospital outside the city and addressed a political rally. On 1 March 2019, a similar visit took place in Kanyakumari district. On 6 March 2019, Modi inaugurated projects, including highways budgeted at ₹5,010 crore, and dedicated a number of completed projects, before speaking at a political rally in Kanchipuram.[5]

Material appeals featured in the campaign as well as policy promises. It was alleged that both sides were distributing cash to voters. The Election Commission seized ₹11.48 crore from associates of the DMK candidate in Vellore and concluded that the money was to be distributed to voters covertly. The commission decided to postpone the election.[6] Elsewhere, the Income Tax Department reported after a raid on an AMMK office, the 'cash was neatly packed in 94 packets/envelopes on which the ward number, number of voters and the amount of ₹300 per voter was written'.[7] In total, the Election Commission seized over ₹500 crore worth of unaccounted cash and precious metals across the state.[8]

The distinction between national and state politics blurred during the campaign. The DMK was hoping that it could remove the AIADMK from office by one means or another. Senior Congress leader P. Chidambaram said that once Congress came to power at the Centre, there would be a change in government in Tamil Nadu.[9] The DMK made large promises during the campaign, including a cancellation of the NEET exams. The discourse of the election campaign was fragmented. Parties made rational appeals to voters, often invoking material interests. The AIADMK made generous offers. They proposed linking the Godavari and Kaveri rivers, and the BJP promised housing for everyone. The DMK promised loan waivers for farmers, writing off educational loans, relieving debt on mortgaged jewels and the implementation of an old pension scheme for government employees.

Also, the DMK highlighted the NYAY scheme, minimum income guarantee, outlined as a national policy by the Congress party. Karti Chidambaram, a Congress candidate for Sivaganga, promised to reduce the DTH monthly charges for television services. Policy was also debated, with the DMK alliance highlighting the negative impact of demonetization and the GST which affected western Tamil Nadu in particular, given the concentration of small-scale industries in the region. Policy campaigners also appealed to sentiment and indulged in hearsay and rumour. The opposition parties frequently referred back to the earlier grass-roots protests and popular grievances.

Whenever the prime minister visited Tamil Nadu, #GoBackModi would trend on Twitter. The DMK promised that when it came to power, probes would be conducted into the death of Jayalalithaa, the Kodanad murders and the Pollachi sexual abuse case. Lurid allegations were made against the DMK by government ministers responding to this negative campaigning. The AIADMK made emotive appeals for support, making much of its erstwhile leader Jayalalithaa, using her popular honorific *Amma* (mother). The EPS government was said to be the government of Amma, following in her footsteps.

Populist ideas were referenced frequently in the campaign. The AIADMK connected itself with the welfare policies advocated and personalized by Jayalalithaa. EPS identified as a farmer and tried to legitimize his government as one which stands up 'for the rights of farmers and the working class people … the welfare of the people'.[10] He claimed to come from a humble background, rising to the office of chief minister from the lowly post of AIADMK branch secretary. EPS contrasted his steady rise with Stalin's dynastic status. Stalin articulated his own populist critique of EPS, '(I)nstead of protecting the people, Tamil Nadu rulers are working hard only to protect themselves.… The Chief Minister is carrying on with his government by being subservient to the Centre.'[11] The DMK offered to protect the state expressed in the slogan '*Tamiḻ māṉam kāppōm*' (let us preserve Tamil pride). Stalin also placed the DMK and Congress on the side of the people, being alert to their needs and poverty.

THE RESULTS

The DMK alliance won 37 out of the 38 Lok Sabha seats in Tamil Nadu with a decisive 54.2 per cent of the vote (Table 17.1). Congress also won the neighbouring Puducherry seat with DMK support. The seven small parties in the alliance did very well, securing 10 seats in the Lok Sabha, and they would be able to use their presence in Parliament to lobby and protest in Delhi.[12] The AIADMK alliance performed poorly, winning 30.2 per cent of the state-wide vote (Table 17.2). The party won a single seat, Theni, where the Deputy Chief Minister OPS backed his son as the candidate. The result showed a continuing improvement for the DMK, which suffered reputational damage during its defeat in the 2011 assembly election. The Lok Sabha results confirmed that the AIADMK is yet to rebuild after the loss of Jayalalithaa. It could not contemplate the prospect of contesting alone (as it did in

Table 17.1 *The DMK Alliance in 2019: Seats Contested, Share of the Vote and Seats Won*

Party	State-Wide Vote Share (%)	Seats Contested	Seats Won
DMK	28.6	19	19
INC	12.8	9	8
CPM	2.4	2	2
CPI	2.4	2	2
VCK*	2.5	2	2
IUML	1.1	1	1
MDMK*	1.3	1	1
KMDK *	1.5	1	1
IJK*	1.6	1	1
Total	54.2	38	37

Source: Calculated by the authors from results posted by the Election Commission of India. Available at http://results.eci.gov.in/ (accessed on 3 October 2019).

Note: *In four seats, the DMK obliged the smaller parties to contest using the DMK election symbol, reducing their profile among the electorate.

Table 17.2 *The AIADMK Alliance in 2019: Seats Contested, Share of the Vote and Seats Won*

Party	State-Wide Vote Share (%)	Seats Contested	Seats Won
AIADMK	17.6	20	1
PMK	5.4	7	0
BJP	3.7	5	0
DMDK	2.2	4	0
PT*	0.8	1	0
TMC (M)	0.5	1	0
Total	30.2	38	1

Source: Calculated by the authors from results posted by the Election Commission of India. Available at http://results.eci.gov.in/ (accessed on 3 October 2019).

Note: *Two small parties, the PT and the PNK, nominated candidates with the two leaves symbol. The PNK is not listed here as it was allocated the Vellore seat, where the election was postponed.

2014 and 2016) and even with allies it lagged behind the DMK. The AMMK did not tear the party apart, but neither did it help the credibility of the AIADMK's new leadership. Furthermore, the connection with the BJP did not lift the AIADMK alliance.

Among the non-aligned parties, the AMMK performed comparatively well in areas where the Thevar caste cluster is concentrated. However, as this group is fairly dispersed, the AMMK could not win a seat in either the Lok Sabha or assembly by-election (Table 17.3). The MNM made some impression, with an overall share of 3.7 per cent of the vote, concentrated in the larger urban areas. The Tamil nationalist Naam Tamilar Katchi (NTK) performed well for a niche party. Its leader Seeman is a well-known figure who argues that the Dravidian legacy is inauthentic.

The AIADMK failed to prove its value as an alliance partner to the BJP, which may prove to be a longer-term problem for the party, as the BJP may shift their strategy in future elections. However, the AIADMK secured its main objective of preserving its administration in Tamil

Table 17.3 *The AMMK, the NTK and the MNM in 2019: Seats Contested, Share of the Vote and Seats Won*

Party	State-Wide Vote Share (%)	Seats Contested	Seats Won
AMMK*	5.2	37	0
NTK	3.9	37	0
MNM	3.7	36	0
Total	12.8	–	–

Source: Calculated by the authors from results posted by the Election Commission of India. Available at http://results.eci.gov.in/ (accessed on 3 October 2019).

Note: *Officially, the AMMK did not register as a political party; it fielded independent candidates, all using a common symbol. After the 2019 election, the party started the registration process.

Table 17.4 *By-election Results*

Party	State-Wide Vote Share (%)	Seats Contested	Seats Won
AIADMK	38.2	22	9
DMK	45.1	22	13
AMMK	7.7	22	0
NTK	3.2	22	0
MNM	2.6	19	0

Source: Calculated by the authors from results posted by the Election Commission of India. Available at http://results.eci.gov.in/ (accessed on 3 October 2019).

Nadu. The party beat the DMK and the AMMK, to win nine seats in the by-elections and hence a majority in the assembly (Table 17.4). The AIADMK has a good chance of serving out a full five-year term and facing elections in 2021. This gives EPS more opportunities to distribute patronage and enhance his personal image. Controlling the government puts the AMMK under pressure and some dissidents have moved to the DMK or returned to the AIADMK already.

The DMK claimed success in the Lok Sabha elections, proving that it had a superior alliance, and demonstrated to its junior allies that it could get them rewards at the Centre, which include the prestige of holding parliamentary seats. If the DMK can hold its alliance together, it should have the edge in the next round of assembly elections. The AIADMK lost vote share and all but one of its seats in the Lok Sabha. EPS kept control of the state government and demonstrated that he was a robust and competent campaigner, while Stalin claimed a decisive victory in the Lok Sabha elections, strengthening his image and authority in the party.

Udhayanidhi, the grandson of Karunanidhi and the son of M. K. Stalin, emerged as a senior DMK leader during the campaign. He is already well known for his film work and used his VIP status effectively. Some candidates met him to seek his blessing after the announcement of the DMK candidate list. During his campaign tour in Tamil Nadu, Udhayanidhi was second only to Stalin in the coverage given to DMK leaders. After the election, Udhayanidhi was appointed as DMK youth wing secretary, a highly prestigious post which his father, Stalin, used to legitimize his leadership. Stalin held the post for a total of 34 years while also taking up other senior positions in the party.

The decisive NDA victory in other parts of India meant that Tamil Nadu lost even more influence in New Delhi. The BJP made no direct gains by allying with the AIADMK, though the party remains determined to break through in the state. The 2021 assembly elections are the next major contest, and the BJP will consider a new strategy. The BJP has long struggled to make a state-wide impact in Tamil Nadu. The political culture of the state is unreceptive to nationalist ideology framed by North Indian leaders. The vehement protests against the scheme for teaching of Hindi, shortly after the elections, revealed the commitment to cultural autonomy. The practice of politics, embedded in grass-roots networks, motivated cadre, and effective brokering by local councillors gives existing parties strength and makes it difficult for incomers to get established.

The 2019 elections contributed to some party system change in the state. The trend towards fission continued with the two new parties, the MNM and the AMMK, picking up nearly 9 per cent of the vote in the Lok Sabha contests. Several smaller parties slipped back, and Vijayakanth's DMDK struggled to negotiate a place in an alliance, taking a last-minute place in the AIADMK alliance. Vaiko's MDMK got one seat in the DMK alliance, and the promise of a further seat in the Rajya Sabha, but it had to contest on the rising sun symbol of the DMK. Among the caste parties, the PMK lost its only Lok Sabha seat, and the Gounder political parties struggled for relevance, largely because Chief Minister Palaniswami is best placed to represent that community.[13]

The 2014 Lok Sabha elections and the 2016 state assembly elections seemed to suggest that the AIADMK had broken the bipolar alliance structure of elections. The AIADMK began to look like a dominant party, winning successive elections with almost no help from junior allies. However, the 2019 elections returned to an earlier pattern of bipolar alliances, with the two main alliances taking 84.4 per cent of the vote. The split in the AIADMK damaged its credibility, with the AMMK campaigning across the state and performing best in areas where Thevar voters are concentrated. The AIADMK got higher proportions of votes in western and northern Tamil Nadu but still did not win any seats from these regions.

CONCLUSION

The 2014 elections left many uncertainties unresolved in Tamil Nadu, with a number of court cases against senior leaders in the DMK and the AIADMK in process. The uncertainty deepened following the deaths of the long-standing leaders of the AIADMK and DMK. However, the picture after the 2019 election is much clearer. Several court cases against senior DMK leaders have been dismissed or have not resulted in convictions, whereas in the case of the AIADMK the conviction and imprisonment of Sasikala decisively altered the leadership succession. While the party split over the issue, Sasikala's family has been removed from the AIADMK and EPS has established himself as the chief minister.

The leadership succession in the DMK was smooth, and the Lok Sabha election victory has enhanced Stalin's reputation. As it stands,

Tamil politics is back on a stable trajectory, with a competitive state assembly election expected in 2021. The BJP has ambitions to expand in Tamil Nadu, with some hoping that it might eclipse the AIADMK. This looks less likely after the 2019 election, though Central pressure on state politicians is likely to continue.

The outcomes in Tamil Nadu revealed that political pluralism is not on the retreat everywhere in India.[14] The series of protests since 2017 show that citizens and grass-roots organizations can feed into the political system in unexpected ways. A review of democracy in the state in 2017 showed ways in which parties seek to control the agenda, but they cannot monopolize power or debate.[15] The party system has remained competitive since the late 1980s, and no party has achieved dominance. Furthermore, the formation of new parties is an indicator of pluralism in the political system. The dependence on electoral alliances reveals the limits of major party influence and openness to new political formations.

The death of Jayalalithaa means the AIADMK is weakened and alliances are once again essential for all parties seeking to win elections. The formation of the AMMK and MNM have further fragmented the party system and created new permutations for alliances in the next assembly and Lok Sabha elections. Within the AIADMK, the party is less centralized than it was under Jayalalithaa, with EPS sharing power with OPS. EPS, as the chief minister, is certainly the most powerful politician in the AIADMK, but he is not the supreme leader of the party. Internal power relations within the AIADMK drastically changed after Jayalalithaa died. The second-level leaders, ministers and MLAs gained more power within the party and the state government. Each MLA vote was precious, given the internal crisis and the thin majority in the assembly majority. During the selection of candidates in 2019, MLAs played a crucial role which was not possible under the leadership of Jayalalithaa.

The DMK is also not a monolithic party. While Stalin is in a position to promote his family, the party remains a dense organization with a well-defined middle-level leadership.[16] It needs to be emphasized that while political pluralism in Tamil Nadu has correlated in the political culture of the state,[17] pluralism should not be confused with an impeccable democratic culture. Rather, pluralism is generated, in part, by a pragmatic approach to politics in which parties know the limit of their influence. A fragmented party system and competitive elections mean that overlooked groups can form new parties and test their support among the electorate. Likewise, smaller parties that are taken for granted can usually change alliances and seek patronage from another large party. It will be a challenge for the DMK to hold its winning alliance together until 2021.

The national context in which Tamil Nadu operates is rather different. The BJP has given some concessions on the status of Hindi and Tamil since 23 May 2019. On other issues, such as NEET and the hydrocarbon project, the Centre has not changed direction. The chief minister can ask hopefully for Central support, but he cannot dictate terms to New Delhi. Union ministries and Central agencies have more freedom to intervene in state politics. Even so, Tamil Nadu has shown some independence from national developments as reflected in the results that favoured the DMK alliance in May 2019.

NOTES

1. Katharine Adeney, 'How Can We Model Ethnic Democracy? An Application to India', mimeo (Nottingham: University of Nottingham, forthcoming).
2. Narendra Subramanian, *Ethnicity and Populist Mobilization: Political Parties, Citizens and Democracy in South India* (New Delhi: Oxford University Press, 1999), 74.
3. K. K. Kailash, 'Dhritarashtra's Embrace: Big and Small Parties in Kerala and Tamil Nadu', *Contemporary South Asia* 27, no. 1 (2019): 73–87.
4. C. Manikandan and Andrew Wyatt, 'Political Parties and Federally Structured Incentives in Indian Politics: The Case of the Pattali Makkal Katchi (PMK)', *Contemporary South Asia* 27, no. 1 (2019): 89.
5. *The Hindu*, 'Prime Minister Inaugurates Ennore LNG Terminal', 7 March 2019. Available at https://www.thehindu.com/news/national/tamil-nadu/prime-minister-inaugurates-ennore-lng-terminal/article26451282.ece (accessed on 20 July 2019).
6. *The Hindu*, 'EC's Elaborate Report to President Led to Vellore Poll Cancellation', 17 April 2019. Available at https://www.thehindu.com/news/national/tamil-nadu/ecs-elaborate-report-to-president-led-to-vellore-poll-cancellation/article26859049.ece (accessed on 19 April 2019).
7. *The New Indian Express*, '₹1.48 Crore Cash Seized from Premises of TTV Dhinakaran's Partyman in Theni, Shots Fired to Disperse Supporters', 17

April 2019. Available at http://www.newindianexpress.com/states/tamil-nadu/2019/apr/17/tamil-nadu-i-t-seizes-rs-148-crore-cash-from-premises-of-ammk-functionary-in-theni-1965437.html (accessed on 18 April 2019).

8. *The New Indian Express,* 'How and Why Cash Polls the Votes in Tamil Nadu Elections', 17 April 2019. Available at https://indianexpress.com/article/opinion/how-and-why-cash-polls-the-votes-in-tamil-nadu-elections-5680135/ (accessed on 18 April 2019).
9. *The Hindu*, 'Stalin Set to Be CM Soon after Rahul Becomes PM', 5 March 2019.
10. *The New Indian Express*, 'AIADMK-BJP Led Government Will Be Farmer-friendly, Says CM Palaniswami', 23 March 2019. Available at http://www.newindianexpress.com/states/tamil-nadu/2019/mar/23/aiadmk-bjp-led-govt-will-be-farmer-friendly-says-cm-1954678.html (accessed on 24 March 2019).
11. *The New Indian Express,* 'Tamil Nadu Rulers Working Hard Only to Protect Themselves: Stalin', 22 March 2019. Available at http://www.newindianexpress.com/states/tamil-nadu/2019/mar/22/tn-rulers-working-hard-only-to-protect-themselves-stalin-1954237.html (accessed on 23 March 2019).
12. Hugo Gorringe shows how the VCK was able to use its position in Delhi between 2009 and 2014 in '"A Voice for the Last and Least": Thirumavalavan and the Viduthalai Chiruthaigal Katchi in the Lok Sabha', *Contemporary South Asia* 27, no. 1 (2019): 103–116.
13. M. Vijayabaskar and Andrew Wyatt, 'Economic Change, Politics and Caste: The Case of the Kongu Nadu Munnetra Kazhagam', *Economic & Political Weekly* 48, no. 48 (2013): 103–111.
14. Andrew Wyatt, 'Political Pluralism in India', mimeo (Bristol: University of Bristol, forthcoming).
15. Andrew Wyatt and C. Manikandan, 'Karunanidhi and Tamil Politics', *Seminar* (2017): 693.
16. C. Manikandan and Andrew Wyatt, 'Elite Formation within a Political Party: The Case of the Dravida Munnetra Kazhagam', *Commonwealth & Comparative Politics* 52, no. 1 (2014): 32–54.
17. Subramanian, *Ethnicity and Populist Mobilization*, 318–322.

Chapter 18

Kerala

The Exception That Proves the Rule?

James Chiriyankandath

Along with the other southern states of Tamil Nadu and Andhra Pradesh, India's southernmost state stood out in the 2019 Lok Sabha elections for returning no members of parliament (MPs) for Prime Minister Narendra Modi's ruling Bharatiya Janata Party (BJP). Not only did Kerala retain the distinction of being the only state of any size in the country not to have ever returned a BJP MP, but it also delivered more seats for the Indian National Congress (INC) than it had ever done—15 with the United Democratic Front (UDF) it led, taking 19 out of the state's 20. It was the only state where Congress reached double figures, returning almost twice as many MPs for the party as any other.

Yet in 1957, in the second Lok Sabha election and the first after the state's creation, Kerala was one of the only two states (the other being Orissa, now Odisha), where Congress failed to win a majority of the seats, a result since repeated in all but five of the following 14 general elections preceding this one. So what explains the party's success in Kerala this time amid abysmal failure elsewhere and, conversely, the BJP's lack of success in the state to date?

THE POLITICAL GEOGRAPHY OF GOD'S OWN COUNTRY

Promoted in tourist brochures as 'God's own country',[1] Kerala was formed in 1956 through the merger of much of two former Hindu princely states to the south, Travancore and Cochin, with parts of Madras state, the district of Malabar and Kasaragod in South Canara district. It brought together the Malayalam-speaking population in what remains the most linguistically homogenous state in India. According to the 2011 census, 97 per cent of Kerala's 33.4 million people spoke Malayalam.[2] Apart from Punjab and several small northeastern states, it is also the state with the least Hindus, Muslims and Christians, whose presence goes back over a millennium, constituting 45 per cent of the population (see Table 18.1). Of the 55 per cent[3] who are Hindu, a fifth belong to either Scheduled Castes and Tribes and the majority of the rest to Avarna (outcaste) Other Backward Classes (OBC) with the Ezhava caste the largest single group.

Kerala is famously distinctive in other respects, long enjoying the highest rates of literacy, life expectancy and gender equity than any other state. Its homogeneity has been diluted in recent decades with many migrant labourers, especially from eastern and northern India, attracted by the higher wages in the state. They are now estimated to exceed two and a half million,[4] more than matching the over two million Keralites employed abroad, the vast majority in the Arab Gulf states.[5] However, the impact of the migration has yet to be reflected electorally with many workers from other states still not registered to vote in Kerala.

Modern forms of political activity in the region were channelled through voluntarist associations based on caste and religion originating in the late 19th century. By the early 20th century, such identities had become well established in Travancore and Cochin with Syrian Christians (the term came from the ancient Syriac rite the local Christians used), Muslims, caste Hindu Nairs and Ezhavas forming distinct categories. This was the outcome of elite mobilization through churches, and religious and caste associations such as the Ezhava Sree Narayana Dharma Paripalana Yogam (SNDP Yogam), founded by the reformer Sree Narayana Guru, and the Nair Service Society (NSS).

Table 18.1 *Religion and Caste in Kerala (by District)*

District (Lok Sabha Seats)	Hindu (Excl. SC/ ST; %)	SC and ST (%)	Muslim (%)	Christian (%)
Kasaragod (Kasaragod)	45.8	7.5+2.5=10.0	37.2	6.7
Kannur (Kannur)	54.9	4.1+0.8=4.9	29.4	10.4
Wayanad (Wayanad)	34.1	4.3+17.4=21.7	37.2	6.7
Kozhikode (Kozhikode, Vadakara)	49.0	7+0.2=7.2	39.2	4.3
Malappuram (Malappuram, Ponnani)	9.4	7.9+0.3=8.2	70.2	2.0
Palakkad (Palakkad, Alathur)	48.8	16.5+1.5=18.0	28.9	4.0
Thrissur (Thrissur)	46.3	11.9+0.2=12.1	17.1	24.3
Ernakulam (Ernakulam, Chalakudy)	36.2	8.5+0.3=8.8	15.7	38.0
Idukki (Idukki)	30.3	14.1+4.5=18.6	7.4	43.4
Kottayam (Kottayam)	41.2	7.7+0.9=8.6	6.4	43.5
Alappuzha (Alappuzha)	59.1	9.4+0.1=9.5	10.6	20.4
Pathanamthitta (Pathanamthitta, Mavelikara)	43.3	13.1+0.5=13.6	4.6	38.1
Kollam (Kollam)	51.7	12.5+0.2=12.7	19.3	16.0
Thiruvananthapuram (Thiruvananthapuram, Attingal)	54.4	11.5+0.6=12.1	13.7	19.1
Kerala	43.8	9.8+1.1=10.9	26.6	18.4

Source: Based on Census of India 2011. Available at https://www.census2011.co.in/data/religion/state/32-kerala.html (accessed on 7 August 2019).

In Malabar, the Nair–Muslim rivalry was an important element in the nationalist movement after the Mappila Muslim rebellion of 1921, and the Muslim League dominated Muslim electoral politics from the mid-1930s.

Related to the development of distinct regionally specific communal identities were radicalizing social reform movements within all the major communities. The latter had significant religious, social, ideological and political effects in the half century preceding the formation of Kerala. These included the spread of radical rationalist and egalitarian ideas, and the widespread development of trade union and peasant movements. These factors fostered the development of a strong communist movement, producing a peculiar combination of communal accommodation and class politics. Together with a cultural heritage based on the Malayalam language, and regional traditions and habits fostered by the area's particular geography, sandwiched as it is by the Arabian Sea and the Western Ghats, this gave rise to a political culture that, while not immune to powerful pan-Indian centripetal influences, maintained a distinctive Malayali flavour.[6]

Kerala's amalgam of a strong regional character, relatively advanced social and educational development, class consciousness, religious and caste identity, and a complex party system contributed to its political volatility. In the first quarter of a century after its formation, no party won a majority in 8 state assembly elections that gave rise to 14 governments, 9 chief ministers and 7 periods of President's rule from the Centre. However, by 1982, the inter-party competition had consolidated into the Congress-led UDF confronting a Left Democratic Front (LDF) spearheaded by the Communist Party of India (Marxist)—CPM. This provided the basis for the most stable state-level multiparty bipolar political system in the country with the two fronts alternating in power.

While secondary constituents have often split and moved in and out of both fronts, the basic contours of the UDF and LDF have remained constant. Apart from the Congress (itself always an uneasy coalition), the main building blocks of the UDF combine have been the Indian Union Muslim League (IUML) and the Kerala Congress (Mani group)—KCM. The League has its powerbase in North Kerala in the Muslim-majority district of Malappuram and adjacent districts of Malabar, while the stronghold of the Kerala Congress[7] group led by the redoubtable octogenarian K. M. Mani (who died just two weeks before polling day in the 2019 election) lies in the Syrian Christian areas of Central Kerala. The LDF's principal constituents have been the CPM, historically strongest in Malabar, and the smaller Communist Party of India. It has principally drawn from the less privileged Ezhavas, and other ritually inferior Hindu castes, as well as poorer Muslims and Catholic and Protestant Christians (of post-16th century convert origins).

The last assembly elections in 2016 saw the UDF government led by Congress's Oommen Chandy ousted by the LDF, allowing the CPM's Pinarayi Vijayan to realize his long-held ambition to become chief minister. That Vijayan and the previous CPM chief minister, V. S. Achuthanandan, are Ezhavas, and Chandy, and his predecessor as Congress's chief minister, A. K. Antony, are Syrian Christians reflects the importance of the respective communities to the two parties. Another indication of the significance of Muslims and Christians in the UDF is the fact that 46 (or 71%) of the 65 Muslim and Christian (of 140) members of the legislative assembly elected in 2016 represented the UDF (nearly four-fifths of UDF legislators). Whereas the LDF won 65 per cent of the seats overall (91), it got 74 per cent (34 of 46) of those in the four districts (Kannur, Palakkad, Alappuzha and Thiruvananthapuram) where Hindus accounted for over 60 per cent of the population and only 33 per cent (14 of 43) of the seats in the four where they were in a minority (Malappuram, Ernakulam, Idukki and Kottayam).[8]

THE BJP IN KERALA—A FISH OUT OF WATER OR LEARNING TO SWIM?

Despite its unexpectedly resounding triumph in increasing both its majority in the Lok Sabha and its percentage of the vote, the fact that the BJP drew a blank in three of the five southern states showed that while a nationally dominant party, it had not been able to sweep all before it. In Kerala, though the BJP-led National Democratic Alliance (NDA) had succeeded in steadily increasing its vote share in the 2010s (see Table 18.2), for the first time winning a seat, Nemom in the state capital, Thiruvananthapuram, in 2016; it was unable to advance further.

Table 18.2 *Kerala Vidhan and Lok Sabha Elections since 1999*

Year	Ruling Centre	Ruling State	UDF Seats	% Vote	LDF Seats	% Vote	NDA Seats	% Vote	Rest Seats	% Vote	%
1999 LS	NDA	LDF	**12**	46.9	8	43.7	0	8.1	0	1.3	70.2
2001 VS	NDA	LDF	**99**	49.1	40	43.8	0	5.0	1	2.1	72.5
2004 LS	NDA	UDF	1	38.4	**18**	46.1	1	12.1	0	3.4	71.4
2006 VS	UPA	UDF	42	43.0	**98**	48.6	0	4.8	0	3.6	72.4
2009 LS	UPA	LDF	**16**	47.7	4	41.9	0	6.4	0	4.0	73.4
2011 VS	UPA	LDF	**72**	45.8	68	44.9	0	6.1	0	3.2	75.1
2014 LS	UPA	UDF	**12**	42.0	8	40.1	0	10.8	0	7.1	73.9
2016 VS	NDA	UDF	47	38.9	**91**	43.3	1	15.0	1	2.8	77.3
2019 LS	NDA	LDF	**19**	47.4	1	35.2	0	15.6	0	1.8	77.7

Source: Based on Election Commission of India. Available at https://eci.gov.in/statistical-report/statistical-reports/ and https://eci.gov.in/general-election/general-elections–2019/ (accessed on 7 August 2019).

Notes: The figures in bold show the majority of seats. VS: Vidhan Sabha; LS: Lok Sabha.

The seeds of the BJP's development in Kerala were planted before Independence.[9] Three Maharashtrian *pracharaks* (full-time propagandists) of the Hindu nationalist parent organization, the Rashtriya Swayamsevak Sangh (RSS), arrived in 1942 and the first Keralite pracharaks emerged a few years later. The pioneering local recruits played key roles in initiating the development of the Bharatiya Jana Sangh (BJS), the BJP's precursor, and other local branches of the Sangh Parivar (family of Hindu nationalist organizations), notably the Vishwa Hindu Parishad, the Bharatiya Mazdoor Sangh (Indian Workers' Union) and the Bharatiya Vichar Kendra (Centre for Indian Thought).

Yet the BJS electoral strength was miniscule and Hindu nationalism very much a peripheral force in the first three decades of Kerala state. The Hindu nationalists did seek to exploit occasional communal flare-ups when they occurred, but failed to make inroads into the complex well-established interplay of communal, caste and class politics. As elsewhere outside the northern Hindi-speaking states, they were hindered by the perception of the RSS and BJS as North Indian outfits pursuing an alien agenda of Hindi–Hindu–Hindutva with little local resonance. A significant handicap they had was that the influential main caste associations, notably the NSS and the SNDP Yogam, with their strong ties to the main political parties, showed little interest in cooperating. The fact that the RSS and BJS membership were disproportionately upper caste Hindu, including non-Malayalis settled in the state, did not help.

The situation only changed somewhat in the 1980s when the Hindu nationalists capitalized on a controversy that erupted in 1983 over a Christian demand to construct a church at Nilakkal on the pilgrimage route to the highland jungle shrine dedicated to the popular syncretic Hindu deity Ayyappa at Sabarimala in Central Kerala. It was claimed that an ancient cross had been unearthed there. Sangh Parivar organizations spearheaded the opposition, launching a Hindu Munnani (Hindu forward movement) to contest the 1984 Lok Sabha and 1987 assembly elections in conjunction with the BJP at a time when the latter was nationally moving to embrace the Ram Janmabhoomi campaign to build a Ram temple at Ayodhya. This yielded limited electoral dividends with the Hindu nationalist combination contesting most of the assembly seats and winning 6.5 per cent of the votes in 1987.

However, their 1987 gains did not presage an electoral breakthrough with the BJP's vote in elections over the next three decades fluctuating between around 5 and 10 per cent. Until 2019, when comparing one assembly election to the next, and one parliamentary poll with the next, the pattern was generally of the BJP gaining when the UDF lost support (1987, 1996, 2004, 2014, 2016) and vice versa (1991, 2001, 2009; see Table 18.2). This tended to bear out a widely held assumption that the disproportionately caste Hindu BJP voters were more likely to be erstwhile supporters of the UDF than of the LDF.

The BJP did have limited success in exploiting its national appeal to expand its electoral support in Kerala. It did so in successive Lok Sabha elections from 1989 to 2004 and, after a setback in 2009, did so again in 2014 and 2019. A major obstacle in the way of the BJP's advance has been its inability to forge the kind of coalition with significant regional parties that it did to its advantage in other states outside the Hindi belt, as with the Shiv Sena in Maharashtra, the Biju Janata Dal in Orissa, the Akali Dal in Punjab and the Telugu Desam in Andhra Pradesh.

The main reasons for this are the well-established lines along which coalition politics in the state have traditionally been drawn and the powerful disincentive for the other parties of risking the alienation of Muslim and Christian voters distrustful of Hindu nationalism. In a bid to win over the lower caste majority of Kerala's Hindus, BJP President Amit Shah encouraged the launch of a new party in 2015, the Bharath Dharma Jana Sena (BDJS), led by Thushar Vellappally, the son of the SNDP Yogam General Secretary Vellappally Natesan. Natesan had welcomed Modi's advent as the BJP's prime ministerial candidate in 2013, hailing him as a leader of OBC origins. Wooed by Shah, he lent the SNDP Yogam's support to the BJP in the 2015 local body elections in which, while still trailing a relatively distant third, it more than doubled its representation.[10]

One problem that the BJP has in Kerala is that it has thrown up few leaders of real calibre or with a high public profile, a fact underlined by the fact that the first and only assembly member it succeeded in returning, O. Rajagopal, was a veteran Jan Sanghite and perennial election candidate in his late 80s. However, in December 2015, Amit

Shah oversaw the election of Kummanam Rajasekharan, the general secretary of the Hindu Aikya Vedi (Hindu United Front), as the party's state president. The charismatic Rajasekharan, a pracharak who had first come to public prominence as the leader of the 1983 Nilakkal agitation, had a reputation as a charismatic RSS hardliner and as an environmental campaigner.

Beyond the political arena, efforts to appropriate and adapt both locally popular Hindu cultural practices and temple traditions, and to aggressively promote an assertive and more homogenized national Hindu identity in the public space, have had success in mitigating the one-time image of the RSS and the BJP as alien north Indian Hindu manifestations.[11] In the 2016 assembly elections the BJP-led NDA, including the BDJS, multiplied its vote share two and a half times, in what was easily its best ever result. By 2018, the RSS was claiming over 4,105 daily *shakhas* and 200,000 active members, and in 2019 the state BJP claimed a membership of 1.5 million (which would represent about half the total vote the NDA won in the Lok Sabha election).[12] That it has not achieved more in spite of propitious national circumstances and a determined effort to expand its support across the Hindu castes shows the considerable challenge the party faced in overcoming Kerala's bifront politics. It may no longer look like a fish out of water, but it is still not swimming freely with much larger fish about.

SABARIMALA, HINDUTVA AND RAHUL: WHY THE LDF AND MODI LOST

Congress President Rahul Gandhi stood and won in his first outing in a Kerala constituency, Wayanad, by a margin (431,770) not much short of what a triumphant Narendra Modi, like Gandhi contesting away from his home state, managed in being re-elected in Varanasi in Uttar Pradesh (479,505). It emphasized the stark contrast between the contest in Kerala and the national one. Here foregrounding the prime minister in the BJP's campaign did little to enhance its performance. In the CSDS-Lokniti Post-poll Survey, Modi trailed Gandhi by 36 per cent as the prime ministerial preference of Kerala voters (47%–11%)—he led him by twelve points nationally (46%–34%). Barely a third expressed satisfaction with the performance of the Central government.[13]

Apart from promoting Modi, the BJP sought to exploit the furious controversy aroused by the LDF state government's avowed determination to respect the September 2018 Supreme Court ruling in favour of a petition that women of menstruating age should be allowed to enter the Ayyappa shrine in Sabarimala. The shrine attracts millions of pilgrims annually, in recent years not just Malayalis but Hindus from across India and beyond.

The court held that the ban violated the constitutional equality of citizens and the right of women to worship. The temple authorities and Hindu organizations, notably those associated with the Sangh Parivar, opposed this and thousands of protesters confronted police to stop women from entering. BJP figures in the forefront included K. Surendran, the party's state general secretary and its candidate in the Pathanamthitta Lok Sabha constituency in which Sabarimala was located. Facing 242 criminal charges, 222 of which were in connection with the agitation, he was jailed for three weeks in December 2018.[14]

After initially supporting the judgement, saying that women should be allowed to go anywhere, Rahul Gandhi backtracked in the face of opposition from the Congress party in the state and said that tradition needed to be protected.[15] While much less aggressive than the BJP in taking this stance, the UDF position proved in retrospect to be in tune with public opinion. Despite Kerala's history of radical social reform and communist politics, as well as positive gender development indicators relative to the rest of the country,[16] society remains influenced by conservative patriarchal attitudes and attachment to tradition. This made the LDF state government's resolute insistence of upholding the Supreme Court ruling fraught with risk.

The CPM claimed that five and a half million women joined in forming a chain of solidarity for women's equality (*vanitha mathil* or women's wall) that spanned the 620 km from one end of the state to the other on New Year's Day 2019. Early the following morning two women under 50, protected by a heavy police presence, entered to worship in the Sabarimala temple.[17] Yet the CSDS-Lokniti Survey found little more than a quarter of those polled supporting the government with the 63 per cent opposed including almost half of those who voted for the LDF.

What was striking was how the constant references to Sabarimala and protecting tradition by BJP leaders failed to translate into electoral support. Even though 46 per cent of those polled by CSDS-Lokniti Survey said it had been an important factor when they were voting, the belief of BJP leaders, 'The Sabarimala issue in Kerala is like Ayodhya in the north'[18] proved misplaced. It had nothing like the effect the Ram Mandir movement had across northern India in the 1990s. Although the BJP attracted the support of more than a third of Nairs, as it had in the last assembly poll, this was matched by the UDF, apparently at the expense of the LDF—Nair support for the LDF was more than halved to 20 per cent. This, together with smaller increases in support from Avarna Hindus who had traditionally disproportionately favoured the LDF, as well as the overwhelming backing of Christians (70%) and Muslims (65%), helped the UDF coast to its very comfortable victory.

Given the unpopularity of the NDA government, the decision that Rahul Gandhi should contest in Kerala boosted the UDF campaign to maximize the UDF's advantage. Modi's jibe about Gandhi finding an 'escape from the Hindu ire', and Shah commenting on the flags waved by the supporters in Gandhi's nomination procession of Congress's UDF ally, the Muslim League, quipping 'when a procession is taken out, you cannot make out whether it is in India or Pakistan',[19] were not well received. These barbed comments about Gandhi having chosen to contest from Wayanad, made by Modi and Shah while campaigning in Maharastra, did the UDF no harm in Kerala. Wayanad and the other four seats (Malappuram, Ponnani, Ernakulam and Idukki) that the UDF won with over half the vote and their biggest margins of between 18 and 40 per cent lay in districts where Muslims, Christians and Scheduled Castes and Tribes formed over 60 per cent of the population (see Tables 18.1 and 18.3).

Months before the election, the BJP decided to focus on four constituencies. They succeeded in winning over a quarter of the votes in these but without coming close to winning. All four possessed major temple complexes: Thiruvananthapuram including the Sree Padmanabhaswamy temple, with Attingal lying just south of the capital; Thrissur with both the famous Vadakkunathan temple and the major pilgrimage centre at Guruvayur; and Pathanamthitta with

Table 18.3 *Kerala Lok Sabha Constituency Results: Per Cent of Votes by Party and Alliance, 2019 and 2014*

Constituency	Party/Alliance	Per Cent Vote 2019	Winning Margin	Per Cent Vote 2014	Winning Margin
Kasaragod	INC/UDF gain	43	4	38	–
(M)	CPM/LDF	39	–	39	1
	BJP/NDA	16	–	18	–
Kannur	INC/UDF gain	50	9	44	–
(M)	CPM/LDF	41	–	45	1
	BJP/NDA	6	–	5	–
Wayanad	INC/UDF	65	40	41	2
(M)	CPI/LDF	25	–	39	–
	BDJS/NDA	7	–	9 (BJP)	–
Vadakara	INC/UDF	49	8	43.4	0.4
(M)	CPM/LDF	41	–	43	–
	BJP/NDA	7	–	8	–
Kozhikode	INC/UDF	46	8	42	2
(M)	CPM/LDF	38	–	40	–
	BJP/NDA	15	–	12	–

Malappuram	IUML/UDF	57	25	51	23
(M)	CPM/LDF	32	–	28	–
	BJP/NDA	8	–	8	–
Ponnani	IUML/UDF	51	19	43	3
(M)	Ind/LDF	32	–	40	–
	BJP/NDA	11	–	9	–
Palakkad	INC/UDF gain	39	1	34 (SJD)	–
(M)	CPM/LDF	38	–	45	11
	BJP/NDA	21	–	15	–
Alathur	INC/UDF gain	52	15	40	–
(M)	CPM/LDF	37	–	44	4
	BDJS/NDA	9	–	9 (BJP)	–
Thrissur	INC/UDF gain	40	9	38	–
(TC)	CPI/LDF	31	–	42	4
	BJP/NDA	28	–	11	–
Chalakudy	INC/UDF gain	48	14	39	–
(TC)	CPM/LDF	34	–	40 (Ind)	1
	BJP/NDA	16	–	10	–

(Continued)

Table 18.3 *(Continued)*

Constituency	Party/Alliance	Per Cent Vote 2019	Winning Margin	Per Cent Vote 2014	Winning Margin
Ernakulam	INC/UDF	51	18	42	11
(TC)	CPM/LDF	33	–	31 (Ind)	–
	BJP/NDA	14	–	12	–
Idukki	INC/UDF gain	54	18	40	–
(TC)	Ind/LDF	36	–	47	7
	BDJS/NDA	9	–	6 (BJP)	–
Kottayam	KCM/UDF	46	11	51	15
(TC)	CPM/LDF	35	–	36 (JDS)	–
	KC/NDA	17	–	5 (Ind)	–
Alappuzha	CPM/LDF gain	41	1	44	–
(TC)	INC/UDF	40	–	46	2
	BJP/NDA	17	–	4 (Ind)	–
Mavelikara	INC/UDF	45	6	45	3
(TC)	CPI/LDF	39	–	42	–
	BDJS/NDA	14	–	9 (BJP)	–

Pathanamthitta	INC/UDF	37	4	41	6
(TC)	CPM/LDF	33	–	35 (Ind)	–
	BJP/NDA	29	–	16	–
Kollam	RSP/UDF	52	16	46	4
(TC)	CPM/LDF	36	–	42	–
	BJP/NDA	11	–	7	–
Attingal	INC/UDF gain	38	4	38	–
(TC)	CPM/LDF	34	–	46	8
	BJP/NDA	25	–	11	–
Thiruvananthapuram	INC/UDF	41	10	34	2
(TC)	BJP/NDA	31	–	32	–
	CPI/LDF	26	–	28	–

Source: Based on Election Commission of India. Available at: https://eci.gov.in/general-election/general-elections–2019/ (accessed on 7 August 2019).

Notes: M: ex-Malabar; TC: ex-Travancore-Cochin; Ind: independent; SJD: Socialist Janata (Democratic) Party; JDS: Janata Dal (Secular); RSP: Revolutionary Socialist Party.

the Sabarimala shrine.[20] The choice may partly have been guided by how the Sangh Parivar had been able to build up support in Kerala by exploiting temple networks. There were also particular local factors at play. Thiruvananthapuram, with its concentration of upper caste Nairs and Tamil Brahmins, had been a seat that O. Rajagopal had come within a whisker of winning for the BJP in 2014. However, this time Kummanam Rajasekharan saw the party's share of the vote cut as celebrity UN diplomat and author turned politician Shashi Tharoor, also a Nair, was re-elected with a majority of almost 100,000. In Thrissur, the BJP was helped by the high profile of its candidate, popular Malayalam film actor Suresh Gopi, who more than doubled the party's vote. In Attingal, another high-profile BJP candidate, Shobha Surendran, the party's leading woman campaigner in the state and a prominent figure in the Sabarimala agitation, may well have assisted the UDF in winning the seat for the first time in 30 years by cutting into the Hindu vote for the LDF.

In the 2016 assembly election, the BJP's alliance with the new BDJS did not dislodge the LDF as the leading choice for Ezhavas with support for the NDA among Ezhavas remaining around 20 per cent. Neither was P. C. Thomas, the leader of a minor Kerala Congress splinter group who had been re-elected to the Lok Sabha for a sixth time in 2004 after having joined the NDA, able to repeat the feat in Kottayam, trailing a distant third. The eve of poll entry into the NDA of the Kerala Janapaksham party set up by P. C. George, a maverick veteran assembly member who had been expelled from the Kerala Congress (Mani group) and whose Poonjar seat lay in the Pathanamthitta constituency,[21] also failed to enable the BJP's K. Surendran overtake the LDF to take second place. The fact that the UDF and LDF combines once again hung together, despite some of the usual inter-and intra-party pre-election stresses and strains, demonstrated the limits in Kerala of the regional alliance strategies that had served the BJP well elsewhere.

The UDF's victories in constituencies such as Attingal, Alathur and Kasaragod that they had not won for around three decades highlighted the importance of how the national focus of Kerala voters, accentuated by Rahul Gandhi's candidacy, neutralized a positive perception of the LDF state government. The CSDS-Lokniti Survey indicated that 70 per cent of voters were satisfied with its performance just eight months after it had faced the challenge of dealing with the worst monsoon floods Kerala had suffered in nearly a century. That this did not help the LDF hold back the UDF advance showed how both the Rahul versus Modi and Sabarimala factors dominated the Lok Sabha vote.

From a national perspective, Kerala in 2019 appears the exceptional Congress victory that proves the rule of the BJP's national dominance. With its unusual religious demography, underpinned by a distinctive history, culture and pattern of social and political development, the state has hitherto proved more resistant than most of the rest of the country to the encompassing appeal of the ideology of Hindu nationalism. Whether this will remain the case if the votaries of that ideology continue to tighten their grip on national institutions, while continuing to mould a pervasive pan-Indian Hindutva culture, is a moot point.

NOTES

1. The phrase is often attributed to the legend of Parashurama, the Brahmin incarnation of the Hindu god Vishnu, having created Kerala by casting his axe into the sea; Adoor K. K. Ramachandran Nair, *Kerala State Gazetteer* vol. 1 (Trivandrum: Government Press, 1986), 4.
2. Available at http://censusindia.gov.in/2011Census/C-16_25062018_NEW.pdf (accessed on 6 August 2019).
3. Available at https://www.census2011.co.in/data/religion/state/32-kerala.html (accessed on 6 August 2019).
4. Garima Maheshwari, 'Migrant Crisis in Kerala: Need to Change the Political Culture', *Economic & Political Weekly* 51, no. 48 (2016): 23–25.
5. Available at https://kerala.gov.in/migration (accessed on 7 August 2019).
6. James Chiriyankandath, 'Hindu Nationalism and Regional Political Culture in India: A Study of Kerala', *Nationalism and Ethnic Politics* 2, no. 1 (1996): 44–66.
7. The Kerala Congress was formed in 1964 by several prominent Syrian Christian and Nair politicians from Central Kerala who broke with R. Sankar, the only Ezhava Congressman to become chief minister; James Chiriyankandath, '"Unity in Diversity"? Coalition Politics in India (with Special Reference to Kerala)', in *Electoral Politics in South Asia*, eds. Subho Basu and Suranjan Das (Calcutta: K.P. Bagchi & Co., 2000), 34.
8. Election Commission of India. Available athttps://eci.gov.in/files/file/3767-kerala-general-legislative-election-2016/ (accessed on 7 August 2019).

9. This section draws on James Chiriyankandath, 'Kerala and the Social and Regional Limits of Hindu Nationalism', in *The BJP and the Compulsions of Politics in India*, eds. Thomas Blom Hansen and Christophe Jaffrelot (Delhi: Oxford University Press, 1998), 202–227.
10. Available at http://lsgelection.kerala.gov.in/lbtrend2015/views/index.php and http://sec.kerala.gov.in/index.php/archives/general-elections-2010 (accessed on 6 August 2019).
11. Latha Jishnu, 'BJP Won't Capture Kerala Yet but RSS Culture Is Sweeping the State', *The Wire*, 18 May 2016. Available at https://thewire.in/communalism/bjp-wont-capture-kerala-yet-but-rss-culture-is-sweeping-the-state (accessed on 5 June 2016).
12. K. R. Rajeev, 'RSS Added 8000 New Members in Kerala Last Year: State Chief', *The Times of India*, 16 March 2018. Available at https://timesofindia.indiatimes.com/city/kozhikode/rss-added-8000-new-members-in-kerala-last-year-state-chief/articleshow/63322319.cms (accessed on 10 August 2019); *The Times of India*, 'BJP Aims to Double Membership in Kerala', 7 July 2019. Available at https://timesofindia.indiatimes.com/city/thiruvananthapuram/bjp-aims-to-double-membership-in-state/articleshow/70110206.cms (accessed on 10 August 2019).
13. K. M. Sajjad Ibrahim, 'Upper Castes and Minority Support Spur UDF to Massive Victory', *The Hindu*, 27 May 2019. Available at https://www.thehindu.com/elections/lok-sabha-2019/upper-castes-and-minority-support-spur-udf-to-massive-victory/article27256482.ece (accessed on 1 June 2019); Jyoti Mishra, 'CSDS-Lokniti Pre-poll Survey: The PM Candidate Effect', *The Hindu*, 20 May 2019. Available at https://www.thehindu.com/elections/lok-sabha-2019/csds-lokniti-pre-poll-survey-the-pm-candidate-effect/article27189621.ece (accessed on 1 June 2019).
14. B. S. Anilkumar, 'Surendran Needed 12 Newspaper Pages to Publish Cases against Him', *The Times of India*, Kochi, 21 April 2019, 5.
15. Anuraag Singh and Amit Agnihotri, 'Sabarimala Verdict: Rahul Gandhi Admits Difference of Opinion between Him and Kerala Congress', *The New Indian Express*, 31 October 2018. Available at http://www.newindianexpress.com/nation/2018/oct/31/sabarimala-verdict-rahul-gandhi-admits-difference-of-opinion-between-him-and-kerala-congress-1892176.html (accessed on 25 January 2019); *The New Indian Express* 'Rahul Gandhi's U-turn on Sabarimala: Now Backs Shrine Tradition', 14 January 2019. Available at http://www.newindianexpress.com/nation/2018/oct/31/sabarimala-verdict-rahul-gandhi-admits-difference-of-opinion-between-him-and-kerala-congress-1892176.html (accessed on 25 January 2019).
16. Ministry of Women and Child Development, Government of India, *Gendering Human Development Indices: Recasting the Gender Development Index and Gender Empowerment Measure for India*. Summary Report (Delhi: Ministry of Women and Child Development, Government of India, 2009), 9. Available at https://www.undp.org/content/dam/india/docs/

gendering_human_development_indices_summary_report.pdf (accessed on 7 August 2019).

17. Adam Withnall, 'Protestors Form 620 km "Women's Wall" in India as Female Devotees Pray at Hindu Temple for First Time', *The Independent*, 2 January 2019. Available at https://www.independent.co.uk/news/world/asia/womens-wall-protest-india-kerala-temple-hindu-pray-supreme-court-sexism-a8708381.html (accessed on 25 January 2019).
18. R. Balashankar, 'Sabarimala Redefined Politics', *The Times of India*, Kochi, 13 April 2019, 2. Balashankar was a member of the BJP Central Committee and a former editor of the RSS mouthpiece *Organiser.*
19. *The Times of India,* 'As the Battle Hots Up, BJP Plays the "Hindu–Muslim" Card', Kochi, 2 April 2019, 4; Vivek Deshpande, 'Amit Shah on Rahul's Wayanad Show: Is It in India or Pakistan?' *The Indian Express*, 10 April 2019. Available at https://indianexpress.com/elections/amit-shah-rahul-gandhi-wayanad-india-pakistan-elections-2019–5667756/ (accessed on 7 August 2019).
20. N. J. Nair, 'BJP to Focus on Four Segments in LS polls', *The New Indian Express*, Kochi, 15 January 2019.
21. *The Times of India*, 'With PC George Joining Force, NDA Gets Two MLAs in Kerala', 11 April 2019. Available at https://timesofindia.indiatimes.com/elections/lok-sabha-elections-2019/kerala/news/with-pc-joining-force-nda-gets-2-mlas-in-state/articleshow/68822405.cms (accessed on 7 August 2019).

D. Northeast

Chapter 19

Assam Polls

The *Hindutva* Wave

Akhil Ranjan Dutta

THE CONTEXT

The 2019 general elections in India were held at a time when Assam was in crisis. The Citizenship Act Amendment Bill (CAB) 2016 was boiling Assam's politics creating unprecedented dissent against the incumbent National Democratic Alliance (NDA) governments both in the state and at the centre led by the Bharatiya Janata Party (BJP). There was a loose coalition of civil and political forces against the BJP on the CAB issue, which proposed to grant citizenship to the illegal migrants of six non-Muslim minority religious communities of Afghanistan, Pakistan and Bangladesh. This proposition was in violation of the Assam Accord, 1985, signed after the anti-foreigners' agitation from 1979–1985. It established 24 March 1971 as the cut-off date for detecting, deleting and deporting foreigners from Assam, which legally became enacted in 1985 through the Amendment of Citizenship Act, 1955.

The Bill was also perceived to have derailed the ongoing process of updating the National Register of Citizens (NRC), 1951, for the state of Assam carried out under the monitoring of the Supreme Court of India in accordance with the provisions of the Assam Accord. Despite the resistance, the government reiterated its commitment to grant citizenship to these non-Muslim communities through a Bill in the Lok Sabha in January 2019, shortly before the Lok Sabha elections. Three ministers from the Asom Gana Parishad (AGP) in the Sarbananda Sonowal ministry in Assam resigned as a protest. Due to political opposition, the Bill could not be introduced in the Rajya Sabha. The BJP during the 2019 election campaign reiterated its commitment to the Bill if returned to power.[1] It was also incorporated in its manifesto.

Despite the public outcry, the BJP improved politically winning nine seats, two more than in 2014. BJP's victory, marked by polarization on religious lines, reduced its major opponent the Congress Party primarily to an East Bengal origin Muslim base as viewed by the electorate. The Congress won three seats maintaining its 2014 tally. All India United Democratic Front (AIUDF), the party that benefitted from polarization of East Bengal origin Muslim votes since the 2006 assembly elections witnessed erosion of its vote banks which evidently shifted towards the Congress. The party which had won three seats in 2014 was reduced to one in 2019.

The BJP registered this landslide victory in Assam despite the unprecedented dissent due to the interplay of social and political forces. These include certain developmental initiatives combined with hyper populism, success of its long-term strategy bringing the tea plantation workers and tribal communities into the *Hindutva* fold, Prime Minister Modi's leadership, its national security campaign capturing the popular imagination, grassroots role of the RSS and its rigid *Hindutva* agenda combined with a cultural and linguistic flavour.

THE VERDICT

The year 2019 marks another consecutive electoral success for the BJP in Assam following its ascendance in 2014. The BJP achieved a landslide victory in the 2016 assembly elections followed by a remarkable performance in the 2018 panchayat elections. Both the 2014 Lok Sabha elections and the 2016 state assembly elections were fought around local issues, which earned a reputation for the BJP being committed towards the state's indigenous people, particularly in the Brahmaputra valley. During both elections, the *Hindutva* agenda was downplayed as folk narratives, cultural ethos and historical legends were featured.[2] In 2019, the *Hindutva* agenda was emphasized by projecting CAB as a saviour of the linguistic and cultural identities of the indigenous people.[3] It also forced AGP, the key regional ally of the BJP, to exit the BJP-led government in January 2019. AGP already had fought the panchayat elections in December 2018 alone. The BJP then succeeded in persuading AGP to return in March 2019, less than a month ahead of the elections. Bodo People's Front (BPF), the other regional ally continued its ties with the BJP despite its reservations over the CAB.

Amidst discontent around CAB on 6 January 2019, the union government established a high-level committee chaired by a retired IAS officer to implement Clause 6 of the Assam Accord which 'suggests that the government has to enact constitutional, legislative and administrative safeguards to protect, preserve and promote the cultural, social and linguistic identity and heritage of the Assamese people.'[4] The nine-member committee including eminent Assamese was expected to submit its report within six months. However, the initiative provoked such strong reactions as being a diversionary tactic that most of the committee members refused to be a part of it.

The mass discontent and protests, however, did not transform into votes either in the panchayat or the Lok Sabha elections. In panchayat elections, the BJP won around 50 per cent seats at all levels.[5] In 2019 Lok Sabha elections, the party won 9 of 10 seats it contested out of 14 in the state. Four seats unsuccessfully went to its two allies—three for AGP and one for BPF. BJP registered 36.05 percent of the votes polled in the state but registered 54.32 percent in the seats it contested. This is more than 20 percent higher than all the other parties (see Table 19.1).

After 1991, the BJP regained both seats in Barak Valley (Karimganj and Silchar), registered its first victory in Lok Sabha elections in the hill districts (autonomous district) and retained six seats (Tezpur, Dibrugarh, Lakhimpur, Jorhat, Guwahati and Mangaldoi) out of seven seats that the party had won in 2014. It lost only in Nowgong constituency to the Congress, which it had won for four consecutive terms before the 2019 elections. Victory in Karimganj constituency with a small margin was considered to be laudable by BJP's political strategists.[6] Shift of the AIUDF votes to Congress also contributed towards the defeat of the AIUDF sitting Member of Parliament (MP) in the constituency.

Table 19.1 *Seats Won and Vote Share of Political Parties*

Parties	Seats Contested	Won	Vote (%)	Vote % per Seat Contested
BJP	10	9	36.05	54.32
AGP	3	0	8.23	32.41
BPF	1	0	2.48	30.2
INC	14	3	35.44	35.44
AUDF	3	1	7.8	33.35
Independents	45	1	4.25	–

Source: Lokniti-CSDS Survey, available at https://www.thehindu.com/elections/lok-sabha-2019/post-poll-survey-bjps-polarisation-strategy-hits-the-mark-in-assam/article27267757.ece (accessed on 26 September 2019).

BJP led in 69 out of 126 assembly segments compared to only 26 for Congress (see Table 19.2).

In both the Hindu Bengalis dominant constituencies in the valley, the BJP used the CAB issue very prominently which pushed the Congress into an embarrassing situation. Officially, the Congress took a firm stand against CAB. However, to woo the Bengali Hindu voters, the Congress veteran and sitting MP of Silchar constituency Sushmita Dev took a position that contradicted her own party's official line.[7] BJP's victory in the autonomous district was also remarkable. Apart from winning the constituency with 61.73 per cent votes by defeating the five times MP and Congress veteran Biren Singh Engti, the BJP registered its lead in all five assembly segments.

The Congress, which won only three seats in the present elections (Kaliabor, Nowgong and Barpeta) was reduced to a party dependent on immigrant Muslims as seen by the public. AIUDF supposedly fought this election with a proclaimed strategy of unity against the BJP, and therefore fielded its candidates only in three constituencies which the party had won in 2014 (Dhubri, Barpeta and Karimganj). The proposed unity, however, did not materialize allegedly due to betrayal by the Congress.[8] The party went from three to one seat.

The Kokrajhar constituency, which is largely under the administrative control of the Bodo Territorial Area Districts (BTAD), and

Table 19.2 *Performance of the Winning Party and the Runner-Up in Lok Sabha Constituencies and Lead in Assembly Segments*

Name of the Constituency	Performance in 2019		Lead in Assembly Segments				
	Winner	Runner-up	Total Assembly Segments	BJP	Cong	AUDF	Others
Autonomous district	BJP (61.73%)	INC (22.94%)	5	5	–	–	–
Barpeta	INC (44.23%)	AGP (34.61%)	10	–	6	–	4 (AGP)
Dhubri	AUDF (42.66%)	INC (29.23%)	10	2	–	8	–
Dibrugarh	BJP (64.94%)	INC (29.04%)	9	9	–	–	–
Guwahati	BJP (57.2%)	INC (37.61%)	10	6	4	–	–
Jorhat	BJP (51.35%)	INC (43.54%)	10	8	2	–	–
Kaliabor	INC (55.18%)	AGP (40.44%)	10	–	5	–	5 (AGP)
Karimganj	BJP (44.62%)	AUDF (41.00%)	8	4	–	4	–
Kokrajhar	Ind. (32.75%)	BPF (30.20%)	10	–	–	–	6 (Ind.) 4 (BPF)
Lakhimpur	BJP (60.49%)	INC (33.18%)	9	8	1	–	–
Mangaldoi	BJP (48.83%)	INC (39.63%)	10	8	2	–	–
Nowgong	INC (49.53%)	BJP (48.41%)	9	6	3	–	–
Silchar	BJP (52.59%)	INC (43.99%)	7	4	3	–	–
Tezpur	BJP (57.48%)	INC (37.08%)	9	9	–	–	–
		Total	126	69	26	12	19

Sources: Compiled from the statistics of Election Commission of India, available at http://results.eci.gov.in/pc/en/constituencywise/ConstituencywiseS033.htm?ac=3 (accessed on 26 September 2019). Disaggregated lead in Assembly segments compiled by Assam Pradesh Congress Committee, Guwahati.

controlled by BJP's ally BPF, returned the non-Bodo independent candidate Naba Kumar Sarania for the second consecutive term, although with a reduced majority from almost 52 per cent to 32.7 per cent in 2014 and 2019, respectively. BPF won 9 out of 10 assembly segments of the constituency in 2016 assembly elections, but won only four assembly segments in the 2019 general elections.

STRIKING FEATURES OF THE 2019 ELECTIONS

1. **Deep roots among the tea tribe communities**
Based on decades of work carried out by the RSS in Northeast India, in general, and Assam, in particular, the BJP succeeded in gaining Hindu support by the tribal and tea tribe communities in the state. An almost complete swing of votes occurred in 2019 by the tea tribe communities, traditional Congress supporters, towards the BJP. The BJP had two tea tribe candidates who polled very well—Rameswar Teli (Dibrugarh) and Pallab Lochan Das (Tezpur). In Dibrugarh, the BJP polled almost 65 per cent of the votes leading in all nine assembly segments as against 29 per cent secured by the Congress candidate. Teli's margin of victory was more than 3.6 lakhs. He defeated the strong Congressman Paban Singh Ghatowar, also a member from the same community who had won the constituency five times and was a state minister both in Narasimha Rao and Manmohan Singh's council of ministers.

BJP's strategy to nominate Pallab Lochan Das, the state minister in the Sarbananda Sonowal's ministry in Assam was both dramatic and strategic. It was reported that BJP's state unit forwarded only the name of Dr Himanta Biswa Sarma, the North East Democratic Alliance (NEDA) coordinator and the state finance minister to the central election committee of the party. The central committee put aside the state unit's single nomination and selected Das as the candidate. The sitting BJP MP, R. P. Sarmah, an old RSS activist who belongs to the dominant Nepali community in the constituency was also denied the ticket.[9] BJP's performance in this constituency too was extraordinary. The party registered more than 57 per cent votes as against 37 per cent by his Congress rival and also led in all nine assembly segments. The margin of victory was over 2.4 lakh votes.

Kamakhya Prasad Tasa, who was the BJP sitting MP from Jorhat constituency, and a member of the tea tribe's community was denied the ticket for the 2019 elections. In this constituency too, where the tea tribes have a substantive presence, the BJP registered a remarkable victory securing more than 51 per cent of the votes polled as against 43.5 per cent by the Congress rival and led in 8 out of 10 assembly segments. The BJP might have played a strategic game plan by putting an Ahom candidate Tapan Kumar Gogoi, former general secretary of All Assam Students' Union (AASU), also an incumbent state minister in Sonowal government, against an Ahom candidate fielded by the Congress. Immediately after the Lok Sabha elections, Tasa was rewarded by electing him to the Rajya Sabha.

In the new union ministry following the 2019 elections, Rameswar Teli became the lone representative from Assam. 'The BJP strategically chose Teli keeping the assembly polls in mind which are just two years away', wrote *The Wire* in its report on the inclusion of Teli, the two time MP from Dibrugarh. In its report titled *Rameshwar Teli's Inclusion in Govt Telling of BJP's Desire to Woo Assam's Tea Tribe*,[10] Pisharoty writes:

> Both in the 2014 Lok Sabha and the 2016 assembly polls, the BJP could become victorious in the Brahmaputra Valley mainly due to the success of the RSS in channeling the tea tribe votes into BJP. With the Assamese community getting vocal against the BJP close to the 2019 Lok Sabha polls due to the Citizenship (Amendment) Bill, it became all the more vital for the BJP to hold on to its tea tribe votes.

In addition to the long-term RSS efforts within the community, the BJP also tried to shift the loyalty of the community from the Congress to the BJP.

A striking feature of the BJP-led state budgets is the numerous schemes announced for the tea tribe community, which has around 35–40 per cent vote share in the Brahmaputra Valley. The schemes favoured the tea tribe community that allegedly could become a solid electoral block for the party. In every budget, the government came up with schemes that also include direct transfer of funds to the people belonging to the community. In 2017, the government launched the *Chah Bagicha Dhan Puraskar Mela*. In January 2018, the government transferred the first tranche of ₹2,500 through Direct Benefit Transfer to over seven lakh bank accounts of tea garden workers across 752 tea gardens. In 2018–2019, additional funds were scheduled to be released including to an expanded list of beneficiaries that include those who have been left out. Additional benefits were allocated for subsidized rice schemes.[11]

The government also introduced a number of populist schemes under *Astadash Mukutar Unnoyonee Mala*, 18 flagship schemes targeting different sections of the society. The government offered free textbooks up to degree level and fee waiver up to postgraduate levels for poor students, one *tola* gold for brides for all communities with a condition of marriage registration as well as further subsidy in rice under the National Food Security Act. These paid electoral dividends to the ruling party.

2. **The RSS at the grassroots**

Explaining the phenomenal success of the BJP in 2019, Bhattacharyya pointed out that 'The traditional bastions of the Congress in Assam's rural areas are being painted with a saffron hue, which helps to explains BJP's phenomenal success in the general elections'.[12] Bhattacharyya was investigating the role of the *Ekal Vidyalayas*, or single-teacher schools, which have mushroomed across almost all districts in Assam. Field reports suggest that the RSS played a significant role in BJP's success as it built up a grassroots network to mitigate the discontent arising out of the CAB 2016. The Sangha reportedly organized around 600 small-scale meetings at the grassroots and distributed 90 lakh leaflets to allay the fear against the CAB 2016.[13] Eminent local persons participated in the meetings.

The RSS has been penetrating Assam's tribal communities as well as mainstream ethnic Assamese communities, particularly through educational and cultural means. A number of educational institutions including Sankardev Sishu Niketan, Ekal Vidyalayas and Vanavasi Kalyan Ashram are working in different locations in the state and have been instrumental in bringing legitimacy to the RSS agenda. In Assam, the RSS appears to have appropriated the name of the great 15th century Assamese poet-saint Sri Sankar Deva by naming its schools after him.[14] Sankardev Sishu Niketan, which has affiliation to Vidya Bharati has a large network in the state with 550 schools that enrol more than 1.60 lakh students.[15] These schools with Assamese medium of instruction are affiliated to the state board (Board of Secondary Education, Assam) providing a reasonably good quality education at affordable fees.

In relatively big towns, the children of middle and upper middle classes gradually switched over to English medium. In small towns and villages, middle and lower income classes resorted to the Shishu Niketans in an environment of major problems with the state-aided schools throughout the state. Apart from the behavioural and cultural training, these schools performed well in final examinations at the secondary level. For example, in 2019 the pass percentage of the Sishu Niketan schools was almost 95 per cent, with more than 130 schools registering 100 per cent success. They have also retained a number of ranks with top 10–20, which are considered to be exceptional in Assam. In 2016, the state education minister publicly declared that these schools would spread to all 2,202 panchayats in the state.[16]

The RSS, under the banner of Purvottar Janajati Shiksha Samiti, established a large network of single-teacher schools named Ekal Vidyalayas. Quoting Karna Gaur, *prabhat pramukh* of the schools in the Northeast, Bhattacharyya has pointed out that about 70 per cent of these schools are located in the tea belt and remaining schools are in the areas inhabited by different tribal communities such as Karbi, Dimasa, Mising, Rabha and Bodo. 'By the end of 2018, as many as 4,650 such schools were established in 22 districts out of a total of thirty-three in the state.'[17] The RSS is now planning to establish these schools in the districts of Dhubri, Nalbari and South Salmara in western Assam having sizeable Muslim populations.

Tea tribes have a decisive role in the electoral politics of the four Lok Sabha constituencies of Jorhat, Dibrugarh, Lakhimpur and Tezpur. BJP victory margins in these constituencies reveal the penetration of *Hindutva* forces into these communities. Ekal Vidyalayas played an important role in this penetration. Apart from the Shishu

Niketans and the Ekal Vidyalayas, the RSS also expanded its network through 'shakhas, Vivekananda schools, balwadis, Kasturba Gandhi Balika Vidyalayas, tuition centres, study circles, vocational training centres and a hospital. The Vanvasi Kalyan Ashram, which works among tribal people, runs eight hostels, 42 nursery schools and coaching centres, holds medical camps and sends tribal teams to out-of-state sports events.'[18]

3. **Polarization on religious and linguistic lines**

> Even as the BJP's campaign strategy remained focused on three major issues: the leadership of Prime Minister Narendra Modi, development activities by the Union government and the performance by the BJP-led government in the state since 2016, the reason for the party's success seems to have been the polarization it achieved.[19]

With RSS networks on the ground and a firmly rooted electoral organization, the BJP succeeded in polarizing the electorate on religious lines. A post-poll survey conducted by Lokniti-CSDS[20] reveals that except for Muslims, all other social categories including the Dalits (66%) and Adivasis (86%) voted for the NDA. A total of 74 per cent Hindus altogether voted for the NDA, and only 16 per cent of them voted for the Congress. A total of 70 per cent Muslims voted for the Congress, a significant trend as only 20 per cent of them voted for the AIUDF. A total of 7 per cent Muslims voted for the NDA. This voting pattern illustrates the failure of the anti-CAB movement to translate into electoral outcomes. The Lokniti-CSDS survey also finds that 75 per cent of Assamese Hindus opposed the Bill. From that total, 56 per cent voted for the BJP and its allies, whereas only 28 per cent voted for the Congress. A total of 25 per cent Assamese Hindus supported CAB, but from that total, 88 per cent voted for the BJP and its allies.

The survey data provides evidence that in a socially diverse state that had undergone decades of ethnic conflict and insurgency, religion cutting across ethnic cleavages can be critically important. BJP's success lies in its ability to neutralize opposition to the CAB and divert the attention of Hindus towards the increase in Muslim population, presumably due to influx from Bangladesh with Congress patronage. This reduced the Congress into a Muslim-dependent party, which is particularly true in the Nowgong constituency. It is the single constituency in Assam which the BJP won for four consecutive terms, from 1999 to 2014. But the BJP lost this Muslim-dominant constituency to Congress in the 2019 elections due to the religious bi-polarization.

The BJP lost it despite leading in six assembly segments out of nine. The Congress won with a lead in only three assembly segments. In two of them, Laharighat and Jamunamukh, which are East Bengal origin Muslim-dominated constituencies, the Congress secured 71 per cent and 83 per cent votes, respectively, as against around 27 per cent and 15 per cent polled by the BJP. The margin of victory was low, less than 17,000. In the case of Kaliabor constituency too, which the Congress won for the seventh consecutive term since 1998, victory was determined by the East Bengal origin Muslim-dominated constituencies, particularly in Dhing and Rupohihat assembly segments, where the party had registered around 90 per cent and 85 per cent votes, respectively. Out of the total 10 assembly segments both the Congress and the AGP, BJP's ally, had a lead in five segments each. The margin of victory was remarkable, more than two lakhs, with the Congress securing 55.80 per cent votes as against 40.89 per cent secured by the AGP.[21]

4. **Modi magic and hype over national security**
In both the 2014 Lok Sabha and 2016 assembly elections, Prime Minister Narendra Modi served as the core BJP campaign rallying point. Glorification of his leadership and creating hype around national security were two key BJP strategies in Assam. Both Modi and BJP President Amit Shah took a keen and active interest in the electoral strategies. Modi campaigned in the state on 4 January, 30 March and 12 April 2019.

He also came on Christmas Day, 25 December 2018, to inaugurate the Dhola–Sadiya Bridge, the longest bridge over the Brahmaputra. Naming the bridge after Dr Bhupen Hazarika, the legendary Assamese musician, and awarding him with the Bharat Ratna evoked state-wide emotional sentiment. On 4 January, Modi addressed a rally in Silchar, primarily aimed at Bengali voters. He assured them that none of the Indian citizens will be left out of the NRC. He also stated that the Citizenship Bill would protect the rights of the Bengali Hindu refugees. On 30 March, he addressed two rallies in upper Assam—one each in the northern and southern banks of the Brahmaputra.

Three issues figured prominently in his campaign: implementation of Clause six of Assam Accord, ST status to six OBC communities and welfare of the tea tribe communities.[22] On 12 April, Mr Modi again came to Assam and addressed two rallies—one in Silchar and the other one in Kendukana in lower Assam. While in Silchar his focus was on CAB, in Kendukana it was on the identity and rights of the indigenous people. Modi got live coverage in electronic media and captured headlines in local dailies. The election campaign glorified Modi's leadership with its poll song *Akou Ebar Modi Sarkar* (Once again the Modi Government). It immediately became viral in social media with the state finance minister singing and dancing and leading street marches across the state.

BJP President Amit Shah campaigned in Assam on 17 February in Lakhimpur, just after the Pulwama bombing on 14 February killing 44 Indian paramilitary soldiers including Assam's Maneswar Basumatary. Shah asserted that both the NRC and CAB are important to save Assam from becoming a state like Jammu and Kashmir.[23] He again came to Assam on 28 March and 6 April and addressed three rallies in central and upper Assam. Basumatary's death evoked patriotic sentiments with the local media providing maximum coverage. He was cremated with full state honours on 17 February 2019.[24] India's Balakot air strike in Pakistan also evoked strong sentiments. All these helped the BJP to counter anti-CAB sentiments.

CONCLUSION

Assam 2019 polls present a number of interesting democratic dimensions. First, there was the growing disconnect between popular sentiments in the civic domain and electoral outcomes. The failure of anti-CAB movement to have an impact on the electoral outcome is a testimony to it. This also signifies a disconnect between higher democratic values and the electoral battles. More importantly, the election strategies on the part of the BJP also indicate that continuing poverty may be advantageous to a competitive party system. The populist agenda for the poor did not evoke the question as to why the incumbent government failed to bring them out of cycles of poverty. Rather, the agenda helped to manufacture layers of beneficiaries which acted as solid vote banks for the ruling party. This has also assisted the process of polarization. All these concerns pose a larger political question: Is there a necessary relationship between elections and substantive democracy? Assam polls do not appear to have answered it positively in these elections.

NOTES

1. In an election rally in Lakhimpur, upper Assam, Amit Shah declared the BJP 'would bring the Citizenship (Amendment) Bill back if it returned to power'. The party also felt 'the Bill was necessary to prevent Assam from becoming a Muslim-majority state like Kashmir'. *The Hindu*, 'Amit Shah Swears by Citizenship Bill' (17 February 2019), available at https://www.thehindu.com/news/national/sacrifices-of-crpf-personnel-wont-go-in-vain-amit-shah/article26296689.ece (accessed on 17 July 2019).
2. Akhil Ranjan Dutta in his analysis of 2014 Lok Sabha elections and 2016 assembly elections in Assam extensively deals with how the BJP used local issues and cultural ethos as electoral strategies. Ranjan Dutta, 'BJP's Consolidation, AIUDF's Polarization and Congress' Defeat in Assam', in *India's 2014 Elections: A Modi-led BJP Sweep*, ed. Paul Wallace (New Delhi: SAGE Publications, 2015), 381–403; Akhil Ranjan Dutta, 'BJP's Electoral Victory in Assam, 2016: Co-opting the Khilonjiyas', *Social Change* 47, no. 1 (2017): 108–124, doi:10.1177/0049085716683114.
3. *The Sentinel*, 'Citizenship (Amendment) Bill Will Prevent Assam from Becoming Kashmir: Himanta Biswa Sarma' (2019), available at https://www.sentinelassam.com (accessed on 17 July 2019).
4. *The Economic Times*, 'Government Sets Up Panel to Implement Clause 6 of Assam Accord' (7 January 2019), available at https://economictimes.indiatimes.com/news/politics-and-nation/government-sets-up-panel-to-implement-clause-6-of-assam-accord/articleshow/67414320.cms (accessed on 17 July 2019).
5. Assam Election Commission, 'Party-wise Results of Counting of Votes for Panchayat Election 2018', press release, 15 December 2018, available at https://www.secassam.in/pdfnoti/Final-Result-21.pdf (accessed on 17 July 2019).

6. In a tweet, Himanta Biswa Sarma, BJP's political strategist in Assam specially mentioned victory in Karimganj constituency. The tweet is available at https://twitter.com/himantabiswa/status/1131522057693360128 (accessed on 17 July 2019). He also mentioned it in a series of his interviews and comments.
7. *Northeast Today*, 'Dual Standard of INC Exposed on the Citizenship (Amendment) Bill' (10 January 2019), available at https://www.northeast-today.in/dual-standard-of-inc-exposed-on-the-citizenship-amendment-bill/ (accessed on 17 July 2019).
8. *The Economic Times*, 'Aiudf Wants Understanding with Congress to stop BJP' (23 March 2019), available at //economictimes.indiatimes.com/articleshow/68541724.cms?from=mdr&utm_source=contentofinterest&utm_medium=text&utm_campaign=cppst (accessed on 17 July 2019); *The Economic Times*, 'Was Betrayed by Congress People: AIUDF's Ajmal' (22 April 2019), available at https://economictimes.indiatimes.com/news/elections/lok-sabha/india/was-betrayed-by-congress-people-aiudfs-ajmal/articleshow/68983510.cms (accessed on 17 July 2019).
9. *News 18*, 'Denied Ticket, BJP's Mission 20 Stands in the Way of Himanta Biswa Sarma and a Delhi Berth' (22 March 2019), available at https://www.news18.com/news/politics/denied-ticket-bjps-mission-20-stands-in-the-way-of-himanta-biswa-sarma-and-a-delhi-berth-2074301.html (accessed on 26 September 2019).
10. Sangeeta Barooah Pisharoty, 'Rameshwar Teli's Inclusion in Govt Telling of BJP's Desire to Woo Assam's Tea Tribe', *The Wire* (31 May 2019), available at: https://thewire.in/politics/rameshwar-teli-inclusion-modi-govt-bjp-assam-tea-community (accessed on 5 June 2019).
11. Himanat Biswa Sarma, *Assam Budget: Budget Speech 2019–20* (Dispur: Finance Department, Government of Assam, 2019), available at https://finassam.in/budget_documents/ (accessed on 26 September 2019).
12. Rajeev Bhattacharyya, 'Saffron Wave in Assam: Ekal Vidyalayas Helped BJP, RSS Establish Strong Roots in Assam's Tribal Areas, Tea Estates', *Firstpost* (24 May 2019), available at https://www.firstpost.com/politics/saffron-wave-in-assam-ekal-vidyalayas-helped-bjp-rss-establish-strong-roots-in-assams-tribal-areas-tea-estates-6696851.html (accessed on 17 July 2019).
13. *The Economic Times*, 'RSS Cleared the Air in Northeast, Assam on Citizenship Bill' (27 May 2019), available at https://economictimes.indiatimes.com/news/elections/lok-sabha/india/rss-cleared-the-air-in-northeast-assam-on-citizenship-bill/articleshow/69511256.cms (accessed on 17 July 2019).
14. Hiren Gohain, 'The BJP's Plans for Assam: An RSS-Run School in Every Panchayat', *The Wire* (15 June 2016), available at https://thewire.in/communalism/the-bjps-plans-for-assam-an-rss-run-school-in-every-panchayat (accessed on 19 March 2019).
15. Information received from Sada Dutta (30 June 2019), who acted as the general secretary of these schools for 9 years. Until the BJP came to power, these schools engaged eminent educationists. Although affiliated to Vidya Bharati,

the presence of the RSS was not prominent. After the BJP came to power in 2016, the RSS increasingly became involved in running the schools.

16. Gohain, 'The BJP's Plans for Assam'.
17. Bhattacharyya, 'Saffron Wave in Assam'.
18. Smita Gupta, 'How the RSS Grew Roots in the North-East', *The Hindu Business Line* (9 March 2018), available at https://www.thehindubusinessline.com/blink/know/how-the-rss-grew-roots-in-the-north-east/article22991950.ece (accessed on 17 July 2019).
19. Hilal Ahmed et al., 'Post-poll Survey: BJP's Polarization Strategy Hits the Mark in Assam', *The Hindu* (28 May 2019), available at https://www.thehindu.com/elections/lok-sabha-2019/post-poll-survey-bjps-polarisation-strategy-hits-the-mark-in-assam/article27267757.ece (accessed on 18 June 2019).
20. Ibid.
21. Compiled from the statistics of Election Commission of India, available at http://results.eci.gov.in/pc/en/constituencywise/ConstituencywiseS033.htm?ac=3 (accessed on 26 September 2019). Disaggregated lead in Assembly segments compiled by Assam Pradesh Congress Committee, Guwahati.
22. *The Economic Times*, 'Narendra Modi Blames Congress for Assam Accord delay in Northeast rally' (30 March 2019), available at https://economictimes.indiatimes.com/news/elections/lok-sabha/india/narendra-modi-blames-congress-for-assam-accord-delay-in-northeast-rally/articleshow/68644339.cms?from=mdr (accessed on 17 July 2019).
23. *The Hindu*, 'Amit Shah Swears by Citizenship Bill'.
24. *The Sentinel*, 'Maneswar Basumatary Cremated with Full State Honour' (17 February 2019), available at https://www.sentinelassam.com/news/maneswar-basumatary-cremated-with-full-state-honour/ (accessed on 17 July 2019).

Chapter 20

Politics of Identity, Regionalism and the BJP

A Synoptic View from Northeast India

Rajesh Dev

REPRESENTING THE REGION: CULTURE, RELIGION AND POLITICS

If we take the winding road from Guwahati—described as the 'gateway to the northeast'—towards Shillong, the picturesque capital of Meghalaya, we would come across numerous statues and large paintings of Christ along the four-lane national highway. Until a few years ago at a particularly sharp bend, about 40 kilometres from Shillong city, one would come across a large painting of Christ with the words, '[W]elcome to Christian state'. The description was perhaps aimed at corralling the difference between this largely Christianized ethnic frontier[1] and the larger Hindu mainland. The growing support for the Bharatiya Janata Party (BJP) in states in this region, therefore, seems to complicate this popular imaginary description.

The region comprising seven[2] states, collectively termed as the 'Northeast', is customarily distinguished from mainland India on the basis of its perceived sense of historical marginality and ethno-cultural and religious differences. The politicization of this perception of difference and marginality has produced competing ethno-political demands, the sheer number, complexity and variety of which led to the region being considered an 'outlier'.[3] In many cases, beginning with the demand of the Nagas, it also led to the construction and privileging of specific religious and cultural selves.[4] This relationship between ethnicity and religion led many observers to logically conclude that a civilizational fault line exists between the region and the mainland, and culture and religion are the foundational template for representing the region.[5]

The debate regarding such stereotypical representations of the region as a single homogenous regional entity 'northeast' is, however, far from settled. While some emphasize the distinctive 'culturo-historical traditions'[6] of communities and the states constituting the region to foreground their discrete identities, others in obvious reference to the partition suggest that the 'region' is a forcible construction dictated by the imperatives of a 'geopolitical accident'.[7] Yet despite these objections, popular imaginary, academic description and administrative policies about this regional artifice continue to be framed around a narrative of shared ethno-cultural and religious difference from the 'mainland' and a bellicose postcolonial history of association with the Indian nation-state.

Ethnic communities and their movements have adopted this narrative to not only interrogate the terms of their cultural incorporation and political affiliation with the Indian State[8] but also imagine a shared sense of regional self-identity as 'northeasterners'. This frame of collective ethno-cultural and religious difference continues to shape popular imaginary and ethno-political claims and movements for autonomy or secession in the region.

A political sociology of regional parties with distinct linguistic, cultural and ethnic interests and support bases will also attribute their formation to this cultural specificity and political identity of the region. Most of the regional parties in these states owe their origins to regional movements for the preservation of regional identity and autonomy. Regional parties such as the erstwhile All Peoples Hill Leaders' Conference (APHLC)[9], the Mizo National Front (MNF)[10], the Indigenous People's Front of Tripura (IPFT)[11] and even a national party with a largely regional presence, the National People's Party (NPP),[12] avowedly identify with the interests and identity projects of specific ethnic groups.

The representation of the region as not only an ethno-cultural but also a religious outlier continues to dominate elementary portrayal of this region. As a result, popular descriptions of the region and the constituting states are shaped by its degree of religious diversity and proportion of religious groups.[13] There is little surprise that such ethno-cultural and religious representation of the region acquires fresh political salience against the backdrop of the rise of the BJP in the region.

It is not my suggestion here, however, that the diffusion effects of this collective self-identification irrefutably shape a uniform regional political culture or constitute a single political field. A cross-state analysis of the region will reveal immense variation in the dynamics and materiality of social identity, politics and electoral competition in each of them.[14] As an instance, the politics of Nagaland and the growing ascendency of the BJP in the state is attributed to a completely different set of local and historical factors than those in Mizoram, both of which are Christian dominated and have a long history of movements for the preservation and protection of ethno-cultural identity.

Moreover, ethnic identity affiliations in each of these states undergo change with their level of aggregation.[15] For instance, within the state of Nagaland, Aos and the Angamis fiercely identify with their respective tribe categories; within India they identify themselves with the Naga nation and collectively both Nagas and Mizos identify themselves as 'northeasterners' within India. These choices at their level of aggregation produce their own dynamics of identity and difference that has implications for electoral competition and political outcomes.

Yet in spite of these internal variations, it is still possible to argue that a broader politics is deeply informed by a collectively imagined region based on the idea of difference. Although it is internalized, it is also contested. Methodologically speaking, framing the debate about the region within this dual process of internalization and contestation enriches our understanding of the individual states as also of the region. In the language of comparative politics, it helps us overcome both a sense of 'false' exceptionalism and/or universalism[16] regarding the history and politics of the region and the constituting states.

How do we then, given this cultural and political context, explain the growth of a party like the BJP which argues for 'one India, one law' in a region where 'difference' has been accorded institutional recognition. How do we explain the political relationships between a party that embodies a majoritarian ethic and a region where the history of state formation manifests the role of innovative constitutional provisions and politico-administrative policies[17] that prohibit the imposition of such an ethic?

This chapter argues that the emergence of the BJP in the region is not alarming, unanticipated or even extensive. And if viewed in the context of certain factors, this development would also seem unsurprising. Such factors would include BJP's affiliation with and the activities of other affiliates of the '*parivar*'[18], the broadening of the party's electoral appeal through regionalization, the dynamics of complex inter-ethnic relation in the region and the inability of the Indian National Congress (INC) to keep pace with the emergence and incorporation of local elites into the party.

The electoral arrival of the BJP in the region began in 1996 in Arunachal Pradesh and Assam, thereafter spreading to other states of the region consolidating its social bases primarily in 'select pockets' in each of the states. Its electoral presence in states beyond Assam began to take more consolidated shape once it learnt to 'induce defections'[19] and effectuate regional alliances by outbidding the Congress. The slow ascendency of the BJP in the region, therefore, corresponds with the growing decline of the Congress which had been a major political force in the region. The in-fighting, factional pressures, resistance to dynasty-based intra-party upward mobility intensified this decline of the Congress and the relative rise of the BJP. Interestingly, in most of the hill states such as Meghalaya, Nagaland, Mizoram and even Arunachal Pradesh, the rise of the BJP not only in terms of seats but also vote share has not been phenomenal.

REFRAMING THE PAST: THE SANGH, THE PARIVAR AND POLITICS IN THE REGION

The political salience of claims to difference and autonomy, that still is the central pivot of politics in the region, became apparent to the '*parivar*' 'decades back'[20] when members from the Rashtriya Swayamsevak Sangh (RSS) 'saw an opportunity to fix the battered limb of a wounded Bharat Mata'[21] and planted the seeds of an 'alternative ideology'[22] during the 'anti-migrants' Assam Movement. In 2003, the BJP government at the centre acknowledged the true weight of this politics when A. B. Vajpayee, as prime minister, candidly recognized the 'unique history of the Nagas'.[23] As the party made national breakthroughs and commenced its expansion in 'northeast', it began to gradually calibrate its elemental ideological postulates with regional cultural and political sensibilities.

Thus, symbols and issues central to the party's political agenda, such as ban on cow slaughter or banning the consumption of beef, Hindutva, Uniform Civil Code, religious conversion or the Ram Temple, are never the privileged idioms of political mobilization in most states beyond Assam. The party rather focuses on a developmentalist narrative[24] arguing that for social and political progress and its integration with the mainland, the region should become an active 'economic gateway' under the Act East Policy.[25] Such emphasis on eclectic developmentalism finds specific empirical illustration in the creation of a separate ministry for the 'development' of the region as also enhanced grants to each of the states for efficiently managing these activities. This is also manifested in the activities of the RSS, and other frontal organizations of the 'Sangh Parivar', such as the Vanvasi Kalyan Ashram, Sewa Bharati, Rashtra Sevika Samiti and Ekal Vidyalayas.[26] These affiliates of the '*parivar*' active in the region, and expanding progressively throughout, are engaged in 'social welfare and developmental tasks' aimed at mainstreaming this 'peripheral and backward' region.

Although a developmental paradigm provides crucial mobilizational and political foil to dissimulate an abiding ideological sub-text, it does not in any ways constrain the party or the affiliates of the '*parivar*' from utilising 'local symbolic inventories' to surmount perceptions about its Hindutva bias[27] and majoritarian image. According to some estimates, there are around 1,088[28] *shakhas* (branches) of the RSS in the entire region. These *shakhas* along with 'innumerable varieties of affiliates'[29] are engaged in discovering, interpreting and appropriating local cultural idioms and symbols within the broader ideas, practices and iconographies of a Hindutva-centric inference of Hinduism.

The process is cogently summed up in an insider's view of the working of the '*parivar*' in the region. It says, 'the challenge for the RSS...was to define, promote and entrench the term Hindu in the consciousness...in such a way that the local histories, myths, idioms, and fables become a part of the Sangh's conception of Hindu nationhood'.[30] The challenge was managed with such missionary assiduity[31] that in a few decades it has come to impact the social and political life in many states of the region. As Jenkins shows in the case of Rajasthan, in these states too, the activities of the '*parivar*' are now accompanied by 'broad ideological adjustments'[32] by the party in ways that suit regional specificities. These adjustments, or what we term as 'strategic moderation', allow the affiliates and the party to access social and political spaces inimical to the core ideology of the party and the broader 'parivar'.

In Arunachal Pradesh for instance, the emergence of revivalist movements among the Adi tribes 'discovering' the concept of '*Donyi-Poloism*' slowly spread among other tribes like the Galo and produced variant forms among the Apatani and Nyishi tribes.[33] In spite of its long history in the state, Christianity had received little social and political salience until recent years when missionary activity among the dominant tribes of the state such as the Adi, Galo, Nyishi, Apatani and Tagin[34] produced collective resistance and construction of identity projects for the revival of authentic cultural and religious selves. Thus, indigenous religious practices like Donyi-Polo, Rangfraism or Intyaism acquired new institutional forms[35] with reformed rituals, practices and iconography encouraged by affiliates associated with the '*parivar*'.[36] The impact of Christianity that has become a dominant force in the state has 'tribe-specific connotations'[37] with implications for political power and public policy in the state.

According to some observers in the parliamentary elections of 2019, this was noticeable in the West Arunachal constituency where Kiren Rijiju, a Buddhist from the Monpa community, stood as a BJP candidate against Nabam Tuki from the Nyishi community, a Christian and Congress candidate. Mr Rijiju claimed that the Arunachal Pradesh Catholic Association (APCA) appealed to members of the Christian faith to vote for Tuki, whom they considered as 'the pillar of Catholic churches in the state'.[38] This alleged appeal and its politicization polarized the electorate and, some say, aided Rijiju. Tapir Gao, a member of the Adi tribe and the BJP candidate and winner from the East Arunachal Constituency was more categorical about the influence and role of religion when he attributed the conversion of tribes to the 'catalytic work of the Congress'[39] identifying, thereby, the Congress as pro-Christian and anti-indigenous faith. That tribe dominance also has a serious impact on electoral competition which is borne by the fact that Nabam Tuki was given the ticket as he belonged to the more dominant Nyishi tribe rather than to the frontrunner Jarjum Ete who belonged to a smaller Galo tribe.

However, this revival and rediscovery of indigenous traditions and practices that create the socio-cultural base for political expansion often subsist in tension with the need to broaden the electoral appeal among the growing number of Christians. Two instances visibly reflect this tension between a purist ideological position pursued by other affiliates of the '*parivar*' and the position of strategic moderation pursued by the party. In 2017, the BJP-led government in the state had to rename the 'Department of Indigenous Faith and Cultural Affairs' more neutrally as the 'Department of Indigenous Affairs' after being pressured by the Arunachal Christian Forum who viewed the former nomenclature as too anti-Christian.[40]

On the other hand, during a recent rally for parliamentary elections, the Chief Minister, Pema Khandu, a Buddhist, expressed his intention to repeal the Arunachal Pradesh Freedom of Religion Act. This announcement was strongly condemned by representatives from indigenous communities and forums who appealed to the RSS to intervene.[41] The chief minister did not act on his announcement and the RSS declined to publicly comment either in favour or against these actions obliquely acquiescing to the need for such ideological compromises.

Similarly in Nagaland, followers of the indigenous religion, Heraka, primarily from the Zeme, Liangmai and Rongmei tribes (also collectively referred to as the Zeliangrong tribe) have been revivified with support from the party and the affiliates of the '*parivar*'. Heraka, an indigenous faith among these tribes, was founded by Jadonang and promoted further by his protégé Rani Gaidinliu.[42] She fought the British in 'Naga territory' and considered Christianity an extension of the colonial state poised to destroy the traditional religion and practice of the Nagas and struggled to establish an indigenous non-Christian 'Naga Raj'.[43]

Various affiliates of the '*parivar*' have been active in Nagaland since the 1970s but only after the formation of the BJP government at the centre and election of state legislators from the party did their association with members of the Heraka faith become visible and politically contentious. During the recent elections to the state assembly and thereafter to the parliament, the discord between the followers of the Heraka faith and the Christians acquired political significance. The sitting Chief Minister, Z. R. Zeliang, was accused of being an RSS sympathizer and a Heraka supporter because he belonged to the Zeliang community. So much so that he had to publicly state he was 'baptised' in 1973 and is still a devout Christian.[44]

An observer,[45] who also happens to be a Christian Naga, believes that Christianized tribes who are in a majority apprehend that being too close to the RSS may allow followers of the Heraka exert new dominance in the politics of the state they have traditionally controlled. This distrust and suspicion, therefore, has inter-tribal connotations for control of state power as traditionally the Aos and Angamis were perceived as dominant groups controlling the levers of power.

Another observer the author spoke to attributes this inter-community contestation over state power to the political competition between Neiphiu Rio, an Angami who wanted to return to state politics and T. R. Zeilang, a Zeliang who was the chief minister at the time. This ultimately resulted in a split in the Naga People's Front (NPF) with

Rio forming a new party, the Nationalist Democratic Progressive Party (NDPP). The BJP during the last state elections in 2017 had an alliance with the NPF but tacitly supported and ultimately formed the government in the state in alliance with the NDPP.

The electoral implications of this contestation between the two communities had become so critical for the BJP in a Christian-dominated state that Ram Madhav, the national general secretary of the party had to publicly acknowledge that it was due to the sacrifices of the missionaries that the people of this region stand tall today.[46] It is little wonder that party workers in the region have come to term the party as 'Bharatiya Jesus Party'.[47] However, the fact that the BJP despite being perceived as anti-Christian was able to electorally expand in Nagaland where powerful church associations influence social and political narratives is a clear indication of the complex mix of cross-cutting and interrelated processes. The tenuous inter-tribal relations and competition for state power by tribal groups and anxieties about Naga political identity produce the political openings that the BJP exploits and which the Congress did in its heydays.

In contrast, this expansion has been very limited in the case of Mizoram, often described as the 'lone sentinel of Christianity'[48] in the region. Except in some Chakma and Reang–Bru dominated constituencies, the BJP or the affiliates of the Sangh have been unable to penetrate the powerful and fiercely Christianized (and homogeneous) civil society and culturo-religious bodies that dominate organized politics and everyday life in Mizoram.[49] Yet the relentless pursuit for political expansion led the party to apply 'a balm of love'[50] through its 'Christian missionary cell'[51] in the state. In Meghalaya too, Sangh affiliates have developed close relationship with indigenous faiths such as the Seng Khasi and the Niamtre of the non-Christian Khasi and Jaintia tribes who consider themselves minorities in a state dominated by their Christian brethren.

This conjunctive process of supporting non-Christian indigenous communities and appearing pro-Christian does produce a contradiction. The BJP creatively manages this by politically positioning itself as 'centrist' and making political trade-offs as in the case of Arunachal Pradesh. Another strategy to convey a 'centrist' message is to support or nominate Christian candidates as in Manipur, Meghalaya and Nagaland. Both these political strategies are counter-balanced by enabling the non-political affiliates of the '*parivar*' to foreground threats to the cultural identity of non-Christian indigenous communities. This division of political and cultural labour not only insulates the BJP from any direct accusation of being partisan but also enables it to strategically utilize it for political purposes. Interestingly, the social and cultural mobilization that follows the activities of the non-political affiliates in the region seems to aid Hindu consolidation in other parts of India. So the joy of winning a 'leftist' Tripura is equally enjoyed with the pain for the oppressed 'Hindu' Reang–Brus in Mizoram by supporters of the party in mainland India.

These synoptic instances from the region underscore not only a deeper tension that the party encounters between 'ideological purity and political pragmatism'[52] as it expands in the region but also provides an insight into the political compulsions of the '*parivar*' for accommodating such ideological compromises. For the '*parivar*' capturing state power even at the cost of short-term ideological compromises is important for deepening its growing social acceptability as also institutionalizing ideological consolidation. An insider account rather boastfully summarizes this regionalization of the party by explaining how

> (I)n spite of being branded as a polarising political force, it (BJP) has a secret recipe that allows it to bond well with strong regionalist, and in some cases, subnational satraps…This secret sauce (is) of unification and subsuming of strong regional sentiments within the accommodative, national politics of the BJP.[53]

MIDDLE CLASS, ELITE INCORPORATION AND POLITICAL EXPANSION

Some explanations for the rise of the BJP agree with the foregoing cultural account. They insist that empirical data reinforce popular assumptions that support for the BJP from sections of the population who do not believe in its core ideology or programmes is due to the activities of its 'non-electoral affiliates'.[54] According to this theory, there is an 'electoral division of labour' between the party and other affiliates of the '*parivar*' such as the Vanvasi Kalyan Ashram and Sewa

Bharati, who engage in 'social welfare services' among those who are unlikely to support the BJP. The 'goodwill' they generate through outreach activities like schools, primary clinics, etc. create the base for political recruitment. And it is inferred that it holds true for the 'northeast' as well.

I argue that a more substantive and alternative line of reasoning must build upon but move beyond facile cultural accounts. And this can be derived from scholarship on political parties, their organizational structures and the ways in which parties recruit and incorporate elite sections of the society. Drawing on Kanchan Chandra, I posit that the BJP engaged in a creative process of 'elite incorporation'[55] through which they gave political life to the cultural symbology and 'goodwill' generated by the other affiliates of the '*parivar*'. An elementary form of the theory's argument is that elites (social and political) would join (or confederate) those parties that provide them with better opportunities and flexibility for upward political mobility. Voter choices would depend on their comparative perception of a party's high or low probability of winning. The caveat, however, is that the incorporation of new elites would be possible when incumbent elites do not fear their own survival. And this would be possible, according to Chandra, in a party that is growing and has a widening resource base to share.

The BJP, under a charismatic and secure leader like Modi has been able to incorporate new elites from a cross-section of the region's communities. This largely has to do with the disillusion of regional elites with the Congress because of its inability to ensure upward mobility of existing elites within the party and accommodate newly emerging elites as an entrenched elite monopolized hierarchies of power and office for political and dynastic interests. The in-fighting, factional rebellion, resistance to dynastic incorporation and centralization of decision-making in a 'high command' diluted the relative authority of powerful regional leaders and resulted in the decline of the party. This provided the BJP with its much-needed political opening, especially in Assam and later beyond that state.

The prominent case of Himanta Biswa Sarma, described as 'one of the towering Congress leaders of Assam' significantly demonstrates how an entrenched hierarchy had institutionalized within the Congress party. Sarma deserted the Congress along with a significant number of sitting legislators from the Congress to become a powerful member of the BJP hierarchy. In spite of its centralized structure, the BJP conceded local authority and power by giving voice and political opening to this disenchanted elite. It also attracted new elites from the rapidly expanding and mobile middle class that emerged among a large number of historically marginal communities in the region during the last decade due to increased developmental activities in the region. The party permitted articulation of their multiple and often cross-cutting interests to protect culture and identity as also fulfil political ambitions and access to expanding state resources.

This strategic concurrence to multiple claims and interests produces, at least at the moment, a durable arrangement where claims for the creation of a Twipraland can be accommodated without losing the support of electorally dominant communities in Tripura; concur to protect indigenous religious faiths without disrupting the claim for more religious freedom of Christians in Arunachal Pradesh or privilege the interests of non-dominant tribes such as Konyaks and Zeliangs together with the promotion of leaders from dominant tribal communities such as the Aos and the Angamis to political office in Nagaland. None of the leaders newly incorporated into the party owe ideological allegiance to the RSS other than a selective deference that ensures their political survival. This institutional incorporation is a significant factor shaping the electoral expansion and success of the BJP and has no bearing on the ideological anchoring of the party in the region. Therefore, the accepted argument that 'saffron rise' owes its origin to the RSS is disputable because beyond Assam, there are no indications of a 'societal or cultural transformation'[56] from below in most of the states of the region. On the contrary, 'strategic moderation' and/or 'ideological adjustments' mark the electoral rise of the BJP in the region.

This chapter argued that the rise of the BJP must be seen against the backdrop of the decline of the Congress in the region and in that context its ability to incorporate and enable regional elites to find fresh political openings. The party in the process aggregated disparate interests and politicized and mainstreamed claims that only had peripheral salience. This assemblage of disparate groups and interests often works at cross-purposes and creates conditions that can be difficult to reconcile politically. As the collective regional resentment against the Citizenship Bill[57] or the continuing political tussle between the BJP and the IPFT[58] demonstrates, this aggregation could only be provisional as the cross-cutting and complex coalition of communities and interests can, at any moment, subvert this newfound stability. For it must be remembered that unlike other states in mainland India where the BJP depends largely on the activities of a committed cadre,[59] in this region the party depends largely on the authority, leadership and social networks of regional elites. Therefore, if the strength of the BJP and its rapid expansion in the region lies in elite incorporation, then here could also lie its weakness.

NOTES

1. Alexander Mackenzie, *History of the Relations of the Government with the Hills Tribes of the North-East Frontier of Bengal* (Calcutta: Government of British India, 1884) 253.
2. When we refer to the 'Northeast' or the Northeastern region, we generally mean the seven states of Assam, Arunachal Pradesh, Meghalaya, Mizoram, Nagaland, Manipur and Tripura. Sikkim does not share any historical or cultural connect with the region. It was added to the Northeast in 2002 by the National Democratic Alliance (NDA).
3. Bethany Lacina, 'Rethinking Delhi's Northeast India Policy', in *Beyond Counter-insurgency. Breaking the Impasse in Northeast India*, ed. Sanjib Baruah (Delhi: OUP, 2009), 332.
4. John Thomas, *Evangelising the Nation. Religion and the Formation of Naga Political Identity* (London: Routledge, 2016), 3.
5. D. R. Mankekar, *On the Slippery Slope in Nagaland* (Bombay: Manaktalas, 1967).
6. Udayon Misra, *The Periphery Strikes Back. Challenges to the Nation-state in Assam and Nagaland* (Shimla: IIAS, 2000), 1. Also see Rajesh Dev, 'Dyed Hair and Flattened Imageries', *The Statesman*, available at https://www.thestatesman.com/supplements/north/dyed-hair-and-flattened-imageries-39736.html (16 February 2014) (accessed on 3 August 2019).
7. B. Pakem, ed., *Regionalism in India (with Reference to North-east India)* (Delhi: Har-Anand Publications, 1993), 9.
8. Rajesh Dev, 'Democracy, Ethnic Fractionalization, and Competitive Politics: The Case of States in Northeast India', in *India's 2009 Elections. Coalition Politics, Party Competition, and Congress Continuity*, eds. Paul Wallace and Ramashray Roy (New Delhi: SAGE Publications, 2011), 355–357.

9. S. K. Chaube, *Hill Politics in Northeast India*, 3rd ed, repr. (Kolkata: Orient BlackSwan, 2017), 107.
10. *The Indian Express*, 'What Is the Mizo National Front?' (11 December 2018), available at https://indianexpress.com/article/what-is/mizo-national-front-mnf-mizoram-results-5488114/ (accessed on 3 August 2019).
11. S. S. Ali. 'Indigenous Peoples Front of Tripura Demands Separate Tribal State', *The Hindu*, available at http://www.thehindu.com/news/national/other-states/indigenous-peoples-front-of-tripura-demands-separate-tribal-state/article5052649.ece (accessed on 3 August 2019).
12. *India Today*, 'Sangma Launches National People's Party, Forms Alliance with NDA', available at https://www.indiatoday.in/india/north/story/pa-sangma-launches-national-peoples-party-npp-forms-alliance-with-nda-150879–2013–01-05 (accessed on 3 August 2019).
13. Samarth Bansal and Smriti Kak Ramachandran, 'Christian Population on the Rise in Arunachal Pradesh, Manipur', *The Hindustan Times* (9 March 2017), available at https://www.hindustantimes.com/india-news/christian-population-on-the-rise-in-arunachal-pradesh-manipur/story-8Go2uITu2BLFJ547MPwohM.html (accessed on 3 August 2019).
14. Dev, 'Democracy, Ethnic Fractionalization, and Competitive Politics'.
15. David Laitin, *Identity in Formation* (Ithaca, NY: Cornell University Press, 1998), 11.
16. Louise Tillin, 'National and Subnational Comparative Politics: Why, What and How', *Journal of Politics* 1, no. 2 (2013): 235–236.
17. Jyotirindra Dasgupta, 'Community, Authenticity, and Autonomy: Insurgence and Institutional Development in India's Northeast', *Journal of Asian Studies* 56, May (1997): 345–370. Also see Kyoko Inoue, 'Integration of the North East: The State Formation Process', in *Sub-Regional Relations in the Eastern South Asia: With Special Focus on India's North Eastern Region*, eds. Mayumi Murayama, Kyoko Inoue and Sanjoy Hazarika (Tokyo: Institute of Developing Economies, 2005), available at https://www.ide.go.jp/library/English/Publish/Download/Jrp/pdf/133_3.pdf (accessed on 4 August 2019).
18. The *Sangh Parivar*, the family, is a collective term usually used to describe the many organizations that are associated with the RSS. They usually include organizations like the Vanvasi Kalyan Ashram, Bharatiya Mazdoor Sangh, Sewa Bharati, Rashtra Sevika Samiti, etc. Even the BJP is seen as a member of the Parivar.
19. S. K. Chaube, *Electoral Politics in Northeast India* (Madras: Universities Press, 1985), 7.
20. Shekar Gupta, 'Assam's 35-Year Saffronisation', *The Print* (3 August 2018), available at https://theprint.in/opinion/writings-on-the-wall/assams-35-year-saffronisation/93004/ (accessed on 10 August 2019).
21. Rajat Sethi and Shubhrastha, *The Last Battle of Saraighat. The Story of BJP's Rise in the North-east* (New Delhi: Penguin India, 2017), 63.
22. Ibid, 27.

23. Rahul Karmakar, 'Atal Bihari Vajpayee, an Understanding Friend of the Nagas', *The Hindu* (18 August 2018), available at https://www.thehindu.com/news/national/other-states/atal-bihari-vajpayee-an-understanding-friend-of-the-nagas/article24720111.ece (accessed on 12 August 2019).
24. The Wire, 'BJP Manifesto 2019', 26, available at https://www.scribd.com/document/405391527/BJP-manifesto-2019#from_embed (accessed on 12 August 2019).
25. R. R. Ziipao, 'Look/Act East Policy, Roads and Market Infrastructure in North-East India', *Strategic Affairs* 42, no. 5 (2018): 476–489.
26. Vanvasi Kalyan Ashram, Sewa Bharati, Ekal Vidyalayas are affiliates of the RSS (*sangh parivar*) working in different sectors like tribal welfare, education, etc. See. F. A. Siddiqui, 'Target Northeast: How RSS Plans to Make Region Saffron', *Hindustan Times*, available at https://www.hindustantimes.com/india/target-northeast-how-rss-plans-to-make-region-saffron/story-YZGPkOBXb6tS301BvpunpJ.html (accessed on 12 August 2019).
27. Rob Jenkins, 'Rajput Hindutva in Contemporary Rajasthan', in *The BJP and the Compulsions of Politics in India*, 2nd edition, eds. T. B. Hansen and C. Jaffrelot (Delhi: OUP, 2001), 101.
28. M. H. Awungashi, 'The Land of the Rising Sangh: The RSS's Expansion into the Northeast', *The Caravan* (1 April 2019), available at https://caravanmagazine.in/reportage/the-rsss-expansion-into-northeast (accessed on 14 August 2019).
29. Parvathy Appaiah, *Hindutva: Ideology and Politics* (Delhi: Deep and Deep Publications, 2003), 12.
30. Sethi and Shubhrastha, *The Last Battle of Saraighat*, 73.
31. Chrisrophe Jaffrelot, *Religion, Caste and Politics* (Delhi: Primus Books, 2010), 196.
32. Jenkins, 'Rajput Hindutva in Contemporary Rajasthan', 102.
33. Sarit K. Chaudhuri, 'The Institutionalization of Tribal Religion Recasting the Donyi-Polo Movement in Arunachal Pradesh', *Asian Ethnology* 72, no. 2 (2013): 259–277.
34. Ibid.
35. Ibid.
36. Awungashi, 'The Land of the Rising Sangh'.
37. Chaudhuri, 'The Institutionalization of Tribal Religion'.
38. *Business Standard*, 'Arunachal Church Body Seeking Votes for Tuki: Rijiju' (7 April 2019), available at https://www.business-standard.com/article/news-ians/arunachal-church-body-seeking-votes-for-tuki-rijiju-119040700538_1.html (accessed on 21 August 2019).
39. Prema Katiyar, 'How Churches in Arunachal Pradesh Are Facing Resistance over Conversion of Tribals', *The Economic Times* (19 November 2017), available at https://economictimes.indiatimes.com/news/politics-and-nation/

how-churches-in-arunachal-pradesh-are-facing-resistance-over-conversion-of-tribals/articleshow/61703687.cms?from=mdr (accessed on 21 August 2019).

40. Prasanta Majumdar, 'Arunachal Pradesh Bows to Christian Pressure: Protection for Indigenous Faith Will Have to Wait', *The New Indian Express* (27 October 2017), available at http://www.newindianexpress.com/nation/2017/oct/27/arunachal-pradesh-bows-to-christian-pressure-protection-for-indigenous-faith-will-have-to-wait-1684171.html (accessed on 22 August 2019).
41. Arunabh Saikia, 'Is BJP Plan to Repeal Arunachal Pradesh's Anti-conversion Law Aimed at Garnering Christian Votes?' *scroll.in* (9 July 2018), available at https://scroll.in/article/885018/is-bjps-plan-to-repeal-arunachal-pradeshs-anti-conversion-law-aimed-at-garnering-christian-votes (accessed on 21 August 2019).
42. Arkotong Longkumer, *Reform, Identity and Narratives of Belonging: The Heraka Movement of Northeast India* (London: Continuum, 2010), 2.
43. Makepeace Sitlhou, 'In Nagaland, a Battle for the Memory of Freedom Leader Rani Gaidinliu Leads to Competing Memorials', scroll.in (1 October 2018), available at https://scroll.in/article/895947/in-nagaland-a-battle-for-the-memory-of-freedom-leader-rani-gaidinliu-leads-to-competing-memorials (accessed on 21 August 2019).
44. P. Majumdar, 'Not Promoting Heraka, I Am Devout Christian: Nagaland Chief Minister T. R. Zeliang', *The New Indian Express* (27 July 2017), available at http://www.newindianexpress.com/nation/2017/jul/27/not-promoting-heraka-i-am-devout-christian-nagaland-chief-minister-tr-zeliang-1634421.html (accessed on 21 August 2019).
45. These observations are of a Naga scholar teaching in a reputed institution in Delhi. The recordings are available with the author.
46. Kallol Dey, 'First Time in Nagaland: Religion Becomes the Talking Point during Elections', *The Indian Express* (24 February 2018), available at https://indianexpress.com/article/north-east-india/nagaland/first-time-in-nagaland-religion-becomes-the-talking-during-elections-5074064/ (accessed on 22 August 2019).
47. Sethi and Shubhrastha, *The Last Battle of Saraighat*, 30.
48. Linda Chhakchhuak, 'Mizoram, "Lone Sentinel of Christianity" and the RSS in a Shadow Ring', *thecitizen.in* (27 November 2018),available at https://www.thecitizen.in/index.php/en/NewsDetail/index/3/15643/Mizoram-Lone-Sentinel-of-Christianity-and-the-RSS-in-a-Shadow-Ring (accessed on 22 August 2019).
49. Shyamal Bikash Chakma and Suraj Gogoi, 'The Bru-Mizo Conflict in Mizoram', *Economic & Political Weekly* 53, no. 44 (November 2018).
50. Abdul Gani, 'How the BJP Is Capitalising the Power of the Church in Christian-Majority Mizoram', *Outlook* (13 August 2019), available at https://www.outlookindia.com/magazine/story/india-news-

how-bjp-is-capitalising-power-of-the-church-in-christian-majority-mizoram/302023 (accessed 23 August 2019).

51. 'To Fight Its Communal Image, BJP Sets up Christian Missionary Cell in Mizoram', The Wire, available at https://thewire.in/politics/bjp-mizoram-christian-missionary-cell (accessed on 21 August 2019).
52. Jenkins, 'Rajput Hindutva in Contemporary Rajasthan', 11.
53. Sethi and Shubhrastha, *The Last Battle of Saraighat*, 76.
54. Tariq Thachil, 'Elite Parties and Poor Votes: Theory and Evidence from India', *American Political Science Review* 108, no. 2 (May 2014).
55. Kanchan Chandra, 'Elite Incorporation in Multi-ethnic Societies', *Asian Survey* 40, no. 5 (2000): 836–865.
56. C. Jaffrelot, 'Vigilantism Is Central to RSS' Mission of Organising Hindus & Defending Their Interests', *The Print* (6 May 2019), available at https://theprint.in/pageturner/excerpt/vigilantism-is-central-to-rss-mission-of-organising-hindus-defending-their-interests/231655/ (accessed on 21 August 2019).
57. *The Times of India*, 'Northeast Erupts over Citizenship Bill, 6 Hurt in Agartala Firing' (9 January 2019), available at https://timesofindia.indiatimes.com/india/northeast-erupts-over-citizenship-bill-6-hurt-in-agartala-firing/articleshow/67445896.cms (accessed on 22 August 2019).
58. Debraj Deb, 'Tripura's Ruling Ally IPFT Says Doors Open for Alliance Talks on ADC Polls with CPI (M)', *The Indian Express* (22 August 2019), available at http://indianexpress.com/article/north-east-india/tripura/tripuras-ruling-ally-ipft-says-doors-open-for-alliance-talks-on-adc-polls-with-cpi-m-5925988/ (accessed on 23 August 2019).
59. Christophe Jaffrelot, 'BJP in Madhya Pradesh', in *The BJP and the Compulsions of Politics in India*, 2nd edition, eds. T. B. Hansen and C. Jaffrelot (Delhi: OUP, 2001), 276.

About the Editor and Contributors

EDITOR

Paul Wallace (PhD, UC, Berkeley), is Professor Emeritus P. S. Consultant on South Asia to various US and Canadian government agencies including the Obama administration. He has received five Smithsonian funded awards for national election studies in India, as well as the Senior Fulbright Award. He was the expert witness on Sikh violence at the 2003 Air India trial in Vancouver, Canada, and before the Supreme Court of British Columbia in 2017. He is the author/editor of nine books, including five on Indian national elections published by SAGE, and over 40 articles. Professor Wallace is a frequent lecturer in India, the United States and Europe, and a commentator for broadcast and print media.

His articles include 'Counterterrorism in India: Khalistan & Kashmir' in *Democracy and Counterterrorism: Lessons from the Past* (2007, edited by Robert Art and Louise Richardson); entries on 'Kashmir' and 'Sikh Terrorism' in *Encyclopedia of World Terrorism* (2011); 'Sikh Militancy and Non-violence', in *Sikhism in Global Context* (2011, edited by Pashaura Singh); 'Punjab, Terrorism & Closure: It "Ain't" Over "Till It's Over"', *Punjab Journal of Politics* (2015); 'Elections and Democracy: The Human Dimension', in *Seven Decades of Indian Elections* (2019, edited by S. Y. Quraishi); and 'Terrorism or Non-violence: Competing Paradigms for Post-Cold War Europe & Russia', in *Globalization and Regime Change: Lessons from the New Russia and the New Europe* (forthcoming 2019, edited by Robin Alison Remington and Robert K. Evanson).

CONTRIBUTORS

Walter Korfitz Andersen did his PhD from University of Chicago, where his dissertation became his first book on the BJP, *The Brotherhood in Saffron*. His second major book on Hindu nationalism is *Messengers of Hindu Nationalism* (2019) co-authored with Shridhar Damle. He joined the P. S. faculty at College of Wooster, also administering programmes for the Great Lakes Colleges Association. He was a senior staff member for a Democrat member of Congress and then joined the US State Department. He was a special assistant to the US Ambassador to India as well as tours in Washington, DC, where he retired in 2004 as the head of the Office of Research for South Asia. He joined the faculty at the School of Advanced International Studies, Johns Hopkins University, becoming the director of its South Asian Studies programmes. He retired in July 2019. He has also taught graduates in IR seminars at Tongji University, Shanghai, since 2010.

Pallavi Bedi is currently working as a Senior Policy Officer, Centre for Internet and Society. She has 11 years of experience in the fields of corporate/commercial law and the intersection of public policy and law. She has worked with Amarch and Mangaldas, and Suresh A Shroff, one of India's leading law firms as well as with the UN Development Programme, Delhi as Project Manager, National Mission on Justice Delivery and Legal Reform, a GOI initiative to ensure faster and more efficient disposal of cases. Her degrees are from the National Law Institute University, Bhopal, and a M.A. in International Law, Fletcher School of Law and Diplomacy in 2011.

Nitin Birmal teaches political science at Dr Ambedkar College, Yerawada, Pune. His work mainly focuses on the political process of Maharashtra, and he has co-authored essays and articles on Maharashtra's elections during past 20 years. His publications include 'Maharashtra: Congress' Dramatic Decline', in *India's 2014 Elections: A Modi-led Sweep* (2015, SAGE, with Suhas Palshikar, edited by Paul Wallace) and 'Coalitions in Maharashtra: Political Fragmentation or Social Reconfiguration?' in *Coalition Politics in India: Select Issues at the Centre and the States* (2014, with Suhas Palshikar and Vivek Ghotale, edited by E. Sridharan).

Anshu N. Chatterjee is an adjunct-faculty member in at the National Security Affairs Department at the Naval Post-graduate School, Monterey, California. Her research focuses on social movements and civil military relations. Her major publications include: 'Civil Scrutiny, Organized Action, and Democratic Consolidation,' with co-author Jyotirindra Dasgupta in Paul Wallace (ed.) India's 2014 Elections: In Modi-led BJP Sweep, Sage, 2015. 'Shifting Lines of Governance: India's Insurgencies and its Civil-Military Relations' in Tom Bruneau and Chris Matei (eds.) Handbook of Civil Military Relations, Routledge, 2012. 'Inequalities in the Public Sphere,' in Asian Ethnicity, Taylor and Francis, 2012 (June).

Sriroop Chaudhuri is Associate Professor, Environmental Studies, School of Liberal Arts and Humanities, Jindal Global University, Haryana. He is Co-director, Center for Environment, Sustainability and Human Development (CESH). He holds MS and PhD from West Virginia University, and was a postdoctoral fellow with Texas A&M University. Sriroop specializes in the eco-sociological ramifications of environmental degradation to understand pitfalls in the institutional governance system and alterations of livelihood strategies among small/marginal communities. A major emphasis of his research is on understanding political entrenchment of policies in developing economies and its impact on sustainable human development paradigms. He takes keen interest in political dynamics in India, as it is the fundamental factor in mobilizing environmental mitigation initiatives. He has over 15 years of teaching/research experience and has published extensively.

James Chiriyankandath (PhD, School of Oriental & African Studies, University of London) is Senior Research Fellow in Indian politics at the Institute of Commonwealth Studies, School of Advanced Study, University of London (since 2009), and Co-editor of the journal *Commonwealth and Comparative Politics* (since 2006). In nearly four decades of research on South Asia and Middle East, he has published on religion, communalism and nationalism, development, electoral and coalition politics, human rights and foreign policy. His publications include *Parties and Political Change in South Asia* (2014, edited), *Electoral Politics in India: A Changing Landscape* (1992, co-edited) and

The Politics of Poverty Reduction in India: The UPA Government, 2004 to 2014 (forthcoming, co-authored). In the last decade, he has authored the entry on South Asia in *The Annual Register*, the authoritative international reference book on world events.

Rainuka Dagar is Professor and Program Director, Afro-Asian Association for Justice Development, an international organization working in the justice sector. Her work focuses on two separate development fields—gender and democratic governance. In the domain of gender, her engagement is with the politics of gender construction, gender positioning and conflict dynamics in multicultural societies, with an application of culturally sensitive methodologies. Her published work includes *Gender Identity and Violence: Female Deselection in India* (2014). Her other domain of work covers an international span in the use of performance measures in public safety and citizen rights.

Jyotirindra DasGupta is Professor Emeritus of Political Science at the University of California, Berkeley. His work has focused on language planning and ethnic mobilization in a comparative perspective. His publications include *Language Conflict and National* (1968) described as 'the first systematic study of language conflict in a developing society and of its consequences for the integrational processes of nation building'; republished in 2018. His major works include *Authority, Priority, and Human Development* (1981) as well chapters relating to development and India's social and political infrastructure in all five of the past volumes in this series on India's national elections.

Prakash Desai is presently Assistant Professor in the Department of Political Science at Goa University, Goa, India. He received his PhD from Jawaharlal Nehru University, New Delhi. His major area of research interest is Indian political thought. His recent publication is 'Quest for Egalitarian Socio-spiritual Order: Lingayats and Their Practices', *Journal of Human Values* (2019).

Rajesh Dev is an Assistant Professor in the Department of Political Science, University of Delhi. His research focuses on democratic theory and constitutionalism, ethnic conflict and politics of identity, and ethnography of law and state. His special area focus is 'Northeast' India.

Akhil Ranjan Dutta is Professor and Head of Department, Political Science, at Gauhati University, Assam. He is Coordinator of the UGC-SAP (DRS II) of the department. He is an academic activist engaged with academic research and socio-political activities concerning human rights and dignity in Northeast India. He has published research articles in social science journals such as *Economic & Political Weekly*, *Social Change* (a SAGE journal) and *Studies in Indian Politics* (a SAGE journal). He is also a regular columnist in Assamese news dailies. He is presently conducting a research project titled 'Contested Urban Space: A Study of Street Vendors in Guwahati (India) and Bangkok (Thailand)', sponsored by Gauhati University. He is also a core author of the SAAPE Poverty Report (2019) titled *Migration in South Asia: Poverty and Inequality*.

Sumit Ganguly is a Distinguished Professor of Political Science and holds the Tagore Chair in Indian Cultures and Civilizations at Indiana University, Bloomington. He is a member of the Council on Foreign Relations and a Fellow of the American Academy of Arts and Sciences. His most recent book is *Ascending India and Its State Capacity* (2017, with William R. Thompson).

Husnain Iqbal is a doctoral student in the Department of Political Science, University of Victoria, working on a dissertation titled 'How China's BRI Is Shaping State Capacity in the Recipient States: The Comparative Case Study of Myanmar and Pakistan'. He completed his MA from the SAARC-run South Asian University, New Delhi, and BA (Hons) Political Science from Forman Christian College, Lahore.

Avinash Kumar teaches at the Centre for Informal Sector and Labour Studies, School of Social Sciences, Jawaharlal Nehru University, New Delhi. His research interests are politics of development, labour movements, social exclusion and marginalization, and Indian political economy. He has published three books: *Criminalisation of Politics:*

Caste, Land and the State (2015); *Revisiting 1956: B R Ambedkar and States Reorganisation* (2014, co-authored) and *The Indian Parliament: A Critical Appraisal* (2014, co-edited).

Pramod Kumar is Professor and Director, Institute for Development and Communication (IDC), Chandigarh. His work focuses on three interrelated political themes: development and governance; conflict management; and practice of democracy through empirical methodologies, analysis of public policy and people's movements. He is a recipient of the prestigious Homi Bhabha Award, 1988–1990. He has authored books and articles on Dalit identity, communal violence, terrorism in Punjab and criminal justice system. His research articles on electoral politics in India include '1998 Elections: Regionalism, Hindutva and State Politics' (1999); 'India's 1999 Elections and 20th Century Politics' (2003); 'India's 2004 Elections: Grassroots and National Perspectives' (2007); 'Decoding the Electoral Verdict in Punjab: The Future of Regional Politics?' (2014) included in different edited volumes by Paul Wallace; *Coalition Politics in India* (2014, edited by E. Sridharan); and 'Punjab Politics: Contesting Identities and Forging Coalitions', *Economic & Political Weekly* (January 2017).

Sajjan Kumar is an independent researcher based in New Delhi. He has a PhD from Centre for Political Studies, JNU. He has co-authored the book *Everyday Communalism: Riots in Contemporary Uttar Pradesh* (2018, with Sudha Pai). His research interests include Indian politics, statecraft, agrarian politics, communalism, cultural politics, state politics and India's homeland security. He has contributed articles in scholarly journals and regularly writes for national newspapers such as the *Hindu*, *Huffington Post*, the *New Indian Express*, the *Indian Express*, *Deccan Herald* and thewire.in.

Devika Malik has been working in media and policy research in India and the US for a decade. After an initial career as a journalist with CNN-IBN, she worked with policy think tanks PRS Legislative Research in India and The Economist Intelligence Unit in the US. She also served as staff for eminent members of Indian Parliament. Devika holds a degree in Journalism from Lady Shri Ram College in Delhi and a Master's in Public Administration from Columbia University in New York.

C. Manikandan is an independent scholar based in Tamil Nadu. His research interests lie in the areas of political recruitment and party politics in Tamil Nadu. He was awarded his PhD by Pondicherry University in 2016.

Pradeep K. Nayak is a civil servant under Odisha government. He holds PhD in law and governance studies from JNU. He is a former fellow at IIAS, Shimla. His recent book is *The State and Land Records Modernisation* (2015). His earlier books are *Party Politics and Communalism: A Study of Ram Janamabhoomi and Babri Masjid Dispute* (1993) and *Communalisation and Tenth Lok Sabha Elections* (1993, co-edited). He has contributed several papers to journals and edited books. His areas of interest are party politics, communalism, public policy, governance studies and Indian society.

Sudha Pai retired as Professor at the Centre for Political Studies and Rector (Pro-Vice Chancellor 2011–2015) of Jawaharlal Nehru University. She was National Fellow, Indian Council of Social Science Research (ICSSR), New Delhi (2016–2017), and Senior Fellow at the Nehru Memorial Museum and Library Teen Murti, New Delhi (2006–2009). Currently, she is heading PRAMAN (Policy Research and Management Network), a research institute that undertakes research on areas such as health, agriculture and education in Gurgaon. Some of her books include *Dalit Assertion and the Unfinished Democratic Revolution: The BSP in Uttar Pradesh* (2002); *Developmental State and the Dalit Question in Madhya Pradesh: Congress Response* (2010); *Handbook on Politics in the Indian States Regions, Political Parties and Economic Reforms* (2013, 2015, edited); and *Everyday Communalism: Riots in Contemporary Uttar Pradesh* (2018, with Sajjan Kumar). She is a regular contributor to the Wire and articles in newspapers.

Suhas Palshikar taught political science at Savitribai Phule Pune University, Pune, till his superannuation in 2016. He is Chief Editor of *Studies in Indian Politics*. His recent publications include 'The Political

Culture of "New" India: Some Contradictions' in *Re-forming India* (2019, edited by Niraja Gopal Jayal) and 'Towards Hegemony: BJP beyond Electoral Dominance', *Economic & Political Weekly* (2018). His works are also published in *Majoritarian State* (2019, edited by Angana P. Chatterjee, Thomas Blom Hansen and Christophe Jaffrelot) and *Indian Democracy* (2017). He co-edited two volumes on 2009 and 2014 elections, *Party Competition in Indian States: Electoral Politics in Post-Congress Polity* (2017; on 2014 elections) and *Electoral Politics in India: Resurgence of Bharatiya Janata Party* (2017). His work focuses on party competition, elections and democratic politics in India. He is also the co-editor of SAGE Series on Politics in Indian States.

Shivaputra. S. Patagundi is a former Professor/Chair of Political Science/Dean of Social Sciences, Karnatak University, Dharwad. His areas of interest are linkages between domestic politics and foreign policy decision-making with reference to the role of political parties and elites, political analysis and international relations. He is author of two books, co-author of two books and co-editor of a book. Professor Patagundi has published more than 35 journal articles and has edited books. He participated in the IPSA World Congress in Montreal (2014), Madrid (2012), Oslo (2008), Fukuoka (2006) and Durban (2003). He is the Founder Registrar, Rani Channamma University, Belagavi, and is an ICSSR Senior Fellow, Centre for Multi-Disciplinary Research, Dharwad.

S. Y. Quraishi joined IAS in 1971, rising to become the 17th Chief Election Commissioner of India. He has had a special focus on people's participation, voters' education and youth involvement in the electoral process, and has been an ardent proponent to grass-roots level election functionaries. Pre-EC, he was Secretary, Ministry of Youth Affairs and Sports, Government of India. His electoral reforms include: creation of a Voter Education Division, Expenditure Monitoring Division and the IIIDEM. He created the National Voters Day and was in the *Indian Express* list of 100 Most Powerful Indians, 2011 and 2012. He is on the Board of Advisors, International Institute of Democracy and Electoral Assistance Stockholm, and was appointed its Ambassador of Democracy in 2017. His major book is *An Undocumented Wonder: The*

Making of the Great Indian Election (2010). Recently, he edited essays on India's electoral democracy, *The Great March of Democracy—Seven Decades of India's Elections* (2019).

Pooja Rani teaches at the Department of Political Science, Gargi College, University of Delhi. She specializes in teaching political theory, Western political thought, and conflict resolution and peace building. Her research interests include gender, land rights, political representation and social justice.

Ghanshyam Shah is an independent researcher, based in Ahmedabad, formerly professor, Jawaharlal Nehru University, New Delhi; Centre for Social Studies, Surat; Fellow in Resident, the Netherlands Institute for Advanced Study, in humanities and social sciences, Wassenaar; National Fellow, Indian Institute of Advanced Study, Shimla; and ICSSR, New Delhi. He has authored/co-authored and edited more than 20 books, including *Democracy, Civil Society and Governance* (2019); *Social Movements in India* (1981, 2004); *Untouchability in Rural India* (2006, co-authored); *Re-reading Hind Swaraj: Modernity and Subalterns* (2012, edited); and *Growth or Development: Which Way Is Gujarat Going?* (2014, co-edited).

Karli Srinivasulu is presently Senior Fellow, ICSSR, New Delhi. He was formerly Professor of Political Science and Dean, Faculty of Social Sciences at Osmania University, Hyderabad, India. His research interests include political theory, agrarian and Dalit movements and public policy. His recent work has been on politics of special economic zones, state business relations and Telangana state movement.

Reeta Chowdhari Tremblay is Professor of Comparative Politics and former Provost/Vice-President Academic at the University of Victoria. Her major areas of research are identity-based politics, secessionist movements (Kashmir) in South Asia and the politics of subaltern resistance and accommodation in post-colonial societies. She has contributed chapters on Jammu and Kashmir to the past three volumes in this series. Her recent publications include *Modi's Foreign Policy* with co-author Ashok Kapur (2017, SAGE) and *Contested*

Governance, Competing Nationalisms, and Disenchanted Publics: Kashmir beyond Intractability? (2017).

Andrew Wyatt is Senior Lecturer in Politics at the University of Bristol, Bristol. His research interests lie in the areas of populism, elites and political parties. His publications include Party System Change in South India (2009). Other books include *Contemporary India* (2010, with K. Adeney); *Party System Change in South India: Political Entrepreneurs, Patterns and Processes* (2009); *The Politics of Cultural Mobilization in India* (2004, edited with J. Zavos and V. Hewitt); and *Decentring the Indian Nation* (2003, edited with J. Zavos).

Index